gilbert

LAW SUMMARIES

CONTRACTS

Twelfth Edition

Melvin A. Eisenberg
Professor of Law
University of California, Berkeley

HARCOURT BRACE LEGAL AND PROFESSIONAL PUBLICATIONS, INC.

EDITORIAL OFFICES: 176 W. Adams, Suite 2100, Chicago, IL 60603

LAW SUMMARIES

REGIONAL OFFICES: New York, Chicago, Los Angeles, Washington, D.C.

Distributed by: **Harcourt Brace & Company** 6277 Sea Harbor Drive, Orlando, FL 32887 (800)787-8717

PROJECT EDITOR
Elizabeth L. Snyder, B.A., J.D.
Attorney at Law

QUALITY CONTROL EDITOR
Dawn M. Barker, B.S.

SUMMARY OF CONTENTS

gilbert
capsule summary
contracts

I. CONSIDERATION

A. INTRODUCTION
Generally, a promise is not enforceable unless it is supported by consideration. Early theories described consideration as a benefit received by the promisor or a detriment incurred by the promisee. Today, most authorities treat consideration as equivalent to "bargain" (*i.e.,* an exchange of promises or a promise for performance where each party views what she gives as the price for what she gets). However, the bargain approach does not explain all situations where promises are enforceable, and so some authorities treat any element that will make a promise or contract enforceable as consideration. Identification of the following six kinds of promises is helpful in analyzing consideration problems . . . . [1]

B. UNRELIED-UPON DONATIVE PROMISES
1. **General Rule:** A promise to make a gift is unenforceable for lack of consideration **unless** it is relied upon or is compensation for a previously conferred benefit that created a moral obligation (or, in some states, is under seal) . . . . [3]
2. **Effect of a Seal:** At common law, a seal made a donative promise enforceable. However, today most states have either statutorily abolished the binding effect of the seal or provided that a seal only raises the **presumption** of consideration . . . . [8]
3. **Effect of Writing:** A writing does **not** make a donative promise enforceable at common law. A few states provide that a donative promise in writing is presumed to have been given for consideration . . . . [11]
4. **Nominal Consideration:** Although not unanimous, the prevailing view is that nominal consideration (*i.e.,* where the parties falsely put their agreement in the form of a bargain) will not make a donative promise enforceable . . . . [13]
5. **Conditional Donative Promises:** A conditional donative promise exists where some condition must be met before the gift is made. It is no more enforceable than any other donative promise even if the condition has been met . . . . [14]
   a. **Conditional donative promise vs. bargain promise:** The test is the manner in which the parties view the condition. If the condition is viewed as a necessary part of making the gift, the promise is donative. However, if performance of the condition is viewed as the price of the promise, there is a bargain . . . . [15]

C. RELIED-UPON DONATIVE PROMISES—DOCTRINE OF PROMISSORY ESTOPPEL
1. **Former Rule—Reliance Irrelevant:** In the past, a donative promise was unenforceable even if it was relied upon . . . . [16]
2. **Modern Rule:** Today, if a donative promise **induces reliance** by the promisee in a manner reasonably expected by the promisor, the promise is enforceable—at least to the extent of the reliance . . . . [17]
   a. **Principle of promissory estoppel:** Where a promisee has relied on a donative promise, the promisor should be estopped (prevented) from pleading lack of consideration. Substantial reliance is not required; the promisor's reasonable expectation of reliance is sufficient . . . . [19]
3. **Reliance as Consideration:** Some authorities (*e.g.,* Rest. 2d) treat "consideration" as equivalent to "bargain"; thus, a relied-upon promise is enforceable

despite the lack of consideration. However, others view promissory estoppel as simply a type of consideration. The ***result*** is the same under either view . . . . . . [23]

D. BARGAIN PROMISES

1. **General Rule—Bargain Constitutes Consideration:** As a general rule, a bargain constitutes consideration. Generally, the law does not require bargained for promises to be of equal value, but gross disparity may be used as evidence of defenses such as unconscionability, incapacity, fraud, duress, etc. Also, adequacy of consideration may be reviewed if an equitable remedy such as specific performance is sought . . . . [24]

2. **Exceptions—Bargains That Are Not Consideration**
   a. **Nominal consideration:** This involves a transaction that has the ***form*** of a bargain but ***lacks the substance*** of a bargain. Nominal consideration will not make a donative promise enforceable . . . . [30]
      (1) **Compare—options and guaranties:** Nominal consideration will make an option enforceable if the option is in writing and proposes fair terms. Similarly, nominal consideration makes a ***written*** guaranty binding. These transactions are usually enforceable because they serve an important commercial purpose and are likely to be relied up– on . . . . [32]
   b. **Promises to surrender or forbear from asserting a legal claim:** This exception gives rise to the problem of whether a bargained-for promise to surrender or forbear from asserting a claim (or the actual surrender or forbearance) constitutes consideration if the claim is not reasonable and/or not held in good faith . . . . [37]
      (1) **Former rule:** Consideration was present only if there was an ***honest and reasonable basis*** for believing the claim valid . . . . [38]
      (2) **Modern rule:** Today sufficient consideration will be found if the promisor's belief in the validity of the claim is ***either*** reasonable or held in good faith . . . . [39]
      (3) **Actual surrender or forbearance:** The same rules that govern promise to surrender or forbear govern the bargained-for ***act*** of surrendering or forbearing . . . . [41]
      (4) **Written release:** Under some state statutes, a written release may constitute consideration ***without*** a reasonable or good faith belief in the claim . . . . [42]
   c. **Illusory promises**
      (1) **General rule for bargains:** A bargain consisting of an exchange of promises (bilateral contract) requires ***mutuality of obligation***; *i.e.*, both parties must be bound or neither is bound . . . . [44]
         (a) **Effect of illusory promise:** If one party makes an illusory promise (a statement in the form but not substance of a promise because it does not limit the speaker's future options) in exchange for the other party's real promise, the rule of mutuality applies and ***neither party is bound*** . . . . [47]
      (2) **Exceptions to the mutuality rule**
         (a) **Unilateral contracts:** The rule of mutuality is ***not*** applicable to unilateral contracts (a promise given in exchange for an act) . . . . [49]
         (b) **Limited promises:** Promises limiting the promisor's options in some way—no matter how slight—are real and are consideration . . . . [50]
         (c) **Voidable promises:** An otherwise real promise is not illusory merely because it is voidable by one party ***as a matter of law*** . . [51]
         (d) **Conditional promises:** A promise which the promisor need only perform if a specified condition occurs is not illusory if the promisor has limited her future options in some way . . . . [53]

(e) **Alternative promises:** Where the *promisor* reserves the right to discharge his obligation by choosing between two or more alternatives, there is consideration only if *each* alternative is sufficient consideration if bargained for alone. Where the *promisee* can choose one of several alternative promises from the promisor, consideration exists if *any* of the alternatives would be sufficient consideration . . . . [54]

(f) **Agreements allowing one party to supply a material term:** At *common law,* such a promise is *illusory.* However, where one party has the power to alter or modify contract terms, many authorities hold that the promise is not illusory since such power is subject to an *implied covenant of fair dealing.* Note that the power to supply (rather than vary) a material term is not illusory where the term must be fixed in relation to an *objective measure* (*e.g.,* market price) . . . . [57]

    1) **U.C.C. provisions:** Today, the U.C.C. explicitly changes the common law by providing that sale-of-goods contracts with unilateral price setting are enforceable if the parties so intend. This power is subject to the duty to exercise it in good faith . . . . [61]

(g) **Implied promises:** The mutuality rule is inapplicable where a promise can be implied in fact or in law from a party's words or actions. A common type of implied promise involves a promise to use one's *reasonable or best efforts* to perform (rule of *Wood v. Lucy*) . . . . [64]

    1) **U.C.C. in accord:** The U.C.C. codifies the rule in *Wood v. Lucy* by providing that, unless otherwise agreed, a lawful agreement for exclusive dealing in *goods* imposes an implied obligation by the seller to use best efforts to promote their sale . . . . [67]

(h) **Requirements and output contracts:** Modern courts and the U.C.C. usually enforce these contracts since the party who determines quantity has limited his options; if he buys or sells at all, he must buy from or sell to the other party . . . . [68]

d. **Legal duty rule—promise to perform act promisor already obliged to perform:** The promise or performance of an act the promisor is already legally obliged to perform does not constitute consideration. This is commonly known as the *legal duty rule* . . . . [76]

(1) **Preexisting public duties**

    (a) **Official duties:** If an official's promised performance is *within the scope of official duties,* neither the promise nor performance thereof is legally sufficient consideration . . . . [79]

    (b) **Other public duties:** Performance of a public duty other than an official duty required by law (*e.g.,* jury service) is treated the same as performance of an official duty . . . . [83]

(2) **Preexisting contractual duties:** Generally, a promise to perform such a duty is not consideration; neither is the performance of the duty. This rule covers the two following types of cases . . . . [84]

    (a) **Performance of preexisting contractual duty for increased payment:** Where A and B have a contract under which A is obliged to perform some act, and B agrees to modify the price he will pay A, but A only promises to render the performance he was already obliged to perform, neither A's new promise to perform nor performance of the same act constitutes consideration for B's promise to pay a greater amount than that set by the original contract. This rule does not apply to the following *exceptions:* . . . . [85]

1) **Promise of different performance:** Consideration exists where A promises to perform an act different from the action he was contractually obliged to perform. Even a slight difference will be sufficient . . . .   [87]

2) **Preexisting duty owed to third party:** Most authorities recognize the existence of consideration where A owes a preexisting contractual duty to someone other than B. And nearly all authorities recognize an exception where a third party's promise runs to A and B *jointly* . . . .   [88]

3) **Defense under original contract:** If A had a valid defense to performing under the original contract, the new promise to perform is sufficient consideration . . . .   [90]

4) **Modification—unanticipated circumstances:** A new promise to pay is enforceable if unanticipated circumstances arise that make modification of the original contract terms *fair and equitable* . . . .   [91]

5) **Modification—sale of goods:** The U.C.C. does *not* require consideration to make binding modifications of contracts for the sale of goods. However, the modifications must be sought in good faith . . . .   [92]

6) **Writing as substitute for consideration:** In a *few* states, a contract may be modified by a subsequent written contract with no new consideration . . . .   [94]

7) **Mutual rescission:** Some courts get around the preexisting legal duty rule by applying the fiction that the parties *mutually rescinded* the original contract and formed a new one . . . .   [96]

8) **Effect of performance:** The legal duty rule is a defense to an action to enforce a contract; if the contract has been fully performed, neither party can use the legal duty rule to recover what it paid unless the party seeking to recover performed under duress (an *improper* threat leaving no reasonable alternative can constitute sufficient economic duress) . . . .   [97]

(b) **Payment of lesser amount as discharge of debtor's full obligation:** Generally, a promise by a debtor to pay less than the full amount he owes creditor in exchange for the creditor's agreement to accept the lesser amount in full satisfaction or discharge of the entire debt is *not* consideration, and the creditor's promise to accept the lesser amount is not enforceable. Exceptions to this rule follow . . . .   [99]

1) **Different performance:** The general rule is inapplicable where the debtor does something different from that which he is obliged to do (*e.g.*, makes early payment) . . . .   [100]

2) **Honest dispute:** If there is an honest dispute as to whether a lesser amount is owed, payment of the lesser sum is consideration for the creditor's discharge in full . . . .   [101]

3) **Unliquidated obligations:** If the amount owed is unliquidated (uncertain), debtor's payment of the lesser amount is consideration for creditor's discharge in full even if the debtor pays no more than he *admittedly* owes. However, if the debtor owes the creditor two *separate debts*, payment of one obligation will not serve as consideration for the creditor's agreement to discharge the other obligation . . . .   [102]

4) **Composition of creditors:** Where a voluntary composition of creditors releases a debtor, consideration may be

E. ACCORD AND SATISFACTION

F. WAIVERS

II. MUTUAL ASSENT—OFFER AND ACCEPTANCE

A. MUTUAL ASSENT
1. **Objective Theory of Contracts:** Whether a bargain has been formed by mutual assent of the parties is determined by examining what a **reasonable person** in the position of each party would be led to believe by the words or conduct of the other party. Although modern contract law rejects the concept that a subjective meeting of the minds is necessary (and instead relies on **manifested intentions**), if both parties subjectively attach the same meaning to a term, that meaning will govern even if it is not a reasonable meaning of the term . . . . [154]
2. **Express and Implied Contracts**
   a. **Express contracts:** In an express contract, mutual assent is manifested in **words of agreement,** oral or written . . . . [155]
   b. **Implied contracts**
      (1) **Implied-in-fact contracts:** If the promises of the parties are inferred from their acts or conduct, or from words that are not explicit words of agreement, the contract is implied in fact . . . . [156]
      (2) **Implied-in-law contracts:** These are cases where a court **fictionally** implies a promise to pay for benefits or services to avoid inequities and unjust enrichment (also known as **quasi-contracts**) . . . . [157]

B. OFFERS
1. **What Constitutes an Offer:** An offer is a manifestation of **present willingness to enter into a bargain**, made in such a way that a reasonable person in the shoes of the person to whom it is addressed would believe that she could **conclude the bargain** merely by giving her assent—*i.e.*, by accepting the offer [159]
   a. **Essential elements:** The essential elements of an offer are . . . . [160]
      (1) **Intent to make a bargain:** Offers must be distinguished from invitations to begin negotiations. Intent is reflected by language and the surrounding circumstances of the statement . . . . [161]
      (2) **Definiteness of terms:** A statement will usually not be considered an offer unless it makes clear the subject matter of the proposed bargain, the quantity involved, and the price . . . . [165]
         (a) **Intent determinative:** Even if an important term is omitted, a statement can still be construed as an offer if the omission does not indicate a lack of intent to conclude a bargain **and** if the court can fill in the missing term by implication . . . . [166]
   b. **Special rules**
      (1) **Advertisements:** Advertisements are generally deemed invitations to deal, rather than offers. However, a **particular** advertisement may be construed as an offer if it is definite in its terms and either the circumstances clearly indicate an intention to make a bargain or the statement invites those to whom it is addressed to take specific action without further communication . . . . [168]
         (a) **Rewards:** An advertisement for a reward is normally construed as an offer . . . . [169]
      (2) **Offering circulars:** These are normally construed as invitations to deal. However, they may be interpreted as offers if a reasonable person in the shoes of the addressee would think the communication had been addressed to him **individually** rather than as one of a **number of recipients** . . . . [170]
      (3) **Auctions**
         (a) **Auction with reserve:** Public notice of the auction and the auctioneer's presenting the goods for sale and calling for bids (putting an item **"on the block"**) are considered invitations to make offers. A bid by a member of the audience is an **offer,**

    (1) **Promise mandatory:** Ordinarily, such an offer can be accepted **only** by a promise, not by an act. There is a possible **exception** where the offeree tenders **full performance** prior to expiration of the offer . . . .

    (2) **Modes of promissory acceptance:** These include a verbal promise, a promise implied in fact by the promisee's conduct, an act designated by the offeror to signify a promise, and, in some situations, silence . . . .

    (3) **Communication of acceptance:** When acceptance is made by a communicated promise, the acceptance and the communicated promise are usually one and the same. However, there are several exceptions: . . . .

       (a) **Mailbox rule:** Where the mail, telegraph, etc. is a reasonable method of communicating an acceptance, the acceptance is usually effective when **dispatched**. This is true even though the acceptance does not actually **reach** the offeror because it is lost in the mails . . . .

       (b) **Waiver of communication:** When the offer provides that the offeree must "accept" or "approve" the offer, but waives notice of such acceptance or approval, a contract is formed when the offeree accepts or approves, even though he does not notify the offeror . . . .

b. **Acceptance of offer for a unilateral contract**

    (1) **Performance mandatory:** Generally, an offer that calls for acceptance by performance of an act can be accepted only by performance, not by a promise . . . .

    (2) **Notice of acceptance:** A unilateral contract is formed by the offeree's performance even though the offeror does not know at the time that the performance has occurred. However, **notice of the completed performance** must be given to the offeror before he becomes obliged to discharge his contractual duties . . . .

       (a) **Sale of goods contracts:** The U.C.C. provides that in sale of goods contracts "where the beginning of a requested performance is a reasonable mode of acceptance, an offeror who is not notified of [such beginning of performance] within a reasonable time may treat the offer as having lapsed before acceptance" . . .

    (3) **Subjective intent of offeree**

       (a) **Performance without knowledge of offer:** The general rule is that performance of the contemplated act by a person who had **no knowledge** of the offer at the time of performance does **not** form a contract. A few cases have made an exception to the general rule for reward offers . . . .

       (b) **Offer not the principal inducement for performance:** Generally, if the actor knows of the offer for a unilateral contract at the time he performs the act called for by the offer, a **contract is formed** even though the offer was not the principal inducement for performance. However, **no contract** is formed if the act is done **involuntarily** (e.g., under duress) . . . .

    (4) **Obligation of offeree:** An offeree's acceptance of a **bilateral** contract binds the offeree as well as the offeror. However, if the offer is for a **unilateral** contract, the offeree is ordinarily not bound, since he never promised anything . . . .

    (5) **Subcontractor's bid:** If a contractor uses a specific subcontractor's sub-bid in determining his own bid, as a matter of contract law, the use of the bid does not constitute acceptance of the sub-bid because the contemplated mode of acceptance in such cases is communicated assent, not the act of using the bid . . . .

7. **Bargains Capable of Being Made Certain:** A bargain lacking an essential term is nevertheless enforceable if it makes reference to an objective standard to be used to fill in the missing term *(e.g.,* output and requirements contracts, custom or usage) . . . . [425]

8. **"Agreements to Agree":** Agreements to agree are bargains in which the parties explicitly reserve some term to be agreed upon in the future. Such agreements were unenforceable at common law, but the modern trend (U.C.C., Rest. 2d) is to enforce them where the parties manifested an intent to conclude a contract. In such a case, if one of the parties fails to reach an agreement as to price, then the price is the reasonable price at the time of delivery . . . . [427]

9. **Bargains Subject to Power of One Party Concerning Performance**
   a. **Unrestricted option:** At common law, if either party retains an unlimited option or right to decide the nature or extent of her performance, her promise is too indefinite to be enforced. However, under the U.C.C., as long as the parties intended to be bound, an agreement for the sale of goods at a price to be fixed by the seller or buyer is enforceable if done in good faith . . [436]
      (1) **Future trend:** Under the Rest. 2d and the U.C.C., it is likely that modern courts will begin to hold that an apparently unrestricted option is not illusory, since it is limited by the general obligation of good faith . [438]
   b. **Alternative promises:** A bargain is not too indefinite because it reserves to a party the right to choose which of two or more performances will be rendered, provided *each* performance imposes an obligation . . . . [439]
   c. **Promise dependent on ability to perform:** A bargain in which a party agrees to perform "as soon as he is *able*" is enforceable if the party's ability to perform is capable of objective determination . . . . [442]

10. **Bargains Where Written Contract Contemplated:** Where parties enter into a bargain on the understanding that a formal contract will be executed and such execution does not occur, the issue then arises as to what function the parties intended the writing to serve . . . . [443]
    a. **Writing as evidentiary memorial:** If it appears that the parties intended the writing only as an evidentiary memorial of the terms of their agreement, and the agreement was fully consummated, the oral agreement is enforceable . . . . [444]
    b. **Writing as consummation of agreement:** The oral agreement is not enforceable if it appears that the parties intended not to be found unless and until a writing was executed . . . . [445]
    c. **Determining intent:** Important factors for determining the parties' intent include: (i) whether the contract is of a type usually put in writing; (ii) whether there are few or many details; (iii) whether the amount involved is large or small; and (iv) whether a formal writing is necessary for full expression . . . .

B. MISTAKE
   1. **Mutual Mistake:** The general rule is that where parties enter into a contract under a mutual mistake as to a *basic assumption of fact,* and the mistake has a material effect on the agreed exchange, the contract is voidable by the adversely affected party . . . . [448]
      a. **Where a party assumes risk of mistake:** Mutual mistake is not a defense where the adversely affected party *bore the risk* that the assumption was mistaken *(e.g.,* both parties *knew* their assumption was *doubtful)* [451]
      b. **Mistake in judgment no defense:** Mutual mistake is also *not* a defense if the mistake concerns *prediction or judgment* . . . . [452]
   2. **Unilateral Mistake:** In contract law, a unilateral mistake refers to a *mechanical* error of computation, perception, etc., made by only *one* of the parties to a contract . . . . [453]
      a. **Nonmistaken party aware of error:** In these situations, the mistake is a *palpable* unilateral mistake which prevents the formation of a contract. It

e. **Surety contract:** Promises made to *another person's* creditor to "answer for" (be responsible for) that person's debt must be in writing. However, if the promise is made *to the debtor,* it is enforceable even though oral . . . . [525]

    (1) **Primary debt by promisor:** The Statute applies only to collateral promises, not to primary contracts which happen to benefit third parties . . . . [526]

    (2) **Main purpose rule:** A surety promise is enforceable, although oral, if it appears that the promisor's *main purpose* in guaranteeing the obligation of another was to secure an advantage or pecuniary benefit *for himself* . . . . [528]

4. **Type of Writing Required**

a. **Memorandum of essential terms:** A writing will satisfy the Statute if it is *signed* by the party to be charged and contains: (i) the identity of the contracting *parties;* (ii) a description of the contractual *subject matter;* (iii) the *terms and conditions* of the agreement; and (iv) in many states, a recital of the *consideration.* The signature may be handwritten, typed, or printed, and if so intended, a party's initials will suffice . . . . [529]

b. **U.C.C. provisions:** In the sale of goods, the writing need only be "sufficient to indicate that a contract for sale has been made" and specify the *quantity* term . . . . [532]

c. **Signatures**

    (1) Agent's signature: Under the original Statute of Frauds, a memorandum was sufficient if signed by an authorized agent of the party to be charged. However, some states have *equal dignity statutes* requiring the agent's authority to be in writing if the principal is to be bound by the agent's signature on a contract . . . . [535]

    (2) **Party to be charged must sign:** Only the signature of the party sought to be held liable must appear. Normally, the signature can appear anywhere on the instrument . . . . [537]

d. **Integration of several documents:** The required writing may consist of several documents, provided each document refers to or incorporates the others, or they are otherwise integrated (*e.g.,* by being physically attached) . . . . [539]

e. **Auction sales:** In auction sales, the auctioneer's memorandum of terms of sale, signed only by the auctioneer, is a sufficient writing to bind both parties . . . . [540]

5. **Effect of Noncompliance with the Statute of Frauds**

a. **Majority view—contract voidable:** Failure to comply with the Statute renders the contract *voidable* (*i.e.,* unenforceable against a party who has not signed the requisite writing), but not void . . . . [541]

    (1) **Effect:** Although suit cannot be brought on an oral contract that is within the Statute, the contract is valid for all other purposes; *e.g.,* if the oral contract is confirmed in a later writing, the contract becomes enforceable against the signing party, even though no new consideration is given. *Note:* Once a contract has been performed on both sides, neither party is entitled to recover what he has given based merely on the fact that the Statute of Frauds was not satisfied . . . . . . [542]

    (2) **No third party defense:** Generally, the Statute may be raised only by a party to the contract, not by a third party . . . . [543]

b. **Minority view—contract void:** In a few states, failure to comply with the Statute renders a contract void . . . . [544]

6. **Recovery in Restitution:** Normally, courts afford restitution for benefits conferred pursuant to a contract unenforceable under the Statute, even where such a contract is deemed to be "void" . . . . [545]

IV. THIRD PARTY RIGHTS AND OBLIGATIONS

a. **Rights of assignee against obligor**
- (1) **Direct action:** An assignee can enforce her rights by direct action against the obligor .... [657]
- (2) **Effect of notice:** Once the obligor has notice of the assignment, he must render performance to the assignee .... [658]

b. **Defenses available to the obligor:** Defenses that are **contract-related** can be asserted against the assignee whether they arise before **or after** notice of the assignment is given. A defense unrelated to the contract can be asserted against the assignee if it **accrues** before the assignee gives the obligor notice of the assignment .... [659]
- (1) **Holder in due course and waiver of defenses:** If a claim is embodied in a negotiable instrument, the assignment of the claim is a "negotiation." If the instrument is negotiated to an assignee who is a holder in due course, the obligor cannot assert against the holder any contract-related defenses (excepted limited defenses, such as duress or incapacity). With nonnegotiable instruments, a similar result can be achieved with waiver-of-defense clauses .... [660]
  - (a) **F.T.C. rule:** The F.T.C. effectively limits both waiver-of-defense clauses and the holder in due course rule in consumer credit sales. Persons who sell consumer goods or services on credit are required to include a notice in consumer credit contracts or notes that the assignee of the contract takes **subject to all claims or defenses** which the consumer debtor could assert against the seller .... [663]
  - (b) **Consumer protection statutes:** Many states have consumer protection statutes that also prohibit such waivers in retail installment contracts involving purchase or lease of consumer goods, so that no assignee can take free of defenses assertable against the seller .... [664]
  - (c) **Modification after assignment:** If the assignor and obligor in good faith modify the contract after notice of the assignment, the traditional view is that the modification does not impair the rights of the assignee. (The U.C.C. is contra as to commercial assignments) .... [665]

c. **Rights of assignee against assignor—warranties:** The law reads into every assignment for consideration three implied warranties by the assignor who warrants .... [669]
- (i) **That the right assigned actually exists and is subject to no limitations or defenses** other than those stated or apparent at the time of the assignment;
- (ii) **That any document or paper** regarding the assignment **is genuine** and what it purports to be; and
- (iii) **That the assignor has the right to assign** (i.e., no prior assignment of the same right) **and will do nothing in the future to defeat the assigned right.**

10. **Priority of Competing Assignees:** Successive assignments of the same right raise the question as to which assignee is entitled to the obligor's performance . [671]

a. **Common law:** Where the **first assignment is revocable**, any subsequent assignment revokes the first assignment and the subsequent assignee prevails. If the assigned claim is represented by a **tangible token**, and the first assignee leaves the token in the assignor's possession, the second assignee prevails .... [672]
- (1) **Other cases:** Other cases are governed by three competing rules: .. [675]
  - (a) **"New York" rule:** Under this rule, the first assignee in point of time prevails .... [676]
  - (b) **"English" rule:** Under this rule, the first assignee to give notice to the obligor prevails .... [677]

2. **Effect of Material Breach:** A material breach always gives rise to an immediate cause of action for breach of the entire contract. And, if the performance was also a condition precedent or concurrent to the other party's duty to perform, that duty is excused . . . . [783]

3. **Effect of a Minor Breach:** A minor breach gives rise to an immediate cause of action for whatever damages were caused by the breach, but **not** a case of action on the entire contract. If the performance was also a condition precedent or concurrent, the minor failure may **suspend,** but does not excuse, the duty of counterperformance . . . . [784]

4. **Material Breach vs. Substantial Performance:** Material breach and substantial performance are similar in that both distinguish between major or important breaches and minor or less important breaches. But the two are used differently. Substantial performance usually is invoked by a party who has breached but seeks the contract price minus a setoff for damages, whereas material breach usually is invoked where one party has breached in a minor way, the other party terminates the contract as a result, and the first party wants to argue that the termination is a default because his breach was not material . . . . [788]

   a. **Substantial performance:** This involves the question: When can a party who has breached bring suit for nonpayment rather than unjust enrichment? [789]

   b. **Material breach:** This involves the question whether a victim of a breach can terminate the contract and be entitled to damages for the whole contract, or cannot terminate the contract and is entitled only to damages for partial breach . . . . [790]

H. ANTICIPATORY BREACH

If either party to a contract repudiates the contract prior to the time set for performance, the other party may treat such anticipatory repudiation as a **present, material breach** of contract and bring an **immediate** action for the entire value of the promised performance . . . . [792]

1. **Acts Sufficient:** The repudiation can be by **words** or by a **voluntary act** that disables the promisor from performing . . . . [793]

2. **Requirement of Unequivocal Repudiation:** An anticipatory repudiation requires a positive, unconditional refusal to perform as promised in the contract. Ambiguous expressions (*e.g.*, "doubt") are insufficient. They may, however, constitute a prospective inability to perform whereupon the other party may suspend counterperformance . . . . [795]

3. **Exception Where Nonrepudiating Party Has Completed Performance:** The doctrine of anticipatory repudiation does not apply where the only remaining duty of performance is a unilateral duty of the repudiating party, especially a duty to pay money in installments . . . . [796]

4. **Retraction:** Generally, the repudiator may retract his repudiation at any time prior to the date set for his performance, unless the innocent party has either **accepted** the repudiation or has changed his position in **detrimental reliance** thereon . . . . [798]

5. **Date for Determining Damages:** Where an anticipatory repudiation occurs and the contract is such that damages are measured by the difference between the contract price and the market price, market price is measured at the time required for performance . . . . [799]

   a. **U.C.C.**

      (1) **Breach by buyer:** Damages for repudiation are measured by the difference between the contract price and the market price at the time and place for tender . . . . [801]

      (2) **Breach by seller:** Here, most courts hold that the buyer is entitled to the difference between the contract price and the market price at the time the buyer learned of the repudiation. A minority measure market price at the time tender was required. Yet another view measures market price a reasonable time after the buyer learned of the breach . . . . [802]

I. CHANGED CIRCUMSTANCES—IMPOSSIBILITY AND FRUSTRATION

J. DISCHARGE

1. **Discharge by Mutual Rescission:** A contract still executory on **both** sides may be discharged by an express agreement between the parties to rescind or call off their deal. Such an agreement is itself a binding contract; *i.e.*, each party is giving up the right to performance by the other, so no other consideration is necessary . . . . [829]

    a. **Formalities:** The rescission may be oral, unless it would work a transfer of title to land or goods within the Statute of Frauds . . . . [832]

2. **Release:** A contract may be discharged by the execution and delivery of a release in which the maker expresses an intention to extinguish contractual rights existing in her favor. The majority of states require adequate consideration for a release . . . . [834]

3. **Accord and Satisfaction**

    a. **"Accord" defined:** An accord is an agreement under which one party to a contract agrees to accept, in full satisfaction of the contract, some performance from the other party other than the performance originally due. Recall, however, that an executory (unexecuted) accord gives rise to special problems. (*See supra*, §§119-122) . . . . [837]

4. **Checks Tendered as "Payment in Full":** When a debtor pays a creditor less than the amount the creditor claims is due, and marks the check "payment in full," the common law held that the creditor must take the check on the terms proffered or return it (*i.e.*, if the creditor crosses out the words and cashes it, there is an accord and satisfaction). The law of full-payment checks is discussed at §109 . . . . [838]

VI. REMEDIES

A. BASIC DAMAGE MEASURES

1. **Damage Measures**

    a. **Expectation damages:** These are based on the contract price and have the purpose of putting the victim of breach in the position he would have been in if the promise had been performed . . . . [841]

        (1) **Incidental damages:** These include expenses such as the seller's costs of shipping goods to and from a buyer who has breached or a buyer's costs of finding substitute goods after a seller breaches. Incidental damages are normally added to the general damage award . . . [842]

    b. **Reliance damages:** These are based on the nonbreaching party's costs and have the purpose of putting the nonbeaching party back into the position she would have been in had the promise not been made . . . . [843]

    c. **Restitutionary (or quasi-contract) damages:** These are based on the reasonable value of a benefit conferred by the promisee on the promisor where: . . . . [844]

        (i)   The benefit was conferred under a contract that turned out to be unenforceable;

        (ii) The promisor is in breach of a contract that turned out to be a losing one for the promisee; or

        (iii) The promisee conferred a benefit on the promisor at a precontractual state while the parties looked forward to (or thought they had) a contract.

B. LIMITATIONS ON EXPECTATION DAMAGES

1. **Principle of *Hadley v. Baxendale*:** A party injured by breach should recover only those damages that (i) should reasonably be considered as arising naturally or in the usual course of things or (ii) might reasonably have been contemplated by the parties at the time the contract was made . . . . [847]

I. RESTITUTIONARY DAMAGES

TEXT CORRELATION CHART

Gilbert Law Summary Contracts	Calamari, Perillo, Bender Contracts 1989 (2nd ed.)	Dawson, Harvey, Henderson Contracts 1992 (6th ed.)	Farnsworth, Young Contracts 1988 (4th ed.)	Fuller, Eisenberg Basic Contract Law 1990 (5th ed.)	Kessler, Gilmore, Kronman Contracts 1986 (3rd ed.)	Knapp, Crystal Problems in Contract Law 1993 (3rd ed.)	Murphy, Speidel Studies in Contract Law 1991 (4th ed.)	Murray Contracts Cases and Materials 1991 (4th ed.)	Rossett Contract Law and Its Application 1988 (4th ed.)
I. CONSIDERATION									
A. Introduction	146-157		38-94		37-38, 279-314	88-90		212	167, 177-178
B. Unrelied-Upon Donative Promises	149-152	196-197, 203-205, 217-218	46-48	2-19	37, 47-51, 285-299	90-93	123-129, 213-216	287-288	168-169, 245-249
C. Relied-Upon Promises—Doctrine of Promissory Estoppel	241-250, 261-277	249-293	94-107, 229-237	22-40, 516	223-225, 282, 308-314	180-225, 230-260	216-251	283-312	228-243
D. Bargain Promises	152-182, 206-228	205-233, 251-259, 295-298, 300-312, 589-591, 596-615	56-60, 71-94, 181-183, 196-197, 317-330, 562-563	41-53, 73-74, 77-166	279-314, 418-470	96-118, 788-793	26-30, 105-150, 158-192, 352-357, 383-410, 910-922	212-233, 245-257, 261-270	167-184, 192-228
E. Accord and Satisfaction	171-180	596-611	323-324, 337-342	136-151	694-703	806-807	999-1003	274-279	213-228
F. Waiver	198-205	286-289, 594-596, 755-760	782-794	151-166		825-833	729-738, 828-839, 1034-1036		206-212, 549-552
G. Moral or Past Consideration	230-240	217-218, 233-248	116-126	167-189	510-551	165-179	30-33, 203-216	312-326	184-192
II. MUTUAL ASSENT— OFFER AND ACCEPTANCE									
A. Mutual Assent	28-30, 84-85, 92, 95-99, 100-101, 113, 783-785	330-340, 357-360	127-137	328-342, 345-349, 476-490	141-179, 238-257	36-51	253-275	41-50	48-53, 94-96
B. Offers	16-33, 72-76, 80-84, 110-145, 259-263	257-258, 349-352, 357-360, 370-373, 377-388, 396-414, 422-425	137-159, 176-190, 215-218	359-410	257-279, 315-348, 357-364, 689-694	51-82, 261-307	276-306, 312, 321-324, 352-369, 373-410, 441-460, 479-512	71-107, 109-126, 175-206	437-495
C. Acceptance	84-110, 122-142	216-217, 228-233, 370-377, 388-396, 425-442, 447-451, 612-614	160-175, 215-218	425-439, 422-447, 461-470	238-257, 320-323, 391-400	61-80	306-373, 391-394	126-167	495-521
D. Time at Which a Communication Between Offeror and Offeree Becomes Effective	110-117	374-375, 384, 435-445	165-175	411-450	257, 348-370	55-61	337-340, 358-369	103-109, 121	500, 521-530
E. Interpretation	288-312	330-340, 498-508	569-591, 644-647	579-594	831-832, 843, 849-851	413-432, 476-493	747-753, 777-803	402-430	53-63
F. The Parol Evidence Rule	278-288, 301-311	457-508	544-569, 596-647	527-578	821-859	451-497	747-776	369-392	258-281

TEXT CORRELATION CHART—continued

Gilbert Law Summary Contracts	Calamari, Perillo, Bender Contracts 1989 (2nd ed.)	Dawson, Harvey, Henderson Contracts 1992 (6th ed.)	Farnsworth, Young Contracts 1988 (4th ed.)	Fuller, Eisenberg Basic Contract Law 1990 (5th ed.)	Kessler, Gilmore, Kronman Contracts 1986 (3rd ed.)	Knapp, Crystal Problems in Contract Law 1993 (3rd ed.)	Murphy, Speidel Studies in Contract Law 1991 (4th ed.)	Murray Contracts Cases and Materials 1991 (4th ed.)	Rossett Contract Law and Its Application 1988 (4th ed.)
III. DEFENSES									
A. Indefiniteness	33-84	349-366	245-252	497-526, 654-683, 691-695	179-201	307-350	411-478	66-71	441-445
B. Mistake	353-367	615-651	356-364		861-910	730-751	479-511	431-453	143-166
C. Contracts Induced by Fraud, Nondisclosure, Duress, or Undue Influence	182-205, 326-353	283-284, 296-298, 488-495, 563-574, 596-603, 647-658	314-318, 330-336, 342-354	47-53, 684-691	74-78, 84-96, 657-663	601-660	528-582	456-466	111-119, 140-143
D. Unconscionability	370-378, 496-499	700-726	364, 379, 385, 401-427	53-67	275, 284, 561, 564-625	660-678, 681-698, 1148,	582-623	466-481	124-136, 774-775
E. Statute of Frauds	757-783, 785-801	95-98, 269-275, 278-281, 957-974	253-288	B-1 to B-39	753-819	1174-1175, 351-412	683-745	329-369	249-258
F. Lack of Contractual Capacity	313-325	235-240, 297, 546-569, 964-965	290-301	176-177		585-601	512-527	261	96-111
G. Illegal Contracts	817-846	145-150, 431, 453-457, 489-495, 516-531, 770-773	440-470		36, 60-61, 76-77, 97-98	698-724	624-682	497-524	71-94
IV. THIRD-PARTY RIGHTS AND OBLIGATIONS									
A. Third-Party Beneficiaries	688-721	877-917	874-923	744-794	1329-1439	1197-1231	1335-1390	753-802	655-678
B. Assignment of Rights and Delegation of Duties	722-756	917-956	924-995	795-846	1441-1558	1231-1259	1279-1334	803-849	678-707
V. PERFORMANCE OF CONTRACT									
A. Obligation to Perform in Good Faith	69-71, 451-465, 502-509, 516-518	308-315, 718-722, 745-746, 773-785	301-302, 606-608, 764-771, 960-964, 979	848-876	201-238	432-439, 510-512	866-867, 888-901, 910-922, 1153-1171	491-497	64-71, 556-557, 910-922
B. Express Conditions	379-409	727-773	74-75, 78-82, 649-670	899-952	978-990, 1021-1059	809-844	804-846	525-539, 545-550, 603-612	537, 541-557, 592-593
C. Implied Conditions	410-439	786-826	670-676, 684-693, 771-772	953-982	985-987, 990-1021	857-870	846-888	549-561, 599-603	556-557
D. Order of Performance	416-417, 518-537	786-823, 853-857	670-676	953-965	983-985	878-889	809-810, 867-872	539-545	535-539, 553-556
E. Doctrine of Substantial Performance	439-447	779-781, 829-830, 837-844	501-506, 694-701	877-898	1050-1051	857-866	44-49, 859-873	574-588	553-556, 975-994
F. Divisible Contracts	447-450	822-825, 857-859	489, 677-678, 710-714, 725-734	974	1038-1039	865-866	873-888	561-565	614-620
G. Material vs. Minor Breach	419-423	844-853	679-683, 694-709, 717-723	974-981	106-110	849-857	859-873, 1028-1034	567-581	535-539, 592-593, 599-620

Gilbert Law Summary Contracts	Calamari, Perillo, Bender Contracts 1989 (2nd ed.)	Dawson, Harvey, Henderson Contracts 1992 (6th ed.)	Farnsworth, Young Contracts 1988 (4th ed.)	Fuller, Eisenberg Basic Contract Law 1990 (5th ed.)	Kessler, Gilmore, Kronman Contracts 1986 (3rd ed.)	Knapp, Crystal Problems in Contract Law 1993 (3rd ed.)	Murphy, Speidel Studies in Contract Law 1991 (4th ed.)	Murray Contracts Cases and Materials 1991 (4th ed.)	Rossett Contract Law and Its Application 1988 (4th ed.)
H. Anticipatory Breach	518-537	38-44, 53-60, 366, 798-802, 805-809, 853-857, 862-871	735-764	983-1027	1269-1328	870-890	1011-1021	591-599	620-653
I. Changed Circumstances—Impossibility and Frustration	538-587	658-700, 750-755, 773-777	809-873	696-743	861-971	751-785	924-987	613-656	557-591
J. Discharge	802-816	286-289, 526-531, 603-611	319-328, 337-342, 363-364	148-151	76-79, 650-703	793-799, 806-807	997-1003		199-228
VI. REMEDIES									
A. Introduction			1-12					657-658	
B. Basic Measures of Damages	588-606, 651-657	1-38, 80-132	108-116, 471-490	192-206, 192-206, 300-325	1061-1069, 1108-1201	891-917, 1025-1073	1036-1085, 1127-1128, 1148-1152, 1128-1152	657, 725-744	282-306, 339-364
C. Limitations on Expectation Damages	588-610	38-80	490-532	236-268	1138-1165, 1269-1328	917-961		659-725	316-338
D. Specific Performance	657-687	151-192, 391-396, 811-818, 871-876	19-35, 302-309, 404, 446, 535-536, 744-745	288-299	1069-1108	1077-1107	426-433, 1156-1163, 1171-1202	744-752	291-296
E. Expectation Damages and Specific Performance in Specific Cases									
1. Contracts for the Sale of Goods	611-620	22-26, 35-38, 53-65, 156-163, 170-173, 179-180, 810-818, 832-835, 859-862	479-485, 490-524, 527-532, 710-724	227-236	1129-1132, 1134-1138, 1165-1171	1158-1195	59-60, 1064-1065, 1085-1107, 1117-1128, 1137-1138	711-725	785-795
2. Contracts for the Sale of Realty	502-506, 657-660		806-807	292-294	478-480, 978, 1073-1074, 291-294	1087		341-345	
3. Employment Contracts	59-72, 606-611, 679-687	44-53, 109-113, 170-184, 277-281, 321-327	62-71, 430-437, 478-479, 492-498, 796-803	236-249	291-294	16-20, 24-31, 531-553, 1118-1120	1004-1009, 1099-1101, 1202-1213	233-242	880-938
4. Construction Contracts and Other Contracts for Services	525-529, 621-625		472, 490-492, 501-506, 520-524	716-723, 780, 783-785	1029-1048	146-151, 1077-1093, 1117-1118	44-49, 1070-1074, 1107-1112, 1195-1202	704-710	950-965, 994-1001
5. Late Performance in Contract for Carriage									

TEXT CORRELATION CHART—continued

Gilbert Law Summary Contracts	Calamari, Perillo, Bender Contracts 1989 (2nd ed.)	Dawson, Harvey, Henderson Contracts 1992 (6th ed.)	Farnsworth, Young Contracts 1988 (4th ed.)	Fuller, Eisenberg Basic Contract Law 1990 (5th ed.)	Kessler, Gilmore, Kronman Contracts 1986 (3rd ed.)	Knapp, Crystal Problems in Contract Law 1993 (3rd ed.)	Murphy, Speidel Studies in Contract Law 1991 (4th ed.)	Murray Contracts Cases and Materials 1991 (4th ed.)	Rossett Contract Law and Its Application 1988 (4th ed.)
F. Nominal Damages G. Liquidated Damages	639-651	119-126, 133-151, 157-158	13-14, 527, 532-543	271-287	1223-1237		1214-1235	693-704	392-414
H. Punitive Damages	625-628, 635-639	22, 26-29, 75-76, 192	5, 36	273-274	1212-1221	987-1001	73-77, 1045-1055		282-289, 422-432
I. Damages for Emotional Distress		73-76	524-526	268-273		973-986	49-56, 1039-1044	682-686	
J. Restitutionary Damages	439-447, 651-654, 657	80-132	115-116, 486, 488	305-325	1186-1188	1050-1073	1074-1085, 1127-1128	733-744	339-364

approach to exams

Just about any contracts exam question can be answered by analyzing five basic questions:

1. **Was a contract made between the parties?** (Formation problems—offer and acceptance, consideration.)

2. **Are there any reasons why the contract should not be enforced as agreed?** (Defenses to formation—indefiniteness, mistake, Statute of Frauds, etc.)

3. **Who has enforceable rights and/or duties under the contract?** (Problems of third-party beneficiaries, assignment and delegation.)

4. **Is there an absolute duty to perform?** (Problems of conditions, changed circumstances, discharge.)

5. **If the contract has been broken, what remedies are available to the innocent party?**

Of course, not all contracts questions will require a thorough discussion of all five issues, but you should consider each of them at least briefly before writing your answer.

For study purposes, be sure to review the more detailed approaches to specific topics in the **_chapter approach sections_** at the beginning of each chapter.

I. **HAS A VALID CONTRACT BEEN FORMED?** To establish an enforceable contract there must be a showing of (i) mutual assent, usually manifested by an **_offer_** and **_acceptance_**; and (ii) **_consideration_**.

A. **Was There an Effective Offer?** Consider the following:

1. **Bargaining Intent:** Does it appear that the offeror was intending to create present contractual rights and duties, or was he merely negotiating or inviting the other party to make an offer? (§§159-164)

2. **Definiteness:** Does the proposal cover, expressly or impliedly, certain essential factors (such as parties, subject matter, price, and time for performance) so that the court can determine what in fact the offeror was intending and whether he intended that a contract would be concluded by acceptance of his proposal? (§§165-166)

B. **Was There an Effective Acceptance?** Consider:

1. **Intent and Manner:** Did the offeree apparently intend, by her words or conduct in response to the offer, to create a contractual relationship between herself and the offeror? And, did the offeree manifest her assent to the offeror's proposal

in the manner required by the offer—*i.e.*, by the doing of an act, or by the giving of a promise? (This raises the distinction between unilateral and bilateral contracts; §253.) Special problems arise where:

a.   The offeree remains **silent**, intending thereby to accept (§§293-305); and

b.   The offeree purports to "accept" the offer in a **manner different** from that requested by the offeror (§§316-327).

2.   **Timeliness:** Did the acceptance become effective prior to the termination of the offer (such termination occurring by revocation of the offer, lapse of time, prior rejection, or counteroffer by the offeree)? (§§180-251)

a.   Where the parties are **dealing at a distance**, special rules (*e.g.*, the "mailbox rule") must be considered as to when an acceptance, revocation, or rejection becomes effective. (§§307-334)

b.   If the offeror has attempted to **revoke**, special rules must be considered as to whether the offer was revocable. (§§225-246)

3.   **Unconditional:** Has the offeree given unqualified assent to the proposal? If not, "acceptance" may operate as a rejection of the proposal and as a counteroffer. (§§196-217)

C.   Was There Legally Sufficient Consideration?

1.   **Bargain:** Did the parties make a bargain? (§§24-28)

a.   Is the consideration promised more than **nominal**? (§§30-36)

b.   Is the promise **illusory**? If the promisor has reserved some right, option, or alternative limiting the obligation, consider whether the right is unqualified (in which case the promise may be illusory). (§§44-75)

c.   Is the promise merely to perform some act that the promisor is **already obliged** to do ? (§§76-114)

2.   **Other Types of Consideration:** If the parties did not make a bargain, was there some other element of consideration?

a.   Was there **foreseeable reliance** on the promise? (§§16-23)

b.   Was there a **waiver** of some nonmaterial condition to the bargain? (§§127-129)

c. Was there a promise to pay based on *moral or past consideration* (*e.g.*, promise to pay debt barred by bankruptcy or the statute of limitations, promise to pay debt based on waiver of a defense, etc.)? (§§130-150)

d. Was there an *accord*? (§§115-126)

e. Was the promise in some *special form* (*e.g.*, under seal) that makes it enforceable? (§§8-12)

II. ARE THERE ANY REASONS NOT TO ENFORCE THE CONTRACT? Assuming that a contract has been formed, consider whether there are any defenses to the enforcement of the contract:

—Indefiniteness (§§401-446)

—Mistake (§§447-468)

—Fraud, nondisclosure, duress, undue influence (§§469-473)

—Unconscionability (§§474-497)

—Lack of a writing (required by Statute of Frauds) (§§498-548)

—Lack of contractual capacity (minors, mental incompetents) (§§549-555)

—Illegality of contract purpose or consideration (§§556-567)

III. DO ANY THIRD PARTIES HAVE ENFORCEABLE RIGHTS AND/OR OBLIGATIONS UNDER THE CONTRACT?

A. **Third-Party Beneficiary:** The "reasonable expectations" induced by the making of the contract may be those of some third party. If so, the third party (as well as the original promisee) may be entitled to enforce the bargain promise made in his or her favor. (§570) In determining the rights of such third parties, consider the following:

1. **Status:** Is the third party more than incidentally benefited by the promises made? Consider the distinction between "donee beneficiaries" and "creditor beneficiaries" vs. "incidental beneficiaries." (§§571-580)

2. **Vesting:** Have the rights of the third party vested? (§§589-591)

3. **Defenses:** What defenses or offsets may be asserted against the third party? (§§582-588)

B. **Assignees and Delegees:** Where, *subsequent* to the original contract, either party seeks to transfer to a third party some right and/or duty provided under the contract, several matters should be considered:

1. **Assignment of Rights**

    a. Are the rights *assignable*? (§§609-622)

    b. What is the *effect* of the assignment (what rights does the assignee have against the obligor, the obligor against the assignor, and what defenses may be asserted by the obligor)? (§§656-670)

    c. If the rights have been assigned successively to several assignees, which one of them has *priority*? (§§671-683)

2. **Delegation of Duties**

    a. Is the duty *capable* of being delegated? (§§687-689)

    b. What is the *effect* of the delegation (what are the liabilities of delegee to obligee, to obligor)? (§§690-699)

IV. **IS THERE AN ABSOLUTE DUTY TO PERFORM?** Once it has been determined that a contract has been made, the question is whether the reasonable expectations induced thereby have been fulfilled; and if not, whether performance has somehow been *excused or discharged* by events subsequent to the formation of the contract. Consider:

A. **Condition vs. Absolute Promise**

1. **Absolute Promise:** Was the promise absolute (*i.e.*, a covenant), or was it subject to some condition? (§§706-717)

2. **Subject to Condition:** If there was a *condition*, ask:

    a. In addition to any *express* conditions, was there any *implied* condition? (§§737-741)

    b. If there were any conditions, have they been *met*?

    c. If a condition has not occurred, has it been *excused* so that there is a duty to perform despite the fact the condition did not occur? (§§728-736)

B. **Present Duty to Perform**

1. **Conditions Precedent:** Have all *conditions precedent* been performed or excused (such as by anticipatory repudiation, prospective inability to perform, substantial performance)? (§§742-809)

2. **Changed Circumstances:** Did the circumstances change so that performance was *impossible* or highly impracticable? (§§810-826)

3. **Frustration:** Did the *purpose or value* of the contract become totally frustrated by some supervening event? (§827)

C. **Discharge of Duty to Perform:** Has the contract been discharged by full performance or some other ground such as rescission, release, accord and satisfaction, or a payment-in-full check? (§§828-838)

V. WHAT REMEDIES ARE AVAILABLE TO THE INNOCENT PARTY? Which remedy will best effectuate the innocent party's reasonable expectations under the contract (damages, restitution, specific performance)?

A. **Damages**

1. **Measure of Damages:** Remember that damages are the most common remedy. Where they are sought, what measure of damages best protects the expectations of the parties? (§§840-844)

2. **Expectation Damages:** What is required to put the injured party into the position he would have been in had the promise been performed? (This depends upon the nature of the contract and the position of the injured party). (§§864-902)

3. **Liquidated Damages:** What is the effect of any agreed measure of damages or any limitation on the measure of damages? (§§904-912)

B. **Specific Performance:** Is the legal remedy (*i.e.*, damages) adequate? If not, consider whether specific performance of the contract would better remedy the breach of contract. (§863)

C. **Restitution:** Would this alternative to damages be a more appropriate remedy? (Plaintiff may recover the reasonable value of the benefit conferred.) (§§924-933)

I. CONSIDERATION

chapter approach

Not every promise is legally enforceable. The concept of **consideration** in contract law concerns what kinds of promises are legally enforceable and what kinds are not. The term "consideration" is used in two related but somewhat different ways. Traditionally, the term is used to mean a legally enforceable bargain. Sometimes, however, the term is used to refer to any element, even a nonbargain element (such as reliance), that makes a promise legally enforceable.

Contracts examination questions typically involve a broken promise. Every question therefore must be preliminarily analyzed to determine if the promise that was broken was legally enforceable—in other words, whether there was consideration.

Because the basic kind of consideration is a bargain—an exchange of promises or a promise for performance—you should begin your analysis by determining whether the broken promise was given as part of a bargain. The answer to that question determines how you should then proceed.

1. Where the broken promise was **not** given as part of a bargain, it is unenforceable unless there is some **other** element that makes it enforceable. The nonbargain elements that may make a promise enforceable are:

   a. **Reliance**—did the promisee rely on the promise to his detriment?

   b. **Past or moral consideration**—was the promise given in recognition of a material benefit previously conferred on the promisor by the promisee?

   c. **Waiver**—did the promise merely waive a nonmaterial condition under a bargain?

   d. **Form**—was the promise in some special legal form, such as under seal in a state that still recognizes the binding force of the seal?

   If any of the these elements is present, the promise may be enforceable even though there was no bargain.

2. If the promise was apparently given as part of a bargain, you should ask yourself the following:

   a. Was the bargain merely **nominal**—*i.e.*, a bargain in form but not in substance? If so, the promise may be unenforceable as essentially a donative promise.

   b. Was the bargain based on a promise to **surrender** or **forbear from asserting** a legal claim? If so, usually it is enforceable only if the claim was reasonable or held in good faith.

   c. Was the promise **illusory**, *i.e.*, a statement that appeared to be a real promise, but in fact did not commit the promisor to any more than what he might later desire to do, or give him a free way out of his apparent commitment? If so, the promise may be unenforceable for lack of mutuality.

d.   Was the promise merely to take an action that the promisor was already ***legally obliged*** to take? If so, the promise may be unenforceable under the preexisting legal duty rule.

A.   INTRODUCTION

1.   **Importance of Consideration:** [§1]   The concept of "consideration" is very important in the law of contracts, because consideration is required to make a promise or contract enforceable.

2.   **What Is Consideration?**

a.   **"Benefit/detriment" approach:** [§2]   At an early stage in contract law, consideration was defined as a benefit received by the promisor (*e.g.*, receiving a television set) or a detriment incurred by the promisee (*e.g.*, delivering a television set). In practice, this definition was not very helpful. First, the definition is overbroad. Second, there are many cases where the definition does not really explain the results, because the law gives a special meaning to the terms "benefit" and "detriment."

b.   **"Bargain" approach:** [§3]   Because of the weaknesses of the early approach to consideration, the next stage of development was to treat consideration as equivalent to bargain. A bargain is an exchange of promises, acts, or both, in which each party views what she gives as the ***price*** of what she gets (*e.g.*, A promises to give B $500 if B will paint A's house: A gives $500 for a paint job and B gives a paint job for $500). The concept that equates consideration and bargain is the so-called ***bargain theory of consideration.***

c.   **"Enforceable element" approach:** [§4]   The bargain theory of consideration also has limits. First, not all bargain promises are enforceable (*see infra,* §§29 *et seq.*). Second, some promises are enforceable even though they are not bargains. Therefore, some authorities treat consideration as equivalent to ***any element***—including but not limited to bargains—that will make a promise or contract ***enforceable***.

3.   **Kinds of Promises Raising Consideration Issues:** [§5]   With the above background in mind, this chapter will examine the kinds of promises that may raise problems of consideration or enforceability. For this purpose, promises can be divided into six broad categories:

a.   Unrelied-upon donative promises;

b.   Relied-upon donative promises;

c.   Bargain promises;

d.   Promises involving an accord and satisfaction;

e. Promises to waive conditions; and

f. Promises based on past or moral consideration.

B. UNRELIED-UPON DONATIVE PROMISES

1. **General Rule:** [§6]   A *donative* (or gratuitous) promise is a promise to make a gift (*e.g.,* A promises to give B a car). The general rule is that a donative promise is *unenforceable* because there is a lack of consideration. [Schnell v. Nell, 17 Ind. 29 (1861)]

   a. **Exceptions:** [§7]   A donative promise may be enforceable if it is under seal (*see infra,* §8), or if it is relied upon (*see infra,* §§17 *et seq.*). In addition, a promise to compensate the promisee for a benefit previously conferred by the promisee or the promisor that gave rise to a moral obligation is not treated as a simple donative promise, and such a promise may also be enforceable (*see infra,* §§130 *et seq.*).

2. **Effect of a Seal:** [§8]   A seal is a piece of wax (or a wafer or some other substance resembling a piece of wax) that is affixed to a written contract, or an indented impression resembling a seal that is made with a tool on a written contract. By statute or decision in many states, a seal may also be written or printed, or may consist of the word "seal," or a pen scrawl (or "scroll"), or some other sign to represent a seal (including the letters "L.S.," which stands for "locus sigilli," meaning "place of the seal" in Latin). At common law, any promise under seal, even a donative promise, is legally enforceable. This rule still holds true where not changed by statute.

   a. **Statutory modification:** [§9]   A large number of states have enacted statutes that either abolish the binding effect of a seal or provide that a seal raises only a presumption of consideration. [*See, e.g.,* Wis. Stat. Ann. §328.57]

      (1) **Presumption statute—promisor must show lack of consideration:** [§10] A statute providing that a seal only raises a presumption of consideration is usually interpreted to mean that if a promisee brings an action on a promise that is under seal, the *promisor* has the burden of proving the absence of consideration. (Normally, a *promisee* has the burden of proving the presence of consideration.)

3. **Effect of Writing:** [§11]   In the absence of a statute, the fact that a donative promise is in writing does not make the promise enforceable. [Hill v. Corbett, 204 P.2d 485 (Wash. 1949)]

   a. **Statutory modifications:** [§12]   However, a few states have statutes providing that a promise in writing is presumed to have been given for consideration. [*See, e.g.,* N.M. Stat. Ann. §20.2-8; Cal. Civ. Code §1614] But this presumption is rebuttable.

4. **Nominal Consideration:** [§13]   Nominal consideration exists when a donative promise is falsely put by the parties into the *form* of a bargain (*e.g.,* A, who wants to promise to make a gift of a car to B, agrees to "sell" B a new car for $1; this is called "nominal" consideration because there is consideration—a bargain—in name only).

Although the authorities are not in accord, the prevailing view today is that nominal consideration will not make a donative promise enforceable (*see infra,* §31).

5. **Conditional Donative Promises:** [§14]   A donative promise is conditional if the promisor intends to confer a gift on the promisee, but the nature of the gift is such that some condition must be fulfilled before the gift is made (*e.g.,* A tells B that she will give B her television if he comes over to her house to get it). A conditional donative promise is no more enforceable than any other donative promise, and this is true even if the condition has been fulfilled, except to the extent that fulfillment of the promise constitutes foreseeable reliance (*see infra,* §§18-21).

   a. **Conditional donative promise vs. bargain promise:** [§15]   A conditional donative promise sometimes looks like a bargain. The difference between a conditional donative promise and a bargain is that in a conditional donative promise, fulfillment of the condition is not the *price* of the promisor's performance. It is sometimes difficult to distinguish a conditional donative promise from a bargain promise. The test is how the *parties view* the condition. If the condition is viewed as simply a necessary part of making the gift, the promise is donative. But if the parties view performance of the condition as the price of the promise, there is a bargain, and the rules applicable to bargains apply.

     (1) **Example:** A telephones B and says, "I have a gift for you. If you come over to my house, you can have it now." B comes over, but A does not give him the gift. A's promise is not enforceable because coming over to A's house was not the "price" of the gift; rather, the parties viewed coming over to the house as the way to take possession of the gift.

     (2) **Compare:** Uncle promises Nephew $5,000 if Nephew will abstain from smoking and drinking until he reaches age 21. Nephew agrees and abstains. Uncle must pay the $5,000. Even if Uncle's motive was altruistic, it was understood that $5,000 was the price Uncle was willing to pay for Nephew's abstention. [Hamer v. Sidway, 124 N.Y. 538 (1891)]

C. RELIED-UPON DONATIVE PROMISES—DOCTRINE OF PROMISSORY ESTOPPEL

Often, a donative promise is relied upon by the promisee.

1. **Former Rule—Reliance Irrelevant:** [§16]   The rule at one time was that reliance was irrelevant; a donative promise was unenforceable even if it was relied upon. [Kirksey v. Kirksey, 8 Ala. 131 (1845)]

2. **Modern Rule:** [§17]   Today, however, the rule is that if a donative promise induces reliance by the promisee in a manner that the promisor should reasonably have expected, the promise will be *legally enforceable*, at least to the extent of the reliance. [Feinberg v. Pfeiffer Co., 322 S.W.2d 163 (Mo. 1959)]

   a. **Restatement (First) section 90:** [§18]   The modern rule stems from section 90 of the Restatement (First) of Contracts ("Restatement First"), which provided that "a promise which the promisor should reasonably expect to induce action or forbearance of a definite and substantial character on the part of the promisee and which does induce such action or forbearance is binding if injustice can be avoided only by enforcement of the promise."

(1) **Principle of "promissory estoppel":** [§19]   The principle of section 90 is sometimes known as the principle of "promissory estoppel." This terminology reflects the idea that where a promisee has relied on a donative promise, for reasons of justice the promisor should be estopped (prevented) from pleading lack of consideration. Under modern law and practice, however, the promisee does not proceed on the theory of estoppel. Instead, reliance is viewed as either a substitute for consideration (when the term "consideration" is reserved for bargains) or as consideration itself (when the term "consideration" means any element that makes a promise enforceable). The term "promissory estoppel" nevertheless remains in wide use as a description of the principle that reliance may make a donative promise enforceable.

b. **Restatement (Second) section 90:** [§20]   Section 90 of Restatement (Second) of Contracts ("Restatement Second") perpetuates Restatement First section 90, with certain changes:

(1) **Remedy may be limited to extent of reliance:** [§21]   Under Restatement First, some authorities argued that if a relied-upon donative promise was enforceable at all, it was enforceable to its **full extent** (*i.e.*, the amount promised, or expectation damages). [Williston, Treatise on the Law of Contracts ("Williston") (3d ed. 1979) §1338, n. 7] However, Restatement Second section 90 makes it clear that damages may be limited **to the extent of the reliance** (*i.e.*, reliance damages), by stating that "the remedy granted for breach may be limited as justice requires." [Rest. 2d §90]

(a) **Example:** Aunt promises to reimburse Nephew $1,000 for opera tickets that Nephew will purchase for his own use. Nephew purchases tickets for $500, and Aunt revokes. Under Restatement First section 90, Nephew might have been entitled to the full extent of the promised sum —$1,000. Under Restatement Second section 90, however, Nephew would be entitled to enforce Aunt's promise only to the extent that the promise was relied upon—$500.

(2) **Substantial reliance not required:** [§22]   Restatement First section 90 required that the reliance be of "a definite and substantial character." Under Restatement Second section 90, it is enough that the promisor should have reasonably expected that the promise would induce reliance.

3. **Reliance as Consideration:** [§23]   Some authorities, including the Restatements, limit the term "consideration" to bargains. According to these authorities, a relied-upon donative promise is enforceable **despite** the absence of consideration—*i.e.*, despite the absence of bargain. However, other authorities treat promissory estoppel as simply a type of consideration. [Feinberg v. Pfeiffer Co., *supra*]

a. **Comment:** This difference in approach is basically a question of nomenclature. The result in any given case is the same under either view—the promise is enforceable.

D. BARGAIN PROMISES

1. **General Rule—Bargain Constitutes Consideration:** [§24]   A bargain is an exchange in which each party views his promise or performance as the price of the other's promise or performance. As a general rule, a bargain constitutes consideration–*i.e.*, a bargained-for promise is enforceable.

   a. **Equal value not required:** [§25]   In most cases, the law does not examine whether a bargained-for promise or performance is commensurate in value with the counterpromise or performance, as long as the contract is not "unconscionable" (*i.e.*, so unfair as to shock the court's conscience; *see infra*, §§475-497). [Batsakis v. Dematsis, 226 S.W.2d 673 (Tex. 1949); Rest. 2d §§71, 72, 79] The theory is that the parties to a bargain are the best judges of its desirability for each of them. The traditional way in which this approach is formulated is that "adequacy of consideration will not be reviewed."

      (1) **Gross disparity as evidence:** [§26]   However, gross disparity between the value of what is done or to be done by each party may be used as *evidence* to support certain *independent* defenses; *e.g.*, incapacity, fraud, duress, etc. (*infra*, §§469 *et seq.*).

      (2) **Unconscionability:** [§27]   Furthermore, under the modern doctrine of unconscionability, courts may directly examine a disparity in value to determine whether the disparity is so great as to be unconscionable. Normally this doctrine is applied to determine whether the *process* that lead to the bargain was unconscionable—*e.g.*, because terms in a form contract were unfairly surprising, or because one party improperly exploited the other's ignorance. In some cases, however, the courts use the doctrine to upset contracts that appear to be so imbalanced as to be oppressive without regard to defects in the bargaining process.

      (3) **Equitable remedies:** [§28]   Furthermore, adequacy of consideration may be reviewed by the courts when an equitable remedy (*e.g.*, specific performance—under which a court orders a party to perform rather than merely to pay damages), rather than a legal remedy, such as damages, is sought. Equity normally requires a showing of fairness and substantial equivalence in value as a condition to granting relief.

2. **Exceptions—Bargains That Are Not Consideration:** [§29]   Although bargains normally constitute consideration and are therefore legally enforceable, there are several types of cases in which bargains or apparent bargains do not constitute consideration (or "lack consideration") and are therefore unenforceable. These cases fall into four major categories:

   (i) *Nominal consideration* (transactions that are bargains in form but not in substance);

   (ii) Promises to *surrender or forbear from asserting a legal claim*;

   (iii) Apparent bargains involving an *illusory* promise; and

(iv) Bargains involving a *preexisting legal obligation.*

a. **Nominal consideration:** [§30]   A transaction is said to involve nominal consideration when a promisor has falsely cast the promise in the *form* of a bargain with the promisee, in an attempt to make the promise enforceable, and although the transaction has the form of a bargain, it lacks the *substance* of a bargain because neither party really views each promised performance as the price of the other.

(1) **Example:** Father promises to give Daughter a house in exchange for one dollar. It is clear that neither Father nor Daughter views the dollar as the price of the house. Rather, the transaction has only the form of a bargain, a form adopted for the obvious purpose of making Father's donative promise legally enforceable. The consideration—*i.e.,* the bargain—is not real; it is only nominal.

(2) **Enforceability of promises given for nominal consideration**

(a) **Donative promises:** [§31]   Although the authorities are not in complete accord, the prevailing view is that nominal consideration will not make a donative promise enforceable. [Schnell v. Nell, *supra,* §6; Rest. 2d §71]

(b) **Options and guaranties:** [§32]   Nominal consideration *will* make options and guaranties enforceable, provided certain conditions are met.

1) **Options:** [§33]   An option is a promise to hold an offer open for a fixed amount of time. Although the cases are split, most courts hold that nominal consideration makes an option binding, at least if the option is in writing and proposes an exchange on fair terms. [Real Estate Co. v. Rudolph, 153 A. 438 (Pa. 1930); Rest. 2d §87; *and see infra,* §195]

a) **Compare—U.C.C. "firm offers":** [§34]   Under the Uniform Commercial Code ("U.C.C."), a written "firm offer" by a merchant to buy or sell goods is irrevocable for the period of time stated in the offer (or if no time is stated, for a reasonable time) without the necessity of any consideration or even a recital of consideration. [U.C.C. §2-205; *and see infra,* §§233-238]

2) **Guaranties:** [§35]   As with options, most courts hold that nominal consideration will make a guaranty binding, at least if the promise is in writing. [Rest. 2d §88]

3) **Rationale:** [§36]   Options and guaranties usually are not donative promises, but rather are promises designed to facilitate or further a proposed bargain. They serve an important commercial purpose and are likely to be relied upon. Therefore, it is not surprising that the law would be ready to enforce such promises even if they are not part of a real bargain. (Note, however, that if an option or a

guaranty lacks both real *and* nominal consideration, it will normally be unenforceable unless either (i) it is relied upon, or (ii) a statute, such as U.C.C. section 2-205, provides for its enforcement; *see infra,* §§233-238.)

b. **Promises to surrender or forbear from asserting a legal claim:** [§37]   A bargained-for promise to surrender or forbear from asserting a claim that is reasonable and held in good faith constitutes consideration. A problem arises, however, when the claim is not reasonable, is not held in good faith, or is neither reasonable nor held in good faith.

(1) **Former rule—honest *and* reasonable belief required:** [§38]   At one time, the courts held that a bargained-for promise to surrender or forbear from asserting a legal claim would constitute consideration only if there was an honest *and* reasonable basis for believing the claim to be valid. [Springstead v. Nees, 125 App. Div. 230 (1908)] This rule was adopted in Restatement First section 76, which provided that "[t]he surrender of, or forbearance to assert, an invalid claim or defense by one who has not an honest *and* reasonable belief in its possible validity" is not consideration. (Emphasis added.)

(2) **Modern rule—honest *or* reasonable belief suffices:** [§39]   The modern rule is that a promise to surrender or forbear from asserting a claim is consideration if the promisor's belief in the validity of the claim is *either* reasonable *or* held in good faith. [Kossick v. United Fruit Co., 365 U.S. 731 (1961)]

(a) **Restatement Second:** [§40]   This rule has been adopted in Restatement Second section 74, which changes the rule of Restatement First section 76 by providing that "forbearance to assert, or the surrender of, an invalid claim or defense is not consideration unless (i) the claim or defense is in fact doubtful because of uncertainty as to the facts or law, *or* (ii) the forbearing or surrendering party honestly believes that his claim or defense is just and may be determined to be valid." (Emphasis added.)

(3) **Actual surrender or forbearance:** [§41]   The rules that govern a bargained-for *promise* to surrender or forbear from asserting a claim also govern a bargained-for *act* of surrendering or forbearing to assert a claim. That is a bargain for the actual surrender of or actual forbearance to assert a claim (as opposed to a bargain for a promise to surrender or forbear) will constitute consideration only where the claim is reasonable or held in good faith.

(4) **Written release:** [§42]   Some authorities take the position that execution of a written release may constitute consideration even if there is neither a reasonable basis for the claim released nor a good faith belief in its validity. [Mullen v. Hawkins, 40 N.E. 797 (Ind. 1895); Rest. 2d §74]

(a) **Example:** Steven Surrender, while a passenger in Nora Negligent's car, is involved in a minor accident resulting from Negligent's lack of care. Surrender, believing he has suffered no injury, makes no claim against Negligent or Negligent's insurer. However, Negligent's insurer is eager to close the file on the case. The insurer therefore approaches Surrender and offers him $200 if he will sign a release. Surrender's execution of the release constitutes consideration even though Surrender does not believe he has a claim.

(5) **Forbearance where no specific period stated:** [§43]   Suppose A agrees, as part of a bargain, to forbear from asserting a legal claim, but no specific period of time is stated during which she must forbear. In such cases, the court will interpret the promise as one to forbear for a *reasonable time*.

(a) **Example:** Suppose B requests A to forbear from asserting a claim that A has against X, and promises to pay A if A forbears and X does not pay. A agrees, and forbears for 11 months. At the end of 11 months, A sues X or otherwise asserts her claim. When X does not pay, A sues B. B defends on the ground that because A asserted her claim against X, she did not keep her part of the bargain. In such a situation, most courts hold that A's promise should not be interpreted as a promise to forbear *forever*, but only as a promise to forbear for a *reasonable* time. [*See* Strong v. Sheffield, 144 N.Y. 392 (1895)] Therefore, if 11 months was a reasonable time, A will prevail in her action against B.

c. **Illusory promises**

(1) **General rule—mutuality of obligation required in bilateral contract:** [§44]   A bargain consisting of an *exchange of promises* is called a *bilateral contract*. (*See* detailed discussion *infra,* §§254-267.) The general rule is that for a bilateral contract to be enforceable, it must have *mutuality of obligation—i.e.,* both parties must be bound. If both parties to a bilateral contract are not bound, neither will be bound. The major impact of the mutuality rule is that an illusory promise is not consideration.

(a) **"Illusory promise" defined:** [§45]   An illusory promise is a statement that has the form of a promise, but is not a real promise in substance. A real promise is a commitment that limits one's future options as compared to one's options immediately before the promise was made. An illusory promise does not limit one's future options. Rather, an illusory promise is an *apparent commitment* that *actually* leaves a "free way out" (*e.g.,* "I will buy wheat from you at $10/bushel *insofar as I want to buy* wheat from you at that price," or "I will buy all my requirements of wheat from you at $10/bushel but *I may terminate my obligation at any time*").

d. **Effect of illusory promise:** [§46]   Under the mutuality rule, if one party makes an illusory promise in exchange for another's real promise, neither party is bound. The first party is not bound simply because he has not made a real promise—nothing he has said limits his future options. The second party is not bound because all she received in exchange for her real promise was an illusory promise, which is not consideration, and a promise without consideration is unenforceable.

(1) **Examples**

    (a) **Promise to do an act "if I want to":** [§47] One common example of an illusory promise is a promise to do a certain act "if I want to." The "promise" is illusory because after making the statement, the "promisor" has not limited his options. He is just as free to do whatever he wants after he makes the statement as he was before he made the statement. He has a free way out by simply deciding that he does not "want" to do the act.

        1) **Example:** On January 1, Seller agrees to sell to Buyer, at $100/ton, all the steel that Buyer orders from Seller until December 31. In exchange, Buyer agrees to buy from Seller, at $100/ton, "all the steel that she decides to order from Seller" until December 31. Seller then refuses to fill Buyer's orders, and Buyer sues. Seller wins. Buyer's "promise" is illusory. All Buyer has said is that she will buy from Seller as much steel as she decides to order from Seller. After making this statement, Buyer is just as free to buy (or refuse to buy) from Seller as she was before she made the statement; she can buy the steel she needs from either Seller or anyone else. Because Buyer's promise is illusory, there is no consideration for Seller's promise, and it is therefore unenforceable.

        2) **Compare:** In the example above, if Buyer had promised to buy from Seller "all the steel she requires," rather than "all the steel she decides to order from Seller," she might be deemed to have made a *real* promise—a promise to purchase her steel requirements *from Seller.* (*See infra,* §§68-75.) In that case, Buyer would be bound because she would have made a commitment that *did* limit her future options. And if Buyer would be bound, Seller would be bound, because the agreement would not lack mutuality.

    (b) **Right to terminate at will without notice:** [§48] Another common example of an illusory promise is a real promise coupled with a power to terminate the obligation under the promise at will and without notice. Such a power gives a free way out and therefore renders the promise illusory. [Miami Coca-Cola Bottling Co. v. Orange Crush Co., 296 F.2d 693 (5th Cir. 1924); Bernstein v. W. B. Manufacturing Co., 131 N.E. 200 (Mass. 1921)]

        1) **Example**: TV Network agrees to sell Avon 20 minutes of advertising time per month, at $5,000 per minute, in exchange for Avon's promise to buy 20 minutes every month. The agreement provides that Avon can cancel without notice at any time. Network then refuses to provide advertising to Avon at the agreed-upon rate, and Avon sues. Network wins. Avon had a free way out, because it could cancel the contract before it had purchased any advertising. Therefore, Avon's promise was illusory and was not consideration for Network's promise.

2) **U.C.C. section 2-309:** U.C.C. section 2-309(3) provides that "termination of a contract by one party except on the happening of an agreed event requires that *reasonable notification* be received by the other party, and an agreement dispensing with notification *is invalid* if its operation would be unconscionable." (Emphasis added.) Under this section, a contractual provision that gives one party to a sale-of-goods contract the right to cancel or terminate may be held subject to an implied requirement of reasonable notification. In that case, a contract that is silent on the issue of notice for termination could not be canceled without reasonable notice, and therefore might not be illusory, because the promise would be binding during the period between the time when notice was given and the time when the notice would be effective. Similarly, an agreement *dispensing* with the necessity of notice may be held invalid under section 2-209(3), and therefore might not render the promise illusory. If the right to cancel is in fact limited under section 2-209(3), and the promise is therefore not illusory, the contract would have consideration and could be enforced by either party.

(2) **Exceptions to mutuality rule**

(a) **Unilateral contracts:** [§49] The doctrine of mutuality is applicable only to *bilateral* contracts (*i.e.*, where a promise is given in exchange for a promise). It is not applicable to *unilateral* contracts. In a unilateral contract, one person makes a promise in exchange for another person's act. The second person is not bound to perform the act, but if she does, the promise becomes enforceable. Thus, in a unilateral contract, it is always true that one party is never bound. Nevertheless, the promise is enforceable. *Rationale*: Unlike the bilateral contract case, where the person who makes the real promise does not get anything in return (except a "meaningless" illusory promise), in the unilateral contract case, the promisor *does* get something in return—the act she bargained for.

1) **Example:** A promises to pay B $200 if B cuts down a tree in A's yard. A makes it clear that she wants B's performance, not merely B's promise. B never promises to cut down the tree, but does so. A must pay B $200, although B was never bound.

(b) **Limited promises:** [§50] If a real promise is made, lack of mutuality is not a defense, *however limited the promise may be.* [Lindner v. Mid-Continent Oil Corp., 252 S.W.2d 631 (Ark. 1952); Gurfein v. Werbelovsky, 118 A. 32 (Conn. 1922)]

1) **Example:** Lindner leased a filling station to Mid-Continent for three years, with an option in Mid-Continent to renew for two more years. Although Lindner was therefore bound for up to five years, Mid-Continent had the right to terminate the lease at any time on 10 days' notice. Lindner claimed the lease lacked mutuality. Held, for Mid-Continent. At the very least, Mid-Continent

bound itself to pay rent for 10 days, and Mid-Continent therefore had made a real promise. [Lindner v. Mid-Continent Oil Corp., *supra*]

2) **Example:** Buyer promises to buy 20 tons of steel per month from Seller at $100/ton, subject to cancellation by Buyer without notice at any time. Buyer's promise is illusory. However, if Buyer also agreed to purchase a minimum of 50 tons, or to cancel only on 30 days' notice, Buyer would have limited her future options, and her promise therefore would constitute consideration.

(c) **Voidable promises:** [§51] A real promise is not rendered illusory merely because the contract is voidable by one party as a matter of law. [Atwell v. Jenkins, 40 N.E. 178 (Mass. 1895); Rest. 2d §78]

1) **Example:** A, who is 17 years old, agrees to buy a two-karat diamond ring from B for $5,000, and B agrees to sell the ring to A for that price. The contract is voidable by A on the ground of infancy (*see infra,* §548), and is therefore unenforceable against her. Nevertheless, B is bound. Although the contract is not enforceable against A, A has made a real promise. The bargain can therefore be enforced *by A* despite the fact that it cannot be enforced *against her*. The same result would follow if the contract was voidable by A (and therefore unenforceable against her) for some other reason, such as the Statute of Frauds.

2) **Compare—void promises:** [§52] It is sometimes said that a promise that is unenforceable by reason of law *is* illusory if the promise is not merely voidable, but void. [*See* Rest. 2d §75] However, this distinction between void and voidable promises is questionable, both in terms of the doctrine and the cases, and in any event very few contracts are completely void (*see infra,* §§548, 559).

(d) **Conditional promises:** [§53] A conditional promise is a promise that the promisor need only perform if a specified condition occurs. Such a promise is a real commitment. The promisor has limited his future options, because if the condition does occur the promisor must perform. Therefore, a conditional promise is not illusory, and constitutes valid consideration. This is true even if the condition is within the promisor's control. [Scott v. Moragues, 80 So. 394 (Ala. 1918)]

1) **Example:** A and B agree that if A acquires a Chevrolet dealership, she will hire B as her sales manager for one year at a salary of $40,000, and B will accept that employment. Although the occurrence of the condition is within A's control (because she need not acquire the dealership), A has nevertheless limited her options. Before A made the agreement, she had the option of acquiring the dealership and hiring anyone she wanted as sales manager. After she made the agreement, if she acquires the dealership she is

bound to hire B as her sales manager. A's promise is therefore not illusory, and is consideration for B's promise.

(e) **Alternative promises:** [§54]   An alternative promise is one in which the promisor can discharge his obligation by choosing between two or more alternatives (*e.g.*, A promises B that he will paint B's porch or B's garage for $500).

1) **General rule—each alternative must constitute consideration:** [§55]   A contract involving alternative promises will be enforceable *only if each* of the performances would have been consideration if bargained for alone.

a) **Example:**   Reader promises Bookseller that if Bookseller gives Reader $100, Reader will either give Bookseller a rare copy of *Tom Sawyer* or straighten out Bookseller's shelves, at Reader's choice. Reader's promise constitutes consideration, because either performance would be consideration.

b) **Example:**   Reader promises Bookseller that if Bookseller gives Reader $100, Reader will either give Bookseller a rare copy of *Tom Sawyer* or serve on a jury if called to jury duty, at Reader's choice. Reader's promise does not constitute consideration because serving on a jury is a legal duty, the performance of a legal duty is not consideration (*see infra,* §§76-83), and therefore each of the alternatives would not constitute consideration standing alone.

2) **Contracts giving promisee the right to choose between alternatives:** [§56]   If, on the other hand, the *promisee* has the right to demand one of several alternative performances from the promisor, a promise to render alternative performances is consideration if *any one* of the alternative performances would be consideration.

a) **Example:**   Reader promises Bookseller that if Bookseller gives Reader $100, Bookseller may choose to have Reader either give Bookseller a rare copy of *Tom Sawyer* or serve on a jury. Because the promisee, Bookseller, could choose to receive the book, Reader's promise is consideration.

(f) **Agreements allowing one party to supply or determine a material term:** [§57]   An agreement may leave open a certain term (*e.g.*, price or quantity) and provide that the term will be supplied or determined by one of the parties in the future.

1) **Common law rule—promise illusory:** [§58]   At common law, the general rule is that if the omitted term is material the promise is illusory.

a) **Example:** A agrees to sell B wheat at a designated price, and the contract provides that A can determine how much wheat he will sell. Under the common law rule, A's promise is illusory, on the theory that A has undertaken no more of an obligation than he might decide to impose on himself at some later date. As a result, under the doctrine of mutuality neither A nor B would be bound. [Washington Chocolate Co. v. Canterbury Candy Makers, 138 P.2d 195 (Wash. 1943)]

2) **Exceptions**

a) **Power to alter terms:** [§59]   A number of decisions hold that if a term is fixed in the contract, but one party is given the power to *alter or modify* the term, the power does not make that party's promise illusory. These cases construe such a power as subject to an *implied covenant of fair dealing.* Therefore, the party with the power to alter the term does not have a free way out, because her power to alter the term is not completely free, but must be exercised in good faith. [Automatic Vending Co. v. Wisdom, 182 Cal. App. 2d 354 (1960)]

b) **Objective standard for establishing terms:** [§60]   Even the power to set (rather than merely to vary) a term does not necessarily render illusory the promise of the party who has the power to set the term if the term must be fixed in relation to an objective measure. For example, a power in a seller to set the price would not render the seller's promise illusory where: (i) the same price must be charged by the seller to all other buyers; or (ii) the contract price is "four cents less than the market price at Town A," or the "posted price charged by the seller" in a given area. [Moore v. Shell Oil Co., 6 P.2d 216 (Or. 1931)]

3) **U.C.C. provisions:** [§61]   The U.C.C. potentially affects the common law rule in several ways.

a) **General obligation of good faith:** [§62]   U.C.C. section 1-203 provides that "every contract or duty within this Act imposes an obligation of good faith in its performance or enforcement." Thus, a party who has the right unilaterally to set term of a sale-of-goods contract is limited by the duty to act in good faith. While section 1-203 does not specifically provide that an agreement that permits a party to set a term of the contract satisfies the requirement of consideration, this result might be reached on the theory that because of the good faith requirement, a party with the right to set a term does not have unlimited discretion, and therefore the promise is not illusory.

b) **Setting price:** [§63]   The U.C.C. has a special rule—beyond section 1-203's general obligation of good faith—if a party is given the right unilaterally to set the price term in a contract for the sale of goods. U.C.C. section 2-305(1) explicitly changes the common law rule by providing that such contracts are **enforceable** if the parties so intend. Under U.C.C. section 2-305(2), the party setting the price has a duty to exercise the power in good faith, whether or not the contract explicitly so provides.

(g) **Implied promises:** [§64] The principle of mutuality is satisfied where, although a party does not seem to have made a promise if regard is had only for the party's explicit words, a promise nevertheless is **implied** (in fact or in law) from the party's words or actions. In such cases, the implied promise serves as consideration just as if it were an explicit promise.

  1) **Implied promise to use reasonable or best efforts:** [§65] A common type of implied promise is an implied promise to use "reasonable efforts" or "best efforts." For example, suppose S promises to give A an exclusive right to market S's services and products, but A does not explicitly promise to market those services and products. S then claims that the contract is unenforceable because it lacks consideration, since A made no promise.

    a) **Rule of *Wood v. Lucy*:** [§66] In the landmark case of *Wood v. Lucy*, Judge Cardozo held that A could enforce a contract of this sort, on the ground that A had made an **implied** promise to use **reasonable efforts** to market S's services and products. [Wood v. Lucy, 222 N.Y. 88 (1917)]

    b) **U.C.C. section 2-306(2):** [§67] In cases involving the sale of goods, U.C.C. section 2-306(2) codifies the rule in *Wood v. Lucy* by providing that unless the parties agree otherwise, a lawful agreement for exclusive dealing in goods imposes an obligation "by the seller to use best efforts to supply the goods and by the buyer to use best efforts to promote their sale."

      1/ **Note:** Because the U.C.C. rule applies only to the sale of goods, *Wood v. Lucy* remains an important precedent in cases involving other areas, such as services or real estate.

(h) **Requirements and output contracts:** [§68] In a **requirements** contract, A agrees to buy all of his requirements of a given commodity from B, and B agrees to sell that amount to A. In an **output** contract, A agrees to sell all of his output of a commodity to B, and B agrees to buy that amount from A.

  1) **Former rule—agreement illusory:** [§69] At one time, some courts treated requirements and output contracts as illusory, on the ground that the buyer in a requirements contract was not obliged to

have any requirements and the seller in an output contract was not obliged to produce any output.

    a) **Exception for established businesses:** [§70]   Many courts, however, held that such contracts were enforceable if the promisor had an established business at the time the contract was made. [Pessin v. Fox Head Waukesha Corp., 282 N.W. 582 (Wis. 1938)]

2) **Modern rule:** [§71]   Today, the courts normally enforce requirements and output contracts regardless of whether the promisor had an established business at the time the contract was made, because the parties really have limited their options. If the buyer in a requirements contract wants to buy *any* of the commodity during the term of the contract, he must buy it all from the seller. If the seller in an output contract wants to produce *any* of the commodity during the term of the contract, he must sell it all to the buyer. [McMichael v. Price, 57 P.2d 549 (Okla. 1936)]

    a) **Example:**   If A promises to buy from B "such coal as I may wish to order from you," A has actually promised nothing since he is still free to buy from anyone else he chooses. His promise is illusory and does not constitute consideration. [Wickham & Burton Coal Co. v. Farmers Lumber Co., 179 N.W. 417 (Iowa 1920)]

    b) **Compare:**   However, if A promises to buy from B "all the coal that I will need" or "all the coal that I require in my business," A's promise *is* consideration. A has restricted his freedom of action, because if A needs any coal, he must buy it from B and no one else.

3) **U.C.C. section 2-306(1):** [§72]   A requirements or output contract that involves the sale of goods (as most such contracts do) is governed by U.C.C. section 2-306(1). This section *assumes* the enforceability of such contracts, and goes on to provide rules governing the performance of such contracts.

    a) **Obligation of good faith:** [§73]   The U.C.C. provides that "a term which measures the quantity by the output of the seller or the requirements of the buyer means such actual output or requirements as may occur *in good faith*." (Emphasis added.) Thus, the party who determines the quantity of requirements or output under such a contract must conduct the business in good faith and according to commercial standards of fair dealing in the trade, so that output or requirements will approximate a reasonably foreseeable figure. [U.C.C. §2-306(1), comment 2]

b) **Limitations on quantity:** [§74]   In addition to the limit imposed by the principle of good faith, U.C.C. section 2-306(1) provides an objective limit. Under that section, "no quantity unreasonably disproportionate to any stated estimate, or in the absence of a stated estimate to any normal or otherwise comparable prior output or requirements, may be tendered or demanded." The Official Comment adds that if an estimate of requirements or output is included in the agreement, it will be treated as "a center around which the parties intend [any] variation to occur." [U.C.C. §2-306(1), comment 3]

c) **Implied promise to remain in business:** [§75]   It might be thought that a seller could avoid the obligation of an output contract, and a buyer could avoid the obligation of a requirements contract, by going out of business, in which event the seller would have no output and the buyer would have no requirements. However, going out of business is itself detrimental. [Brightwater Paper Co. v. Monadnock Paper Mills, 161 F.2d 869 (1st Cir. 1947); McMichael v. Price, *supra*] Furthermore, the freedom to go out of business may be limited by the obligation to perform in good faith. As a general rule, if a party to an output or requirements contract goes out of business for reasons *other than* the profitability of the contract in question, there is no breach of the duty to perform in good faith. However, a shutdown motivated by the unprofitability of the contract in question may violate the duty. Thus, a shutdown by a requirements buyer for lack of orders might be permissible, whereas a shutdown merely to curtail losses under the contract in question might not be. [*See* U.C.C. §2-306(1), comment 2]

e. **Legal duty rule—promise to perform act promisor already obliged to perform**

(1) **General rule:** [§76]   Another exception to the principle that bargains are consideration is that a promise to perform an act that the promisor has a pre-existing legal duty to perform (*i.e.,* a legal duty that preexisted the new promise) does not constitute consideration even if bargained for. This is often referred to as the legal duty rule. The same rule applies to the actual performance of such a duty. [Rest. 2d §73]

(a) **Example:** A agrees to construct a factory for B for $5 million. When the factory is 75% completed, A determines that because of a rise in the price of building materials, construction will be much more expensive than A had anticipated, and tells B that he will not complete the job unless B agrees to pay $6 million. At this point, getting a substitute contractor would be very time-consuming, and the resulting delay in the completion of the plant would cause a significant loss of profits to B. B therefore agrees to pay $6 million rather than $5 million. B's promise is unenforceable.

(b) **Complainant:** [§77]   Normally, the person who asserts the legal duty rule is the person who has ***not*** made the promise to perform a preexisting legal duty. For example, in the example above, B has not promised to perform a preexisting legal duty, because he had no preexisting legal duty to pay A $6 million instead of $5 million. Rather, B argues that his promise is unenforceable because all that he received in exchange for the promise to pay $6 million was A's promise to perform (or A's actual performance) of a preexisting legal duty, and because such a promise (or performance) is not consideration, B's new promise is not enforceable.

(2) **Types of preexisting legal duties:** [§78]   There are two principal categories of preexisting legal duties: ***public duties*** (*e.g.*, the duty of a judge to preside fairly or the duty of a witness to testify truthfully) and ***contractual duties*** (*e.g.*, A promises to wash B's car for $5 and then the parties "modify" the price to $8; washing the car is A's contractual duty). Application of the legal duty rule differs somewhat between the two categories.

   (a) **Preexisting public duties**

      1) **Official duties:** [§79]   Under the preexisting legal duty rule, the promise of an official to perform an act that falls within the scope of the official's duties is not consideration, and neither is the actual performance of such an act. [Gray v. Martino, 103 A. 24 (N.J. 1918)]

         a) **Example:** A, a police officer, promises B, a merchant who owns a store on A's beat, that she will keep an eye on B's store in exchange for B's promise to pay her $50 a month. B's promise is unenforceable because the promised performance is within the scope of A's official duties.

         b) **Action within scope of official duties:** [§80]   The legal duty rule is applicable to a promise by an official whenever the action is within the ***scope*** of the official's duties, even though performance by the ***specific*** act is not legally required.

            1/ **Example:** Suppose that in the above example, A promises to use part of her lunch hour to keep an eye on B's store. Because keeping an eye on B's store is within the scope of A's official duties, B's promise to pay A $50 a month is unenforceable even though A is not legally required to watch B's store during lunch.

         c) **Action not within scope of official duties:** [§81]   The legal duty rule is not applicable where the act performed by the official is not within the scope of official duties, even though it is similar to those duties. [Harris v. More, 70 Cal. 502 (1886); Rest. 2d §73]

1/ **Example:** A, a San Francisco police officer, is on vacation in Arizona, staying at B's hotel. A agrees with B to spend three hours a day watching the hotel lobby, in exchange for a free room. Since the promised performance is not within the scope of A's official duties (because those duties do not apply in Arizona), B's promise is enforceable.

d) **Pretense of bargain not sufficient:** [§82] The legal duty rule cannot be avoided by a bargain that merely pretends to call for a performance outside the scope of an official's duties. The difference between the official duty and the promised performance must be real and material, not a slight difference contrived to make the contract enforceable. [Rest. 2d §73]

2) **Other public duties:** [§83] Performance of a public duty required by law, other than an official duty, is treated in the same way as is performance of an official duty. [Van Boskerck v. Aronson, 197 N.Y.S. 809 (1923); Rest. 2d §73, comment b]

a) **Example:** A and B make an agreement under which A promises to tell the truth as a witness in a suit that B has brought against C, and B promises to pay A $1,000 in exchange. A tells the truth in the suit, but B refuses to pay. A sues B for the $1,000. B prevails because every citizen has a public duty to tell the truth as a witness, and so A's promise to tell the truth is not consideration.

(b) **Preexisting contractual duties:** [§84] The general rule is that a promise to perform, or the actual performance of, a preexisting contractual (as opposed to public) duty that is owed to the promisee is *not* consideration. The cases covered by this branch of the legal duty rule tend to fall into two patterns: (i) those in which A is under a contractual duty to render some performance to B, and B agrees to pay A *more* for the very same performance, and (ii) those in which Debtor owes some amount to Creditor, and Creditor agrees to accept *less* than that amount *in full discharge* of Debtor's obligation to Creditor.

1) **Performance of preexisting contractual duty for increased payment**

a) **General rule—no consideration:** [§85] Assume two parties, A and B, have a contract under which A is under a duty to render a certain performance to B. A and B then agree to a *modification* of the contract under which A promises only to render the same performance, but B agrees to pay more than the amount he originally agreed to pay. Under the legal duty rule, A's new promise to render the performance is not consideration for the promise by B to pay a greater amount than was set out in the original contract, and A therefore cannot enforce the modification against B. [Lingenfelder v. Wainwright Brewery Co., 15 S.W. 844 (Mo. 1890)] The same rule applies to A's actual performance, as opposed to A's promise to perform. That is, under the legal duty rule, neither A's promise to perform, nor his actual performance, of a preexisting contractual duty to B is consideration for B's promise to pay more for the same performance.

b) **Exceptions:** [§86]   In many cases, the legal duty rule is not in accord with generally accepted commercial practice, at least when the preexisting legal duty is contractual rather than official or public. Therefore, the courts have recognized a number of exceptions to the rule as it applies to a modification of a contract.

1/ **Promise of different performance:** [§87]   The legal duty rule is inapplicable to a modification that involves the performance of an act that is similar to, but *different from*, the performance required under the preexisting contract. Furthermore, because the courts do not favor the legal duty rule, even a relatively slight difference between the performance required under the modification and the performance required under the preexisting contract will suffice to constitute consideration.

a/ **Example:**   A agrees to construct a house for B for $430,000. Under the contract, the house is to have pine doors. A and B then modify the contract so that the doors will be made of redwood, and B will pay $450,000. The modification is enforceable.

2/ **Preexisting duty owed to third party:** [§88]   The legal duty rule is also usually inapplicable where the preexisting contractual duty is owed to *someone other than the promisee.* [Joseph Lande & Sons, Inc. v. Wellsco Realty, Inc., 34 A.2d 418 (N.J. 1943); Rest. 2d §74]

a/ **Example:**   A contracts with B to construct a commercial building by July 31. T, a prospective tenant in the building, is eager to ensure that the building is completed on schedule. Accordingly, T promises to pay A $5,000 if A completes construction by July 31. A completes the building by July 31, but T refuses to pay. The contract is enforceable, because at the time T made the promise to A, A was under a contractual duty to B, not to T.

b/ **Minority position:**   A few authorities do not recognize an exception to the legal duty rule in such a case, on the ground that when A makes the promise to T, A is under a preexisting legal duty to perform, even though the duty does not run to T. [De Cicco v. Schweizer, 221 N.Y. 431 (1917)] Even this minority view, however, recognizes an exception to the legal duty rule where T makes a promise to A and B *jointly*—i.e., where T promises something to A and B in return for their joint promise to perform the contract, or in return for their actual joint performance. [De Cicco v. Schweizer, *supra*] The rationale is that A and B had a legal right to mutually rescind their preexisting contract. Therefore, by jointly agreeing to perform at contract, they promised to do something they were not previously obliged to do—i.e., they promised to refrain from mutually rescinding their contract.

3/ **Availability of a defense under original contract:** [§89]   The legal duty rule is also inapplicable if A, who promises to do no more than was required under the original contract, had a valid defense under the original contract (for example, mutual mistake). In such a case, A was not legally obliged to render any performance because of the defense, and so her promise is not simply a promise to perform a preexisting legal duty.

a/ **Example:**   A and B enter into an oral agreement under which B agrees to sell A a parcel of land for $450,000. The agreement is unenforceable against either party under the Statute of Frauds. B states that he will not convey the parcel for $450,000, but will convey it for $500,000. A agrees, and the agreement is put into writing. A's promise is enforceable, because as a result of the Statute of Frauds, B was not under a preexisting legal duty to convey the parcel for $450,000.

4/ **Fair and equitable modification in light of unanticipated circumstances:** [§90]   Most courts now also hold that the legal duty rule is inapplicable to a modification of an ongoing contract, if the modification is based on *unanticipated circumstances,* and is *fair and equitable* in view of the circumstances. This exception is applicable even if the unanticipated circumstances would not provide a defense of "impossibility" or "changed circumstances" under the preexisting contract. [Linz v. Shuck, 67 A. 286 (Md. 1907); Rest. 2d §87]

a/ **Example:**   A agrees to excavate a cellar for B for $6,000. A unexpectedly encounters subsoil hardpan, and so notifies B. The unanticipated subsoil conditions do not give A a defense for nonperformance of the contract. (*See infra*, §§810 *et seq.*) Nevertheless, in view of the unanticipated circumstances, which significantly increase A's costs, B agrees to pay A an additional $2,000 for the excavation. This increase is fair and equitable in view of the unanticipated greater difficulty of performance. The contract, therefore, is enforceable.

5/ **Modification of contract for the sale of goods:** [§91] Under U.C.C. section 2-209(1), an agreement modifying a contract for the *sale of goods* is binding *without consideration*. Thus, the legal duty rule is inapplicable to contracts for the sale of goods.

   a/ **Fairness not explicitly required:** [§92] Unlike the exception for modifications that are fair and equitable in view of unanticipated circumstances (*supra*, §91), U.C.C. section 2-209 is not explicitly limited to agreements that are fair and equitable in view of circumstances not anticipated when the contract was made. However, the modification must meet the general test of "good faith" under U.C.C. section 1-203 (*supra*, §62), so that a modification that is not fair and equitable would probably not be binding. [U.C.C. §2-209, Comment]

   b/ **Distinguish—waivers:** [§93] Although a *modification* of a contract is enforceable without consideration under U.C.C. section 2-209, a *waiver* of a right under a contract is enforceable without consideration only if the waiver is *not validly withdrawn.* (The distinction between a waiver and a modification, and the circumstances under which a waiver may be validly withdrawn, are discussed *infra*, §129.)

6/ **Writing as substitute for consideration:** [§94] In a few states, a contract may be enforceably modified by a writing even though no new consideration is given. [Cal. Civ. Code §1697]

7/ **Surrender of "power to breach" as consideration:** [§95] A few courts have gotten around the legal duty rule by concluding that performance of a preexisting contractual duty by A is consideration because A's continued performance constitutes a surrender of A's power to breach the original contract—*i.e.*, A's power to incur a liability for damages for nonperformance, instead of actually going to the trouble and expense of performance. [Munroe v. Perkins, 26 Mass. 298 (1830)]

a/ **Criticism:** This view has been heavily criticized on the ground that A may have the *power* to breach the contract, but A does not have the *right* to do so, and there is no consideration unless a legal *right* is surrendered. [Corbin on Contracts ("Corbin") (1st ed. 1963) §182]

8/ **"Mutual rescission":** [§96]   A few other courts have gotten around the legal duty rule by concluding that the new promise constitutes a mutual rescission of the pre-existing contract and the formation of a new contract. [Schwartzreich v. Bauman-Basch, Inc., 231 N.Y. 196 (1921); Watkins & Son v. Carrig, 21 A.2d 591 (N.H. 1941)] However, the finding of a mutual rescission is usually fictional. In effect, courts that adopt this reasoning simply undercut the legal duty rule.

9/ **Effect of performance:** [§97]   The legal duty rule is a defense to an action to enforce a promise to pay more money for a previously agreed-upon performance in which the only consideration for the promise to pay more is the promise to perform (or the performance of) the preexisting legal duty. However, once such a contract has been fully performed, the legal duty rule has no application, and the promisor cannot recover the extra money paid unless she paid under duress (*see* below). (An analogy would be the rule that unrelied-upon donative promises lack consideration. That rule prevents enforcement of a promise to make a gift, but once the gift is delivered, the consideration rule becomes irrelevant, and the gift cannot be recovered.)

a/ **Preexisting legal duty coupled with economic duress:** [§98]   However, if a contract not only lacks consideration under the legal duty rule, but also is made under economic duress, then the party who was under duress usually *can* recover the extra payment. A contract is made under economic duress if a promisor's assent is induced by an *improper* threat by the promisee that leaves the promisor no reasonable alternative. Although a threat to break a contract is improper, such a threat does not constitute economic duress unless it leaves the promisor with no reasonable alternative.

1] **Example:** A is under contractual duty to construct an addition to B's factory for $10,000. Before performance has begun, B says that he will render the performance only if A will pay B $12,000. At this point, there are other contractors who could take B's place. A agrees to B's terms. B renders the performance, and A pays $12,000. Because other contractors were available, A was not under economic duress at the time she made the new agreement and the payment. Even after she made the new agreement, A could have refused to pay $12,000, under the legal duty rule (unless an exception to the rule was applicable), but once she paid the $12,000 she cannot recover the difference between $12,000 and $10,000.

2] **Compare:** Same facts as above, but after performance has begun, B threatens to walk off the job unless paid $12,000 on the spot, B cannot be quickly replaced by another contractor, and A will lose a substantial amount of money if the addition to the factory is delayed. Under these circumstances, the new agreement and the payment are made under economic duress, and A can recover the extra $2,000 from B.

2) **Payment of lesser amount as discharge of debtor's full obligation**

a) **General rule—no consideration:** [§99] The second common type of case to which the legal duty rule applies is the case in which Debtor agrees to pay less than the full amount owed to Creditor in exchange for Creditor's agreement to accept the lesser amount in full satisfaction or discharge of the debt. The same general rule applies in this case as where B promises to pay A more for rendering a performance that A is already contractually obliged to perform. Debtor's payment of the lesser sum is *not* consideration because Debtor is doing only what he has a preexisting legal duty to do. Therefore, Creditor's promise to accept the lesser sum as full payment is not enforceable. As a result, after Debtor has paid the smaller amount, Creditor can sue for the balance, despite the fact that Creditor agreed to accept the smaller amount in full discharge of Debtor's obligation. [Foakes v. Beer, App. 9 Cas. 605 (1884)]

1/ **Example:** Debtor owes Creditor $100,000, which was due on January 1. On January 15, Debtor offers to pay Creditor $90,000 if Creditor will agree to accept that amount in full satisfaction of the $100,000 debt. Creditor agrees and Debtor pays $90,000 to Creditor. Creditor then sues Debtor for $10,000, representing the difference between the $100,000 owed and the $90,000 paid. Debtor defends on the ground that the debt has been discharged. Creditor wins. Since Debtor owed Creditor $100,000, Debtor's payment of $90,000 did not constitute consideration for Creditor's agreement to accept that amount in full satisfaction of Debtor's debt. The agreement therefore is not binding, and the discharge is not a defense to Debtor's suit.

b) **Exceptions**

1/ **Different performance:** [§100] The general rule is inapplicable if the debtor does something *different* from that which she is obliged to do; *e.g.*, debtor pays a lesser sum *before* the full obligation is due or renders a service in lieu of paying money. [Jaffray v. Davis, 124 N.Y. 164 (1891)]

2/ **Honest dispute:** [§101] If there is an honest dispute whether Debtor owes Creditor a debt, payment by Debtor of a lesser amount than that claimed by Creditor *is* consideration for a discharge in full. [Rest. 2d §73; *and see supra,* §39]

3/ **Unliquidated obligations:** [§102] Furthermore, even where there is no honest dispute whether Debtor owes Creditor a debt, if the *amount* of the debt is unliquidated (*i.e.*, uncertain), payment of an amount that is less than Creditor claims *is* consideration for a discharge of the debt in full. [Rest. 2d §74]

a/ **Payment of amount admittedly due:** [§103] This exception applies even though Debtor pays no more than he *admittedly* owes. [Tanner v. Merrill, 65 N.W. 664 (Mich. 1895)]

1] **Example:** B, a plumber, performs plumbing services for A. A requested B to perform these services, but the parties did not discuss B's charges in advance. B claims that on the basis of her standard charges, A owes $500. A admits that he must pay for B's services (*see infra,* §156), and that he should pay at least $200. A offers to pay $200 if B will accept that amount in full satisfaction of her entire claim. B argues, but accepts, and A pays the $200. B then sues for the $300 balance that she claims is due. A wins. Since the debt was unliquidated, the payment of $200 was consideration for B's agreement to accept that amount in full satisfaction of A's obligation, even though A did not dispute that he owed at least that much.

b/ **Separate debts:** [§104] However, if Debtor owes Creditor two *separate* obligations, one liquidated and one not, payment of the liquidated obligation will not serve as consideration for Creditor's agreement to discharge the unliquidated obligation. [Rest. 2d §74]

1] **Comment:** This exception depends on drawing on a distinction between (i) cases involving two separate debts, and (ii) cases involving one debt, part of which is admittedly due and part of which is contested. In practice, however, it is frequently difficult to determine into which category a given case involving two debts falls. The best guideline is whether the two debts arose out of one contract or transaction, or more than one. If the two debts arose out of one transaction, they are likely to be related; if they arose out of more than one transaction, they are likely to be separate. However, even separate transactions may be closely related (as in the case of a series of related sales in the course of an ongoing relationship between the buyer and the seller), and in such a case the total debts arising out of the related transactions may be considered as one debt for purposes of applying the rule concerning the settlement of unliquidated obligations.

4/ **Composition of creditors:** [§105] A composition of creditors is an agreement *among* creditors to settle with a debtor on certain terms. Where a composition releases the debtor in exchange for part payment, consideration may be found in the creditors' mutual agreement to accept lesser sums than those actually due. In this situation, the debtor is a third-party beneficiary of the composition agreement. [Massey v. Del-Valley Corp., 134 A.2d 602 (N.J. 1957); *see also infra*, §§568-574]

5/ **Agreement not to file a bankruptcy petition:** [§106] Payment by Debtor of a lesser amount than that owing may constitute consideration for a promise to give a discharge in full if Creditor's purpose in agreeing to give a full discharge is to induce Debtor not to declare bankruptcy. In such a case, Debtor has forgone the exercise of a legal right. [Hanson v. McCann, 20 Cal. App. 43 (1904)]

6/ **Written release:** [§107]   Statutes in several states provide that a written release by a creditor will operate to extinguish the original debt. [*See, e.g.,* Cal. Civ. Code §§1524, 1541]

7/ **Executory contracts:** [§108]   There is a split of authority concerning the effect of payment of a lesser amount than is due in the case of a contract that involves further performance (*e.g.,* payments of reduced rentals under an ongoing lease). Some authorities hold that in such cases, an agreement to accept lesser payments in full satisfaction of the payments already due is enforceable to the extent that it is *executed* (*i.e.,* as to those payments made and accepted). [*See, e.g.,* Julian v. Gold, 214 Cal. 74 (1931)] Other authorities hold that because performance of a preexisting legal duty is no more consideration than a promise to perform, the differentials on payments already made can be recovered. [*See, e.g.,* Levine v. Blumental, 186 A. 457 (N.J. 1936)]

8/ **Full-payment checks:** [§109]   A special problem occurs where A, who owes B an unliquidated obligation, tenders a check to B as full payment for B's claim. For example, the check may state "This check is in full payment [or full settlement] of a liability to you for" a given transaction. Such checks are known as "full-payment checks." Suppose that B cashes the check, but then sues to recover the balance of the claim.

   a/ **Common law:** [§110]   The common law rule was that cashing a full-payment check constituted an accord and satisfaction that discharged the entire debt. This was true even if the check was for no more than the amount A admittedly owed.

   b/ **U.C.C.:** [§111]   There is a split of authority on the issue of whether the U.C.C. changes the common law rule that cashing a full-payment check discharges the entire debt when the party cashing the check either notifies the other party or notes on the check that it is not accepted as payment in full.

      1] **U.C.C. provision:** [§112]   U.C.C. section 1-107 provides that "A party who with explicit reservation of rights performs or promises performance or assents to performance in a manner demanded or offered by the other party does not thereby prejudice the rights reserved. Such words as 'without prejudice,' 'under protest' or the like are sufficient."

2] **Majority view:** [§113] The majority view is that U.C.C. section 1-107 does **not** change the common law rule, so that B's act of cashing a full-payment check discharges A even if B cashes the check "under protest" or "with reservation" of his rights. However, there is a strong minority view the other way.

3] **Notice required:** [§114] Even under the majority view, cashing a full-payment check will not discharge A unless B had reasonable notice that the check was intended to be in full satisfaction of the debt, and there was a good faith dispute concerning the debt.

E. ACCORD AND SATISFACTION

Loosely related to the legal duty rule are the rules concerning "accord and satisfaction."

1. **"Accord" Defined:** [§115] An "accord" is an agreement under which one party to a contract—A—agrees to accept in full satisfaction of an obligation owed to A under the contract by the other party—B—some performance other than the performance that was originally due.

   a. **Example:** B owes A $1,000 under a contract. B promises to give her car to A in settlement of the debt, and A agrees to accept the car in settlement of the debt. This agreement is an accord.

   b. **Type of obligation:** [§116] An accord might involve B's doing only what she was already legally obliged to do. Usually, however, as in the example above, both parties agree to do something that they were not obliged to do. (In the example above, B was not obliged to give A her car, and A was not obliged to accept the car in lieu of the $1,000 debt.)

2. **"Satisfaction" and Executory Accord Defined:** [§117] A "satisfaction" is the "execution" (performance or fulfillment) of an accord. An "executory accord" is an accord that has not yet been "satisfied" (performed or fulfilled).

   a. **Effect of satisfaction:** [§118] The satisfaction of an accord discharges both the accord and the original contractual duty. Thus, in the example above, if B gives her car to A the accord is discharged and so is B's original duty to pay A $1,000.

   b. **Effect of executory accord:** [§119] It might be thought that even before satisfaction, an accord is a fully enforceable modification of the original contract, because if each party to a contract agrees to do something **different** from what he or she was obliged to do, the legal duty rule normally would not apply. For purely historical reasons, however, that is not the law.

(1) **Traditional rule:** [§120] The traditional legal rule is that an executory accord is unenforceable. This rule is inconsistent with the bargain principle, because an executory accord is a bargain, and bargains are normally enforceable. As a result, although in theory the traditional rule is still the law, the rule is hedged with a number of exceptions and distinctions, so that in practice the rule has little bite.

(2) **Modern rules**

    (a) **"Substituted contract":** [§121] In some cases, an executory accord is treated as a "substituted contract" (*i.e.*, a contract under which the *promise* of a substituted performance *is accepted as a full and immediate satisfaction* of the original duty). If an accord is a substituted contract, the accord itself is said to be a satisfaction and therefore immediately discharges the original contract. Whether an accord is a substituted contract is said to be a question of the parties' intent. The modern rule is that in resolving doubts in this regard, a court is less likely to find that an accord was a substituted contract if the original duty was to pay money, was undisputed, was unliquidated, and had matured. Correspondingly, the courts are more likely to find that an accord was a substituted contract if the duty under the original contract did not have such characteristics. [Rest. 2d §281, comment e.]

        1) **Example:** A claims that B is obliged to deliver two horses to A in exchange for agricultural services A rendered to B. B admits that he owes A something for the services, but denies that he is obliged to deliver two horses. The parties make an agreement under which B promises to deliver one horse to A and A agrees to accept the horse as payment of B's debt. The accord is likely to be treated as a substituted contract, and therefore is itself a satisfaction, because the duty under the original contract was not to pay money, was disputed, and was unliquidated.

        2) **Compare:** Same facts as above, but A claims that B agreed to pay $900 for A's services, and B does not dispute the claim. The accord is not likely to be treated as a substituted contract, because the duty under the original contract was to pay money, was not disputed, was liquidated, and had matured.

    (b) **Where accord not itself a satisfaction:** [§122] Even where an executory accord is not a substituted contract, so that the original contract is not discharged, the accord nevertheless has three significant effects:

        1) **Suspension of rights under original contract:** [§123] First, under the modern rule an executory accord operates to suspend A's rights under the original contract during the period in which B is supposed to perform the accord.

        2) **Suit for breach of accord:** [§124] Second, if B tenders performance under the executory accord and A refuses to accept it, B

can sue A for damages for breach of the accord. B may also be able to sue for specific performance or for an injunction against A bringing suit on the original contract, or may be able to prevent A from suing on the original contract on the theory that the accord suspends the original contract.

3) **Suit under either agreement:** [§125]   Third, if B fails to tender performance under the executory accord, A can sue B under either the old contract or the accord. [Rest. 2d §281]

4) **Application:** [§126]   B owes A $1,000, and the parties subsequently agree that in settlement of the $1,000 obligation, B will give A her car on June 1. Because the original performance was an undisputed obligation to pay a fixed sum of money, the accord will probably not be treated as a substituted contract, and B's duty to pay the $1,000 therefore will not be discharged unless there is evidence that the parties intended it to be. However, B's duty is suspended until June 1. Thus:

   a) *If B delivers the car and A accepts it*, A has performed the executory accord, and there is a satisfaction that discharges both the accord and B's prior duty to pay $1,000.

   b) *If B breaches the executory accord by failing to deliver the car*, A may recover a judgment for the $1,000 or, at her option, may seek damages for the failure to deliver the car.

   c) *If A breaches the executory accord by bringing an action to recover* the $1,000 prior to June 1, B may go into equity to enjoin A's proceeding until June 1. [Union Central Life Insurance Co. v. Imsland, 91 F.2d 365 (8th Cir. 1937)]

   d) *If A breaches the executory accord by refusing to accept the car* when it is tendered on June 1 and bringing an action for the $1,000 thereafter, B can bring an action for breach of the accord, and may be able to sue for specific performance or an injunction to block A's suit on the ground that the original contract is suspended even after June 1. [Dobias v. White, 80 S.E.2d 23 (N.C. 1954)]

F.   WAIVER

1. **Definition:** [§127]   A waiver occurs when a party to a contract promises to render the performance under the contract even though a certain contractual condition to her obligation to perform under the contract has not occurred.

2. **Enforceability:** [§128]   A waiver is enforceable if it is given in exchange for separate consideration. It is also enforceable (subject to the possibility of retraction, below) *without separate consideration* if (i) the waived condition was not a material part of the agreed-upon exchange; and (ii) uncertainty of the occurrence of the condition was

not an element of the risk assumed by the party who gave the waiver. [Rest. 2d §84(i)]

a. **Example:** B employs A to build a house for $400,000, payable no later than December 10, upon the production by that date of an architect's certificate, signed by B's architect, Xaviar, that the house has been completed according to contract specifications. A builds the house, but Xaviar rightfully refuses to give the certificate because the house is defective in several respects. On December 15, B says to A, "My architect Xaviar rightfully refused to give you a certificate, but because the defects are not serious, I will pay you the full $400,000." B's waiver is enforceable, because production of the architect's certificate was not a material part of the agreed-upon exchange.

b. **Example:** Acme Insurance Company insures B for $100,000 against B's becoming disabled while traveling. The policy is payable only if B or his beneficiary gives Acme written notice of loss within 30 days after the loss occurs. B is disabled in an auto accident, but does not give Acme notice until 34 days after the accident. Acme informs B that this notice is sufficient, thereby waiving the 30-day condition. Acme's waiver is enforceable, even though B gave no consideration for the waiver, because the provision concerning notice was not a material part of the agreed-upon exchange, and uncertainty about receiving notice was not an element of the risk assumed by Acme.

c. **Compare:** Same facts as in b., above, but B is disabled while working at home, and Acme waives the requirement that the accident occur while traveling. Acme's waiver is unenforceable, because the condition that the disablement occur while traveling was a significant element of the risk assumed by B.

3. **Retraction:** [§129]   Even though a waiver is otherwise enforceable, it can be *retracted* if each of four conditions is met:

(i)   The *waiver was not given for separate consideration*;

(ii)   The *other party has not changed position* in reliance on the waiver;

(iii) The *waiver relates to a condition to be fulfilled by the other party* to the contract, rather than by a third party; *and*

(iv) The *retraction occurs before* the time that the waived condition was supposed to occur *and* the party who gave the waiver either (a) gives notice of her intention to retract while there is still a reasonable time for fulfilling the condition, or (b) provides a reasonable extension of the time in which to perform.

[Rest. 2d §84(2)]

a. **Example:** Assume that in the example concerning the architect's certificate (*supra,* §128), B attempts to retract the waiver. The retraction would be ineffective for two reasons. First, the waiver did not relate to a condition that was to be fulfilled by the other party to the contract, A, but by a third person—Xaviar, B's architect. Second, at the time the waiver was given, the time for fulfilling the condition (*i.e.,* the time for producing the certificate) had already passed.

b. **Compare:** Assume that in the Acme insurance policy example (*supra,* §128), Acme waived the requirement of written notice four days after the accident and then attempted to retract its waiver the day after the waiver was given and before A has changed his position. Here, the retraction is effective because it was not given for separate consideration, was not relied upon, related to a condition to be fulfilled by A, and occurred before the time the waived condition was supposed to occur and while there was still a reasonable time for fulfilling the condition.

G. MORAL OR PAST CONSIDERATION

1. **Definition:** [§130]   A promise is said to be given for "moral" or "past" consideration when the promisor's motivation for making the promise is a *past* benefit to the promisor or detriment to the promisee that gave rise to a *moral* obligation, but no *legal* obligation, to make compensation. Such a promise is similar to a pure donative promise (*supra,* §6) in that the promise is not bargained for and is altruistic. However, such a promise differs from other donative promises insofar as it is rooted in the motive to make compensation on the basis of a past transaction that gave rise to a moral obligation to make compensation.

2. **Traditional Rule:** [§131]   The traditional rule is that a promise based on moral or past consideration is simply a donative promise, and as such, is unenforceable. [Mills v. Wyman, 3 Pick. 207 (Mass. 1825)]

3. **Exceptions:** [§132]   However, there are certain well-established exceptions to the traditional rule. These traditional exceptions concern a promise to pay a debt barred by the statute of limitations, a promise to perform a voidable obligation, and a promise to pay a debt discharged by bankruptcy.

   a. **Promise to pay debt barred by statute of limitations:** [§133]   A promise to pay a debt barred by the statute of limitations is enforceable despite the absence of any new consideration from the promisee. [Rest. 2d §82]

      (1) **Action is on new promise:** [§134]   In such cases, it is the *new* promise, *not* the old debt, that is enforceable. Therefore, if the debtor promises to pay less than the amount of the barred debt, or promises to repay the debt only in installments or only under stated conditions, that is all she is obliged to do. [Brown v. Hebb, 175 A. 602 (Md. 1934); Rest. 2d §82]

         (a) **Example:** A owes B a debt of $1,000, but the statute of limitations has run on the debt. A then writes B, "I realize I still owe you $1,000, and I will pay it." B can enforce the promise.

         (b) **Example:** A writes to B, "I realize I owe you $1,000 and I will pay it to you if I am promoted to a better job." The promise can be enforced only if A is promoted since it is the new promise, not the old debt, that is enforceable.

         (c) **Example:** A writes to B, "I realize I owe you $1,000, and I will pay you $800." B can recover only $800 since it is the new promise, not the old debt, that is enforceable.

(2) **Effect of acknowledgment or part payment:** [§135] The new promise need not be explicit. A promise to pay a debt barred by the statute of limitations will normally be implied from an unqualified acknowledgment that the debt is owing, or from a part payment of the debt. [Rest. 2d §82; Corbin §216]

    (a) **Implication from acknowledgment or part payment not determinative:** [§136] In such a case, it is not the acknowledgment or part payment that is decisive, but the implication of a promise from the acknowledgment or part payment. Therefore, if such an implication cannot fairly be drawn, no action will lie.

        1) **Example:** A owes B $5,000, but the debt is barred by the statute of limitations. B asks A to pay, and A writes, "I acknowledge that I owe you that money, and I should pay it to you by all rights, but you'll never get a cent." B has no cause of action, because although A acknowledged the debt, a promise to pay cannot be implied. [Rest. 2d §82]

        2) **Compare:** Same facts as above, except that A writes, "I'm sorry I haven't paid, but I had no extra money last year." The court might treat this statement as an unqualified acknowledgment of the debt that will give rise to an implied promise. [Buescher v. Lastar, 61 Cal. App. 3d 73 (1976)]

(3) **Requirement of a writing:** [§137] A promise to pay a debt barred by the statute of limitations does not fall within the Statute of Frauds as originally enacted. Therefore, at common law a promise to pay a debt barred by the statute of limitations does not need to be in writing to be enforceable. However, most states have now adopted special Statute of Frauds provisions, known as "Lord Tenterden's Acts," that provide that a promise to pay a debt barred by the statute of limitations is not enforceable unless the promise is in writing or a part payment has been made. [*See, e.g.*, Mass. Gen. Laws ch. 260, §§13, 14]

(4) **New promise made before statute of limitations has run:** [§138] The rules set forth above are also generally applicable to a new promise, an acknowledgment, or a part payment that is made *before* the statute of limitations has run on the old debt. In such a case, the statute of limitations on the new promise will begin to run from the date of the new promise, acknowledgment, or part payment.

b. **Promise to perform a voidable obligation:** [§139] A promise to perform a voidable obligation (known as a *ratification*) is enforceable despite the absence of new consideration, as long as the new promise is not subject to the same privilege or defenses as the original obligation. [Rest. 2d §85]

(1) **Example—infancy:** A and B reside in state S, where the age of majority is 18. Just before A turns 18, she enters into a contract with B. Two weeks after A turns 18, she promises B that she will perform the contract. The con-

tract is enforceable against A even though there is no consideration for A's new promise. [*See* Rest. 2d §85]

(2) **Example—fraud:** A is defrauded by B into entering into a contract to purchase Redacre. A learns of the fraud but still wants Redacre, and A promises B that she will perform. The contract is enforceable against A even though there is no consideration for A's new promise. [*See* Rest. 2d §85]

c. **Promise to pay a debt discharged by bankruptcy**

(1) **Under contract law:** [§140]   As a matter of *contract law* a promise to pay a debt discharged by bankruptcy is treated like a promise to pay a debt barred by the statute of limitations, with certain exceptions:

(a) **Acknowledgment and part payment:** [§141]   Although a promise to pay a debt barred by the statute of limitations may be implied from an acknowledgement or part payment, in most states a promise to pay a debt discharged by bankruptcy will *not* be implied from a mere acknowledgment or part payment—*i.e.,* a promise to pay a debt discharged by bankruptcy will be enforceable only if it is *express*. [Rest. 2d §83]

(b) **Requirement of a writing:** [§142]   Although a promise to pay a debt barred by the statute of limitations normally must be in writing, as a matter of contract law most states do *not* require that a promise to pay a debt discharged by bankruptcy be in writing to be enforceable. [*See* Zabella v. Pakel, 242 F.2d 452 (7th Cir. 1957)] However, such a requirement is statutorily imposed in a few states.

(2) **Under bankruptcy law:** [§143]   The Bankruptcy Reform Act of 1978 severely changed the contract law rules concerning a promise to pay a debt that is discharged by bankruptcy. The reasons for these changes were the unequal bargaining position of debtors and creditors, and the creditors' superior experience in bankruptcy matters. Under the Act, a promise to pay a debt that has been discharged by bankruptcy is normally enforceable only if a number of very stringent conditions are met. These include the following requirements:

(a) The new promise must be *made before the discharge*;

(b) The new agreement must contain a clear and conspicuous statement advising the debtor that the *agreement may be rescinded* at any time prior to discharge, or within 60 days after the agreement is filed with the court, whichever occurs later;

(c) The new agreement must be *filed with the court*, and if the debtor was represented by an attorney, must be accompanied by a declaration or affidavit of the attorney stating that the agreement represents a fully informed and voluntary agreement by the debtor and does not impose an undue hardship on the debtor or a dependent of the debtor; and

(d) In a case concerning an individual who was not represented by an attorney, the ***court must determine that the agreement does not impose an undue hardship*** on the debtor or a dependent of the debtor and is in the best interest of the debtor.

4. Modern Rule—Promise to Pay Moral Obligation Arising Out of Past Economic Benefit to Promisor

a. **In general:** [§144]   Beyond the three core cases of promises to pay debts barred by the statute of limitations, voidable at law, or discharged by bankruptcy, the principles that govern past or moral consideration are still in the process of development. The emerging modern rule is that a promise based on a moral obligation *is* enforceable, even if it does not fall within one of the three core cases, *if* the promise is based on a ***material benefit*** (usually meaning an economic benefit) ***previously conferred*** by the promisee upon the promisor, provided the benefit gave rise to an obligation—even if only a moral obligation—to make compensation.

(1) **Older view—promise unenforceable:** [§145]   At one time, the tendency was to hold that such a promise was not enforceable, on the basis of the traditional rule that a promise based on past or moral consideration was unenforceable as a donative promise (*supra, §131*). [*See, e.g.,* Harrington v. Taylor, 36 S.E.2d 227 (N.C. 1945)]

(2) **Modern view:** [§146]   However, the modern tendency is to hold that a promise based on a ***material benefit*** conferred on the promisor by the promisee that gave rise to a moral obligation *is* enforceable, at least up to the value of the benefit conferred. [*See, e.g.,* Webb v. McGowin, 168 So. 196 (Ala. 1935)]

(a) **Example:** A voluntarily intervenes on B's behalf to save B from injury or death, but A himself is seriously injured as a result of his efforts. B later promises to pay A's hospital expenses. B's promise is enforceable because it is based on a past material benefit that gave rise to a moral obligation to make compensation.

(b) **Restatement position:** [§147]   This position is adopted by the Restatement Second, which provides that "a promise made in recognition of a benefit previously received by the promisor from the promisee is binding to the extent necessary to prevent injustice," but is not binding "to the extent that its value is disproportionate to the benefit." [Rest. 2d §86]

(c) **State statutes:** [§148]   The issue of past or moral consideration is affected by statute in some states. For example, a New York statute provides that past consideration is valid to support a written promise if the consideration is expressed in writing, is proved to have been given or performed, and would have been valid consideration if it was present rather than past consideration. [N.Y. Gen. Obligations Law §5-1105]

And a California statute provides that "a moral obligation originating in some benefit conferred upon the promisor . . . is . . . a good consideration for a promise, to an extent corresponding with the extent of the obligation, but no further or otherwise." [Cal. Civ. Code §1606]

b. **Benefits conferred gratuitously:** [§149] Even under the modern view, a promise to make compensation for a past benefit conferred will not be enforceable if that benefit was conferred as a *gift*, because there is no moral obligation to repay the value of a gift. [Rest. 2d §86]

(1) **Example:** A's wealthy elder sister, B, gives A a new car for his twenty-first birthday. Later, A promises to pay B the value of the car. A's promise is unenforceable.

c. **Promise based on expense incurred by promisee:** [§150] Even under the modern view, a promise based on a moral obligation will normally not be enforced where the promisor did not receive a material (*i.e.*, economic) benefit—even if the promisee incurred expenses. [Old American Life Insurance Co. v. Biggers, 172 F.2d 495 (10th Cir. 1949); Mills v. Wyman, *supra*, §131]

(1) **Example:** A's adult son, S, falls ill while away from home. Without having been requested to do so by A, B takes care of S, but S dies. B then writes A to tell him of S's death, and points out that he expended $300 on S's behalf. A writes back and promises to pay B $300. A's promise is unenforceable, because he did not receive a "material" (*i.e.*, economic) benefit from B's action.

(2) **Caveat:** The above example is a borderline case. Contract law has given increasing recognition to the reliance interest, and may come to recognize it in this situation too. Also, in some cases an expense of the promisee may be treated as a benefit to the promisor so as to make the promise enforceable.

5. **Promise to Pay Fixed Amount in Liquidation of a Legal Obligation:** [§151] Suppose A asks B, a local handyperson, to paint A's garage while A is on vacation. A states that she will pay B when she returns, but the price is not discussed. B paints the garage, and when A returns she makes an express promise to pay B $500. A clearly has *some* liability to B, because when services are rendered with an expectation of payment and at the request of another, there is an implied-in-fact duty to pay the reasonable value of the services (*see infra,* §156). The problem is whether A's express promise is enforceable, or whether B can sue only for restitution.

a. **Acceptance by promisee constitutes bargain:** [§152] If B *accepts* A's promise, there is a bargain between A and B to substitute a liquidated amount for an unliquidated obligation, and there is consideration.

b. **Split of authority where no acceptance:** [§153] If, however, B does not specifically accept A's promise, the courts are divided:

(1) Some cases hold that the new promise is *merely evidence of what is reasonable compensation*. [Old American Life Insurance Co. v. Biggers, *supra*; Conant v. Evans, 88 N.E. 438 (Mass. 1909)]

(2) However, other cases hold that the ***promise defines the extent of the promisor's implied-in-fact duty***. Under this view, the promise may be enforceable without regard to the actual value of the services rendered. [*In re* Bradbury, 105 App. Div. 250 (1905); Estate of Hatten, 288 N.W. 278 (Wis. 1940)]

II. MUTUAL ASSENT—OFFER AND ACCEPTANCE

chapter approach

Unless a contracts question specifically states that the parties made a contract, the answer to the question should address whether a contract was formed. This usually requires a determination of whether there was consideration (as discussed in Chapter I) and whether there was an offer and acceptance. This Chapter discusses offer and acceptance. You should watch for the following five situations:

1. ***The question sets out the texts of two or more communications***—In that case, consider whether each communication was an invitation to bid, an offer, a revocation, an acceptance, an inquiry, a conditional acceptance, a counteroffer, or a rejection. When considering the category of each communication, keep in mind that:

    a. Frequently there is ambiguity as to what legal category a communication falls into. If that is the case, the ambiguity must be explored in your answer.

    b. The interpretation of each item in a series of communications is related to the interpretation of earlier items in that series. For example, if you determine that the first communication in a series is an invitation to bid, the question you should ask about the second communication is whether it is an offer or another invitation to bid. If, however, you determine that the first communication in a series is an offer, the question you should ask about the second communication is whether it is an acceptance, a conditional acceptance, a counteroffer, an inquiry, or a rejection.

    c. A response to an offer that purports to be an acceptance must be examined to determine whether it (i) is timely; (ii) is in the proper form (*e.g.,* does the offer require acceptance by a promise or by an act?); and (iii) does it deviate from the offer in any way. If a response that purports to be an offer deviates from the offer in any way, it is normally not an acceptance unless (i) it simply spells out an implication of the offer or (ii) the transaction involves a contract for the sale of goods, in which case the response may be an acceptance, even though it differs from the offer, by virtue of U.C.C. section 2-207.

    d. After determining the category into which each communication falls, you should determine the legal effect of each communication. For example, an offer creates a power of acceptance in the offeree; a rejection terminates the power of acceptance; a conditional acceptance normally terminates the power of acceptance (except under the U.C.C.); a counteroffer terminates the offeree's power of acceptance, but creates a new power of acceptance in the original offeror; and an acceptance concludes a bargain if the acceptance is timely and in proper form.

2. ***The question sets out the dates on which two or more communications were sent between the parties***—In that case, be sure to consider whether a purported acceptance was timely according to the period for acceptance, if any, expressly required under the offer, or if no period was expressly required under the offer, whether the acceptance was within a reasonable time.

3. ***The question states that a party made an offer that was then revoked***—In that case, the question will normally raise the issue of whether the revocation was effective:

   a. ***If the revocation crosses paths*** with an acceptance, you must determine whether the acceptance was sent in a timely manner and by an appropriate medium. If so, the acceptance is effective on dispatch but the revocation is effective only on receipt.

   b. Alternatively, the problem may be whether the offeror had the ***right to revoke***. The general rule is that an offer is revocable, but there are important exceptions:

      (1) If the offer is for a ***unilateral contract***, it is not revocable if the offeree began performance prior to the revocation.

      (2) If the offer is for a ***bilateral*** contract, it may not be revocable if (i) the offeree gave consideration (*i.e.,* if the offer was an option); (ii) the offer is in writing and recites nominal consideration; (iii) the offeree has relied upon the offer in a foreseeable way; or (iv) the offer was for the sale of goods and therefore fell within the U.C.C.

4. ***The question involves an offer by one party but no explicit acceptance by the other***—In that case, be sure to consider the issue of ***silence*** as acceptance.

5. ***The question states that an offer or acceptance was lost or delayed in the mail***—In that case, the question will normally raise the issue of the effect of the loss or delay. Generally, an acceptance is effective on dispatch, but all other communications are effective only on receipt.

Finally, if you determine that a contract was formed you might find that the contract raises problems of interpretation. Also, if the agreement ***has*** been reduced to a written form, watch for parol evidence rule problems. If the contract has ***not*** been reduced to written form, watch for Statute of Frauds problems.

A. MUTUAL ASSENT

For a contract to be formed, there must be mutual assent.

1. **Objective Theory of Contracts:** [§154]   In determining whether mutual assent has been achieved for contract law purposes, the test to be applied (with certain limited exceptions; *see, e.g., infra,* §§439-440) is the ***objective*** theory of contracts—*i.e.,* what a ***reasonable person*** in the position of each of the parties would be led to believe by the words or conduct of the other party or the words of a written contract. This means that words or conduct are normally interpreted according to what a reasonable person, standing in the shoes of the addressee, would understand the words or conduct to mean and ***not*** according to what the addressor (the speaker or the actor) subjectively meant to convey or what the addressee (the person to whom the words or conduct were addressed) subjectively understood them to mean.

a. **Rationale—protection of parties' reasonable expectations:** At one time, contract theory seems to have required an actual "meeting of the minds" to form a contract. This implies a subjective element to contract formation. Modern contract law has rejected the concept that an actual, subjective meeting of the minds is necessary to form a contract, because the importance of protecting the parties' reasonable expectations in relying on a promise and the need for security and certainty in business transactions make it imperative that each contracting party be able to rely on the other party's *manifested* intentions, without regard to her thoughts or mental reservations. [Rest. 2d §18; Brant v. California Dairies, Inc., 4 Cal. 2d 128 (1935)]

(1) **Compare:** Notwithstanding the rise of the objective theory of contracts, courts often continued to speak of a "meeting of the minds." When modern courts use that term, however, it is simply a shorthand phrase for the formation of a contract, and does not require an actual or subjective meeting of the minds.

b. **Application:** Accordingly, there is a sufficient manifestation of assent whenever a party uses words or acts that he knows, or has reason to know, the other party would reasonably interpret as an offer or acceptance, and the other party does so interpret them. [Rest. 2d §19] For example, an offer made by A to B purely in jest will result in a binding contract if B reasonably believes that A was serious. [Plate v. Durst, 24 S.E. 580 (W. Va. 1896)]

c. **Exception:** If *both* parties subjectively attach the same meaning to a term, that meaning will govern even if it is not the reasonable meaning of the term. (This exception is largely theoretical, however, because normally when there is a dispute about interpretation, each party asserts a *different* meaning, and the question is which of those different meanings is reasonable, or at least more reasonable.)

2. **Express and Implied Contracts**

a. **Express contracts:** [§155] If mutual assent is explicitly manifested in oral or written words of agreement, the resulting contract is said to be *express*.

b. **Implied contracts**

(1) **Implied-in-fact contracts:** [§156] If the promises of the parties are inferred from their acts or conduct, or from words that are not explicitly words of agreement, the contract is said to be *implied in fact*. Although implied, such contracts are true contracts. The mutual assent is inferred, but it is real, not fictional. [Rest. 2d §4]

(a) **Example:** Auctioneer A conducts a "Dutch auction" of a vase. (In a Dutch auction, the auctioneer starts with a high price, and reduces the price step-by-step until a member of the audience bids by raising a hand. That bidder "wins" the auction.) When the price for the vase falls to $190, bidder B raises her hand, and A knocks down the hammer. A and B have an implied-in-fact contract, under which B must pay $190 for the vase.

(b) **Example:** A asks B, a plumber, to repair A's sink. B does so. There is an implied-in-fact contract under which A must pay B his usual rates for such a job, provided the rates are reasonable.

(2) **Implied-in-law contracts:** [§157] To be carefully distinguished from contracts implied in fact are contracts *implied in law*. A contract is said to be "implied in law" where one party is required to compensate another for a benefit conferred in order to avoid unjust enrichment. Unlike implied-in-fact contracts, implied-in-law contracts are not real contracts. The basis for implied-in-law contracts is unjust enrichment, not assent. The term "contract" is used only because, for purely technical reasons, the English courts historically classified these cases under a contract heading, by *fictionally* implying a promise to pay for benefits or services rendered, to prevent unjust enrichment, even though no such promise was ever made or intended. (*See infra,* §§391-392.)

(a) **Example:** A, a doctor, sees B lying in the street unconscious and renders medical services. When B recovers, A bills B. B is liable for the reasonable value of A's services. As a matter of policy, the law will fictionally imply a request by B for A's services.

B. OFFERS [§158]

Most contracts are formed by *offer and acceptance*. Therefore, the first step in analyzing a contracts problem usually is to determine whether an offer has been made.

1. **What Constitutes an Offer?** [§159] An offer is a manifestation of present willingness to enter into a bargain, made in such a way that a reasonable person in the shoes of the person to whom the manifestation is addressed would believe that she could *conclude a bargain* merely by giving assent in the manner required. [Rest. 2d §24] The manifestation may be by words or by an act. Because an offer is usually made by words, the simpler term "statement" will be used herein instead of the term "manifestation."

a. **Two essential elements:** [§160] To be legally sufficient as an offer, a statement must meet two criteria, each of which is discussed in detail below:

(i) *Intent* to enter into a bargain; and

(ii) *Certainty* and definiteness of terms.

(1) **Intent to enter into a bargain**

(a) **Offer vs. invitation to deal:** [§161] The fact that a statement looks toward a bargain does not make the statement an offer if it is clear from the language or circumstances that the statement reflects merely an intent to begin negotiation. Such statements are called *"preliminary negotiations"* or *"invitations to negotiate"* or *"invitations to deal,"* rather than offers.

1) **Words suggesting negotiations:** [§162] Typically, words such as "Are you interested . . . ?," or "Would you give . . . ?," "I quote . . .," or "I would consider . . ." suggest only preliminary negotiations or invitations to deal. [Elkhorn-Hazard Coal Co. v. Kentucky River Corp., 20 F.2d 67 (6th Cir. 1927)]

    a) **Example:** A asks B whether B would sell a certain store property for $30,000. This is not an offer. B replies, "I would not be selling for under $40,000." This is also not an offer, but merely an invitation to A to negotiate.

2) **Words suggesting an offer:** [§163] On the other hand, words such as "I will sell (or buy)," "I offer," or "I bid" suggest that an offer is intended.

3) **Words not conclusive:** [§164] However, the words used in a statement are not conclusive by themselves. Depending on the circumstances, a statement using the word "offer" may be construed as an invitation to deal, and a statement using the word "quote" may be an offer. (*See supra,* §152.)

(2) **Certainty and definiteness of terms:** [§165] Another index to whether a statement constitutes an offer is whether its terms are sufficiently ***certain and definite***. Although what constitutes sufficient certainty and definiteness varies considerably with the circumstances, and although an offer need not cover all possible contingencies, generally speaking a statement will not be considered an offer unless it makes clear: (i) the subject matter of the proposed bargain; (ii) the price; and (iii) the quantity involved.

    (a) **Intent determinative:** [§166] Even the omission of one of the above terms does not necessarily preclude a statement from being an offer, if the statement otherwise evidences an intent to conclude a bargain, the omission does not indicate a lack of such intent, and the court can fill in the omitted term by implication. (*See* discussion on definiteness of terms, *infra,* §§401 *et seq.*)

b. **Special rules:** [§167] Some types of statements are governed by special rules.

(1) **Advertisements:** [§168] The general rule is that advertisements are normally deemed to be invitations to deal, rather than offers. [Craft v. Elder & Johnston Co., 38 N.E.2d 416 (Ohio 1941)]

    (a) **Rationale:** The general rule governing advertisements is usually based on one or more of the following three grounds:

        1) ***Advertisements are usually indefinite*** as to quantity and other terms;

        2) ***Sellers ought to be able to choose*** with whom they will deal; and

3) ***Advertisements are typically addressed to the general public,*** so that if an advertisement was considered to be an offer, a seller might find the offer "overaccepted"—*i.e.,* the number of persons who "accepted" might exceed the number of items that the advertiser had available for sale.

(b) **Exceptions:** Although the general rule is that advertisements are normally deemed to be only invitations to deal, a particular advertisement may be construed as an offer. Such a construction is most likely if the advertisement is definite in its terms, and either (i) the circumstances clearly indicate an intention to make a bargain, (ii) the advertisement invites those to whom it is addressed to take a specific action without further communication, or (iii) overacceptance is unlikely. [Lefkowitz v. Great Minneapolis Surplus Store, 86 N.W.2d 689 (Minn. 1957)]

1) **Example:** Rare Books, Inc. publishes the following advertisement in *The New York Times Book Review:* "Rare Books, Inc. will pay $100 for every copy of the first edition of Sinclair Lewis's *Main Street* sent to us by January 1, 1983." This advertisement is an offer. It is definite in its terms and invites those to whom it is addressed to take a specific action (sending in the book) without further communication. Since Rare Books has signified an intention to buy any and all of the first editions, there is no significant problem of overacceptance.

2) **Example:** A department store runs the following advertisement in the newspapers: "Saturday, 9 A.M. Sharp, 3 Brand New Fur Coats Worth Up to $1000, $100 each, First Come, First Served." This is also an offer. Again, it is definite in its terms, and invites those to whom it is addressed to take an action (being first in line) without further communication. Since the number of available coats are specified, there is no significant problem of overacceptance. [Lefkowitz v. Great Minneapolis Surplus, *supra*]

3) **Rewards:** [§169] An advertisement that a reward will be paid (*e.g.,* a reward for the return of lost property or for the capture of a criminal) is normally construed as an offer. (*Cf. infra,* §276.) The act is specified; there is a clear intention that those who see the advertisement will rely on it; and since only one person normally can claim a reward, there is no significant problem of overacceptance.

(2) **Offering circulars:** [§170] "Offering circulars" are general mailings sent out by merchants to a number of potential customers, setting forth the terms on which a merchant is ready to deal. Offering circulars are treated like advertisements; *i.e.,* they are normally construed as invitations to deal, but they ***may*** be construed as offers in a given case. The usual test is whether a reasonable person in the shoes of the addressee would think the communication had been addressed to him ***individually*** (in which case it will be treated as an offer), or only as ***one of a number*** of recipients (in which case it will be treated as an invitation to deal). Use of the word "offer" usually, but not al-

ways, suggests an offer. Use of the word "quote" usually, but not always, suggests an invitation to deal.

(a) **Example:** A receives a printed letter from B stating, "We are authorized to offer Michigan fine salt in full carload lots of 80 to 95 barrels, delivered at your city, at 85 cents per barrel." Because the letter does not appear to be directed at A individually, it is merely an invitation to deal, despite use of the word "offer." [Moulton v. Kershaw, 18 N.W. 172 (Wis. 1884)]

(b) **Example:** A sends an inquiry to B asking B's price for Mason jars. B replies, "We quote you Mason fruit jars, pints $4.50, quarts $5.00 for immediate acceptance." Because the response was directed to A individually, it is an offer despite use of the word "quote." [Fairmount Glass Works v. Crunden-Martin Woodenware Co., 51 S.W. 196 (Ky. 1899)]

(3) **Auctions**

(a) **Auction with reserve:** [§171] The usual auction (sometimes called an auction "with reserve") is subject to the following rules:

1) **Putting an item on the block:** [§172] The act of an auctioneer in putting an item "on the block" (*i.e.,* putting an item up for sale) and calling for bids is not an offer. Rather, putting an item on the block is considered an invitation to make offers. Because putting an item on the block is not an offer, a bid by a member of the audience is not an acceptance (but rather, an offer). Therefore, the auctioneer may withdraw the item even after the bidding has begun, unless and until the auctioneer has actually "hammered down" (*i.e.,* accepted) a particular bid. [U.C.C. §2-328(3)]

2) **Bids:** [§173] A bid by a member of the audience is an offer, which can be accepted by the auctioneer's "hammering it down."

a) Because an offer is normally revocable (*see infra,* §§219 *et seq.*), until a bid is accepted by being hammered down, the ***bid may be withdrawn*** (revoked).

b) Each new bid (offer) ***automatically discharges*** all earlier bids. [U.C.C. §2-328(2),(3); Payne v. Cave, 3 Term R. (K.B.) 148 (1789)] Thus, if a bid is withdrawn before it is hammered down, the auctioneer is not free to accept earlier bids.

(b) **Auction without reserve:** [§174] Certain different rules apply to an auction that is announced to be "without reserve." In such an auction, once the auctioneer calls for bids on an item, the item cannot be withdrawn unless no bid is made within a reasonable time. [U.C.C. §2-328(3)] However, ***bids*** in an auction "without reserve" are treated the same way as bids in a normal auction (*i.e.,* the bids can be withdrawn at any time before being hammered down).

(c) **Determining whether auction is "with" or "without" reserve:** [§175] An auction is deemed to be "with reserve," and therefore subject to the normal rules, unless the terms of the auction state that it is to be without reserve. [U.C.C. §2-328] Thus, the usual auction is with reserve, and the auctioneer may reject any and all bids, and withdraw any item from sale at any time before the hammer has fallen.

(4) **Putting contracts out for bid:** [§176] A government agency or a private firm may put a contract "out for bid"—*i.e.,* the agency or firm may let it be known, by formal publication or otherwise, that it contemplates entering into a contract for a certain performance, such as building a warehouse or purchasing office equipment. The agency or firm typically publishes or otherwise makes available the contract specifications, and asks potential contractors or suppliers to submit bids that state the price at which the contractor or supplier would render the performance. (Individuals may also put out contracts for bid, such as a contract to build a private residence.) Similarly, contractors who plan to submit bids may themselves request bids from subcontractors on defined portions of the work (*e.g.,* on the carpentry portion of a construction contract).

(a) **Legal status:** [§177] Putting out a contract for bids usually is *not* deemed to be an offer. However, the bids submitted in response to such a submission usually *are* considered offers.

1) **Example:** A, a general contractor who wants to make a bid on a school construction job, requests plumbing subcontractors to give her bids on the plumbing part of the job. This request is not an offer to the subcontractors. A is therefore free to decline all of the subcontractors' bids, or to accept a bid other than the lowest bid. However, bids by the subcontractors are offers to A. [Drennan v. Star Paving Co., 51 Cal. 2d 409 (1958); *see also infra,* §228]

(b) **Interpretation:** [§178] As in the case of advertisements and offering circulars, the rules governing contract bidding involve matters of interpretation. Therefore, depending on the language and circumstances, putting a contract out for bids might be interpreted as an offer [*see, e.g.,* Jenkin's Towel Service, Inc. v. Fidelity-Philadelphia Trust Co., 161 A.2d 334 (1960)], while a bid might be interpreted as only an invitation to deal [*see* Leo F. Piazza Paving Co. v. Bebeck & Brkich, 141 Cal. App. 2d 226 (1956)]. However, such interpretations are *very* exceptional.

2. **Legal Significance of an Offer:** [§179] The legal significance of determining that a particular statement is an offer is that an offer creates a ***power of acceptance*** in the addressee. Therefore, if a statement constitutes an offer, the addressee has the power to ***conclude a bargain*** (and thereby enter into a contract and ***bind*** the offeror) merely by giving assent in the appropriate manner (*see infra,* §252).

3. **Termination of Power of Acceptance—In General:** [§180] An offeree can conclude a bargain by giving assent only if his power of acceptance has not been termi-

nated. Termination of the offeree's power of acceptance may result from any of the following causes:

(i)   Expiration or lapse of the offer;

(ii) A rejection;

(iii) A counteroffer;

(iv) A qualified or conditional acceptance by the offeree;

(v)   A valid revocation of the offer by the offeror; or

(vi) By operation of law.

a.   **Termination of power of acceptance by expiration or lapse of the offer:** [§181]   Perhaps the most common manner in which the power of acceptance is terminated is through *expiration* or *lapse*. The rules governing this method of termination depend in part on whether a time period is fixed in the offer itself.

   (1)   **Where time for acceptance is fixed in the offer:** [§182]   If the offer states that it will be "held open," or "is good," or the like, for a certain period of time, the offeree's power of acceptance expires or lapses at the end of that period without any further action by the offeror. [Rest. 2d §41]

      (a)   **Interpretation of stated time period:** [§183]   Suppose an offer sent through the mail or by telegram states that it will be held open for 10 days. Does this mean 10 days after the offer was *sent,* or 10 days after it was *received?* There is very little authority on this issue, but what case law exists indicates that unless the offer otherwise provides, the time runs from the day of *receipt,* at least if the offer was not delayed in transmission. [Caldwell v. Cline, 156 S.E. 55 (W. Va. 1930)]

         1)   **Delay in transmission:** [§184]   Suppose the offer was delayed in transmission. If the offeree had no reason to know of the delay, the same rule applies. However, if the offeree *knew or should have known* of the delay (as where an offer dated March 1 is received on March 19), the time period begins to run from the day on which the offeree *would have received* the offer if the delay had not occurred. [Rest. 2d §49] This is true even though the delay in transmission was the offeror's fault (as where the offeror carelessly misaddressed the letter).

   (2)   **Where no time for acceptance is fixed in offer:** [§185]   If the offer does not state a period of time during which it will remain open, the offeree's power of acceptance expires or lapses after the expiration of a reasonable time. [Loring v. City of Boston, 48 Mass. (7 Metc.) 409 (1844)]

      (a)   **What constitutes a reasonable time?** [§186]   What constitutes a reasonable time depends on the circumstances: *e.g.,* the subject matter of the offer, the rapidity of price fluctuation for that subject matter, the medium through which the offer is made (face-to-face, letter, telegram, and so forth), and business custom. [Rest. 2d §41]

1) **Face-to-face and telephonic bargaining:** [§187]   When the parties bargain *face-to-face or by telephone*, the time for acceptance ordinarily does not extend beyond the end of the conversation, unless a contrary intention is indicated (*e.g.,* if the offeror says, "Well, think it over . . ."). [Rest. 2d §40]

2) **Offer sent by mail:** [§188]   When an offer is sent *by mail*, an acceptance mailed by midnight on the day of receipt is timely, unless the circumstances indicate otherwise. [Rest. 2d §41] However, an acceptance may be timely even if it is sent later, provided it is sent within a reasonable time under the circumstances and the offer does not restrict the time, such as by requiring an answer by return mail. But remember that a different rule might apply where the offer is delayed in transmission and the offeree knows or should know of the delay. (*See supra,* §184.)

b. **Termination of offer through rejection by offeree:** [§189]   A rejection is a statement by an offeree that he intends not to accept the offer. An offeree's power of acceptance is terminated by a rejection, even though the power of acceptance would not otherwise have lapsed. [Goodwin v. Hidalgo County Water Control & Improvement District No. 1, 58 S.W.2d 1092 (Tex. 1933)]

(1) **Example:** On January 2, A offers to paint B's portrait in February for $3,000, the offer to be held open until January 11. On January 5, B *rejects* the offer. On January 7, B changes her mind and accepts the offer. The acceptance is ineffective, since B's power of acceptance was terminated on January 5 by her rejection.

(2) **Rationale—protection of offeror:** [§190]   When an offeree rejects the offer, the offeror is likely to believe the offeree is no longer interested and may therefore take actions that he would not have taken if he thought the offeree might accept. For instance, in the example above, after B rejected the offer, A might have contracted to paint someone else's portrait in February.

(3) **Exception for options:** [§191]   Several authorities take the position that in the case of an *option*, a rejection during the option period does *not* terminate the offeree's power of acceptance, *i.e.,* his right to "exercise the option." [Ryder v. Westcoat, 535 S.W.2d 269 (Mo. 1976)] The rationale is that the offeree has a *contractual right* to have the offer held open during its term (*see infra,* §226). However, even under these authorities, the offeror would be protected if he *relied* on the rejection.

c. **Termination of power of acceptance by counteroffer:** [§192]   A counteroffer is an offer made by an offeree to an offeror that concerns the same subject matter as the original offer, but differs in its terms. A counteroffer terminates the offeree's power of acceptance, on the same rationale that applies to rejections. [Livingston v. Evans, [1925] 4 D.L.R. 769 (Can.); Rest. 2d §39]

(1) **Example:** Same facts as in the portrait example, except that on January 5, B responds, "I will give you $2,000." This is a counteroffer and terminates B's power of acceptance.

(2) **Inquiries and requests:** [§193]   The offeree's power of acceptance is ***not*** terminated by an ***inquiry*** concerning the offer or by a ***request*** for different terms. [Stevenson, Jaques & Co. v. McLean, 5 Q.B.D. 346 (1880)]

   (a) **Example:** Assume the same facts as in the example above, except that on January 5, B responds, "Does the price you quote include framing?" This is an inquiry, not a counteroffer, and does not terminate B's power of acceptance.

   (b) **Test:** [§194]   A test in distinguishing between a counteroffer and an inquiry is whether a reasonable person in the offeror's shoes would think that the communication from the offeree was ***itself an offer*** that could be accepted. For example, B's question about framing is obviously not itself an offer.

(3) **Exception for options:** [§195]   In the case of an ***option***, a counteroffer made during the option period does ***not*** terminate the offeree's power of acceptance—*i.e.,* his right to "exercise the option." [Humble Oil & Refining Co. v. Westside Investment Corp., 428 S.W.2d 92 (Tex. 1968)]

   (a) **Rationale:** The offeree has a ***contractual right*** to have the offer held open during its term (*see infra,* §226).

d. **Termination of power of acceptance by conditional or qualified acceptance:** [§196]   A purported acceptance that adds to or changes the terms of the offer is known as a ***conditional or qualified*** acceptance.

(1) **Legal effect—general rule:** [§197]   Except in the case of contracts for the sale of goods (*infra,* §206), a conditional or qualified acceptance generally terminates the offeree's power of acceptance, on the same rationale as that applicable to counteroffers. [Minneapolis & St. Louis Railway v. Columbus Rolling Mill, 119 U.S. 149 (1886)]

   (a) **Example:** On January 2, A makes a written offer to B to sell his house, Amberacre, for $50,000, the offer to be held open until January 11. On January 5, B replies in writing, "I accept your offer on condition that you install a new front door at Amberacre." B's reply constitutes a conditional or qualified acceptance and terminates his power of acceptance.

   (b) **Status as counteroffer:** [§198]   A conditional or qualified acceptance, like a counteroffer, is itself an offer, which can be accepted by the original offeror.

(2) **Exceptions to general rule**

(a) **Acceptance coupled with request:** [§199] An unconditional acceptance coupled with a *request* is a valid acceptance and forms a contract. [Culton v. Gilchrist, 61 N.W. 384 (Iowa 1894)]

    1) **Example:** Same facts as the Amberacre example, above, except that on January 5, B replies, "I accept your offer gladly. I do hope that you will install a new front door before I take possession." B's response is an acceptance, because in this example the installation of a new front door is merely a request, not a condition.

(b) **"Grumbling" acceptances:** [§200] A "grumbling" acceptance is an acceptance accompanied by an expression of dissatisfaction. (For example, "Send the goods on, but I sure wish you could give us a better price.") A grumbling acceptance is a valid acceptance and forms a contract as long as the expression of dissatisfaction stops short of actual dissent. [Johnson v. Federal Union Surety Co., 153 N.W. 788 (Mich. 1915)]

(c) **Implied terms:** [§201] An offeree's power of acceptance is not terminated by an acceptance that is conditional or qualified in *form*, but in *substance* merely spells out an implied term of the offer. [Rest. 2d §59]

    1) **Example:** Same facts as the Amberacre example, above, except that on January 5, B replies, "I accept your offer on condition that you convey marketable title." B's reply is not a conditional acceptance because it is an implied term of a seller's offer that marketable title will be conveyed, and B's reply merely spells out that implication.

(d) **U.C.C. provision:** [§202] In the case of a contract for the sale of goods, U.C.C. section 2-207(1) changes the common law rule by providing that "a definite and seasonable expression of acceptance . . . operates as an acceptance *even though it states terms additional to or different from those offered or agreed upon,* unless acceptance is *expressly* made conditional on assent to the additional or different terms." (Emphasis added.) This provision is discussed at length *infra,* §§206 *et seq.*

(3) **The mirror image rule:** [§203] At common law, an acceptance had to be a "mirror image" of the offer. In other words, if a purported acceptance deviated from the offer in any way—even in an immaterial way—it was deemed a qualified or conditional acceptance and did not form a contract; instead, it had the legal effect of a counteroffer. [Poel v. Brunswick-Balke Collender Co., 216 N.Y. 310 (1915); *see supra,* §196]

(a) **Form contracts and the last shot rule**

1) **The problem:** [§204] The mirror image rule had a particularly strong bite in the case of form contracts. Typically, merchant sellers and merchant buyers transact by exchanging preprinted forms, usually called Sales Orders, Purchase Orders, or Confirmations. The most important terms of the transaction—such as a description of the subject matter of the contract, the quantity, the price, the delivery date, and the terms of payment—normally are typed onto each form and normally correspond. However, other terms—such as warranties—will be preprinted on each form in fine print. Invariably, the printed terms of a seller's form will differ from the printed terms of the buyer's form, because each form is drafted to favor the party who prepared it. Nevertheless, if the typewritten terms on the forms agree, the seller will normally ship the goods described, and the buyer will normally accept the goods, even if the printed terms of the forms differ.

2) **Common law last shot rule:** [§205] On the facts described above, under the common law mirror image rule there is no contract at the time the goods are shipped, because the two forms differ. Since no contract was formed, the seller is under no obligation to ship any goods. However, if the seller does ship the goods, he is deemed to have shipped them pursuant to the last form. Similarly, the buyer is under no obligation to accept the goods that were shipped, but if she does accept the goods, she is deemed to have accepted them pursuant to the last form. Thus at common law, where the seller's form and the buyer's form differ, the last form is deemed to be a conditional acceptance and therefore a counteroffer, and shipment and acceptance of the goods is deemed to be an acceptance of that counteroffer. This approach is known as the last shot rule, because under this approach the terms of the contract are those set out in the last form, which could be either the seller's form (if the transaction was initiated by the buyer's Purchase Order) or the buyer's form (if the transaction was initiated by the seller's Sales Order).

a) **Example:** Buyer sends Seller a Purchase Order for 1,000 desk chairs. Seller sends back a Sales Order. The typed terms of the Purchase Order and the Sales Order agree, but the printed terms differ. Seller then ships the chairs, and Buyer accepts them. Under the common law mirror image rule, a contract was not formed by exchanging the Sales Order and Purchase Order, because the Sales Order would be deemed a conditional acceptance. However, a contract would be deemed to have been formed by the shipment and acceptance of the chairs. The terms of the contract would be those set out in the Sales Order (the last form sent), because the seller would be deemed to have shipped the goods on the terms of the Sales Order, and the buyer would be deemed to have accepted the goods on those terms.

b) **Compare:** Same facts as in the example above, except that the transaction is initiated by a Sales Order sent by Seller, followed by a Purchase Order sent by Buyer. On these facts, under the last shot rule of the common law, the shipment and acceptance of the goods would form a contract on the basis of the terms in the Purchase Order.

(4) **U.C.C. rule:** [§206]   The U.C.C. has changed the mirror image rule as regarding contracts for the sale of goods, so that "a definite and seasonable expression of acceptance . . . operates as an acceptance *even though it states terms additional to or different from those offered or agreed upon,* unless acceptance is expressly made conditional on assent to the additional or different terms." [U.C.C. §2-207(1)]

(a) **Sale of goods:** [§207]   As indicated above, U.C.C. section 2-207 is applicable only to contracts for the sale of *goods* (although some courts might apply it to other contracts by analogy). [*See In re* Doughboy Industries, Inc., 17 App. Div. 2d 216 (1962)]

(b) **Form contracts:** [§208]   Although in theory U.C.C. section 2-207 is applicable to all contracts for the sale of goods, the section was really designed to deal with the problem raised by form contracts. Therefore, as a practical matter, in determining whether section 2-207 is applicable in a given case, the courts may take into account whether a form contract is involved (*see infra,* §480).

(c) **"Definite expression of acceptance":** [§209]   U.C.C. section 2-207(1) leaves open what constitutes a definite expression of acceptance, and the cases have not definitively settled the issue. It is clear that the offeree's response must *purport* to be an acceptance to qualify as a definite expression of acceptance under this section. It is also clear that since the very purpose of section 2-207 is to *change* the mirror image rule, just because a response to an offer diverges from the offer in *some* way—even a *material* way—does not mean the response is not a definite expression of acceptance under section 2-207. However, if an offeree's response diverges from the offer in its critical, typed-in terms—such as the description of the subject matter, price, or quantity—the response probably will not be considered a definite expression of acceptance within the meaning of section 2-207.

1) **Example:** On January 2, A sends B a form Purchase Order for 1,000 barrels of nails at $20/barrel, delivery on February 1, payment in 30 days. B replies by sending A a form Sales Order which confirms all the principal terms of A's offer. However, on the reverse side of the Sales Order are various printed terms, one of which provides that "any claims arising under this Sales Order must be submitted to arbitration under the rules of the American Arbitration Association." A's Purchase Order did not include such a provision. Despite the fact that B's Sales Order varies from A's

offer in this way, there is a contract under U.C.C. section 2-207. (For the *effect* of the added provision, *see infra,* §213.)

2) **Compare:** Same facts as in the example above, except that the typewritten terms on the face of B's Sales Order provide for delivery on April 1, not February 1, as stated in the Purchase Order. There is no contract. Although B has purported to accept A's offer, B's response cannot be fairly characterized as a "definite expression of acceptance."

3) **"Written confirmation":** [§210] Under U.C.C. section 2-207(1), the rules applicable to a definite expression of acceptance are also applicable to a written *confirmation* of a prior agreement.

(d) **"Acceptance expressly made conditional":** [§211] U.C.C. section 2-207(1) by its terms is inapplicable if an acceptance is "expressly made conditional on the offeror's assent to the additional or different terms in the acceptance."

1) **Example:** Same facts as example 1), *supra,* §209, except that B's Sales Order states, "This Sales Order is expressly made conditional on the buyer's assent to additional and different terms contained herein." There is no contract under section 2-207(1).

2) **Note:** A contractual provision that conforms to the conditional assent clause of section 2-207(1) has a very dramatic effect: it prevents the formation of a contract that would otherwise be formed under the section. Accordingly, the courts read the conditional assent clause very strictly, and do not apply the clause unless the relevant provision of the contract is almost word-for-word in the language of the clause. Thus a provision in a purchase order that "the acceptance of your purchase order is subject to all of the conditions of this sales order" might not prevent contract formation since it does not conform strictly to the conditional assent clause of section 2-207(1) (*see supra,* §209).

(e) **Effect of additional or different terms:** [§212] Assuming there is a definite and seasonable expression of acceptance that is not expressly conditional on the offeror's assent to additional or different terms, as indicated above, under U.C.C. section 2-207 a contract is formed despite the presence of the additional or different terms in the acceptance. The next question is the effect of such additional or different terms. In determining the effect, U.C.C. section 2-207 draws a distinction between "additional" terms (*i.e.,* terms that add to the offer but do not *contradict* it) and "different" terms (*i.e.,* terms that *contradict* the terms of the offer). [U.C.C. §2-207(2)]

1) **Additional terms:** [§213] Under U.C.C. section 2-207(2), *additional* terms contained in the acceptance are to be construed as

proposals for additions to the contract. *If the parties are both merchants*, these proposed additional terms become part of the contract, unless:

(i) The offer *expressly limits acceptance to the terms of the offer*;

(ii) The *additional terms would materially alter the contract*; or

(iii) The *offeror notifies the offeree within a reasonable time that he objects* to the additional terms.

a) **Example:** Same facts as example 1), *supra,* §209, except that the relevant term of B's Sales Order provides, "Any complaints concerning the nails must be made in writing within 12 months after the nails have been received." If A does not notify B that he objects to this term, it would probably become part of the contract. Both A and B are merchants; A's offer did not expressly limit acceptance to the terms of the offer; and the additional term would probably not materially alter the contract.

b) **Compare:** Same facts as in the example above, except that B's Sales Order contains a term on the reverse side disclaiming all warranties. There is a contract under section 2-207(1). However, the disclaimer does not become part of the contract under section 2-207(2) because it would materially alter the contract.

c) **Merchant:** Under the U.C.C., a "merchant" is a person who deals in the kind of goods involved in the transaction or who otherwise holds himself or herself out as having knowledge or skill peculiar to the practices or goods involved in the transaction. [U.C.C. §2-104(1)]

2) **Different terms:** [§214] Under U.C.C. section 2-207(2), *different* terms contained in the acceptance (*i.e.,* terms that *contradict* provisions of the offer) do *not* become part of the contract, even if they are not material.

a) **Example:** Same facts as in example 1), *supra,* §209, except the reverse side of A's Purchase Order provides that complaints by the buyer shall be deemed effective whether made orally or in writing, while the reverse side of B's Sales Order provides that complaints by the buyer must be made in writing. Under U.C.C. section 2-207(1), there is a contract. However, under U.C.C. section 2-207(2), the term in B's sales order requiring complaints to be made in writing is not included, because it contradicts the terms of A's offer.

b) **Knockout rule:** [§215]   Although *different* (contradictory) terms do not become part of the contract, they may have an important effect. Under an emerging rule known as the "knockout rule," different terms in an acceptance "knock out" the terms in the offer that they contradict. The contract then consists of the terms on which the offer and the acceptance agree, plus terms implied by law under the U.C.C.

c) **Dropout or "first shot" rule:** [§216]   Not all authorities support the knockout rule. Under a minority view, if there is a definite and seasonable expression of acceptance, so that a contract is formed under section 2-207(1), terms in the acceptance that contradict the terms of the offer simply drop out. The contract then consists of the terms of the offer and those *additional* (but not *different*) terms of the acceptance that qualify under section 2-207(2) (*supra*, §213). Under this view, a "first shot" analysis replaces the "last shot" analysis of the common law. Recall that under the common law, if a contract is not formed by an offer and acceptance, but performance occurs, there will be a contract on the terms of the last form; *see supra*, §205. Under the minority (non-knockout) view of section 2-207(2), if a contract is formed under section 2-207(1) there will be a contract on the terms of the first form.

d) **"Mistake" theory:** [§217]   Some authorities take the position that different terms should be treated just like new terms under section 2-207(2)—*i.e.*, they are proposals that automatically become part of the contract between merchants, subject to the three exceptions discussed *supra* (§213)—on the theory that there is a mistake in the drafting of section 2-207(2). The basis for this theory is that even though section 2-207 provides only that *additional* terms become part of the contract between merchants, section 2-207(1) provides that *additional or different* terms will not prevent an acceptance from being effective, and Comment 3 to section 2-207 states that whether "*additional or different* terms become part of the contract depends on the provisions of subsection (2)." Thus, the theory goes, the term "or different" must have been omitted from section 2-207(2).

1/ **Comment:** The mistake theory is very weak. It is true that either section 2-207(2) or the Official Comment is in error, but there is no reason to believe that it is the Code that is in error; the drafters should have conformed the Official Comment to the statute. The argument might have some force if there were no possible justification for distinguishing between "additional" and "different" terms in section 2-207(2), so that the only way to explain the omission of "or different" is as a typographical error.

However, there is a very obvious reason for the omission of "different" terms from section 2-207(1): Under section 2-207, an additional term does not become part of the contract if it will materially alter the contract. A different term would always alter the contract. Thus, presumably, the drafters did not refer to "different" terms in section 2-207(2) because such a reference would have been fruitless, since a "different" term would always fail the test of the subsection.

(f) **Formation of contract by conduct of the parties—U.C.C. section 2-207(3):** [§218]   Suppose that in a case involving the sale of goods, a contract is not formed under U.C.C. section 2-207(1), either because the offeree's response is not a definite expression of acceptance or because the offeree's purported acceptance contains a conditional assent clause. At this point, either party can walk away. Assume, however, that the parties proceed to perform as if they had a contract; that is, the seller ships the goods and the buyer accepts them. In such a case, although there is no contract under U.C.C. section 2-207(1), there is a contract under U.C.C. section 2-207(3), which provides that "conduct by both parties which recognizes the existence of a contract is sufficient to establish a contract for sale *although the writings of the parties do not otherwise establish a contract.*" (Emphasis added.)

e. **Termination of power of acceptance by revocation:** [§219]   A *revocation* is a retraction of an offer by the offeror. The general rule is that a revocation terminates the offeree's power of acceptance, provided of course that the offer has not already been accepted.

(1) **When revocation is effective:** [§220]   Under the great weight of authority, a revocation is effective only when received by the offeree. [Rest. 2d §42] (Recall that, in contrast, an acceptance is usually effective on dispatch.)

(a) **Minority view:** [§221]   By statute, California and a few other states follow a minority view under which a revocation is effective on dispatch.

(2) **Communication of revocation:** [§222]   To be effective, a revocation must normally be communicated by the offeror to the offeree (unless a statute, like that of California, provides otherwise).

(a) **Exception—offer to the public:** [§223]   An offer made to the public at large, such as a reward, can normally be revoked by publishing the revocation in the same medium as that in which the offer was made. Such publication terminates the power of acceptance even of those persons who saw the offer but did not see the revocation. [Shuey v. United States, 92 U.S. 73 (1875)]

(b) **Exception—indirect revocation:** [§224]   An offer is deemed revoked, despite the absence of direct communication between the offeror and the offeree, if the offeree obtains reliable information that the offeror has taken action showing that he has changed his mind. (This is often known as an "indirect revocation," or "the rule of *Dickinson v. Dodds*.") [Dickinson v. Dodds, 2 Ch. D. 463 (1876)]

1) **Example:** On January 2, A offers to sell Blackacre to B for $40,000, the offer to be held open until January 10. On January 5, B learns from her own real estate broker that A has sold Blackacre to a third party. On January 6, B hands A a written acceptance of A's offer. The acceptance is ineffective. The fact that B obtained reliable information that A changed his mind has the same effect as a revocation. [Dickinson v. Dodds, *supra*; Rest. 2d §43]

(3) **Revocability of "firm offers":** [§225]   A firm offer is an offer that by its express or implied terms is to remain open for a certain period (*e.g.,* "This offer is good until January 10," or "You have two weeks to decide whether to accept"). The general rule is that a revocation of a firm offer, prior to the expiration of the period during which it was to remain open, has the same effect as the revocation of an ordinary offer—*i.e.,* such a revocation terminates the power of acceptance despite the fact that the offer by its terms was to remain open. [*See, e.g.,* Dickinson v. Dodds, *supra*] However, this rule is subject to some large and important exceptions.

(a) **Example:** On January 2, A makes B a written offer to sell B his property, Orangeacre, for $50,000. A's offer provides, "This offer will be held open until January 10." On January 5, A revokes the offer. On January 7, B hands A a written acceptance. The acceptance is ineffective, because A's revocation terminated B's power of acceptance.

(b) **Rationale—no consideration:** The rationale of the firm offer rule is that the term of the offer that states that the offer will be held open for a certain period is, in effect, a promise by the offeror to hold the offer open for the designated period. As discussed above, a promise without consideration is not binding. (*See supra,* §1.) Therefore, the promise to hold the offer open for a fixed period is not binding, and the offer is just as revocable as it would have been if the offeror had not promised to hold it open for a certain period.

(c) **Exceptions**

1) **Options:** [§226]   Because the general rule is based on the rationale that there is no consideration for the offeror's promise to hold the offer open for a certain period, if the offeree *gives consideration* for the promise, the offer is *irrevocable* for the stated period. [Humble Oil & Refining Co. v. Westside Investment Corp., 428 S.W.2d 92 (Tex. 1968)] A firm offer in which consideration has been given for the promise to hold the offer open for a certain period is called an "*option*."

2) **Nominal consideration:** [§227]   Even if there is no true consideration for a firm offer, under the majority rule the offer is irrevocable if it *recites* a purported or *nominal* consideration—at least if

the offer is in writing and proposes an exchange on fair terms within a reasonable time. [Rest. 2d §87(1)(a)]

3) **Reliance:** [§228] A firm offer is also irrevocable where the offeror should reasonably have expected that the offer would induce reliance by the offeree prior to acceptance, and such reliance occurs. [Drennan v. Star Paving Co., *supra,* §177]

a) **Example:** Contractor C plans to bid on a contract to construct a school building for School Board. Bids are to be submitted to School Board by 5:00 p.m. on February 1, and will be opened that evening. Before making up her own bid, C asks various subcontractors, including S, to give her sub-bids for paving the schoolyard. On January 31, S gives C a written bid to do the paving for $24,000, and states that this bid will be held open for acceptance by C until February 3. C uses S's paving bid in making up her own bid, and early on February 1, C submits her bid to School Board. When the bids are opened at 5:00 p.m. on February 1, C's bid is the lowest, and C is immediately awarded the contract by School Board. At 9:00 a.m. the next day, before C has expressly accepted S's sub-bid, S calls C and attempts to revoke the sub-bid. The attempted revocation is ineffective. S should have expected that C would rely on S's paving bid in making up the terms of C's own bid. Therefore, S's promise to hold its sub-bid open until February 3 is enforceable, and the sub-bid is irrevocable until that date.

b) **Implied promise to hold offer open:** [§229] A promise to hold an offer open may be implied rather than express. For example, in the above example even if S had not explicitly promised to hold its paving bid open until February 3, there would be an implied promise to hold it open until a reasonable time after School Board awarded the contract.

c) **Effect of rule:** [§230] Under the foregoing rule, subcontractor S is bound to perform if general contractor C gets the contract, but normally C would not be bound to give the subcontract to S even if C uses S's bid in making its bid and is awarded the contract. This has been criticized as "commercial imbalance." [*See* 19 U. Chi. L. Rev. 237 (1952)]

    1/ **Note:** In certain limited cases, however, C may be bound to S. (*See infra,* §§281-282.)

d) **Older view:** [§231] Some cases have allowed an offeror to revoke a firm offer notwithstanding the offeree's reliance. However, most of these are older cases, and probably would not be followed today. [*See, e.g.,* James Baird Co. v. Gimbel Bros., 64 F.2d 344 (2d Cir. 1933)]

e) **Restatement view:** [§232] Restatement Second has explicitly adopted the rule that reliance on a firm offer makes the offer irrevocable, at least to the extent necessary to avoid injustice. Under Restatement Second section 87, "an offer which the offeror should reasonably expect to induce action or forbearance of a substantial character on the part of the offeree before acceptance and which does induce such action or forbearance is binding as an option contract to the extent necessary to avoid injustice." [Rest. 2d §87]

4) **Contracts for the sale of goods—U.C.C. section 2-205:** [§233] Under U.C.C. section 2-205, a signed, written offer by a *merchant* to buy or sell goods, which gives assurance that it will be held open, is not revocable for lack of consideration during the time stated (or if no time is stated for a reasonable time), provided that such period of irrevocability can in no event exceed three months.

a) **Operation of U.C.C. section 2-205:** [§234] For U.C.C. section 2-205 to be applicable, the following conditions must be satisfied:

1/ **Written and signed:** [§235] The offer must be in writing, and must be signed by the offeror-merchant. If the offer is on a form prepared by the offeree, the provision to hold the offer open must be separately signed by the offeror.

2/ **Irrevocability:** [§236] The offer must state that it is irrevocable. However, the offer need not state the time during which it is irrevocable. If no time is stated and all the other requirements of section 2-205 are met, the offer will be irrevocable for a reasonable time, not to exceed three months.

3/ **Sale of goods:** [§237] Like all other provisions of U.C.C. Article 2, section 2-205 relates only to contracts for the sale of goods.

4/ **Merchant offeror:** [§238] Unlike most provisions of Article 2, section 2-205 is limited to offers by *merchants*.

a/ **Example:** On January 2, A, the owner of a textile company, makes a written offer to sell her personal grand piano to B for $3,000. The offer provides that it will be held open until January 10. On January 4, A revokes her offer. The revocation is effective. In selling her personal piano, A is not a merchant within the meaning of section 2-104. (*See supra*, §213.) Therefore, section 2-205 is inapplicable and, assuming that B has not foreseeably relied on A's offer, the offer is revocable under the general common law rule.

(4) **Revocability of offers for unilateral contracts:** [§239]   An offer that is to be accepted by *performance of an act* is known as an offer for a *unilateral* contract. (In contrast, an offer that is to be accepted by a promise is known as an offer for a *bilateral* contract.) Special problems are raised when a person who has made an offer for a unilateral contract attempts to revoke it after performance has begun but before performance has been completed.

    (a) **Old rule—offer revocable until performance is complete:** [§240] It was formerly said to be the rule that an offer for a unilateral contract was revocable until the offeree had completed performance of the act specified in the offer. Under this rule, an offer for a unilateral contract was deemed revocable even though the offeree began performance of the act in reliance on the offer, as long as performance had not yet been completed. [Petterson v. Pattberg, 248 N.Y. 86 (1928)]

        1) **Example:** It was said that if A offered B $50 to cross the Brooklyn Bridge, A could revoke when B was halfway across. [26 Yale L.J. 136 (1916)]

        2) **Rationale:** The rationale of the old rule was that an offer for a unilateral contract can be accepted only by performance of an act, and because an offer is revocable until accepted, until the act was completed the offer was revocable.

        3) **Note:** Not all courts followed this rule. [*See, e.g.*, Braekenbury v. Hodgkins, 102 A. 106 (Me. 1917)—performance having begun, offeror not allowed to revoke promise to leave her farm to her daughter and son-in-law if they would care for her during her life]

    (b) **Modern rule—offer for unilateral contract not revocable after performance has begun:** [§241]   Modern courts reject the old reasoning. Under the modern rule, an offer for a unilateral contract cannot be revoked once performance has begun unless the performance is not completed within a reasonable time.

        1) **Rationale:** The rationale of the modern rule is that an offer for a unilateral contract includes an implied promise to hold the offer open for a reasonable time if the offeree makes a substantial beginning of performance prior to revocation, and that the beginning of performance in reliance on this implied promise renders the offer irrevocable.

    (c) **Restatement Second section 45:** [§242]   The modern rule is embodied in Restatement Second section 45, which provides that "(1) Where an offer invites an offeree to accept by rendering a performance and does not invite a promissory acceptance, an option contract is created when the offeree tenders or begins the invited performance or tenders a beginning of it. (2) The offeror's duty of performance under any option contract so created is conditional on completion or tender of the invited performance in accordance with the terms of the offer." Section 45 is widely followed by the courts. The following three aspects of the rule embodied in section 45 are noteworthy:

1) **Offer open for reasonable time:** [§243]   Under section 45, the offeror impliedly promises that once performance has begun, she will hold the offer open for the time stated in the offer, or if none, for a reasonable time. Thus the offeror *can* revoke before the offeree begins performance (subject to possible exception in case of reliance *other* than performance; *see supra,* §232), and can even revoke *after* the offeree begins performance if the offeree does not complete performance within the time given or a reasonable time.

2) **Preparation vs. performance:** [§244]   A problem may arise when the offeror revokes after the offeree has begun *preparing* to perform, but before the offeree has actually begun *performing*. For example, if the offer calls for the building of a shed, under the preparation/performance distinction, section 45 would not be applicable if the offeree has only purchased lumber, but section 45 would be applicable if the offeree has begun to put up the shed.

   a) **Restatement First:** [§245]   The Comment to Restatement First section 45 stated that preparation, as opposed to part performance, was not sufficient to make an offer for a unilateral contract irrevocable.

      1/ **Comment:** The preparation/performance distinction is often simpler to state than it is to apply. Furthermore, it is not clear that courts will always make the distinction.

   b) **Restatement Second:** [§246]   Although the Comment to Restatement Second section 45 continues to draw a distinction between preparation and performance, the Comment also recognizes that the offeree's preparation may constitute *reliance* of a type that contract law should protect. Such reliance may prevent revocation under the principle reflected in Restatement Second section 87 (*see supra,* §232), even if section 45 is inapplicable because performance has not begun.

      1/ **Significance:** Since preparation to perform is likely to constitute reliance that may make the offer irrevocable under section 87, why does Restatement Second draw a distinction between preparation and performance under section 45? The answer seems to be that under Restatement Second if the offeree in a unilateral contract has begun *performance*, so that the rule embodied in section 45 is applicable, the offeree should normally be entitled to *expectation* damages if the offeror revokes. However, if the offeree has simply begun *preparation*, so that the case falls under the principle of section 87, the offeree may be entitled only to *reliance* damages. (On these two measures of damages, *see infra,* §§841-843.)

f. **Termination of power of acceptance by operation of law: [§247]** An offeree's power of acceptance may also be terminated by operation of law through the death or incapacity of the offeror or as a result of changed circumstances.

   (1) **Death or incapacity of offeror: [§248]** An offeree's power of acceptance is terminated by the offeror's death or incapacity, ***whether or not*** the offeree ***knows*** of the death or incapacity. [Rest. 2d §48]

      (a) **Example:** On January 2, A sends B a written offer to buy B's property, Orangeacre, for $50,000, the offer to be held open until January 11. On January 5, A dies. On January 7, B, unaware of A's death, mails an acceptance of A's offer. The acceptance is ineffective, because B's power of acceptance was terminated on January 5 by A's death.

      (b) **Example:** Same facts as in the example above, except that on January 5, A becomes incompetent by reason of a stroke. Again, B's acceptance is ineffective.

      (c) **Options: [§249]** Note, however, that death or incapacity of the offeror does ***not*** terminate the offeree's power of acceptance under an ***option*** (*i.e.,* an offer in which the offeree has given the offeror consideration to hold the offer open for a fixed period of time), at least where individual performance by the decedent was not an essential part of the proposed contract. So, for example, the grant of an option to purchase property is binding on a decedent's estate. [Rest. 2d §37]

         1) **Unilateral contracts: [§250]** The rule embodied in Restatement Second section 45, *supra,* also prevents termination of the offeree's power of acceptance by the offeror's death or incapacity once the offeree has begun performance.

            a) **Rationale:** An option is not terminated by the offeror's death or incapacity, and under Restatement Second section 45, once performance has begun an offer for a unilateral contract is treated like an option.

            b) **Example:** On January 2, A writes to B, "If you promise to paint my country house dark green by January 15, I will pay you $2,000. Let me know your answer by January 10." On January 4, A dies, unbeknownst to B. On January 5, B sends a letter accepting A's offer. B's acceptance is not effective. A's offer was for a bilateral contract, and B's power of acceptance was therefore terminated by A's death.

        c) **Compare:** Same facts as in the example above, except that A writes B, "If you paint my country house dark green by January 15, I will pay you $500." On January 3, B begins painting the house. B's power of acceptance is not terminated by A's death. A's offer was for a unilateral contract, and when B began performance, the offer became irrevocable under the principle embodied in section 45.

    (2) **Changed circumstances:** [§251] The offeree's power of acceptance may also be terminated by operation of law as a result of certain very limited types of changed circumstances, such as supervening illegality of the proposed contract or destruction of its subject matter. (*See* the discussion of changed circumstances *infra,* §§810-827.)

C. ACCEPTANCE [§252]

Assuming there is an offer and the offeree's power of acceptance is still open, the next question is whether the offer has been accepted. Three major issues are raised in connection with this question:

(i) What *kind* of acceptance is required (promise or act);

(ii) When can *silence* operate as an acceptance; and

(iii) What is the effect of a purported acceptance that deviates from the terms of the offer?

1. **Is Offer for Unilateral or Bilateral Contract?** [§253] An offer may require acceptance by either a promise or an act.

    a. **Acceptance of offer for bilateral contract:** [§254] An offer that requires acceptance by a promise is called an offer for a *bilateral contract.*

        (1) **In general—promissory acceptance required:** [§255] The general rule is that an offer that requires acceptance by a promise can be accepted *only* by a promise, not by an act—although the required promise may be either express or implied, and in some cases a promise can be implied from an act (*see infra,* §260) [*See* White v. Corlies, 46 N.Y. 467 (1871)] As it is sometimes put, the offeror is master of his or her offer.

           (a) **Example:** On January 2, A says to B, "I promise to pay you $500 if you promise to paint my garage dark green and to finish the job by January 10. I must have your promise by January 5." B makes no promise, but on January 4, while A is away for the weekend, B begins painting A's garage. On January 5, A (who is unaware that B has begun painting) calls B and revokes the offer. There is no contract. A's offer was for a bilateral contract and could be accepted only by B's promise. Because B had made no promise prior to the revocation, the revocation was effective. (B's reliance does not limit A's power to revoke, because it was unreasonable for B to begin painting A's garage before accepting A's offer, and only reasonable reliance prevents an offeror from revoking.)

(b) **Compare:** While A and B are next to A's fence, A says to B, "I will give you $200 if you agree to paint this fence." B immediately picks up a paint brush and begins to paint the fence. A contract is formed. A's offer required an acceptance by promise, but under the circumstances a promise can be implied from B's act.

(c) **Possible exception—tender of full performance:** [§256] Despite the general rule that an offer for a bilateral contract can be accepted only by a promise, it is sometimes said that such an offer can be accepted, without a promise, by *full performance* prior to termination of the offeree's power of acceptance.

    1) **Two views**

        a) **Restatement First:** [§257] The major support for this exception was Restatement First section 63, which provided that a contract was formed where an offer called for acceptance by a promise and the offeree (i) fully performed, or tendered full performance, before his power of acceptance had terminated; and (ii) notified the offeror of that fact within the time allowed for accepting by promise.

            1/ **Example:** A writes to B, "I will pay you $100 for plowing Flodden Field if you will promise me by the end of Monday to finish the work no later than a week from Monday." B makes no promise, but begins and completes plowing Flodden Field on Sunday and notifies A on Monday that the plowing has been completed. Restatement First section 63 took the position that on these facts, a contract was formed.

            2/ **Rationale:** In such a case the offeror is not prejudiced by getting the "wrong" kind of acceptance, because she gets more than, or at least as much as, she bargained for.

        b) **Restatement Second:** [§258] Restatement Second has dropped Restatement First section 63 on the theory that the rule in section 63 involved a departure from the basic principle that the offeror is master of his offer. [Rest. 2d §62] Thus, the status of the rule embodied in Restatement First section 63 is now uncertain.

(2) **Modes of promissory acceptance:** [§259] Note that even though an offer for a bilateral contract can be accepted only by a promise, the promise need not necessarily be *verbal*.

(a) **Promise implied from promisee's act:** [§260] As discussed above, in some cases, a promise may be implied in fact from the promisee's conduct (*see supra,* §156).

1) **Example:** A says to B, "I promise to pay you $500 if you promise to paint my garage dark green." B nods her head yes. Under these circumstances, there is a contract. B's nodding of her head is a promise to perform the painting job and constitutes an acceptance of A's offer.

2) **Example:** Same facts as in the example above, except that when A makes his offer, B does not nod her head. Instead, she immediately (and in sight of A) picks up a paintbrush and begins painting A's garage dark green. Again, there is a contract. Under the circumstances, B's act of beginning to paint is equivalent to nodding her head yes. It constitutes a promise to perform the painting job and is therefore an acceptance of A's offer.

(b) **Act designated by offeror to signify a promise:** [§261]   A comparable case is that in which the offer provides that the offeree can do some act to *signify* her promise. In that case, performance of the act constitutes a *promissory* acceptance.

1) **Example:** A sends B a written offer to buy B's car for $900. The offer states, "If you want to accept my offer, let me know by leaving your car in my driveway on Thursday." B can accept by parking her car in A's driveway on Thursday. If B does so, a bilateral contract is formed.

2) **Note:** In such cases, doing the act specified for signifying acceptance is not the bargained-for consideration. It merely evidences the return promise (*e.g.,* in the example above, to sell the car for $900).

3) **Limitation:** The offeror cannot put the offeree in the position where if the offeree does an act that she might very well do anyway, she will be deemed to have accepted the offer. For example, in the example above, if A had written, "If you want to accept my offer, let me know by parking your car in your own garage on Thursday," and B goes home that evening and parks her car in her own garage with no intent to accept A's offer, there is no contract.

(c) **Silence as acceptance:** [§262]   In some situations, a promissory acceptance may even be inferred from the offeree's silence (*see infra,* §§293-305).

(3) **Communication of acceptance of bilateral contract offer:** [§263]   The problem of whether an offeree must communicate acceptance normally does not arise in the case of an offer for a bilateral contract, because normally such an offer can be accepted only by a communicated promise. However, there are several cases in which this is not true:

(a) **Mailbox rule:** [§264]   Under the so-called "mailbox rule" (discussed *infra,* §307), where use of the mail, telegrams, or the like is a reasonable method of communicating an acceptance, the acceptance normally is effective when *dispatched*. This is true even though the acceptance does not actually *reach* the offeror because it is lost in the mails. [Rest. 2d §56]

(b) **Waiver of communication:** [§265]   In some cases, the offer provides that the offeree must "accept" or "approve" the offer, but *waives communication* of the acceptance or approval. In such cases, a contract is formed when the offeree accepts or approves even though he does not communicate the acceptance. [International Filter Co. v. Conroe Gin, Ice & Light Co., 277 S.W. 631 (Tex. 1925); Rest. 2d §56]

1) **Example:**   On November 1, A gives an order to B Company's traveling sales representative for a water purifying machine, shipment to be made on or about December 1. The order provides, "This order becomes a contract when approved by an executive officer of B Company at its home office." On November 3, an executive officer of B Company enters a notation of approval on the order. On November 4, before B has given notice of its approval, A calls B and attempts to revoke the offer. The revocation is ineffective because a contract was formed on November 3, when the notation was made.

2) **Note:** [§266]   It may, however, be an implied condition in such cases that *notice* of the acceptance be sent by the offeree within a reasonable time after the acceptance is effective, so that the offeror knows the contract is on. If such a condition is implied, a contract would be *formed* when the offeree approves the offer, so that the offer would no longer be revocable. However, the contract would not be *enforceable* unless the offeree gave notice of the acceptance within a reasonable time thereafter.

3) **Implied waiver:** [§267]   Communication of an acceptance may also be impliedly waived in cases where *silence* may constitute acceptance (*see infra,* §§293-305).

b. **Acceptance of offer for unilateral contract:** [§268]   An offer that calls for acceptance by performance of an act is known as an offer for a *unilateral contract*. Such an offer can be accepted only by performance—not by a promise.

(1) **Example:**   A says to B, "I am going away until next Friday. If you have painted my garage dark green by the time I return, I will pay you $500. Don't bother to promise or not promise that you will do it: I am just telling you that if you do it, I will pay." B replies, "It's no bother to promise—I promise to paint the garage." An hour later (and before B begins to paint), A revokes the offer. The revocation is effective. No contract was formed by B's promise, because A's offer could be accepted only by an act. Restatement Second sections 45 and 89 (*supra,* §§242 and 232) do not prevent A from revoking because B had not begun to perform and had not otherwise relied on the offer.

(2) **Notice of acceptance:** [§269]   The issue of notice of acceptance is most likely to arise in the case of unilateral contracts. In the case of a bilateral contract, a promissory acceptance is normally required—subject to the limited exceptions discussed *supra* (§§256-258)—and the acceptance itself will therefore normally be a notice of acceptance. In the case of an offer for a unilateral contract, however, a contract may be formed by beginning or completing performance, even though the offeror does not immediately know that performance has begun or been completed. Therefore, a problem of notice to the offeror may arise in unilateral contract cases.

    (a) **Notice of completed performance required:** [§270]   The general rule is that although a unilateral contract is *formed* when the offeree completes performance, the offeror's *obligation* under the contract is subject to the implied condition that he receive notice of the offeree's performance within a reasonable time thereafter. Thus, if an offeree under a unilateral contract performs in full, but fails to notify the offeror within a reasonable time after completion that she has completed performance, a contract will be formed by the performance, but the offeror's obligation under the contract will be discharged by the failure to give notice. [Bishop v. Eaton, 37 N.E. 665 (Mass. 1894)]

        1) **Example:** On April 1, A writes to B as follows: "If you guarantee to any creditor of my brother X that X will pay any debt he may incur, I will reimburse you for any losses you suffer as a result of the guarantee." On March 1, B guarantees to Y, a creditor of X, a debt that X incurs. On March 3, before B has given A notice of the guarantee, A telephones B and revokes the offer. The revocation is ineffective. A contract was formed when B completed performance by making the guarantee. Although B was obliged to notify A that she had made the guarantee within a reasonable time after doing so, a reasonable time had not elapsed before A tried to revoke.

        2) **Compare:** Same facts as in the example above, except that B never gives notice to A of the guarantee until she is sued by Y two years later. A is not bound. A contract between A and B was formed when B gave the guarantee, but A's obligation under the contract was discharged by B's failure to give notice to him within a reasonable time.

        3) **Diligence in giving notice:** [§271] It is sufficient that the offeree uses reasonable diligence to give notice of completed performance. If the offeree uses such diligence, the offeror will be bound even though for some fortuitous reason (such as loss of a letter in the mails), the notice does not actually reach the offeror. [Bishop v. Eaton, *supra*]

        4) **Exceptions:** [§272] An offeree under a unilateral contract who has completed performance is not required to give notice of that fact to the offeror if either:

(i) The offeror expressly or impliedly waives notice;

(ii) The performance would come to the offeror's attention within a reasonable time in the normal course of things and the offeror has not explicitly required notice; or

(iii) The performance actually comes to the offeror's attention within a reasonable time.

[Midland National Bank v. Security Elevator Co., 200 N.W. 851 (Minn. 1924); Rest. 2d §54]

(b) **Contracts for the sale of goods:** [§273]   In most cases the offeree under a unilateral contract need only notify the offeror that performance has been *completed*—not that performance has begun. However, in the case of a contract for the sale of goods, U.C.C. section 2-206(2) provides that "where the beginning of a requested performance is a reasonable mode of acceptance, an offeror who is not notified of [such beginning of performance] within a reasonable time may treat the offer as having lapsed before acceptance."

(3) **Subjective intent of offeree:** [§274]   An offer for a unilateral contract contemplates acceptance by performance of an act. Suppose the act called for by an offer is performed by either (i) a person who has no *knowledge* of the offer or (ii) a person who knows of the offer but who is *principally motivated* to perform by some reason other than the offer. The two situations are treated differently.

(a) **Performance without knowledge of offer**

1) **General rule—contract not formed:** [§275]   The general rule is that in the case of an offer for a unilateral contract, performance of the requested act by a person who had no knowledge of the offer at the time she performed the act does not form a contract. [Broadnax v. Ledbetter, 99 S.W. 1111 (Tex. 1907)]

a) **Example:** A offers a reward of $50 for his lost wallet. Without knowing of the reward, B finds A's wallet and returns it to A. B cannot collect the reward.

2) **Minority rule:** [§276]   A few cases have held that in the case of a reward offer, a contract is formed even though the offeree had no knowledge of the offer, on the theory that persons should be encouraged to take virtuous action in hope of receiving a reward. [Dawkins v. Sappington, 26 Ind. 199 (1866)]

a) **Statutory rewards:** [§277]   Also, it is sometimes held that knowledge is not required in the case of a reward that is offered by statute, on the ground that liability in such a case is statutory rather than contractual. [Choice v. Dallas, 210 S.W. 753 (Tex. 1919)]

(b) **Offer not the principal motive for performance**

1) **General rule—contract formed:** [§278]   If the actor knows of an offer for a unilateral contract at the time he performs the act called for by the offer, the general rule is that a contract is formed even though the offer was not the principal motive for performing the act. [Williams v. Carwardine, 4 B. & R. Adol. 621 (1833); Corbin §58]

   a) **Example:** Same facts as in the example at §275, except that B knew of the reward but returned the wallet principally because of ethical considerations. B is entitled to collect the reward.

2) **Exception—involuntary acceptance:** [§279]   Performance of the act requested by an offer for a unilateral contract might not form a contract if the act is done *involuntarily.* [Vitty v. Eley, 51 App. Div. 44 (1900)]

   a) **Example:** A offers a reward for information leading to the arrest of the person who committed a certain crime. B, a friend of the criminal, knows of the reward and is interrogated by the police. During the interrogation, B is forced by threat of prosecution into giving information that leads to the arrest of the true perpetrator. B might not be able to collect the reward.

(4) **Obligation of offeree:** [§280]   As stated previously, an offeree's acceptance of an offer for a *bilateral* contract binds the *offeree* as well as the offeror. However, if the offer is for a *unilateral* contract, the offeree's beginning of performance obliges the *offeror* to hold the offer open (*see supra,* §241), but does not ordinarily oblige the *offeree* to complete performance, because the offeree has never promised anything.

(a) **Exception:** In some cases, an offeree who has begun to perform under an offer for a unilateral contract should know that the beginning of performance is likely to come to the offeree's notice, and that the offeree is likely to treat the beginning of performance as an implied promise by the offeree to complete the performance. This is most likely to be true where the offeree's failure to complete performance will make the offeror worse off than he would have been if the offeree had not begun. For example, if the performance consists of transporting goods, and the offeree begins to transport the goods, there is an implied promise that he will not abandon the goods midway. Since the offer is for a unilateral contract, an implied promise to complete once performance has begun will not create a bilateral contract, because the offer can be accepted only by an act. However, if the offeror relies upon such an implied promise by the offeree, that reliance might make the implied promise enforceable under the reliance principle. [Rest. 2d §90]

(5) **Use of subcontractor's bid:** [§281]   Suppose a general contractor uses a specific subcontractor's sub-bid in making up his own bid. Does the general contractor's conduct in using the sub-bid constitute an acceptance of the sub-bid, so that a contract is formed, in which the general contractor's obligation to perform is conditioned on the award of the contract to the general contractor? As a matter of *contract* law, the answer is no, because the contemplated mode of accepting the sub-bid is assent by the general contractor, not by the act of using the bid. [Southern California Acoustics Co. v. C.V. Holder, Inc., 71 Cal. 2d 719 (1969); Williams v. Favret, 161 F.2d 822 (5th Cir. 1947)]

(a) **Statutory approaches:** [§282]   However, in some states, *statutes* provide that a general contractor who bids on a *government* job must include with his bid a list of all subcontractors whose sub-bids he has used, and that except under designated circumstances, the general contractor may not substitute any subcontractors for those he has listed. If the general contractor makes an impermissible substitution, the subcontractor whose sub-bid was used can bring suit against the general contractor *under the statute*. [Southern California Acoustics Co. v. C.V. Holder, Inc., *supra*]

c. **Summary of consequences of unilateral vs. bilateral contract offer:** [§283] As a practical matter, there are two particularly important consequences of whether an offer is for a unilateral or a bilateral contract.

(1) **Mode of acceptance:** [§284]   The first consequence concerns whether the mode of acceptance used by an offeree was proper. For example, if, in response to an offer, the offeree performs an act without having made a promise, and claims a contract was formed, the offeror might deny that a contract was formed on the ground that the offer was for a bilateral contract. Similarly, if the offeree makes a promise but does not begin to perform, the offeror might deny that a contract was formed on the ground that the offer was for a unilateral contract.

(2) **Revocability:** [§285]   The second consequence concerns whether an offeree who has begun performance without having made a promise is protected against termination of his power of acceptance by revocation or death of the offeror. If the offer was for a unilateral contract, such an offeree will be protected under the rule of Restatement section 45. However, such an offeree may not be protected if the offer was for a bilateral contract. Although reasonable reliance on an offer might make the offer irrevocable even if the offer is for a bilateral contract, beginning to perform before making a required promissory acceptance might not constitute reasonable reliance.

(a) **Note:** In many cases, even these problems do not arise, either because acts can often be interpreted as a promise (*see* §261, *supra*), or because offers can often be accepted by *either* a promise or an act (*see infra,* §288).

d. **Offers calling for acceptance by either a promise or an act:** [§286] The analysis until now has assumed that an offer is for *either* a bilateral or a unilateral contract. However, in many cases the offer is ambiguous as to whether an offer requires acceptance by a promise or by an act.

(1) **Example:** A says to B, "I will give you $500 to paint my house." It is ambiguous whether this is an offer for a bilateral contract to be accepted by a promise ("I accept"), or for a unilateral contract to be accepted by performance (painting the house).

(2) **Restatement First rule:** [§287] Restatement First provided that in case of doubt whether an offer called for acceptance by a promise or by an act, it was to be presumed that the offer invited the formation of a *bilateral* contract by a promissory acceptance. [Davis v. Jacoby, 1 Cal. 2d 370 (1934)]

   (a) **Criticism:** The Restatement First rule created a problem where there was doubt about what kind of acceptance was required, and the offeree interpreted the offer as calling for acceptance by an act and began performance. Under the Restatement First rule, where there was doubt about what type of acceptance was required, an offer was presumed to require acceptance by a promise. Therefore, the beginning of performance by the offeree had no legal significance, and accordingly, where there was such doubt, the offeror would therefore be free to revoke even after performance had begun.

(3) **Restatement Second rule:** [§288] Because of the unfairness of this result, Restatement Second adopts a different rule: In case of doubt, an offer is interpreted as inviting acceptance by *either* a promise *or* performance. Under this rule, if there is doubt about whether the offer requires acceptance by a promise or by performance, the offeree is protected no matter which interpretation he places upon the offer.

   (a) **U.C.C. in accord:** [§289] Similarly, in the case of contracts for the sale of goods, U.C.C. section 2-206(1)(a) provides that "unless otherwise unambiguously indicated by the language or circumstances . . . an offer to make a contract shall be construed as inviting acceptance in any manner . . . reasonable in the circumstances."

      1) **Orders for prompt shipment:** [§290] The general rule of U.C.C. section 2-206(1)(a) is applied in section 2-206(1)(b) to the specific case of "an order or other offer to buy goods for prompt or current shipment." Under section 2-206(1)(b), such an order is construed as inviting acceptance either by a prompt promise to ship or by the prompt or current shipment of the goods. (However, if the offeree chooses to accept by shipping the goods, and the offeror is not notified "within a reasonable time" that shipment has begun, the offeror may treat his offer as having lapsed before acceptance.) [U.C.C. §2-206(1)(b); *see* Sales Summary]

a) **Shipment of nonconforming goods:** [§291] The seller's shipment of goods will be deemed an acceptance even if the goods shipped are "nonconforming" (*i.e.,* not up to the specifications set forth in the buyer's offer). In such a case, the shipment is simultaneously an acceptance of the buyer's offer and a breach of the resulting contract. However, if the shipper "seasonably notifies the buyer that the shipment is offered only as an *accommodation* to the buyer," then there is no breach if the goods are nonconforming. In such cases, the shipment of nonconforming goods is not construed as an acceptance, but only as a counteroffer. [U.C.C. §2-206(1)(b); *see* Sales Summary]

2. **Silence as Acceptance**

a. **General rule:** [§292] The general rule is that the silence of an offeree does not constitute acceptance. [Royal Insurance Co. v. Beatty, 12 A. 607 (Pa. 1888)]

(1) **Rationale:** The purpose of this rule is to prevent an offeror from placing an offeree involuntarily in a situation where the offeree must either take an affirmative action to reject the offer or else become liable on a contract.

b. **Exceptions:** [§293] There are a number of exceptions to the general rule that silence will not constitute acceptance. In most of these exceptions, the offeree is *not involuntarily* put into a situation where she must either take an affirmative action to reject the offer or else become liable on a contract.

(1) **Offeree leads offeror to believe that silence will constitute acceptance:** [§294] Silence will constitute acceptance where the *offeree*, by her own prior words or conduct, gave the offeror reason to interpret her silence as an acceptance. [Hobbs v. Massasoit Whip Co., 33 N.E. 495 (Mass. 1893); National Union Fire Insurance Co. v. Ehrlich, 122 Misc. 682 (1924); Rest. 2d §69]

(a) **Example:** A, a rare book collector, tells B, a rare book dealer, "You know what kind of books interest me. If you run across any, send them to me with a proposed price. If I do not return the book promptly, you may deem it accepted at the price you state." B sends a book with a stated price of $300. A receives it, does not return it promptly, and says nothing. As a result of her earlier statement, A's inaction constitutes acceptance, and she is contractually bound to pay B $300.

(2) **Silence coupled with subjective intent to accept:** [§295] Silence will constitute acceptance where the offeror has said that silence will constitute acceptance and the offeree remains silent, subjectively intending to accept. [Rest. 2d §69; *see* International Filter Co. v. Conroe Gin, Ice & Light Co., *supra,* §265]

(a) **Example:** On January 2, A writes to B, "I will send you lithographs by messenger from time to time, with a stated price. If I do not hear from you within five days, I will deem the lithographs accepted at that price." B does not reply. On February 1, A sends B a lithograph by messenger with a stated price of $300. B inspects the lithograph and forms a subjective intent to accept A's offer in accordance with A's letter of January 2. B's subjective intent constitutes acceptance of A's offer, and B is contractually bound to pay A the stated price. If B had not formed a subjective intent to accept she would not be bound, provided she did not exercise dominion over the lithograph. (*See infra,* §296.)

(3) **Exercise of dominion:** [§296]   An offeree who improperly *exercises dominion* over goods sent to him for approval, inspection, or the like is contractually bound to purchase the goods at the proffered price, unless that price is manifestly unreasonable—even if the offeree does not have a subjective intent to accept. [Louisville Tin & Stove Co. v. Lay, 65 S.W.2d 1002 (Ky. 1933); Indiana Manufacturing Co. v. Hayes, 26 A. 6 (Pa. 1893); Rest. 2d §69]

    (a) **Example:**   Same facts as in the lithograph example above, except that B does not form a subjective intent to accept A's offer of the lithograph. Nevertheless, B sends the lithograph to her son at college, telling him to hang it in his dormitory room. B is contractually bound to pay A $300.

        1) **Note:**   Of course, if goods are sent for inspection, *mere* inspection does not constitute an improper exercise of dominion.

    (b) **Statutory exceptions:** [§297]   A federal statute now provides that "Except for free samples clearly and conspicuously marked as such, and merchandise mailed by a charitable organization soliciting contributions, the mailing of unordered merchandise . . . constitutes an unfair method of competition and an unfair trade practice." Any merchandise mailed in violation of this statute "may be treated as a gift by the recipient, who shall have the right to retain, use, discard, or dispose of it in any manner he sees fit without any obligation whatsoever to the sender." [39 U.S.C. §3009] Similar statutes have been enacted in several states. [*See, e.g.,* Cal. Civ. Code §1584.5] These statutes in effect overturn the "exercise of dominion" rule in the cases to which they apply.

(4) **Solicitation of offer by offeree:** [§298]   Silence may also result in the formation of a contract where (i) the *offeree* has solicited the offer and drafted its terms; (ii) the offer, as drafted by the offeree, is so worded that a reasonable person in the offeror's position would believe that the *offer was to be deemed accepted* unless the offeree notifies the offeror that the offer is rejected; and (iii) the *offeror relies* or is likely to have relied on the reasonable belief that lack of a prompt rejection constituted an acceptance.

    (a) **Solicitation of orders for goods:** [§299]   For example, where a seller sends out traveling salespersons to take "orders" by customers (which are technically offers by the customers) on order forms prepared by the seller, and the order is so worded that the customer would reasonably believe that she can deem the order accepted unless notified otherwise, the seller may be under a duty to fill the order unless he specifically rejects it within a reasonable time. [Cole-Mclntyre-Norfleet Co. v. Holloway, 214 S.W. 817 (Tenn. 1919); Ammons v. Wilson & Co., 170 So. 227 (Miss. 1936)]

(b) **Applications for insurance:** [§300]   A comparable case arises where an applicant applies for an insurance policy on a form provided by the insurer; the insurer holds the application for an unreasonably long time without making a decision; and the applicant suffers a loss while the insurer is holding the application. Here the applicant is technically the offeror, but many cases hold that the insurer is liable if it fails to reject the application in a timely manner—at least if the application was in good order and the loss occurred after the expiration of a reasonable time in which the insurer should have made a decision. [Kukuska v. Home Mutual Hail Tornado Insurance Co., 235 N.W. 403 (Wis. 1931)]

   1) **Rationale:**   The insurer should know that the applicant will rely on reasonably expeditious processing, because while the applicant is waiting to hear from the insurer, as a practical matter he usually cannot make application to other insurers.

(5) **Late acceptance:** [§301]   A late acceptance has the legal effect of a counteroffer—*i.e.,* a late acceptance does not conclude a bargain, but is treated as an offer that can be accepted by the original offeror. (*See infra,* §314.) In addition, however, if an offeree sends an acceptance after a reasonable time for acceptance has elapsed (so that it is late), but within a period that the offeree might plausibly regard as reasonable, courts have held that good faith and fair dealing require the original offeror to notify the original offeree that the acceptance was too late. If the original offeror does not give such notice, the offeree's late acceptance/counteroffer will be deemed accepted by the original offeror's silence. [Phillips v. Moor, 71 Me. 78 (1880); Rest. 2d §70]

(6) **Implied-in-fact contracts:** [§302]   In the context of the general rule that silence does not constitute acceptance, "silence" means *inaction*. (*See supra,* §260.) Thus *communicated action* does not constitute silence, for purposes of this rule, even if the action is nonverbal.

(a) **Example:**   A bids $150 for a painting at an auction. After waiting a few seconds, the auctioneer says, "Do I hear more?" and then knocks the hammer down. A's bid is an offer, and B's action in knocking down the hammer is an implied-in-fact acceptance of that offer.

(b) **Example:**   A writes a note to B, a plumber, requesting B to repair A's leaky faucet. B comes the next day while A is home, and proceeds to make the repair. A's request is an offer to pay B's usual rates, provided they are not unreasonable. B's conduct in making the repair is an implied-in-fact acceptance of that offer.

(c) **Implied-in-fact offer and acceptance:** [§303]   In some cases, both the offer and the acceptance may be implied in fact from nonverbal actions.

1) **Example:** A passes B's fruit and vegetable store every day on the way to work and buys an apple. One day, A is late. She grabs an apple; holds it up to B, who nods; and runs off to catch her bus. The conduct of A and B results in an implied-in-fact contract for the sale of the apple at B's posted price.

2) **U.C.C.:** Likewise, under the U.C.C. conduct by both parties that recognizes the existence of a contract for the sale of goods is sufficient to establish a contract, even though the writings of the parties do not otherwise establish a contract. [U.C.C. §2-207(3); *see supra*, §218]

(7) **Unjust enrichment or quasi-contract:** [§304]   Under the principle of *unjust enrichment* or *quasi-contract*, in a variety of cases liability may be imposed on a person who receives a benefit from another, even in the absence of a promise to pay for the benefits. A plaintiff can recover in restitution or quasi-contract if he can show that:

(i)   He has conferred a benefit on the defendant;

(ii)   He conferred the benefit with the expectation that he would be paid its value;

(iii)   The defendant knew or had reason to know of the plaintiff's expectation; and

(iv)   The defendant would be unjustly enriched if he were allowed to retain the benefit without paying its value.

(a) **Example:** A begins to build a party wall (*i.e.*, a wall that straddles the boundary between two properties) on the boundary between A's property and B's property. A reasonable person in B's position would know that, because B will have legal ownership of half the wall (since the wall is partly on B's side of the boundary line), A expects B to pay for half the value of the wall. B says nothing and lets A continue to work. B is liable for half the value of the wall. [Day v. Caton, 119 Mass. 513 (1876)]

(b) **Failed contract:** [§305]   Note that the four requirements discussed above need not be proved where a quasi-contract remedy is sought because an attempted contract has failed (*e.g.*, because of noncompliance with the Statute of Frauds). All that must be proved is the failed contract and unjust enrichment that would result absent the quasi-contractual remedy.

D. TIME AT WHICH A COMMUNICATION BETWEEN OFFEROR AND OFFEREE BECOMES EFFECTIVE

1. **In General:** [§306]   When parties are not negotiating orally, it often becomes important to determine when a communication, such as an acceptance, a revocation, or a rejection, takes effect. The rules vary according to what type of communication is involved. In general, and subject to the exceptions described below, all communications except an acceptance are effective *on receipt*. An acceptance is effective *on dispatch*.

2. **Acceptance—"Mailbox Rule":** [§307]   Although a promise normally must be communicated to be effective, for reasons of policy the general rule is that an acceptance is effective on dispatch, *i.e.,* even before it has been received. This rule is known as the rule of *Adams v. Lindsell,* or the "mailbox" rule. [Adams v. Lindsell, 106 Eng. Rep. 250 (1818)]

   a. **Rationale:**   Such a rule (i) encourages contracting by parties at a distance from each other, by making the offeree just as secure as if the contract were made face-to-face and (ii) creates a contract at the earliest possible moment.

   b. **Exception for options:** [§308]   Some authorities, including the Restatement, take the position that in the case of an *option,* an acceptance (or "exercise" of the option) is not effective until *received.* [Cities Service Oil Co. v. National Shawmut Bank, 172 N.E.2d 104 (Mass. 1961); Scott-Burr Stores Corp. v. Wilcox, 194 F.2d 989 (5th Cir. 1952); Rest. 2d §63] However, other courts apply the mailbox rule even to the exercise of options. [Palo Alto Town & Country Village v. BBTC Co., 11 Cal. 3d 494 (1974); Shubert Theatrical Co. v. Rath, 271 F. 827 (2d Cir. 1921)]

   c. **Requirements necessary to satisfy the mailbox rule:** [§309]   To be effective upon dispatch, the acceptance must be dispatched in a *timely* and *proper* manner. [Rest. 2d §63]

      (1) **Timely dispatch:** [§310]   Whether dispatch is timely depends in part on whether the offer specifies a period of time for acceptance.

         (a) **No time specified for acceptance:** [§311]   If no period of time for acceptance is specified in the offer, the offeree must accept within a reasonable time (*see supra,* §185).

         (b) **Specified period for acceptance:** [§312]   If a period of time is specified in the offer, then unless otherwise specified the time period begins running *when the offer is received,* and the acceptance must be dispatched within that time period. [Caldwell v. Cline, *supra,* §183]

         (c) **Time of dispatch, not receipt, important:** [§313]   If the acceptance is dispatched within the specified time period, it is timely even if in the normal course of delivery it will be (and is) received by the offeree after the specified period. [Falconer v. Mazess, 168 A.2d 558 (Pa. 1961)]

1) **Example:** A lives in Atlanta and B lives in New York. The course of post between Atlanta and New York is two days. On January 2, A mails a written offer to B. The offer states that it will remain open for 10 days. A's letter arrives on January 4. The 10-day time period begins running on January 4. B's acceptance will be timely if it is dispatched by mail on or prior to January 14.

(d) **Consequences of late dispatch:** [§314]   If an acceptance is not dispatched in a timely manner and arrives too late, it is ineffective as an acceptance. However, it does serve as a counteroffer and therefore creates a power of acceptance in the original offeror.

1) **Note:** Under certain circumstances, the original offeror's failure to *reject* the late acceptance/counteroffer will operate as an acceptance by silence (*see supra*, §301).

(e) **Options:** [§315]   Remember that some authorities do not apply the mailbox rule where the offer is an option. According to those authorities, if the offeree has a specified period of time in which to exercise the option, the acceptance must be *received* (not merely dispatched) within that period.

(2) **Proper manner:** [§316]   Assuming an acceptance has been dispatched in a timely fashion, the next question is whether it has been dispatched in a proper manner.

(a) **Appropriate care:** [§317]   To begin with, the acceptance must be dispatched with appropriate care—that is, correctly addressed, in a proper envelope or container, with postage or delivery charges prepaid. [Rest. 2d §66; Shubert Theatrical Co. v. Rath, *supra,* §308]

(b) **Medium of communication:** [§318]   The offeree must also dispatch the acceptance by an appropriate medium of communication. What constitutes an appropriate medium depends in part on whether the offeror has suggested or prescribed a medium of acceptance.

1) **Where offeror does not suggest or prescribe medium of acceptance**

a) **Traditional rule:** [§319]   The traditional rule was that where the offeror did not prescribe or suggest the medium of acceptance, an acceptance would be effective on dispatch only if the offeree used a medium of communication that the offeror had "expressly or impliedly authorized." For example, the offeror was deemed to impliedly authorize the medium by which he sent the offer. [Henthorn v. Fraser, [1892] 2 Ch. 27]

b) **Modern rule:** [§320]   The modern rule is that unless otherwise specified an offer is deemed to invite acceptance by any medium "reasonable in the circumstances." [Rest. 2d §30; U.C.C. §2-206(1)(a)]

1/ **"Reasonable" medium:** [§321] A medium of communication is normally reasonable if it is the one used by the offeror (unless the offer specifies otherwise), or if it is customary in similar transactions at the time and place the offer is received. [Rest. 2d §65]

2/ **Other factors:** [§322] If the medium does not meet one of these two tests it may still be reasonable, depending on such circumstances as the speed and reliability of the medium, the prior course of dealing between the parties, and usage of trade. [Rest. 2d §65]

   a/ **Use of mail:** [§323] Acceptance by mail is ordinarily reasonable when the parties are negotiating at a distance, even if the offer is not made by mail, unless there is a special reason for speed, such as rapid price changes.

      1] **Example:** A lives in Los Angeles and B lives in San Francisco. A makes a face-to-face offer of employment to B in Los Angeles, and gives B two days to consider the offer. B says she will go back to San Francisco and think about it. That evening, B posts an acceptance by mail from San Francisco. The acceptance is effective on dispatch. Since the parties live in different cities, A should have contemplated that B would use the mails. In any event, except in unusual situations, such as those involving a subject matter whose price fluctuates rapidly, the mails are a customary means of conducting business negotiations.

         a] **Note:** Acceptance by telegram is also ordinarily reasonable when the parties are negotiating at a distance, although there is some authority contra. [*Compare* Rest. 2d §65 *with* Dickey v. Hurd, 33 F.2d 415 (1st Cir. 1929)] Today, acceptance by fax or E-mail would also probably be deemed reasonable in the ordinary case.

2) **Where offeror suggests medium of acceptance:** [§324] If the offeror explicitly suggests a medium of acceptance, use of that medium is always appropriate. Failure to use a suggested medium may (but does not necessarily) mean that the medium that is used is unreasonable.

3) **Where offeror prescribes medium of communication:** [§325] If the offeror *prescribes* a medium of communication, no contract will be formed *unless* that medium is used.

a) **Example:** A offers to sell her land to B on certain terms, and states, "You must accept this offer, if at all, in person at my office at noon, tomorrow." B's power of acceptance can be exercised *only* in the manner A has designated. Acceptance in any other manner is a mere counteroffer. [Rest. 2d §60]

b) **Interpretation:** [§326] Language that appears to prescribe a medium of acceptance may be interpreted only to suggest that medium. In such cases, the offeree can use some other medium, but if that other medium is not reasonable under the circumstances, the acceptance will be effective only if it arrives no later than would an acceptance sent through the suggested medium. [Rest. 2d §60]

1/ **Example:** A mails an offer to B in which A says, "Accept by return mail." Because there is ordinarily no reason why an offeror would insist on use of the mail to the exclusion of all other media, the offer would probably be interpreted (i) to suggest rather than require use of the mails; (ii) to require that an acceptance by any other medium arrive as soon as a letter would have arrived; and (iii) to require that the acceptance be in writing. Therefore, a written acceptance sent on time by any other means would create a contract on dispatch if the means of communication was reasonable. If the means of communication was not reasonable, the acceptance would be effective if it arrived as soon as a letter sent by return mail would have arrived. [Rest. 2d §60] If such an acceptance is sent on time and arrives on time, it will be deemed effective on dispatch.

(c) **Consequence of using unreasonable medium or failing to use reasonable care in dispatching acceptance:** [§327] Failure to use reasonable care in dispatching an acceptance does not necessarily mean that no contract is formed, unless there was a failure to use a *required* medium. However, if the medium employed is not a reasonable one, or if reasonable care was not employed in dispatching the acceptance, the acceptance will not be effective unless it actually *arrives*.

1) **Note:** However, as noted above, if an acceptance is dispatched through an unreasonable medium, but on time, and it arrives on time, it is treated as operative on dispatch, just as if it were properly sent.

d. **Significance of mailbox rule:** [§328] Assuming that an acceptance is properly dispatched, so that the mailbox rule is applicable, a number of consequences may follow, depending on the context:

(1) **Crossed acceptance and revocation:** [§329]   In most states, a revocation is effective only on receipt. (*See infra,* §335). Therefore, under the mailbox rule if an *acceptance* is *dispatched* before a *revocation* is *received,* a contract is formed. This is true even though the acceptance is dispatched after the revocation is dispatched and received after the revocation is received.

    (a) **Minority view:** [§330]   Statutes in a few states, including California, provide that a revocation is effective on *dispatch.* (*See infra,* §337.) In such states, a contract is formed if the acceptance is dispatched first, but not if the revocation is dispatched first. [Cal. Civ. Code §1587]

(2) **Lost or delayed acceptance:** [§331]   Suppose a properly dispatched acceptance is lost or delayed by the carrier, so that it does not arrive at all, or arrives late. Under the mailbox rule, the acceptance is nevertheless effective and a contract is formed. In other words, under the mailbox rule the *risk of loss or delay* in transmission of a properly dispatched acceptance is on the *offeror.*

    (a) **Note:** There is authority for the proposition that even though a contract is formed despite the fact that the acceptance does not arrive, the *offeror's duty to perform* under the contract is conditional on receipt of notice that he is obliged to perform and must begin performance. Under these authorities, even though a contract is formed, the offeror's failure to perform will not be a breach unless and until he receives such a notice. [Haas v. Myers, 111 Ill. 421 (1884); Rest. 2d §63]

(3) **What law governs?** [§332]   The general choice-of-law rule is that a contract is governed by the law of the state in which the contract was formed. Under the mailbox rule, a contract is formed when the acceptance is dispatched. Therefore, under the mailbox rule a contract will be governed by the *law of the state in which the acceptance was dispatched.* [Perry v. Mt. Hope Iron Co., 5 A. 632 (R.I. 1886)]

(4) **Effective date of obligation to perform:** [§333]   In some cases, it is important to determine when the parties' obligation to perform becomes effective. Under the mailbox rule, the obligation to perform becomes effective when the acceptance is dispatched. [Taylor v. Merchant's Fire Insurance Co., 50 U.S. (9 How.) 390 (1850)]

    (a) **Example:** On January 2, A, a resident of Atlanta, Georgia, mails an application for life insurance to B Insurance Company of Hartford, Connecticut. A's application constitutes an offer. The course of post between Atlanta and Hartford is two days. On January 5, B accepts A's application by mailing a policy to her. A dies on January 6, before receiving the policy. A was covered by the policy at the time of her death, because the dispatch of the policy constituted an acceptance, and therefore under the mailbox rule a contract was formed on January 5, prior to A's death.

e. **Offeror's power to negate the mailbox rule:** [§334] An offeror can negate the mailbox rule by providing in the offer that the acceptance will be effective only on receipt. However, the offeror must use clear language to achieve that result.

    (1) **Example:** A lives in California and B lives in Massachusetts. A makes a written offer to B by mail, which concludes, "If you agree to this offer and will telegraph me on receipt of this, I will order my agent in Boston to begin performance. Telegraph me 'Yes' or 'No.' If 'No,' I will go to Boston and make other arrangements. If a telegram from you is not in my hands within 10 days, I shall conclude 'No.' " B sends a properly dispatched telegraphic acceptance, but it fails to arrive. There is no contract, because the language of the offer negates the mailbox rule. [*See* Lewis v. Browning, 130 Mass. 173 (1881)]

3. **Revocation:** [§335] As noted above, the general rule is that a revocation is effective only *upon receipt*, subject to statutory exceptions in a few cases. [Stevenson, Jaques & Co. v. McLean, *supra,* §193]

    a. **Crossed acceptance and revocation:** [§336] Because an acceptance is effective on *dispatch*, but a revocation is effective only on *receipt*, if an offeree dispatches an acceptance after the offeror dispatches a revocation but before the revocation arrives, a contract is formed. [Stevenson, Jaques & Co. v. McLean, *supra*; Henthorn v. Fraser, *supra,* §319; and *see supra,* §329]

4. **Rejection:** [§337] The general rule is that a rejection of an offer is effective only *upon receipt*. [Rest. 2d §40]

    a. **Where offeree sends both rejection and acceptance:** [§338] Special problems arise when an offeree first dispatches a rejection, and later changes his mind and dispatches an acceptance. The result in such cases depends partly on whether the rejection or the acceptance arrives first.

        (1) **Rejection arrives first:** [§339] If the rejection arrives before the acceptance, there is no contract, even if the acceptance was dispatched before the rejection arrives. In other words, the *mailbox rule does not apply* in this case. [Rest. 2d §40]

            (a) **Rationale:** [§340] When the offeror receives the rejection without having yet received the acceptance, his expectation is that negotiations have terminated. That expectation should be protected.

            (b) **Effect of later-arriving acceptance:** [§341] Although the later-arriving acceptance in such a case will not be effective as an acceptance, it will be effective as a *counteroffer,* creating a power of acceptance in the original offeror.

        (2) **Acceptance arrives first:** [§342] If the rejection arrives *after* the acceptance, a contract *is* formed.

(a) **Rationale:** When the offeror receives the acceptance without having yet received the rejection, his expectation is that a contract is formed. Again, that expectation should be protected.

(b) **Effect of later-arriving rejection:** [§343] The later-arriving rejection in such a case is not effective as a rejection and does not relieve the offeree of liability under the contract. However, the offeror may regard the rejection as a repudiation of the contract. If the offeror *does* so regard the rejection, and relies upon his belief that the contract has been repudiated, the offeree will be estopped from enforcing the contract.

5. **Repudiation of Acceptance:** [§344] A repudiation of an acceptance is a communication by an offeree who has previously dispatched an acceptance, stating that the offeree does not intend to be bound by the acceptance. That is, the offeree first dispatches an acceptance and then changes his mind and dispatches a repudiation. A repudiation therefore differs from a rejection. In a rejection, the offeree turns down the offer. In a repudiation, the offeree "turns down" his own earlier acceptance. By its nature a repudiation therefore can be dispatched only after an acceptance is dispatched, because before the acceptance is dispatched there is nothing to repudiate.

When an offeree sends both a repudiation and an acceptance, the governing rules are comparable to the rules that govern the case in which an offeree sends both a rejection and an acceptance. In both cases, the result turns in large part on which communication arrives first.

a. **Acceptance arrives first:** [§345] If an acceptance arrives before a repudiation of an acceptance arrives, a contract is formed.

(1) **Rationale:** When the acceptance arrives, the offeror's expectation is that a contract is formed. That expectation should be protected.

(2) **Effect of later-arriving repudiation:** [§346] The later-arriving repudiation in such a case is not effective to relieve the *offeree* of liability under the contract. However, the *offeror* may regard the offeree's repudiation of the acceptance as a repudiation of the contract. If the offeror does so regard the rejection, and relies upon his belief that the contract has been repudiated, the offeree will be estopped from enforcing the contract.

b. **Repudiation arrives first:** [§347] Suppose now that the repudiation arrives first. Under a strict application of the mailbox rule, a contract would still be formed, because under the mailbox rule an acceptance is effective on dispatch, and the acceptance was dispatched before the repudiation arrived. The Restatement takes just this position. [Rest. 2d §63] However, the cases are split on the issue whether a contract is formed if the repudiation arrives first. [*Compare* Morrison v. Thoelke, 155 So.2d 889 (Fla. 1963)—contract formed, *with* Dick v. United States, 82 F. Supp. 326 (Ct. Cl. 1949)—contract not formed]

(1) **Rationale:** Because the offeror receives the repudiation first, her expectation is probably that no contract is formed. If that was the rule, however, an offeree could speculate at the offeror's expense by mailing an acceptance

and then watching the market while the letter traveled through the mail. If the market moved in the offeree's favor, she could let the acceptance ride, so that a contract would be formed. If the market moved against her, she could send a repudiation by an overtaking (faster) means of communication. The Restatement rule, that a contract is formed even when the repudiation arrives first, is intended to prevent such speculation by binding the offeree as soon as she dispatches her acceptance.

(2) **Effect of repudiation:** [§348]   At least under the Restatement rule, the earlier-arriving repudiation does not prevent formation of a contract. However, because the offeror receives the repudiation first, he may regard it as a rejection, and rely upon it. If he does, the offeree will be estopped from asserting that a contract was formed.

6. **Withdrawal of Acceptance:** [§349]   A withdrawal of an acceptance occurs when the offeree dispatches an acceptance and then manages to *retrieve* the acceptance before it reaches the offeror. For example, the offeree might retrieve a mailed letter of acceptance from the post office. There is very little law on this issue, but the Restatement takes the position that the mailbox rule is still applicable in such a case—*i.e.,* a contract is formed when the acceptance is dispatched, and the withdrawal is therefore ineffective. [Rest. 2d §63] Most courts would probably agree. [*See* G.C. Casebolt Co. v. United States, 421 F.2d 710 (Ct. Cl. 1970)]

   a. **Note:** There is a practical problem in such cases: Because the offeror never receives the acceptance, he may never learn that the offeree had dispatched the offer and then withdrawn it.

7. **Crossed Offers:** [§350]   Suppose A writes to B on January 2 that she will sell Orangeacre to B for $40,000, and coincidentally on the same day B writes to A that he will buy Orangeacre for $40,000. Is there a contract? This kind of situation is called "crossed offers" or "crossed offer and acceptance." The general rule is that a contract is *not* formed by crossed offers, on the theory that an offer is not effective until received, and cannot be accepted until it is effective. [Tinn v. Hoffman, 29 L.T.R. (n.s.) 271 (1873)]

   a. **Previous agreement:** [§351]   However, a different result may follow where the parties had previously agreed upon all but one minor point, and then in crossed letters they each propose identical terms on that point. [Asinof v. Freudenthal, 195 App. Div. 79 (1921)]

E. INTERPRETATION

1. **General Rule:** [§352]   A contract can be based on either words or conduct. Words or conduct that are addressed by one party (the addressor) to another (the addressee) can be called an "expression." The general rule of interpretation in contract law is that where the interpretation of an expression is in issue, the expression should be given an *objective* interpretation. This means that the expression should be given the interpretation a reasonable person standing in the addressee's shoes would put upon it, rather than the interpretation that the addressor subjectively intends.

a. **Application—reasonable person knowing what addressee knows:** [§353] In applying the objective test, the question should be not simply how a generalized reasonable person in the addressee's shoes would interpret the relevant expression, but what interpretation would be given by a reasonable person knowing all that the addressee knew. Accordingly, if the parties are in a special trade, the interpretation must include the usages of the trade. Similarly, if the addressee knows special circumstances that would give the expression a different meaning than it would normally be given, those circumstances would be relevant in an objective interpretation.

(1) **Example:** A is an employee of B under a 10-month contract expiring on December 31. On December 15, A asks B to renew the contract for another 10 months, stating that if B does not renew, A will immediately take steps to find a new job. B replies, "Don't worry, you're all right," and A says, "O.K." A subjectively interprets the conversation to be an agreement on a new contract. B does not. A's interpretation is more reasonable than B's; consequently, there is a contract. [Embry v. Hargadine-McKittrick Dry Goods Co., 105 S.W. 777 (Mo. 1907)]

2. **Exceptions:** [§354] There are several major exceptions to the normal rule of objective interpretation.

a. **The *Peerless* rule:** [§355] One exception occurs where an expression is susceptible of two *equally reasonable* meanings, and each party understands the expression differently. This was the famous *Peerless* case. In that case, both parties used the term "ex ship Peerless," each thinking there was only one ship Peerless. In fact there were two ships Peerless, and each party subjectively intended a different Peerless. The rule in such cases is that if both parties subjectively attach different, equally reasonable, interpretations to their expressions, no contract is formed.

(1) **Note:** The *Peerless* rule is limited to cases where two or more meanings are *equally reasonable*. If an expression is susceptible of two or more meanings, but only one meaning is reasonable, or one meaning is more reasonable than the other, then the objective theory prevails and the interpretation is based on the reasonable or more reasonable meaning, provided that that is the meaning that one of the parties intended.

(2) **Note:** Subjective interpretation is also relevant where both parties have the same subjective interpretation. A jointly held subjective interpretation will govern, even if it differs from a reasonable interpretation.

3. **Extrinsic Evidence:** [§356] Questions often arise whether "extrinsic evidence"— *i.e.,* evidence outside the contract itself, such as conversations between the parties and surrounding circumstances—may be admitted in aid of interpreting a contract.

a. **Traditional rule:** [§357] The traditional rule was that if there was no ambiguity in a written contract on its face, and no special meaning attached to the words of a written contract by custom or usage, the terms of the contract were to be interpreted only according to their "plain meaning," and extrinsic evidence was inadmissible. [Rowe v. Chesapeake Mineral Co., 156 F.2d 752 (6th Cir. 1946)]

b. **Modern rule:** [§358]   Today, however, there is an increasing tendency to be more liberal, and allow extrinsic evidence to show what the parties intended by their words, without regard to their "plain" meaning or a prior showing of ambiguity.

(1) **Rationale:** No language is infallible; what is "plain" to the judge may not have been "plain" to the parties. Whether a contract is ambiguous cannot be determined unless and until all the relevant circumstances have been considered. [Pacific Gas & Electric Co. v. Thomas Drayage & Rigging Co., 69 Cal. 2d 33 (1968)]

4. **Course of Performance, Course of Dealing, Usage, and Usage of Trade:** [§359] Course of performance, course of dealing, usage, and usage of trade are all relevant in issues of interpretation.

a. **Course of performance:** [§360]   Where a contract involves repeated occasions for performance by either party, with knowledge of the nature of the performance and opportunity for objection to it by the other party, a course of performance of the contract that is accepted or acquiesced in without objection is relevant to determine the meaning of the agreement. The parties themselves know best what they meant by the words of their agreement, and their actions under that agreement is the best indication of what that meaning was.

b. **Course of dealing:** [§361]   A course of dealing is a sequence of conduct between the parties *prior to the contract* (*e.g.,* a sequence of earlier contracts between the parties) that is fairly to be regarded as establishing a common basis of understanding for interpreting their expressions. Unless otherwise agreed, a course of dealing between the parties may give meaning to, supplement, or qualify their contract.

c. **Usage:** [§362]   A usage is a habitual or customary practice. An agreement is interpreted in accordance with a relevant usage if each party knew or had reason to know of the usage. An agreement is supplemented or qualified by a reasonable usage if each party knows or has reason to know of the usage.

(1) **Example:** A, an ordained rabbi, is employed by B, an orthodox Jewish congregation, to officiate as cantor at specified religious services. At the time the contract is made, it is the practice of such congregations not to use music, and a contrary practice would violate A's religious beliefs. At a time when it is too late for A to obtain substitute employment, B adopts a contrary practice. A refuses to officiate. The practice is part of the contract, and A is entitled to the agreed compensation.

d. **Usage of trade:** [§363]   A usage of trade is a usage regularly observed in a vocation or trade. Unless otherwise agreed, a usage of trade in the vocation in which the parties are engaged gives meaning to, supplements, or qualifies their agreement.

(1) **Example:** A contracts to sell B 10,000 shingles. By usage of the shingle trade, in which both A and B are engaged, two packs of a certain size consti-

tute 1,000 shingles, although the packs do not actually contain 1,000 shingles. Unless otherwise agreed, "1,000" in the contract means two packs.

e. **Priorities:** [§364] Express terms are given greater weight than course of performance, course of dealing, usage, and usage of trade. Course of performance is given greater weight than course of dealing, usage, or usage of trade. Course of dealing is given greater weight than usage or usage of trade.

F. THE PAROL EVIDENCE RULE

1. **The Problem:** [§365] Often, although an agreement has been put in writing, one party claims there was *also* an earlier oral or written agreement, or a contemporaneous oral agreement, that was not included in the writing but was intended to be part of the contract. In such cases, the admissibility of the alleged agreement turns on the applicability of the parol evidence rule.

2. **The Rule:** [§366] Stated simply, the parol evidence rule provides that where there is a fully integrated contract (*see infra*), parol evidence (*see infra*) will not be allowed into evidence to *vary, add to, or contradict* the terms of the writing. [Hayden v. Hoadley, 111 A. 343 (Vt. 1920)]

   a. **What constitutes an "integration"?** [§367] Before the parol evidence rule applies, it must appear that the parties intended the writing in question to be an *"integration"*—*i.e.,* to be the final and complete expression of (or "to integrate") their agreement. There is disagreement, however, on how intent is to be determined for this purpose.

      (1) **"Face of the instrument" test:** [§368] The traditional view was that a writing would be treated as an integration if taken as a whole and *on its face* it appears complete. [70 A.L.R. 752; Gianni v. R. Russel & Co., 126 A. 791 (Pa. 1924)] This view has been associated with Williston. The judge assumes the position of a reasonable person to make this determination.

      (2) **"Any relevant evidence" test:** [§369] However, today many or most courts follow a competing test that is associated with Corbin. Under this test, a writing is deemed to be an integration if the parties *actually intended* it to be an integration. The writing itself is given no unique force; the court will consider *any* relevant evidence to determine whether the parties actually intended the writing as the final and complete expression of their agreement. [Masterson v. Sine, 68 Cal. 2d 222 (1968); Rest. 2d §209]

      (3) **Application of competing theories:** [§370] The Williston "face of the instrument" test is a "generic," objective test that requires the judge to impose upon the parties the terms of the written contractual documents as understood by a reasonably intelligent person. This leads to a broad application of the parol evidence rule and consequently leads to the exclusion of parol evidence. The Corbin "any relevant evidence" test is an individualized test that requires the judge to fix the legal relations of the parties in accordance with their actual intention, even when the "forms" they employed suggest otherwise. This leads to a narrower application of the parol evidence rule and con-

sequently leads to the admission of parol evidence. As stated above, the tendency is to follow the Corbin view, but many cases still follow the Williston view.

b. **What constitutes parol evidence?** [§371]   If there is a writing that is an integration, evidence of an *alleged earlier oral or written agreement* that is within the scope of the writing, or *evidence of an alleged contemporaneous oral agreement* that is within the scope of the writing, constitutes "parol evidence." An alleged agreement that such evidence concerns may be called a "parol agreement" and may be excluded from evidence if it would add to, vary, or contradict one contractual written agreement.

3.   **Exceptions:** [§372]   The parol evidence rule is subject to a number of exceptions.

a. **Separate consideration:** [§373]   Even if a writing *is* determined to be an integration, parol evidence is admissible if the written integration and the alleged parol agreement are each supported by *separate consideration*.

b. **Collateral terms:** [§374]   Parol evidence is admissible if the alleged parol agreement was *"collateral"* to the written integration. This test is not very helpful, because a determination whether the agreement was "collateral" is conclusory.

c. **"Naturally omitted" terms:** [§375]   A widely accepted modern rule, adopted in the Restatement, is that parol evidence is admissible if it concerns a naturally omitted term; *i.e.*, a term that would naturally be omitted from the writing. Under the Restatement, a term will be treated as a naturally omitted term if:

(i)   The terms of the alleged parol agreement *do not conflict* with the written integration; *and*

(ii)   The alleged parol agreement concerns a subject that might naturally be made as a separate agreement and omitted from the integration; *i.e.*, a subject that similarly situated parties would not ordinarily be expected to include in the written agreement.

[Rest. 1st §240; *and see* Rest. 2d §216]

(1)   **Two approaches:** [§376]   The same approaches that are used to determine whether a writing is an integration (*see supra*, §§368-370) are used to determine whether a parol agreement concerns a subject that would be the natural subject of a separate agreement.

(a)   **Williston generic approach:** [§377]   Under the Williston "generic" approach, the court does not give much weight to the individual circumstances of each particular case, but instead treats cases generically to determine whether an abstract reasonable person would naturally have omitted the term in question from the writing and instead make the term a separate agreement.

(b) **Corbin individual circumstances approach:** [§378] Many modern courts follow the Corbin approach, and give an expansive reading to the Restatement rule by taking into account all of the circumstances of the individual case in determining whether a parol agreement concerns a subject that might naturally be the subject of a separate agreement.

(c) **Application of competing approaches:** [§379] Application of the Williston approach leads to broad application of the parol evidence rule and consequently leads to exclusion of parol evidence. Application of the Corbin approach leads to more liberal admission of parol evidence because the party who seeks to have the parol evidence admitted can point to some special feature of her case that explains why, given all the particular circumstances, it was natural for the parties to have made a separate parol agreement. Just as the tendency of modern courts is to focus on the parties' actual intent in determining whether a writing is an integration (*see supra*, §369), so too the tendency of modern courts is to take into account all of the circumstances of a particular case to determine whether the parol agreement is one that would be the natural subject of a separate agreement.

1) **Example:** A written employment contract gave an employer an unrestricted right to terminate an employee's employment. Nevertheless, parol evidence was held to be admissible to show that the employer orally promised not to terminate the employee as long as the employee was "doing a good job," on the ground that the oral promise was a "natural subject for separate agreement." [Brawthen v. H&R Block, 28 Cal. App. 3d 131 (1972)]

(2) **Comment:** The modern views concerning the "natural subject of a separate agreement" rule and the test to determine what constitutes an integrated contract result in courts being more ready to admit parol evidence than were courts in the past. However, even if the parol evidence rule is given very liberal treatment it still has a bite, because under the rule, the judge, rather than the jury, makes determinations of whether parties situated like the parties might naturally have made the parol agreement. Furthermore, even though the long-run tendency may be toward liberalization in the application of the parol evidence rule, the courts still regard the rule as important and apply it to bar parol evidence in many cases.

(3) **Contradictory terms:** [§380] An oral agreement that *contradicts* a written agreement usually will not fall within the "might naturally be omitted" test. However, there are two views on what "contradicts" means for these purposes.

(a) **Logically inconsistent terms:** [§381] Some courts essentially treat parol evidence as contradictory only if it is *logically inconsistent* with the written agreement that constitutes an integration. Under this view, if, for example, a written contract provides for the sale of 10,000 widgets, an alleged parol agreement that *8,000* widgets will be sold would be treated as contradicting the written agreement, because an obligation to sell 8,000 widgets is logically inconsistent with an obligation to sell 10,000 widgets. However, evidence of a parol agreement that "**up to 10,000**" widgets will be sold might not be viewed as contradicting the written agreement, because "10,000" and "up to 10,000" are not logically inconsistent.

    (b) **Reasonably harmonious terms:** [§382]   Other courts, however, treat parol evidence as contradicting a written agreement if the parol evidence is not *reasonably harmonious* with the writing. Under this view, evidence of a parol agreement that "up to 10,000" widgets will be sold might be viewed as contradicting the written agreement, because it would not be reasonably harmonious with the writing.

d. **U.C.C. test:** [§383]   The U.C.C. is even more liberal than the Restatement. Under the U.C.C., in the case of contracts for the sale of goods, parol evidence is admissible unless the matter covered in the alleged parol agreement "*certainly would have been included*" in the written agreement. [U.C.C. §2-202, Comment 3 (emphasis added)]

e. **"Partial" integration:** [§384]   Even where a writing is not a *complete* integration, it may be a "partial" integration—*i.e.,* an integration of the *subjects actually covered* in the writing. A partial integration is controlling on those subjects that it covers, but it does not bar parol evidence on subjects that it does not cover.

f. **Lack of consideration:** [§385]   Parol evidence is admissible to show a lack of consideration.

g. **Fraud, duress, or mistake:** [§386]   Parol evidence is admissible to show fraud, duress, or mistake. Furthermore, under the law of misrepresentation, a person who makes a promise that he has no intention of performing commits "promissory fraud." Applying this concept to the parol evidence rule, many courts hold that under the fraud exception to that rule, it is permissible to introduce evidence of a parol promise if the promise was made with no intention to perform it.

h. **Existence of a condition precedent to legal effectiveness of written agreement:** [§387]   Parol evidence is admissible to prove that there was a condition precedent (written or oral) to the *legal effectiveness* of a written agreement. [Hicks v. Bush, 10 N.Y.2d 488 (1962)] Note, however, that parol evidence is not admissible to *add* a condition to the obligation to render performance under a *legally effective contract*.

    (1) **Example:** A and B sign a written instrument whereby they will merge their respective corporations into a single new holding company. The written instrument provides that A will subscribe for 425,000 shares of stock in the new holding corporation, and B will subscribe for 1 million shares. A does not perform, and B brings suit. In response, A claims that the parties orally agreed that the written instrument was not to be legally effective as a contract until "equity expansion funds" of $675,000 had first been procured from third parties. The evidence is admissible because it concerns a condition to the legal effectiveness of the contract.

(2) **Compare:** Same facts as in the last example, except that A does not allege that the instrument was not a legally effective contract, but instead alleges only that the parties orally agreed that A's *duty to perform* under the contract was conditioned on B's contribution of $675,000 in new equity funds. This parol evidence is inadmissible. It does not fall within the exception applicable to the last example, because the alleged parol agreement modifies an admitted legally effective contract by adding a condition to performance under the contract, rather than showing that there was a condition to the writing becoming a legally effective contract.

(3) **Comment:** As the above examples suggest, the exception to the parol evidence rule allowing evidence of a parol agreement that the writing will not be a legally effective contract unless some condition occurs—is very tenuous because there is only a narrow and unclear line between (i) evidence of an agreement that a written instrument will not become *effective* unless a certain condition is fulfilled (which falls within the exception and is admissible) and (ii) evidence of an agreement that *performance under an admittedly effective contract* is subject to a condition (which does not fall within the exception and is not admissible).

i. **Evidence to explain or interpret terms of written agreement:** [§388] The parol evidence rule does not bar admission of extrinsic evidence to show *what the parties meant* by the words used in their written agreement. The rationale of this exception to the rule is that such evidence explains the written agreement, rather than adding to, varying, or contradicting the written agreement. To qualify under the exception, the evidence may not be in the form of a promise or agreement, but rather must be in the form of background discussion, surrounding circumstances, or the like. Technically, extrinsic evidence concerning interpretation is not parol evidence at all, because it does not concern alleged parol *agreements* but only extrinsic evidence *other than agreements.* However, such evidence may be barred by the "plain meaning rule"—the rule that if there is no ambiguity in a written contract on its face, and no special meaning attached to the words of a written contract by custom or usage, the terms of the contract are to be interpreted only according to their "plain meaning," and extrinsic evidence is inadmissible either to interpret the contract or to establish that the contract is ambiguous. The courts often lump together the plain meaning rule and the parol evidence rule, because both rules concern evidence that is outside a written agreement. (*See supra,* §371.)

(1) **Modern rule:** [§389] Today, there is an increasing tendency to be more liberal and allow extrinsic evidence to show what the parties intended by their words, without regard to the "plain meaning" of the words. (*See supra,* §369.)

(a) **Example:** A agrees to indemnify B against "any injury to property," caused while A is repairing B's machinery. Extrinsic evidence is admissible to show that this term means injury to the property of third persons, not injury to B's own property. [Pacific Gas & Electric Co. v. Thomas Drayage, 69 Cal. 2d 33 (1968)]

(b) **Limitation:** The process of "interpretation" cannot be used to **contradict** the terms of the written instrument. Either party might claim that he "didn't mean" what he said. To allow extrinsic evidence in such cases could effectively destroy the parol evidence rule. Accordingly, oral evidence bearing on interpretation is admissible only if the interpretation does not contradict the words in the writing or, to put it differently, is an interpretation that the words in the writing **will bear**. However, what constitutes a contradiction is itself ambiguous. (*See supra*, §§380-382.)

(2) **Course of performance, course of dealing, and usage:** [§390] Extrinsic evidence is also admissible to show any special meanings attached to words used in the written agreement deriving from course of performance, course of dealing, or usage. Courts are becoming increasingly liberal in admitting such evidence, even when it contradicts the **implications** that would otherwise be drawn from the writing, and sometimes even when the evidence seems to contradict the writing itself. For example, in *Columbia Nitrogen Corp. v. Royster,* 451 F.2d 3 (4th Cir. 1971), the court held that evidence of course of dealing and usage of trade was admissible to show that an apparently firm obligation to purchase phosphate was merely a projection to be adjusted according to market forces. [*See also* Southern Concrete Services, Inc. v. Mableton Contractors, Inc., 407 F. Supp. 581 (N.D. Ga. 1975)—contra]

(a) **Comment:** Strictly speaking, evidence of course of dealing, course of performance, or trade usage is not parol evidence, because it does not concern agreements **between** the parties. Furthermore, in contracts for the sale of goods, U.C.C. section 1-201(3) defines "agreement" to mean "the bargain of the parties in fact as found in their language or by implication from other circumstances **including** course of dealing or usage of trade or course of performance as provided in this Act." Literally, therefore, under the U.C.C. course of dealing, course of performance, and trade usage are not parol evidence outside the agreement, but are **part** of the agreement. On this view, course of dealing, course of performance, and trade usage are admissible even if they **contradict** the writing. Courts are increasingly tending toward this view by admitting such evidence, at least if the evidence is not **logically inconsistent** with the explicit language of the agreement. However, some courts still view the admissibility of such evidence as a parol evidence rule issue, and exclude such evidence on that ground if there is a lack of reasonable harmony between the course of dealing, course of performance, or trade usage, on the one hand, and the writing on the other.

(3) **Filling in gaps**

(a) **Traditional approach:** [§391] Under the traditional approach, where a written contract left a gap as to some term (*e.g.*, time of performance), parol evidence would be admitted on the issue of what was a **reasonable term** for the court to imply, but parol evidence was not admissible to show that the parties had **actually reached an agreement** concerning the subject matter of the gap. [Hayden v. Hoadley, *supra, *§366]

(b) **Modern approach:** [§392]   Modern courts are increasingly disposed to admit parol evidence of agreements concerning gaps under the "interpretation" exception to the parol evidence rule as long as the evidence does not squarely contradict the contract language. Some cases admit parol evidence even though the evidence contradicts the implication of law that would be drawn in the absence of the parol evidence. For example, in *Masterson v. Sine, supra,* §369, parol evidence was held admissible to show that the parties had made an agreement that an option was intended to be exercised only by the optionee, although in the absence of such evidence the normal rule is that the right to exercise an option is freely assignable.

j. **Modifications:** [§393]   A *later* oral agreement that modifies a *previously existing* written contract does *not* fall within the parol evidence rule, because the modification is subsequent to, rather than prior to or contemporaneous with, the written agreement. Therefore, the fact that a modification is oral does not make it unenforceable under the parol evidence rule.

(1) **Consideration:** [§394]   Of course, such an agreement still needs consideration to be enforceable (except in contracts for the sale of goods; *see supra,* §92).

(2) **Statute of Frauds:** [§395]   Furthermore, even if a modification is not invalid for lack of consideration, it must still comply with any applicable provision of the Statute of Frauds (*see infra,* §§498 *et seq.*).

(3) **Contractual requirement of a writing:** [§396]   In some cases, a written contract contains a provision requiring that any modification of the contract be in writing. Under common law, such provisions are not normally given effect to prevent the enforcement of an oral modification of a contract containing such a provision, if the modification is otherwise legally enforceable (*i.e.,* if the modification has consideration and need not be in writing under the Statute of Frauds). [Teer v. George A. Fuller Co., 30 F.2d 30 (4th Cir. 1929)]

(a) **Rationale:**   The rationale for not giving effect to such a provision at common law is that if the modification has consideration, it is a new contract, and the new contract implicitly includes a mutual agreement to abandon the requirement of a writing set out in the old contract.

(b) **U.C.C.:** [§397]   Under the U.C.C., in the case of a contract for the sale of goods, if the original contract excludes modification or rescission except by a signed writing, then a modification or rescission must be in writing. [U.C.C. §2-209(2)]

1) **Waiver:** [§398]   However, the U.C.C. also provides that an oral modification of a contract for the sale of goods that is unenforceable because it is required to be in writing, either under the Statute of Frauds or under a provision of the original contract, can "operate as a *waiver.*"

a) **Requisites of waiver:** [§399] It is not clear what is required to make an oral modification that should have been in writing enforceable on the ground that it "operate[s] as a waiver." Under one view, a modification will operate as a waiver, within the meaning of section 2-209(2), only if relied upon. Under a competing view, a modification will operate as a waiver if it involves the knowing surrender of a legal right, whether or not relied upon. [U.C.C. §2-209(4), (5)]

b) **Significance of competing views:** [§400] The significance of the difference in views is as follows. Under U.C.C. section 2-209(5), a waiver that relates to *prospective performance* can be retracted before it has been relied upon, but a waiver related to *past performance* cannot be retracted. Under the view that an oral modification can "operate as a waiver" only if it has been relied upon, it does not matter whether the modification relates to a past or a present performance; in either case, the oral modification will be effective only if relied upon. In contrast, under the view that a modification can operate as a waiver if it involves the knowing surrender of a legal right, an oral modification would be effective, even if not relied upon, if it related to past performance, and would be effective even if it related to prospective performance unless retracted.

III. DEFENSES

chapter approach

After you determine that a contract has been formed, you must next determine whether the contract is unenforceable by reason of some *defense* related to the *formation* of the contract. (Defenses concerning the *performance* of the contract will be considered in Chapter V.) The most important of these defenses are indefiniteness, mistake, fraud, nondisclosure, duress, undue influence, unconscionability, the Statute of Frauds, lack of capacity, and illegality.

1. *Indefiniteness*—For a bargain to be enforceable, its terms must be sufficiently definite to evidence that the parties have concluded a deal (rather than merely engaging in preliminary negotiations), and to enable the court to determine the terms of the bargain with sufficient certainty to fashion a remedy for breach.

   If you see a question that involves a bargain in which the parties have failed to specify price, quantity, or payment terms, or have stated that a formal contract will follow, you should always consider the defense of indefiniteness. You must also be aware, however, that often courts will fill in gaps by the process of implication, so that merely because a contract has gaps does not mean that it will fail on the ground that it is too indefinite. If the contract is for the sale of goods, it will fall within the U.C.C., which includes a number of "gap filler" provisions.

2. *Mistake*—Whenever a question involves a promise that is made under some kind of false impression, other than one induced by fraud or nondisclosure, there is likely to be an issue of mistake. These issues fall into five categories:

   a. A *mutual mistake* occurs where the parties made a contract under a shared mistake concerning a *basic assumption of fact* on which the contract was made. In such cases, the adversely affected party is normally entitled to rescission *unless* he bore the risk of the mistake.

   b. A *unilateral mistake* occurs when something goes wrong with the mental machinery of *one* of the parties, as where one of the parties makes a mistake in computation. Such a mistake is a ground for rescission if the nonmistaken party *knew or should have known* of the mistake, so that the mistake was "palpable." Some courts hold that even if a unilateral mistake is not palpable, the mistaken party is liable only for reliance (rather than expectation) damages.

   c. A *mistranscription* occurs where an error was made in transcribing an oral agreement into writing. In such cases, either party is entitled to have the writing corrected through the remedy of reformation.

   d. A *misunderstanding* occurs where (i) the parties made a contract under the mistaken impression that their language was unambiguous, when in fact it was ambiguous; (ii) each party gave the language a different interpretation; and (iii) each party's interpretation was equally reasonable. In such cases, the general rule is that neither party is liable.

e. A ***mistake in transmission*** occurs where an intermediary, such as a telegraph company, makes an error in transmitting an offer or acceptance. Normally, if the party receiving the message ***knew or should have known*** of the error, there is no contract.

3. ***Fraud, Nondisclosure, Duress, Undue Influence***—In some cases, a party acts under a mistaken impression as a result of the other party's fraud or nondisclosure. ***Fraud*** is ***always*** a defense. ***Nondisclosure*** is normally ***not*** a defense, unless the parties were in a relation of trust or confidence or under certain other limited circumstances. A contract is voidable on the basis of ***duress*** if consent was induced by physical force or the threat of physical force, or by other wrongful threats. ***Undue influence*** is unfair persuasion of a party who is under the domination of the person exercising the persuasion, or who by virtue of the relation between them is justified in assuming that that person will not act in a manner inconsistent with his welfare. If a party's manifestation of assent is induced by undue influence by the other party, the contract is voidable by the victim.

4. ***Unconscionability***—A contract may also be unenforceable on the ground of unconscionability. Although a contract may be deemed unconscionable because it is grossly lopsided, most unconscionability problems involve ***unfairness in the bargaining process***, such as the use of a form contract that contains unfairly surprising terms (terms that a reasonable person would not expect, or that are not written clearly). Be especially aware of unconscionability issues in any question that involves a standard form contract, particularly one with a disclaimer of warranties or a clause exculpating a party from liability for negligence.

5. ***Statute of Frauds***—Always ask yourself whether a contract in a question is or is not in writing. If the contract ***is*** in writing, the question may raise a parol evidence rule problem. (*See* §§365-400, *supra*.) If the contract is ***not*** in writing, you must ask yourself whether the contract falls within the Statute of Frauds. In particular:

    (i) Is the contract for the sale of an ***interest in land***?

    (ii) Is the contract for the ***sale of goods*** at a price of ***$500 or more***?

    (iii) Is the contract in ***consideration of marriage***?

    (iv) By its terms, can the contract ***not be performed within one year*** of the making of the contract?

    (v) Is the contract one of ***suretyship***?

    If the contract falls into one of these categories and is not in writing, it is unenforceable unless it is "taken out" of the Statute by an appropriate written memorandum signed by the party against whom suit is brought, by part performance, or by reliance.

6. ***Lack of Capacity***—If a party to an agreement lacks capacity to contract, the resulting agreement may be voidable. Capacity issues may arise in contracts with a minor or contracts with a person suffering under a permanent or temporary mental incapacity.

7. ***Illegality***—A contract may be unenforceable if it is illegal.

A. INDEFINITENESS

1. **General Rule—Certainty of Terms Required:** [§401]   An apparent bargain will not be enforced if (i) the court concludes that the parties had not really completed bargaining, but rather had engaged only in preliminary negotiation, or (ii) even though the parties thought they had a bargain, it is so indefinite that a court cannot determine its material terms with reasonable certainty or fashion an appropriate remedy for breach.

2. **Test:** [§402]   The mere fact that an agreement leaves gaps does not render it fatally indefinite; almost all contracts leave some gaps. For the agreement to be unenforceable on the ground of indefiniteness, either the indefiniteness must be such as to show that the parties did not regard themselves as having completed a bargain, or the court must be unable to fill the gaps through the process of *implication*.

   a. **Example:** An agreement to convey title to a specific parcel of land is not too indefinite; although no mention is made as to *quality* of title. The courts will imply a promise to convey "marketable" title.

   b. **Example:** Similarly, an agreement to paint a house will normally not be rendered indefinite because it sets no time for completion—a "reasonable time" for completion will be implied.

   c. **Compare:** However, an agreement to build "a house," where no plans or specifications are given, would normally be too indefinite to be enforced. "Reasonable" plans cannot be implied. [*See* Stanton v. Dennis, 116 P. 650 (Wash. 1911)] Therefore, the courts normally would not have a sound basis for implying what constitutes a "house" for purposes of a given contract. (Even here, however, the result might be different if there *were* a basis for such an implication; *e.g.*, if the house was to be one of a number of tract houses that are all virtually identical.) [*See* City Stores Co. v. Ammerman, 266 F. Supp. 766, *aff'd*, 394 F.2d 950 (D.C. Cir. 1967)]

3. **Part Performance:** [§403]   As a practical matter, what constitutes sufficient definiteness is very much a question of judgment. One factor that often affects this judgment is whether the contract has been partly performed. Generally speaking, a court might enforce a contract that has been partly performed even though it might have held the same contract too indefinite if the contract had not been partly performed. (*See infra,* §424.)

4. **Examples of Recurring Types of Omissions**

   a. **Price**

      (1) **Omission of price:** [§404]   Under the older cases, a gap as to price was usually fatal, on the theory that courts could not infer what price the parties intended. However, under many modern cases and the U.C.C. (*see infra,* §417), if the contract is *totally silent* as to price a reasonable price can be implied, *provided* the court is satisfied that the parties intended to conclude a contract and there is some objective standard (*e.g.*, fair market value) for determining a reasonable price. [Bendalin v. Delgado, 406 S.W.2d 897 (Tex. 1966)]

(a) **Intent to conclude a contract:** [§405]   Even under the more liberal modern trend, a court will not enforce the bargain unless it determines that the parties intended to conclude a contract. The omission of price may be deemed evidence that the parties were still in preliminary negotiation. [Western Homes, Inc. v. Herbert Ketell, Inc., 236 Cal. App. 2d 142 (1965)]

(2) **Definite standard provided by the contract:** [§406]   Omission of price is not a problem if the contract provides a definite standard by which the price is to be determined (*e.g.*, the seller's posted price or a fixed price adjusted for inflation under a designated index).

(3) **Indefinite standard provided by parties:** [§407]   If the parties do not simply *omit* any reference to price, but instead attempt to define the price through a standard that is itself indefinite, the courts tend to refuse enforcement. *Rationale:* In such cases it cannot be inferred that the parties intended a "reasonable price." [Walker v. Keith, 382 S.W.2d 198 (Ky. 1964)]

(a) **Example:** A proposal to furnish services at cost "plus a fair profit" would probably be unenforceable for indefiniteness, because a court cannot determine either what is an objectively fair profit or what profit the parties would have intended as fair. [Gaines v. R.J. Reynolds Tobacco Co., 174 S.W. 482 (Ky. 1915)]

(b) **Note:** A different result may be reached under the U.C.C. (*See infra,* §417.)

b. **Time for performance**

(1) **General rule—reasonable time implied:** [§408]   A gap as to time of performance is rarely fatal. Instead, the courts will usually fill the gap by implying that the contract is to be performed within a reasonable time. [Automatic Sprinkler Co. v. Sherman, 294 F. 533 (5th Cir. 1923)]

(a) **Test of reasonableness:** [§409]   What is a reasonable time will depend on the nature of the contract, custom and usage in the community, and prior dealings between the parties.

(2) **Special cases**

(a) **Employment contracts:** [§410]   In an employment contract whose duration is not specified, the usual rule is that the contract is *terminable at will* by either party. [Atchison, Topeka & Santa Fe Railway v. Andrews, 211 F.2d 264 (10th Cir. 1954)]

1) **Rationale—no basis for setting reasonable period:** [§411] Employment involves personal relationships, and it would be objectionable to force either party to continue in such a relationship against his will, unless the parties have so provided.

2) **Stated pay period not controlling:** [§412]   A statement of pay period does not change the usual rule; *i.e.,* the fact that the employee's salary or other compensation is payable weekly, monthly, or annually does not mean that the employment is to last that long. Instead, such a statement is deemed only to set the employee's rate of pay while the employment continues.

   a) **Note:** Some courts interpret a stated pay period as the *minimum* length of employment. These courts take the position that if, *e.g.,* the parties stipulated an annual salary, they must have intended the employment to last at least a year. [11 A.L.R. 469]

3) **Agreement for "permanent" employment:** [§413]   Even agreements for a "permanent" job or employment "for life" or "for so long as the employee chooses" are usually interpreted to be terminable at the will of either party. [35 A.L.R. 1432; Ruinello v. Murray, 36 Cal. 2d 687 (1951)]

   a) **Note:** There are cases in which an agreement for "permanent" employment (or any other indefinite period) will be interpreted literally. These are usually cases in which either (i) the agreement *specifically limits* the employer's power to fire the employee (*e.g.,* "permanent employment except in case of improper performance by employee"), or (ii) the circumstances clearly indicate that the parties really did have permanent employment in mind (*e.g.,* the employee takes a very low salary in early years, with promise of a significant share of the profits in later years if the business is successful, or the employee releases a claim against the employer in exchange for the promise of permanent employment). [Drzewiecki v. H & R Block, Inc., 24 Cal. App. 3d 695 (1972)]

(b) **Distributorship and franchise contracts:** [§414]   Where the duration of a distributorship or franchise contract is left open (*e.g.,* Manufacturer A appoints B its exclusive sales representative, but no period of time is specified or indicated) the law implies that the contract will last a "reasonable" time, which is often interpreted to be the time it will take the distributor to recover his investment. [Allied Equipment Co. v. Weber Engineered Products, 237 F.2d 879 (4th Cir. 1956)]

5. **U.C.C. Provisions:** [§415]   The U.C.C. adopts very liberal rules on indefiniteness in contracts for the sale of goods, and also includes a number of "gap filler" provisions. To begin with, U.C.C. section 2-204 provides that "even though one or more terms are left open, a contract for the sale of goods does not fail for indefiniteness if the parties have intended to make a contract and there is a reasonably certain basis for giving an appropriate remedy."

   a. **Gap fillers:** [§416]   Other sections of the U.C.C. fill gaps by providing designated terms that govern if there is a certain type of gap, or by providing how a certain kind of gap should be filled. Thus under the U.C.C. the following rules apply:

(1) **Price:** [§417]   Under U.C.C. section 2-305(1), if the parties "so intend" they can conclude a contract for sale even though the price is not settled. In such a case, the price is a reasonable price at the time for delivery if: (i) nothing has been said as to price, (ii) the price is left to be agreed upon by the parties and they fail to agree, or (iii) the price is to be fixed in terms of some standard set by a third person or agency (such as a market), and it is not so set.

   (a) **Note:** Under U.C.C. section 2-305(1), where the parties intend not to be bound *unless* the price is fixed or agreed upon, and the price is not fixed or agreed upon, then there is no contract. In such cases, the buyer must return any goods already received or, if unable to do so, must pay the reasonable value of the goods at the time of delivery, and the seller must return any portion of the price paid on account.

(2) **Place of delivery:** [§418]   Under U.C.C. section 2-308, if the place of delivery for goods is not specified, the place of delivery is the seller's place of business. (However, in the case of identified goods that the parties know are in some other place, that other place is the place of delivery.)

(3) **Time for shipment or delivery:** [§419]   Under U.C.C. section 2-309, if the time for shipment or delivery is not specified, delivery is due in a reasonable time.

(4) **Time for payment:** [§420]   Under U.C.C. section 2-310, if the time for payment is not specified, payment is due at the time and place at which the buyer is to receive the goods.

(5) **Duration of contract:** [§421]   Under U.C.C. section 2-309, if a contract provides for successive performances, but is indefinite in duration, the contract is valid for a reasonable time but either party may terminate the contract at any time unless otherwise agreed.

(6) **Effect of gap-filler provisions:** [§422]   In summary, under the U.C.C., in theory a bargain may be enforceable even though it omits the price, the place of delivery, the time for shipment or delivery, the time for payment, and the duration of the contract. Remember, however, that the U.C.C. gap filler provisions are applicable only "if the parties have intended to make a contract and there is a reasonably certain basis for giving an appropriate remedy" (*supra,* §415). Where too many terms are missing, the court may conclude that the parties did *not* intend to make a contract, but rather they were only engaged in preliminary negotiations.

6. **Modern Trend Toward Liberalization:** [§423]   Modern authorities are beginning to apply the U.C.C. approach to contracts generally (rather than only to contracts for the sale of goods). Under this trend, courts that believe the parties intended to make a contract are generally more willing to imply reasonable terms to fill the gaps than they

were in the past. The trend is reflected in Restatement Second, which provides: "As a standard of reasonable certainty, it is enough if the terms provide a basis for determining the existence of a breach and for giving an appropriate remedy." [Rest. 2d §33]

7. **Indefiniteness Cured by Part Performance:** [§424]   An agreement that would otherwise be refused enforcement as too indefinite may be enforced if the parties have begun performance. [Bettancourt v. Gilroy Theatre Co., 120 Cal. App. 2d 364 (1953)]

    a. **Rationales:** Enforcement of indefinite agreements on the basis of part performance is generally grounded on one or more of the following theories:

        (1) Part performance pursuant to the agreement shows that the parties believed they had completed a bargain, and were not still in preliminary negotiations;

        (2) The greater the extent to which performance has already occurred, the more unjust it is to let one of the parties off the hook, and therefore the more ready the court will be to imply missing terms; and

        (3) Performance may fill a gap left in the contract by showing what the parties believed the relevant term was.

    b. **Example:** An agreement between S and B that S will sell B 500 bushels of beans per month at $2 a bushel for 12 months may be fatally defective where S has many types of beans for sale, because there is no indication of grade, type, and quality. But if S subsequently sends, and B accepts, several deliveries of No. 4 red pinto beans, this part performance identifies the subject matter of the contract and therefore supplies the requisite degree of certainty. [*See* Brown-Crummer Investment Co. v. Arkansas City, 266 P. 60 (Kan. 1928)]

8. **Bargains Capable of Being Made Certain:** [§425]   In some cases, the parties do not fix a material term in the contract, but do set a method for fixing the term. Such a bargain is enforceable if it makes reference to an objective standard that is to be used to fix the missing term.

    a. **Standards for determining price:** [§426]   For example, bargains in which A agrees to sell to B at a price "as then quoted on the grain exchange," or "the same as that in the Ajax Co. contract" are enforceable. [Kladivo v. Melberg, 227 N.W. 833 (Iowa 1930)]

    b. **Output and requirements contracts:** [§427]   A bargain in which A agrees to supply B with "all your requirements of coal" or to sell B "the entire output of my plant" is sufficiently certain. Both "requirements" and "output" may be objectively determined. [Twin City Pipe Line Co. v. Harding Glass Co., 283 U.S. 353 (1931)]

        (1) **Caveat:** *See supra*, §73, concerning the interpretation of such contract.

    c. **Custom or usage:** [§428]   Terms may also be rendered certain by reference to local custom or usage. For example, an offer to execute a conveyance "in the usual form" is sufficiently certain. In such a case, the standard is the type of conveyance that is usual in the community. [Bondy v. Harvey, 62 F.2d 521 (2d Cir. 1933)]

9. **"Agreements to Agree":** [§429]   Frequently, parties make an agreement in which they explicitly reserve some essential term to be determined in the future, not by reference to an objective standard, but by their future agreement. Such an agreement is known as "an agreement to agree." If the term involved is material, the traditional rule is that the agreement is unenforceable; *i.e.*, the traditional rule is that such an agreement gives rise to no legal obligation unless and until the parties actually reach agreement on the relevant term. [Ridgway v. Wharton, 6 Clark's H.L. 238 (1857); Autry v. Republic Productions, Inc., 30 Cal. 2d 144 (1947)]

   a. **Rationale—the courts will not make a contract for the parties:** [§430]   The rationale of the traditional rule is that the courts can neither force the parties to agree nor determine what they would agree upon. Furthermore, in such cases it is said that there is no room to imply a "reasonable" term because the parties have not simply left a gap but have provided a specific gap-filling mechanism (their agreement), which has failed.

   b. **Complete omission of term:** [§431]   The result under the traditional rule is that if the parties make no provision at all for a material term, such as price, the courts might infer a reasonable term and uphold the contract (*supra*, §417). However, where the parties provide that the term is "to be agreed upon," under the traditional rule the agreement usually will not be enforced.

   c. **Minor terms reserved:** [§432]   However, where the term "to be agreed upon" is a *minor* one, the contract will generally not be rendered unenforceable. For example, a construction contract for a large office building that is otherwise sufficiently certain as to its terms will not be rendered fatally indefinite because some relatively minor architectural detail is "to be agreed upon." [Rest. 2d §33]

   d. **U.C.C. provision:** [§433]   As in cases where the parties simply leave a gap, the U.C.C. is very liberal as to the effect of an agreement to agree. Under U.C.C. section 2-305, in a contract for the sale of goods an agreement to agree on price does not render a bargain unenforceable, provided the court finds that the parties intended to conclude a contract. In such a case, if the parties fail to reach an agreement as to price, then the price is "a reasonable price at the time of delivery."

   e. **Future trend:** [§434]   The Restatement takes the same position as the U.C.C. regarding enforcement of agreements to agree on price. [*See* Rest. 2d §33] Since modern courts have tended to apply the U.C.C. by analogy to contracts not involving the sale of goods, and since the Restatement is very influential with the courts, the trend among modern courts will probably be to depart from the traditional rule and enforce a contract that leaves a material term to future agreement, provided the parties have manifested an intent to conclude a contract.

10. **Bargains Subject to Power of One Party Concerning Performance:** [§435]   Questions frequently arise as to whether a bargain is sufficiently definite where one party has reserved some power concerning performance.

a. **Unrestricted option**

(1) **Common law:** [§436]   At common law, if either party retains an unlimited power to decide the nature or extent of his performance, his promise is considered "illusory," and thus fails as adequate consideration for a counterpromise. (*See supra*, §44).

   (a) **Example:** A makes an employment agreement with B under which A will pay B "such wages as I wish" [Gulf Colorado & San Francisco Railway v. Winton, 7 Tex. Civ. App. 57 (1894)], or A agrees to buy services from B at a price "solely within our discretion" [Davis v. General Foods Corp., 21 F. Supp. 445 (S.D.N.Y. 1937)]. Under the traditional rule, these contracts would be unenforceable, as illusory.

(2) **U.C.C. position:** [§437]   Under the U.C.C., if it appears that the parties intended to be bound, an agreement for the sale of goods at a price to be fixed by the seller or by the buyer *is enforceable.* [U.C.C. §2-305; *supra,* §63] The U.C.C. provides that the party who is to fix the price does not have unlimited discretion; the price must be fixed in good faith. [U.C.C. §2-305] If the party who is to fix the price refuses to specify a price, or unreasonably fixes a price, the other party can either cancel the contract or set a reasonable price himself.

   (a) **Example:** S sells 10 tons of coal to B for delivery next winter, the price to be fixed by S at time of delivery. Under the U.C.C., the contract is enforceable. S must fix the price in good faith; if S fails to do so, B can cancel the contract or enforce the contract at a reasonable price.

(3) **Future trend:** [§438]   As in the case of agreements to agree, the Restatement takes the same position as the U.C.C. on a power to set a term [Rest. 2d §33], and it is likely that modern courts will begin to hold that an apparently unrestricted power to set price is not illusory because it is limited by the general obligation to perform contracts in good faith.

b. **Alternative promises:** [§439]   A bargain is not too indefinite merely because it reserves to a party the right to choose which of two or more performances will be rendered, provided that *each* performance would constitute consideration when taken alone (*supra,* §§54-56).

(1) **Promisee's option:** [§440]   Thus, a bargain in which A agrees to sell to B "my horse or my cow, whichever you choose, for $100" is enforceable.

(2) **Promisor's option:** [§441]   So is a bargain in which A agrees to sell "my horse or my cow, whichever I choose, for $100." If the seller refuses to deliver either, the buyer is entitled to damages based on the less valuable animal. [Rest. 2d §34] However, if the promisor has an option to take an action that would *not* constitute consideration, the contract is unenforceable. Thus where A agrees that if B pays her $100, A will either sell B her horse or serve on a jury the next time she is called, the contract is unenforceable. Since service on a jury is simply performance of a legal obligation, it does

not constitute consideration under the legal duty rule, and a bargain that reserves in the promisor the right to perform alternatives is not enforceable unless *each* of the alternatives constitutes consideration.

    c. **Promise dependent on ability to perform:** [§442]   A bargain in which A agrees to pay B "as soon as I am *able*" is enforceable because A's financial ability to pay is capable of objective determination. [Van Buskirk v. Kuhns, 164 Cal. 472 (1913)]

11. **Bargains Where Written Contract Contemplated:** [§443]   A special problem that is related to indefiniteness occurs where parties enter into a bargain on the understanding that a formal written contract will be executed, and that does not occur. The question then arises, what was the parties' intent in providing for the written instrument?

    a. **Writing as evidentiary memorial:** [§444]   If it appears that the parties intended the writing only as an *evidentiary memorial* of the terms of their agreement, and that the bargain, although not yet formally memorialized, is complete, then the bargain is enforceable, assuming that there is no Statute of Frauds problem (*see infra*, §§498 *et seq*.). [Saunders v. Pottlitzer Bros. Fruit Co., 144 N.Y. 209 (1894); Goad v. Rogers, 103 Cal. App. 2d 294 (1951)]

    b. **Writing as consummation of agreement:** [§445]   If, however, it appears that the parties intended not to be bound unless and until a writing was executed (*i.e.*, if it appears that the writing was intended to be the *consummation* of the negotiations) then the bargain is *not* enforceable. [Stanton v. Dennis, *supra*, §402; Rest. 2d §27; 165 A.L.R. 752]

    c. **Determining intent:** [§446]   In determining whether the parties intended the written contract to be a memorial of their agreement or a consummation of their negotiations, important factors to consider are: (i) whether the contract is of a type usually put in writing; (ii) whether there are few or many details; (iii) whether the amount involved is large or small; and (iv) whether a formal writing is necessary for full expression. [Mississippi & Dominion Steamship Co. v. Swift, 29 A. 1063 (Me. 1894); Rest. 2d §27]

      (1) **Note:** Sometimes there are special circumstances indicating that the primary intention was simply to memorialize the bargain—*e.g.*, where the negotiations consisted of a series of letters, and the purpose of the proposed writing appeared to be simply to collect all the terms together in one instrument.

B. MISTAKE [§447]

Mistake in contract law falls into five categories, known as "mutual mistake," "unilateral mistake," "mistake in transcription," "misunderstanding," and "mistake in transmission."

1. **Mutual Mistake:** [§448]   In ordinary language, the term "mutual mistake" means a shared mistake made by both of the parties to a contract. As used in contract law, however, the term normally refers to a special kind of mutual mistake, namely, a mistaken assumption shared by both parties as to the conditions of the outside world.

a. **Older test:** [§449]   At one time, courts held that the test for whether mutual mistake constituted a defense was whether the mistake concerned the "substance" or "identity" of the contract's subject matter (in which case the contract would be voidable), or only its "accidents" or "collateral attributes" (in which case the contract would *not* be voidable). [*See, e.g.,* Sherwood v. Walker, 33 N.W. 919 (Mich. 1887)] Such distinctions were neither very illuminating nor easily workable, and few if any courts would now use this test.

b. **Modern rule:** [§450]   The modern rule is that where parties enter into a contract under a mutual mistake concerning a *basic assumption of fact* on which the contract was made, the contract is voidable by the adversely affected party if the mistake has a material effect on the agreed exchange and the adversely affected party did not bear the risk that the assumption was mistaken. [Griffith v. Brymer, 19 T.L.R. 434 (1903); Rest. 2d §152]

(1) **Example:** On May 5, A contracts to sell her famous race horse, Apex, to B. Unbeknownst to either party, Apex had died on the night of May 4. The contract is voidable by B, because both parties were mistaken as to a basic assumption on which the contract was made (*i.e.,* that Apex was alive), the mistake is material, and the mistaken assumption was not one as to which B, the adversely affected party, bore the risk of mistake.

(2) **Example:** A leases Blackacre to B for one day for the purpose of conducting a rock concert on the property. Unbeknownst to either party, a municipal ordinance had just been enacted that effectively prevents such use of Blackacre. The lease is voidable by B, because both parties were mistaken as to a basic assumption on which the contract was made (*i.e.,* that concerts could be held on Blackacre), the mistake is material, and the assumption was not one as to which B, the adversely affected party, bore the risk of mistake.

c. **Where a party assumes risk of mistake:** [§451]   Under the modern rule, mutual mistake is not a defense where the adversely affected party *bore the risk* that the assumption in question might be mistaken. [Rest. 2d §154] A common instance of this type of case occurs where the parties knew that the relevant assumption was *doubtful*. According to Restatement First, "where the parties know that there is doubt in regard to a certain matter and contract on that assumption, the contract is not rendered voidable because one is disappointed in the hope that the facts accord with the wishes. The risk of the doubtful fact is then assumed as one of the elements of the bargain." [Rest. 1st §502, comment]

(1) **Example:** B agrees to buy from S a tract of land situated in a remote desert area. S states that she believes she has good title to the land, but she makes no representation that she has good title, and the contract provides only that S will convey such title as she has. B also believes that S has good title to the land, but B makes no title search, as S knows. It turns out that S does not have good title. B does not have a defense of mutual mistake, because he knew that there was an element of doubt as to the assumption that S owned the land. [Rest. 2d §154, Ill. 1]

d. **Mistake in judgment no defense:** [§452]   Similarly, a contract is not voidable on the ground of mutual mistake if the mistake concerns *prediction* or *judgment*, for example, if both parties erroneously think the market price of potatoes will go down, or that a horse one is buying from the other is not fast enough to race.

2. **Unilateral Mistake:** [§453]   A second type of mistake in contract law is *unilateral mistake*. In ordinary language, the term "unilateral mistake" means a mistake made by one, rather than both, of the parties to a contract. As used in contract law, however, the term normally refers to a special kind of unilateral mistake, namely, a *mechanical* error of computation, perception, or the like. For example, where one party submits a bid to the other based on an error in addition, so that the bid is unintentionally low, there has been a mechanical error in computation. Similarly, if A says, "I will buy that box for $6," and B accepts thinking A has offered $60, there has been a mechanical error in perception. Most unilateral mistake cases concern errors in computation.

a. **Nonmistaken party aware of error:** [§454]   If the nonmistaken party either *knew or should have known* of the other party's mechanical mistake, the mistake is said to be a *"palpable"* unilateral mistake. A palpable unilateral mistake makes the contract *voidable* by the mistaken party. "One cannot snap up an offer knowing that it was made in mistake." [Tyra v. Cheney, 152 N.W. 835 (Minn. 1915); Peerless Glass Co. v. Pacific Crockery & Tinware Co., 121 Cal. 641 (1898)]

   (1) **Actual knowledge not necessary:** [§455]   It is sufficient that the nonmistaken party *should have known* of the mistake, as where one bid is substantially and inexplicably lower than all others.

      (a) **Example:** A bids $700,000 on a construction project. The next lowest bid is $1,700. This substantial difference in price is sufficient to charge the nonmistaken party with knowledge that A's bid reflected an error in computation. Therefore, the contract is voidable by A. [*See* Kemper Construction Co. v. Los Angeles, 37 Cal. 3d 696 (1951)]

   (2) **Analysis:** [§456]   The rule that a palpable unilateral mistake of computation, or the like, prevents contract formation is often said to be an exception to the objective theory of contracts, because the mistake is subjective. However, the purpose of the objective theory is to protect the promisee's reasonable expectations. If the promisee knew or should have known that the promisor made a unilateral mistake of computation or the like, she does not have a reasonable expectation that a contract was formed.

   (3) **Errors in judgment:** [§457]   The rule concerning palpable unilateral mistake applies only to mechanical errors, such as errors in computation or the like. It does not apply to *errors in judgment* as to the value or quality of the work done or goods contracted for.

      (a) **Example:** A offers to sell her car to B for $500, and B accepts. B knows that A's car has a market value of $1,500 and that this fact is unknown to A. The contract is enforceable.

   Nonmistaken party unaware of error: [§458]   If the nonmistaken party neither knew nor had reason to know of the other party's unilateral mistake, the majority rule is that there is a binding contract.

(1) **Damages:** Under this rule, if the mistaken party discovers the mistake and refuses to perform, the nonmistaken party is entitled to expectation damages (*see infra,* §841). [Crenshaw County Hospital Board v. St. Paul Fire & Marine Insurance Co., 411 F.2d 213 (5th Cir. 1969)]

(2) **Modern trend:** [§459]   However, a number of modern cases hold that if the mistaken party notifies the other party of a unilateral mistake before the nonmistaken party has changed her position in reliance, the mistaken party can rescind the contract. [St. Nicholas Church v. Kropp, 160 N.W. 500 (Minn. 1916)] Furthermore, some of the modern cases hold that even if the nonmistaken party *has* changed her position, her recovery will be limited to damages required to compensate her for her reliance. While these cases are in the minority, they appear to represent the trend of decision.

3. **Mistranscription:** [§460]   The third type of mistake, *mistranscription*, occurs where the parties make an oral agreement which they reduce to a signed writing, but through some clerical mistake the writing does not correctly embody the oral agreement. In such cases, the aggrieved party is entitled to the equitable remedy of *reformation*. Under this remedy, the writing is reformed by the court so that it corresponds to the oral agreement. However, to obtain reformation the aggrieved party must prove his case not merely by the usual "preponderance of the evidence" but by "clear and convincing" evidence. [Goode v. Riley, 28 N.E. 228 (Mass. 1891); *see also* Remedies Summary]

4. **Misunderstanding:** [§461]   The fourth kind of mistake, *misunderstanding*, arises where an expression (consisting of words or conduct) is susceptible of two different but equally reasonable interpretations, and each party's subjective intention concerning the expression differs from that of the other party. In such a case, no contract is formed. (*See supra,* §355.) Note that this rule is inapplicable where one party's interpretation is *more reasonable* than the other's. In such cases, the fact that the two parties subjectively intend two different meanings does not prevent contract formation. Instead, a contract is formed, and its meaning is the meaning intended by the party whose interpretation is more reasonable.

5. **Mistakes in Transmission by Intermediary:** [§462]   The fifth kind of mistake concerns cases in which an offeror uses an intermediary—such as the telegraph company or an interpreter—to transmit a communication, and the intermediary makes a mistake in transmitting the communication. Normally this type of mistake involves a mistransmitted offer.

   a. **Offeree aware of mistake:** [§463]   As in the case of a unilateral mistake, if the offeree knew or should have known of the mistake—for example, because of the magnitude of the discrepancy between an offered price and the market price—he cannot "snap up" what he knows to be an erroneous price. Accordingly, if he attempts to accept, a contract will not be formed. [Germain Fruit Co. v. Western Union, 137 Cal. 598 (1902)]

   b. **Offeree unaware of mistake:** [§464]   Where the offeree neither knows nor should know of the mistake, there is a split of authority:

(1) **Majority view:** [§465]   The majority view is that a contract is formed on the terms conveyed to the offeree by the intermediary. Some courts rationalize this result on the theory that the intermediary acts as the agent of the offeror, and the offeror is liable for the acts of the agent. [Des Arc Oil Mill v. Western Union Telegraph Co., 201 S.W. 273 (Ark. 1918)] The problem with this rationale is that the intermediary is usually an independent contractor, not an agent. Other courts adopt the rationale that the offeror chose the intermediary who caused the error; where one of two innocent parties must suffer, the one who caused the loss should bear the burden thereof; and that by choosing the intermediary, the offeror caused the loss. [Ayer v. Western Union, 10 A. 495 (Me. 1887)] This rationale, however, breaks down where the offeree was the first to use the particular intermediary (*e.g.*, by telegraphing an inquiry to the offeror). Besides, using a particular intermediary is often a reasonable thing to do.

(2) **Minority view:** [§466]   Under the minority view, no contract results where there is an error in transmission, on the ground that the parties have neither objectively nor subjectively reached an agreement. [Strong v. Western Union, 109 P. 910 (Idaho 1910)]

(3) **Intermediary's liability:** [§467]   Under either view, the intermediary may be liable for negligence (and perhaps also for breach of its contract of transmission) for any loss suffered by either party. Thus, the primary effect of either the majority or minority view may simply be to determine which party must sue the intermediary. However, a remedy against an intermediary is not always satisfactory. Intermediaries, such as telegraph companies, usually limit their liability for error as part of the transmission contract, and such limitations on liability have generally been upheld. [54 A.L.R. 1363]

c. **Practical significance:** [§468]   The practical significance of mistakes in transmission by an intermediary has probably been much reduced by changes in modes of communication. Most of the intermediary cases involve telegrams that are incorrectly typed by the telegraph company. With the advent of overnight mail, fax, and E-mail, the use of telegraph companies or other intermediaries who must type out a message seems to have drastically declined. Most mistakes in transmission today are therefore likely to involve either clerical errors by the offeror or a failure of the offeror's or offeree's equipment. The rules concerning such errors have not yet emerged, but it is likely that each party will be responsible for its own clerical errors and for errors caused by its own equipment.

C. CONTRACTS INDUCED BY FRAUD, NONDISCLOSURE, DURESS, OR UNDUE INFLUENCE

1. **Fraud:** [§469]   If either party has defrauded the other into executing the contract there is no real consent, and the contract is therefore voidable by the innocent party. [Rest. 1st §477] (As to what constitutes "fraud," *see* Torts Summary.)

a. **Misrepresentation:** A material misrepresentation by one party also makes the contract voidable by the innocent party. A misrepresentation is material if it would be likely to induce a reasonable person to assent, or if the person who makes the misrepresentation knows that it would be likely to induce the other party to assent.

2. **Nondisclosure:** [§470]   The general rule is that a party who proposes a contract does not have an obligation to affirmatively disclose facts concerning the subject matter of the contract. However, disclosure of material facts is required if the prospective parties are in a fiduciary relationship or a relationship of trust or confidence. Disclosure may also be required, even in the absence of such a relationship, where a material fact is known to one party by virtue of his special position and could not be readily determined by the other party in the exercise of normal diligence. For example, if a seller of a house, by virtue of his special position as owner of the house, knows of a nonapparent termite infestation, the seller may be obliged to disclose the infestation to a prospective buyer, especially if the parties reside in an area in which buyers normally do not commission termite inspections before purchasing homes.

3. **Duress:** [§471]   A contract is voidable on the ground of duress where consent was induced by physical force or threats of force, or by other *wrongful* threats. [Rest. 1st §§492-495]

   a. **Economic duress:** [§472]   A threat to withhold something another party badly needs or wants is not in itself duress, because it is not wrongful to refuse to contract or to agree to contract only on very favorable terms. But economic duress is a valid defense to the enforcement of a contract where:

   (i) One party commits or *threatens to commit a wrongful act*, including a breach of contract, that would place the other in a position that would seriously threaten his property or finances, unless the other party enters into a contract; and

   (ii) *No adequate means are available to avoid or prevent the threatened loss*, other than entering into the contract.

   (1) **Example:** B engages A as tax counsel to resist a large tax deficiency assessed against him by the Internal Revenue Department. A waits until just before the deadline for filing a reply with the Department, and then forces B to sign a very high contingency fee agreement by threatening that unless B agrees to the fee, A will not file the necessary papers, and B would thus be liable for the full assessment. At this point, it is too late for B to find another lawyer who would make a timely filing. The agreement is unenforceable on the ground of economic duress. [Thompson Crane & Trucking v. Eyman Co., 123 Cal. App. 2d 904 (1954)]

4. **Undue Influence:** [§473]   Undue influence is unfair persuasion of a party, A, who is under the domination of the person exercising the persuasion, B, or who by virtue of the relation between them is justified in assuming that B will not act in a manner inconsistent with A's welfare. If a party's assent is induced by the other party's undue influence, the contract is voidable by the victim.

   a. **Example:** Attorney convinces Client, a senile person, to sell to Attorney certain of Client's personal property at an unfair price. An undue influence defense will likely succeed here, since by virtue of the attorney-client relationship, Client was justified in assuming that Attorney would act in Client's best interests.

D. UNCONSCIONABILITY [§474]

The principle of unconscionability is a relatively new and very important doctrine whose impact is growing, but whose precise scope is still uncertain.

1. **Development of Doctrine—U.C.C.:** [§475] Although traces of a doctrine of unconscionability can be found at early common law, the doctrine in its modern form was introduced into contract law by U.C.C. section 2-302.

   a. **U.C.C. section 2-302:** [§476] U.C.C. section 2-302 provides that "if a court as a matter of law finds a contract or any clause of the contract to have been unconscionable at the time it was made, the court may refuse to enforce the contract, or it may enforce the remainder of the contract without the unconscionable clause, or it may so limit the application of any unconscionable clause as to avoid any unconscionable result." (Note that under section 2-302 it is normally up to the trial judge, rather than the jury, to decide whether a contract or provision is unconscionable.)

   b. **Extension:** [§477] Strictly speaking, U.C.C. section 2-302 is applicable only to contracts for the sale of goods. However, since the original promulgation of the U.C.C., courts have generally held that the principle of unconscionability is applicable to all contracts, and the principle is now also embodied in Restatement Second section 208.

2. **Meaning and Scope of Doctrine:** [§478] Despite the general acceptance of the principle of unconscionability, its meaning and scope are still uncertain. Many commentators draw a distinction between "procedural" unconscionability (*i.e.,* an unconscionable *bargaining process)* and "substantive" unconscionability (*i.e.,* contract *terms* that are unconscionable without regard to the process by which those terms were reached, because they are lopsided). [113 U. Pa. L. Rev. 435 (1965)]

   a. **Comment:** This distinction is very helpful, because most cases in which the doctrine of unconscionability is applied to invalidate a contractual clause involve *procedural* unconscionability.

3. **Unfair Surprise:** [§479] Many (and perhaps most) cases of unconscionability involve *"unfair surprise."* Unfair surprise occurs where the party who drafts the contract includes a term in the contract, having reason to know that the term does not accord with the other party's fair expectations. This is an example of procedural unconscionability, since inclusion of such a term without calling it to the other party's attention involves an unfair bargaining process. [U.C.C. §2-302, Comment]

   a. **Adhesion contracts:** [§480] Unfair surprise is particularly likely in printed form adhesion contracts—*i.e.,* contracts in which the parties occupy substantially unequal bargaining positions, and the party in the inferior bargaining position is forced to "adhere" to the terms in the other's printed form on a "take it or leave it" basis, rather than having terms dickered out. [Wheeler v. St. Joseph Hospital,

63 Cal. App. 3d 345 (1977); 16 Kans. L. Rev. 303 (1968)] Typical examples of form adhesion contracts include life insurance policies, loan agreements, and residential leases. Unfair surprise may result because a given term in the form is contrary to reasonable expectations as to what provisions a contract of the general *type* would involve, and the term is not pointed out and explained; because the term is written in obscure language; or both.

b. **Party's lack of knowledge of provisions in contract**

(1) **Traditional view:** [§481]   The traditional rule was that each party to a contract was charged with knowledge of its provisions; *i.e.*, each was bound by what he signed, whether or not he read, understood, or even knew of the provisions in question. Under this rule, there was no doctrine of unfair surprise.

(2) **Modern rule:** [§482]   Modern cases, however, tend to hold that, at least when a form adhesion contract is involved, a contracting party is bound only by those provisions that are not unfairly surprising. [California State Auto Association v. Barrett Garages, Inc., 257 Cal. App. 2d 71 (1967)]

    (a) **Example:** A, the owner of a department store, requests B Insurance Company to issue a liability insurance policy covering A's premises. B agrees to do so. The policy, as issued, includes a provision that excludes liability arising out of the use of elevators, although B knows that A's store has elevators. A reasonable person in A's position would expect a premises-liability policy to include liability for all accidents on the premises, including elevator accidents. B does not call A's attention to the exclusion. The exclusion is unconscionable as unfairly surprising and will not be enforced. [Portella v. Sonnenberg, 74 N.J. Super. 354 (1962)]

    (b) **Example:** A Insurance Company insures B's residential property, including homeowner's liability. A provision of the policy excludes liability to domestic employees, but the wording of the provision is so obscure that its effect would not be understood by a reasonable person in B's position and is not understood by B. The exclusion is unconscionable as unfairly surprising and will not be enforced.

(3) **Comment—protection of weaker party:** The harsher or more one-sided the provision in question, the more scrupulous the courts usually are in requiring that the weaker party had actual knowledge of the provisions.

4. **Substantive Unconscionability:** [§483]   The extent to which the courts will apply a doctrine of substantive unconscionability—unconscionability based on lopsided terms, without regard to defects in the bargaining process—is still unresolved.

a. **U.C.C.:** [§484]   The Comment to U.C.C. section 2-302 states that "[t]he principle [of unconscionability] is one of prevention of oppression and unfair surprise . . . and not of disturbance of allocation of risks because of superior bargaining power."

b. **Restatement Second:** [§485]   The Comment to Restatement Second section 208 takes the position that it *is* possible for a contract to be oppressive taken as a whole, despite the fact that there is no weakness in the bargaining process, but adds that unconscionability ordinarily involves other factors as well as overall imbalance. [Rest. 2d §208, Comment]

c. **Cases:** [§486]   Although most unconscionability cases have involved an unfair bargaining *process*, a few cases have invalidated the price term of a contract on the basis that the price charged was unconscionable—*i.e.*, that the buyers were being charged far more for goods than the goods were actually worth. [American Home Improvement, Inc. v. MacIver, 201 A.2d 886 (N.H. 1964)]

   (1) **Example:** A contract for encyclopedias sold door-to-door (with sales largely directed toward consumers of limited education and economic means) was held unconscionable where it was shown that the price charged was roughly two and one-half times the reasonable market price of the books. [Kugler v. Romain, 279 A.2d 640 (N.J. 1971)]

5. **Examples of Unconscionability:** [§487]   The following are examples of provisions that have been attacked as unconscionable in various settings:

a. **Exculpatory clauses:** [§488]   An exculpatory clause is a clause releasing a party from liability for injury caused by his actions. Such clauses often raise problems of unconscionability.

   (1) **Intentional wrongs:** [§489]   An exculpatory clause relieving a party from liability for his own intentional wrongs is usually held violative of public policy and hence illegal. [Cal. Civ. Code §1688]

   (2) **Negligence:** [§490]   Provisions relieving a party from liability for his own negligence raise greater difficulty.

      (a) **Injuries to the person:** [§491]   In general, the courts tend to strike down exculpatory clauses excusing a party from liability for personal injuries resulting from his negligence, at least if the parties did not have equal bargaining positions or if the public interest is involved.

         1) **Examples:** Thus, a provision in a hospital admission form waiving any claims by the patient for medical malpractice against the hospital or attending doctors was held void as against public policy. [Tunkl v. Regents of University of California, 60 Cal. 2d 92 (1963)] Similarly, clauses in employment agreements exculpating the employer for negligently causing injury to the employee in the course of employment have usually been held unenforceable as against public policy. [Rest. 1st §575]

         2) **Exceptions:** However, such clauses are sometimes upheld where the court finds that the injured party did have a choice during the bargaining process. [Garretson v. United States, 456 F.2d 1017 (9th Cir. 1972)—experienced ski-jumper signed entry blank for a

ski-jumping tournament that contained a clear and prominent clause releasing sponsors of the tournament from liability for injuries the ski-jumper might sustain]

(b) **Injuries to property:** [§492] Provisions that relieve a party from liability for lost profits or injury to property caused by the party's negligence are frequently upheld, provided the injured party had some choice and no unfair surprise was involved (*see infra*, §§495-497). [Mayfair Fabrics v. Henley, 222 A.2d 602 (N.J. 1967); Sweeney Gasoline & Oil Co. v. Toledo, Peoria & Western Railroad, 247 N.E.2d 603 (Ill. 1969)] For example, the courts have tended to uphold exculpatory clauses in contracts between advertisers and the telephone company for ads in the Yellow Pages, where the clause limits the advertisers' damages for the telephone company's errors and omissions to an amount equal to the cost of the advertisement. [Gas House, Inc. v. Southern Bell Telephone Co., 221 S.E.2d 499 (N.C. 1976); Willie v. Southwestern Bell Telephone & Telegraph Co., 549 P.2d 903 (Kan. 1976), *but see* Allen v. Michigan Bell Telephone Co., 171 N.W.2d 689 (Mich. 1969)]

b. **Disclaimers and limitations of warranty liability:** [§493] Certain warranties are implied in contracts for the sale of goods (*e.g.*, a warranty of title; a warranty of merchantability—which generally warrants that goods sold by merchants are fit for their ordinary purposes; and a warranty of fitness for particular purpose—which warrants that goods will be fit for a particular purpose if the seller knows the particular purposes for which the goods are to be used). A seller may try to limit warranty liability in two different ways, and such limitations are not necessarily unconscionable.

(1) **Disclaimers:** [§494] First, the seller may attempt to disclaim (*i.e.*, negate) the warranty altogether. U.C.C. section 2-316 provides that to exclude or modify the implied warranty of merchantability, the *language must mention merchantability* and, in the case of a writing, the disclaimer must be conspicuous. To exclude the implied warranty of fitness, the language *must be in writing and conspicuous.*

(2) **Limitation of remedies:** [§495] U.C.C. section 2-719(1)(a) provides that agreements for the sale of goods may limit the buyer's remedies. Thus, instead of disclaiming a certain warranty, the seller may limit liability for breach of warranty. For example, the agreement may limit the buyer's remedies for breach of warranty to repair and replacement of defective goods. U.C.C. section 2-719(1)(a) is subject to two major exceptions:

(a) **Where exclusive remedy fails of its purpose:** [§496] First, U.C.C. section 2-719(2) provides that "where circumstances cause an exclusive or limited remedy to fail of its essential purpose, remedy may be had as provided in this Act." This provision is most commonly invoked where the contract limits remedy to repair and replacement and the seller neither repairs nor replaces within a reasonable period of time.

(b) **Where there is personal injury:** [§497]   Second, U.C.C. section 2-719(3) provides that consequential damages may be limited or excluded unless the limitation or exclusion is unconscionable, but that "limitation of consequential damages for injury *to the person* [resulting from] consumer goods is prima facie unconscionable." (U.C.C. section 2-719(3) adds that limitation of damages where the loss is *commercial* is not prima facie unconscionable.)

1) **Application:** Although U.C.C. section 2-719(3) provides that a limitation on consequential damages for injury to the person resulting from consumer goods is only "prima facie" unconscionable, in practice such a limitation is almost invariably viewed as unconscionable by the courts. [*See, e.g.,* Collins v. Uniroyal, Inc., 315 A.2d 15 (N.J. 1974)]

E.   STATUTE OF FRAUDS

1. **In General:** [§498]   Absent a statute otherwise, oral contracts are enforceable. However, a type of statute known as a "Statute of Frauds" commonly requires certain types of contracts to be in a writing signed by "the party to be charged," that is, by the party against whom enforcement of the contract is sought. These statutes stem from the English Statute of Frauds of 1677. If an oral contract falls within one of the categories of contracts that must be in writing under the Statute of Frauds, the contract is said to be "within the Statute"—*i.e.,* the Statute of Frauds is a defense to enforcement of the contract *unless some exception* to the Statute applies. If an exception does apply, it is said that the contract is "taken out of the Statute"—*i.e.,* the Statute is then not a defense by virtue of the exception. In short, if a contract is "within the Statute" it is unenforceable against a party who has not signed a written contract, unless some exception (like part performance) takes the contract "out of the Statute," in which case the contract *is* enforceable.

2. **Purpose:** [§499]   The basic purpose of the Statute of Frauds is to prevent fraud and perjury by persons who might falsely claim that a contract was made, when it was not.

3. **Types of Contracts that Must Be in Writing:** [§500]   Following the original English Statute of Frauds, modern American Statutes of Frauds commonly require at least five categories of contracts to be in writing: (i) contracts for the sale of an interest in land; (ii) contracts for the sale of goods (now covered by the U.C.C.); (iii) contracts in consideration of marriage; (iv) contracts not to be performed within one year from the making thereof; and (v) contracts of suretyship.

a. **Contracts for sale of interest in land:** [§501]   Under the Statute of Frauds, a contract for the sale of land or of any interest therein must be in writing.

(1) **Leases:** [§502]   Leases are covered by the sale-of-an-interest-in-land provision of the Statute, unless explicitly excepted. However, many Statutes of Frauds provide that leases for one year or less do not have to be in writing. [*See* Cal. Civ. Proc. Code §1971]

(2) **What constitutes "interest in land"?** [§503]   It is often difficult to determine just what constitutes an "interest in land" within the meaning of the

Statute of Frauds. In general, what constitutes an interest in land under the Statute is determined by whatever test is furnished by the law of property as to what constitutes such an interest.

(a) **Note:** A contract to **share the profits** or **proceeds** from the purchase or sale of land is **not** within the Statute, because it is **not** a contract for **sale** and does not promise to convey an **interest in land**.

(3) **Part performance doctrine:** [§504] Part performance of an oral contract for the sale of an interest in land operates somewhat differently on sellers and purchasers.

(a) **Sellers:** [§505] A seller who has performed her side of an oral contract for the sale of an interest in land, by conveying the interest to the buyer, can recover the purchase price even though the contract is not in writing.

(b) **Purchasers:** [§506] Part performance by the purchaser of an interest in land may take a contract out of the Statute for purposes of **equitable relief**—*i.e.*, a suit for specific performance (which seeks an order from a court to a party to perform under a contract). As applied to contracts for the sale of an interest in land, however, the traditional part-performance exception to the Statute of Frauds does not apply to an action at law—*i.e.*, an action for damages—as against the seller.

1) **Requirements under traditional rule:** Under the traditional rule, the exception to the sale-of-land provision for part performance by a purchaser is applicable only if the purchaser, with the consent of the seller, either: (i) made a valuable improvement on the land, or (ii) took or retained possession **and** paid a part of the purchase price.

2) **Reliance doctrine:** Under modern law, as an aspect of the development of the reliance principle in the Statute of Frauds area (*see infra,* §§546-548), part performance that does not meet the traditional test, but that constitutes reliance, may be sufficient to estop the other party from pleading the Statute of Frauds. On this theory, part performance may be relevant even where the action is at law; *i.e.*, for damages.

b. **Contracts for the sale of goods—U.C.C. section 2-201:** [§507] The modern Statute of Frauds provision applicable to sales of goods is set forth in U.C.C. section 2-201. Under section 2-201, a contract for the sale of any goods for the price of **$500 or more** must be in writing.

(1) **"Goods" defined:** [§508] "Goods" includes all tangible movable property. It does not include intangible securities or services.

(2) **Exceptions:** [§509] However, certain exceptions are recognized in U.C.C. section 2-201. Under these exceptions, an oral contract for the sale of goods priced over $500 **will** be enforced where one of the following occurs:

    (a) **Receipt and acceptance of goods:** [§510]   The buyer receives and accepts all or part of the goods (in which case the contract becomes enforceable as to the goods accepted and received) [U.C.C. §2-201(3)(c)];

    (b) **Part payment:** [§511]   The buyer makes part payment for the goods (in which case the contract is enforceable as to the goods for which payment has been made) [U.C.C. §2-201(3)(c)];

    (c) **Special manufacture:** [§512]   The contract calls for the manufacture of special goods for the buyer not suitable for sale to others in the ordinary course of the seller's business, and the seller makes a "substantial beginning" in the manufacture of the goods or commitments for their procurement [U.C.C. §2-201(3)(a)];

    (d) **No objection to confirmation:** [§513]   The contract is *between merchants*; within a reasonable time a written confirmation, which satisfies the Statute of Frauds as to the sender, is sent; and the party receiving the confirmation does not dispatch a written objection thereto within 10 days [U.C.C. §2-201(2)]; or

    (e) **Admission:** [§514]   The contract is admitted by the party against whom enforcement is sought "in his pleadings or testimony in court" [U.C.C. §2-201(3)(b)—not in effect in California].

(3) **Modifications:** [§515]   A modification of a contract for the sale of goods is within the Statute of Frauds if the new agreement that results from putting together the original contract and the modification is within the Statute.

    (a) **Example:** Seller orally agrees to sell Buyer two used cars for $900. Before the time for delivery, Seller and Buyer orally modify the contract so that Seller will sell only one of the cars, for $450. The modification is not within the Statute of Frauds.

    (b) **Compare:** If the original contract was to sell one car for $450, and the contract was then orally modified to cover two cars for $900, the modification would be within the Statute of Frauds.

(4) **Other U.C.C. provisions:** [§516]   U.C.C. section 2-201, above, is limited solely to contracts for the sale of goods. However, other U.C.C. provisions require a written contract for other types of transactions.

    (a) **Assignments:** [§517]   U.C.C. section 9-203 provides that, with certain exceptions, *assignments* for consideration are unenforceable unless the assignor has signed a written agreement describing the assigned debt.

    (b) **Securities:** [§518]   U.C.C. section 8-319 provides that contracts for the sale of securities must be in writing (or at least evidenced by a written confirmation) to be enforceable, regardless of the amount or value of the security involved. [U.C.C. §8-319]

    (c) **General intangibles:** [§519] U.C.C. section 1-206, a *residual* Statute of Frauds provision, covers transactions for the sale of personal property that are not covered by specific U.C.C. provisions such as sections 2-201, 8-319, and 9-203, *supra—e.g.*, the sale of "general intangibles" such as royalties or copyrights. Under section 1-206, a contract for the sale of such property is not enforceable beyond $5,000 in amount or value of remedy.

   (5) **Sale of goods vs. contract for services:** [§520] Often a contract requires the supplying of goods as well as a rendering of services. For Statute of Frauds purposes, it must then be determined whether the contract is primarily for the sale of goods or primarily for the rendering of a service. A contract does not come within the sale-of-goods provision of the Statute merely because it involves an incidental supply of goods, like a contract to repair a television set in which the repairer also furnishes parts. Conversely, a contract does not fall outside the sale-of-goods provision merely because it requires an incidental furnishing of services, like a contract to sell an air-conditioner in which the seller also does installation. In doubtful cases, the issue is what is the "*predominant factor*" of the contract.

c. **Contracts in consideration of marriage:** [§521] Under the Statute of Frauds, contracts in consideration of marriage must be in writing. This provision of the Statute is interpreted to refer to marriage-settlement contracts and prenuptial contracts that include financial provisions. The provision is *not* interpreted to apply to simple mutual promises between prospective spouses to marry. These contracts are (somewhat arbitrarily) considered to be "contracts to marry" rather than "contracts in consideration of marriage." (Note, however, that in many or most states suit can no longer be brought by one fiance against another for breach of a promise to marry.)

   (1) **Example:** Mother orally promises Friend that if he marries Daughter, she (Mother) will give the couple $10,000 after the wedding. Friend and Daughter marry. The promise is not enforceable under the Statute of Frauds because it was not in writing.

   (2) **Compare:** A and B orally agree to marry. The agreement is not within the Statute of Frauds, because each promise to marry is deemed to be in consideration of the other promise to marry, not in consideration of marriage itself.

   (3) **Compare:** F and M, the father of the groom and the mother of the bride, orally agree that if the marriage takes place they will each give $5,000 to the couple. The agreement is not within the Statute of Frauds, because each promise to give is deemed to be given in consideration of the other's promise to give, not in consideration of marriage.

d. **Contracts that cannot be performed within one year of making:** [§522] Under the "one-year provision" of the Statute of Frauds, contracts that *by their terms cannot be performed within one year* from the making thereof must be in writing. The one-year period begins at the date the contract is *made,* not when performance is promised. [2 Corbin §444]

(1) **Statute not applicable if performance within one year is possible although unlikely:** [§523]   A contract that will probably take more than one year to perform, or even seems to envision performance over more than one year, may nonetheless be *capable* of being fully performed within one year. Such a contract is not within the Statute, and therefore is enforceable even though oral.

    (a) **Examples:** The following oral contracts would not be within the one-year provision (subject to the caveat below) because they are capable, although unlikely, of being performed in one year:

        (i)   A promise to take care of another person until she dies.

        (ii) A promise to pay a pension until death. [Leonard v. Rose, 65 Cal. 2d 589 (1967)]

        (iii) A promise to service and maintain equipment "as long as you need it." [Warner v. Texas Railway, 164 U.S. 418 (1896)]

        (iv) A promise of "lifetime" employment.

        1)   **Caveat:** Some statutes require "lifetime" contracts to be in writing. [*See* N.Y. Gen. Oblig. Law §5-701]

(2) **Exception for part performance:** [§524]   Even if a contract cannot be performed within one year, the great weight of authority holds that once the contract has been *fully performed on one side*, it will be enforceable even though oral.

    (a) **Example:** By an oral agreement, A promises to maintain B's property for two years, and B promises to pay A $5,000 at the end of that time. A fully performs. B's promise to pay $5,000 can be enforced.

    (b) **Rationale:** Even if the contract was not enforceable, the party who performed could sue in restitution for the benefit conferred. (*See infra*, §525.) Allowing suit on the contract itself avoids the difficulty of measuring the value of the benefit conferred.

e. **Suretyship contracts:** [§525]   Under the suretyship provision of the Statute of Frauds, promises made to a creditor of another person—a debtor—to "answer for" (*i.e.*, to be responsible for or guarantee) the debtor's obligation must be in writing, subject to some important exceptions:

(1) **Promises to debtor:** [§526]   If the promise is made to *the debtor* (*e.g.*, "I promise to pay your obligation to your creditor"), the promise does not fall within the suretyship section of the Statute of Frauds. Such a promise is therefore enforceable even though oral, assuming there is consideration. [Rest. 2d §123]

(2) **Primary debt by promisor:** [§527]   The Statute of Frauds applies only to promises that are "collateral" to a third person's obligation, not where the

"primary" contract is between the promisor and the promisee, even though the contract incidentally benefits a third party.

    (a) **Example:** A orally instructs X, a department store, "Send a Z vacuum cleaner to B, and bill it to me." In such case, the primary contract is between A and X. The contract is therefore enforceable even though oral.

(3) **Main purpose rule:** [§528]   A suretyship promise is enforceable, even though oral, if it appears that the promisor's *main purpose* in guaranteeing the obligation of another was to secure an advantage or pecuniary benefit *for himself.* [Rest. 2d §116]

    (a) **Example:** Subcontractor S refuses to furnish further labor and materials in the construction of O's house because the credit of the principal contractor, P, is bad. To get her house completed, O orally guarantees S that she will pay all amounts owed by P to S if P does not pay. O's promise is enforceable. Her main purpose was not to aid S, but to get her own house completed. [Kampman v. Pittsburgh Construction & Engineering Co., 175 A. 396 (Pa. 1934)]

4. **Type of Writing Required:** [§529]   Normally, the Statute of Frauds can be satisfied by any sort of writing signed by the party to be charged. Even a letter will do; a formal contract is not required. However, the writing must constitute a *"memorandum"* of the *essential terms* of the agreement and must be *signed* by the "party to be charged." To put this differently, even if an oral agreement is of a type that is required to be in writing under the Statute of Frauds, and is therefore "within" the Statute, the existence of a sufficient memorandum, signed by the party to be charged, will take the contract "out of" the statute.

a. **Essential terms:** [§530]   To satisfy the Statute, a memorandum normally must include:

    (i) The identity of the *contracting parties*;

    (ii) A description of the *subject matter* of the contract; and

    (iii) The *terms and conditions* of the agreement.

b. **Recital of consideration:** [§531]   Many states provide that a writing will not satisfy the Statute of Frauds unless it states "the consideration." Normally this requirement has little meaning, because a writing that fails to state what each party was to do would probably be insufficient to satisfy the Statute of Frauds in any event. The major application of this requirement is to contracts of suretyship, where the writing often states the surety's promise without stating the consideration for that promise.

c. **U.C.C. provisions:** [§532]   In contracts for the sale of goods, which are governed by the U.C.C., a writing can satisfy the Statute of Frauds even though it is less complete than is usually required. Under the U.C.C., there need only be "some writing sufficient to indicate that a contract for sale has been made" and specifying the *quantity* term. Such a writing will suffice even though it omits or incorrectly states the price, time and place of payment, and quality of the goods, and even if the quantity term is incorrectly stated. However, the contract will not be enforceable beyond the quantity of goods specified in the writing. [U.C.C. §2-201; *and see* Sales Summary]

(1) **Written confirmations:** [§533]   The U.C.C. also provides that if one merchant sends a written confirmation of a contract to another merchant in a form sufficient to bind the sender, the recipient is bound unless he objects within 10 days following receipt—even though the recipient merchant never signed anything. [U.C.C. §2-201(2); *see supra*, §509]

d. **Signature:** [§534]   The signature on the requisite writing need not be handwritten to satisfy the Statute of Frauds; it can be typed or printed. A party's initials may also be a sufficient signature if intended as such.

(1) **Agents' signature:** [§535]   The original Statute of Frauds expressly provided that a memorandum was sufficient if signed by an authorized agent of the party to be charged. It was not required that the agent's authority to sign also be in writing. Thus, if A orally authorized B to buy land on her behalf, and B signed a land purchase contract "A, by her agent B," A was bound.

(a) **Equal dignity statutes:** [§536]   However, some states have "equal dignity" statutes. Under such statutes, if a contract is required by law to be in writing under the Statute of Frauds, a principal is bound to a contract signed by the agent only if the agent's authority is also in writing. [*See, e.g.*, Cal. Civ. Code §2309]

(2) **Party to be charged must sign:** [§537]   Only the party sought to be held liable must have signed a writing. The fact that the party seeking to enforce the contract has not signed a writing is immaterial.

(a) **Example:** Vendor and Purchaser make an oral agreement for the sale of land. Purchaser signs a memorandum that satisfies the Statute of Frauds, but Vendor does not. Vendor can enforce the contract, even though Purchaser cannot.

(3) **Location of signature:** [§538]   Normally, the signature (however made) can appear anywhere on the relevant instrument. However, a few statutes say that the writing must be "subscribed." Some courts applying such statutes have required a signature at the bottom of the writing.

e. **Integration of several documents:** [§539]   The requisite writing or memorandum may be composed of several documents, provided each document refers to or incorporates the others or the documents are otherwise integrated (*e.g.*, by being physically attached).

f. **Auction sales:** [§540]   Sales at auction are usually oral. However, the auctioneer's written memorandum of the terms of a sale is held to be a sufficient writing against both the buyer and the seller, on the theory that in making the memorandum the auctioneer is the agent of both the buyer and the seller. [Rest. 2d §135]

5. **Effect of Noncompliance with the Statute of Frauds**

   a. **Majority view—contract unenforceable but not void:** [§541]   In most states, failure to comply with the Statute of Frauds renders a contract *voidable—i.e.*, unenforceable against a party who has not signed the requisite writing—but not void. [U.C.C. §2-201; Rest. 2d §138; Walter H. Leimert Co. v. Woodson, 125 Cal. App. 2d 186 (1954)]

      (1) **Effect:** [§542]   Under this view, although a suit cannot be brought on an oral contract that is within the Statute, the contract is valid for all other purposes. For example, if the oral contract is confirmed in a later memorandum, the contract becomes enforceable against the party who signed the memorandum even though no new consideration is given (*supra*, §113). Similarly, once a contract that falls within the Statute of Frauds has been performed on both sides, neither party is entitled to recover back what he has given. [Rest. 2d §145]

      (2) **Third party cannot raise defense of Statute of Frauds:** [§543]   The Statute of Frauds normally may be asserted only by a party to the contract, not by a third person. Thus, if A orally promises to convey Blackacre to B, and gives B immediate possession of the property, including the right to rents payable from tenant T, T cannot refuse to pay the rent to B on the ground that B's contract was oral.

   b. **Minority view—contract void:** [§544]   In a few states, the Statute provides failure to comply with the Statute renders a contract *void.* Under this view, the Statute of Frauds might be a defense to the formation, not merely the enforcement, of a contract. [Ward v. Ward, 30 P.2d 853 (Colo. 1934)] In general, however, the courts have not put much weight on whether a given Statute of Frauds provides that contracts that fail to comply with the Statute are "void."

6. **Recovery in Restitution:** [§545]   Normally, a party who has conferred a benefit pursuant to a contract that falls within the Statute of Frauds can recover in restitution for the value of the benefit, even if he cannot enforce the contract.

   a. **Rationale:** A suit to recover the benefit is not technically within the Statute of Frauds. The Statute says that no action shall lie to enforce contracts that fall within it. A suit to recover the value of a benefit is not an action to enforce the contract, but an action in restitution or quasi-contract. Moreover, it would be unjust to permit a party to retain benefits received under the contract without paying for them.

   b. **Distinguish part performance exceptions:** [§546]   In certain cases, part performance (or full performance on one side) creates an exception to the Statute of Frauds, and makes a contract enforceable—either in full, as in sale-of-land cases (*see supra*, §504) or in part, as in sale-of-goods cases (*see supra*, §509). As pointed out above, even if the law did not recognize these part performance exceptions, a party who has rendered performance could recover the value of the benefit conferred. The significance of the part performance exceptions is that where such an exception is applicable, it allows the performing party to sue *on the contract*, for expectation damages, rather than merely in restitution or quasi-contract, for the value of the benefit conferred.

(1) **Caveat:** Remember that only certain kinds of part performance result in the enforceability of a contract that falls within the Statute (*see supra*, §§504, 510). If part performance does not make a contract enforceable, the remedy remains a suit in restitution for benefit conferred.

7. **Reliance on Contracts Within the Statute of Frauds**

   a. **Reliance on the contract:** [§547] The traditional rule was that reliance on a contract that is within the Statute of Frauds does not create an exception to the Statute—*i.e.*, reliance does not take the contract out of the Statute—except insofar as the reliance involves part performance of the kind that takes a contract out of the Statute. However, a growing number of modern cases hold that reliance itself by one party may estop (preclude) the other from asserting the Statute of Frauds as a defense.

      (1) **Example:** B orally agrees to buy a group of used cars from S, and S transports the cars across the country to deliver them to B. B then refuses to proceed with the purchase. During the interim, the used car market has fallen sharply. B is estopped to rely on the Statute as a defense, because if the contract is not enforced, S would suffer an unconscionable loss as a result of her reliance. [Goldstein v. McNeil, 122 Cal. App. 2d 608 (1954)]

   b. **Restatement in accord:** [§548] Restatement Second adopts the position that reliance by one party on a contract that is within the Statute of Frauds may estop the other party from pleading the Statute as a defense. In particular, Restatement Second section 139 provides that where a contract is within the Statute of Frauds, but the promisor has induced action or forbearance by the promisee so that "injustice can be avoided only by enforcement of the promise," the promise is enforceable. [Rest. 2d §139] Under the Restatement rule, whether a promise that falls within the Statute of Frauds should be enforced because of reliance depends upon the availability and adequacy of other remedies, particularly restitution; the extent to which the promisee's detrimental reliance was substantial, reasonable, and foreseeable; and the extent to which the oral agreement is corroborated by the reliance or other evidence.

F. LACK OF CONTRACTUAL CAPACITY

1. **Minors:** [§549] A contract made by a minor (an "infant"; in most states, a person younger than 18) is voidable at the minor's option, although the minor may enforce the contract against the adult.

   a. **Restitution:** [§550] In general, a minor is not even liable for the value of benefits he has received under the contract, although if he disaffirms the contract he must return anything that he received under the contract and still retains at the time of disaffirmance. However a minor *is* liable in restitution for the reasonable value of *necessaries* furnished to him.

(1) **"Necessaries":** "Necessaries" includes food, clothing, shelter, and whatever else is needed for the minor's subsistence, health, comfort, or education, taking into consideration the minor's age, status, and condition in life.

(a) **Note:** In some states, a minor is liable for the reasonable value of necessaries furnished to him or purchased by him only if he is emancipated from his parents, or if his parents are unable to provide the necessaries. [*See* Cal. Civ. Code §36]

2. **Mental Incapacity**

a. **Traditional rule:** [§551]   The traditional rule is that a person lacks the mental capacity to contract *only if* his mental processes are so deficient that he lacks understanding of the nature, purpose, and effect of the transaction. [95 A.L.R. 1442]   This is sometimes referred to as the "cognitive test." Under this test, which is the majority rule, psychological or emotional problems that affect a party's judgment or reason do not constitute in themselves mental incapacity for contract law purposes. Rather, the psychological condition must actually deprive the party of an understanding of what he is doing. [Smalley v. Baker, 262 Cal. App. 2d 824 (1968)—manic depressive held competent]

b. **Restatement rule:** [§552]   The Restatement adopts a more liberal rule. Under the Restatement, a party lacks capacity if he is *"unable to act in a reasonable manner,* and the other party has *reason to know* of his condition."* [Rest. 2d §15]   This is sometimes referred to as the "affective test."

c. **Effect of incapacity:** [§553]   A contract entered into by a person lacking mental capacity is voidable by him (or a guardian acting on his behalf), but not by the other contracting party.

(1) **Void vs. voidable:** In many states, if the person has been *adjudicated* insane or mentally incompetent his contracts are void, rather than merely voidable. [*See, e.g.,* Cal. Civ. Code §40]

d. **Restitutional liability for necessaries:** [§554]   A person who lacks mental capacity (or his estate) *is* liable in restitution for the value of any necessaries furnished to him.

3. **Drunken or Drugged Persons:** [§555]   Drunkenness and drugs raise problems of *temporary* incapacity. Each case must be judged on its own facts. The test, however, remains the same—whether the person was so intoxicated or drugged as to be unable to understand the nature, purpose, and effect of what he was doing. [Rest. 2d §16; Backus v. Sessions, 17 Cal. 2d 380 (1941)]

G. ILLEGAL CONTRACTS

1. **In General:** [§556]   If a proposed contract is legal at the time an offer is made but becomes illegal before acceptance of the offer, the intervening illegality terminates the

offer as a matter of law. If a contract is made, and is legal when made, but becomes illegal thereafter, the contract is discharged (*see infra*, §812).

2. **What Constitutes Illegality?** [§557] A contract is illegal if either the consideration or the object of the contract is illegal. Some contracts are illegal because expressly prohibited by statute (*e.g.*, gambling contracts and contracts in restraint of trade). Other contracts are illegal because they violate public policy (*e.g.*, contracts to defraud or injure third parties).

   a. **Indirect aid in accomplishment of an illegal act:** [§558] An otherwise valid contract is not illegal merely because its performance will indirectly aid in the accomplishment of an illegal act, provided the illegal act does not involve a serious crime or great moral turpitude. For example, a seller can recover the price of furniture even though she knows the furniture was purchased for an illegal gambling casino, provided the seller herself does nothing in furtherance of the unlawful design. Similarly, a lender can recover money loaned even though he knew the borrower intended to use the money for illegal gambling, provided the lender takes no part in the gambling.

3. **Effects of Illegality:** [§559] An illegal contract is void, and the general rule is that if a contract is illegal the courts will not intercede to aid either party. Therefore, if the contract is executory, neither party can enforce it. If the contract is partly performed, neither party can recover in restitution for benefits conferred. The rationale is that the public importance of discouraging such transactions outweighs considerations of possible injustice between the private parties. [Rest. 1st §598] However, there are some important exceptions to this rule:

   a. **Severable portion may be enforced:** [§560] First, if the agreement is "severable" into legal and illegal portions, and the illegal portion does not go to the "essence of the bargain," the legal portion may be enforced. [Rest. 1st §606] An agreement is severable for these purposes only where it expressly requires performance in distinct installments or portions and a separable consideration is provided for each such portion (*see infra*, §§772 *et seq.*).

   b. **"Locus penitentiae" doctrine:** [§561] Second, some decisions hold that where one party to an illegal contract repents and repudiates the contract before any part of the illegal purpose is carried out, that party may obtain restitutionary recovery for the value of what he gave in performance. [Rest. 1st §605; Wasserman v. Sloss, 117 Cal. 425 (1897)]

   c. **Not "in pari delicto":** [§562] Third, a party who has conferred a benefit under an illegal contract may be entitled to bring suit in restitution for the value of the benefit conferred if that party is not guilty of serious moral turpitude and is not as blameworthy as the other party. In such cases, the relatively innocent party is said to not be "in pari delicto." This exception is *inapplicable* if the contract is *malum in se* (against good morals). [Smith v. Bach, 183 Cal. 259 (1920)]

      (1) **Where one party is member of protected class:** [§563] If one party to a contract that is illegal by reason of statute is a member of the class for whose benefit the statute was enacted, that party is usually not considered in pari

delicto. Thus, an employee who works a greater number of hours than permitted by statute is not in pari delicto with his employer and can recover for his extra services. Similarly, an investor who purchases stock issued in violation of the "blue sky law" (*i.e.*, state securities statutes) is not in pari delicto with the corporation and may recover the purchase price paid for the stock. [Randal v. Beber, 107 Cal. App. 2d 692 (1951)]

d. **Contract malum prohibitum:** [§564] Restitutionary recovery may also be available if the contract is only ***malum prohibitum*** (against some statute or regulation but not involving any offense to good morals). In such cases, the courts will not enforce the illegal contract, but they may permit a party to obtain restitution for benefits conferred. [Rest. 1st §604]

   (1) **Example:** A hires B to do part-time work, knowing that B is a city employee and that a city ordinance prohibits city employees from accepting part-time jobs. B may recover from A in restitution for the value of her services because violation of the ordinance does not involve an affront to public morals. [Vick v. Patterson, 158 Cal. App. 2d 414 (1958)]

   (2) **Example:** A usurious contract is also only malum prohibitum. The lender therefore can usually recover the principal sum loaned, although the usurious interest will not be enforced. [Haines v. Commercial Mortgage Co., 200 Cal. 609 (1927)]

e. **Licensing requirements:** [§565] Statutes frequently require persons to obtain a license or permit from an appropriate governmental authority in order to engage in a specified business or occupation (such as doctor, attorney, contractor, or stockbroker). If an unlicensed person contracts to perform services, whether the contract is enforceable depends upon the purpose of the licensing statute.

   (1) **License for protection of public:** [§566] If the purpose of the licensing requirement is to protect the public from unqualified persons (*i.e.*, to assure that license holders have certain minimum qualifications), a contract negotiated by an unlicensed person relating to the business is usually held illegal, and the person will be denied recovery in restitution for the value of the services.

      (a) **Note:** Even in this kind of case, if a party has ***substantially complied*** with the licensing laws, that compliance will generally be held sufficient. Courts will not allow the other party to the contract to avoid obligations under the contract merely because of technical violations (*e.g.*, late renewal of permit), as long as the public has received substantially the protection contemplated by the licensing laws. [Latipac v. Superior Court, 64 Cal. 2d 278 (1966)]

   (2) **License for fiscal regulation or taxation:** [§567] If a licensing requirement is imposed primarily for purposes of fiscal regulation or taxation, rather than to protect the public from unqualified persons, contracts entered into by the unlicensed person are usually held enforceable notwithstanding the lack of a license.

(a) **Example:** Cities usually require that a business license be obtained by persons engaged in business in the city, but such licensing is normally for revenue raising purposes, and the cities do not pass on the qualification of the licensees. Failure to obtain a license is generally held not to render contracts entered into by the unlicensed person unenforceable.

IV. THIRD-PARTY RIGHTS AND OBLIGATIONS

chapter approach

Once you have established that an enforceable contract has been formed, you should next consider whether any third parties (*i.e.*, persons not parties to the contract) have any rights or duties under the contract. The classes of third parties who may have rights or duties under a contract are third-party beneficiaries, assignees of contractual rights, and persons to whom contractual duties have been delegated.

If a question sets out a contract that provides for a performance to be rendered to someone, or will benefit someone, other than a party, you have a third-party beneficiary situation. To decide whether this third party has the right to enforce the contract, you must:

— *Classify the third party* as an "incidental" or an "intended" beneficiary (or, under the older terminology, as an "incidental," "donee," or "creditor" beneficiary);

— *Consider whether any defenses may be available* to the promisor; and

— If the promisor and the promisee *have attempted to modify* the contract, determine whether, if the third party has a right to enforce the contract, the *rights of the third party have vested*.

If a question sets out a situation where one of the original parties to the contract has transferred rights or delegated duties under the contract to a third person, you have an assignments problem. In that case, consider:

— *Whether the rights may be assigned* or the duties delegated; and

— *The effect* of the assignment or delegation on the various parties.

A. THIRD-PARTY BENEFICIARIES

1. **In General:** [§568] The question often arises whether a person who was not a party to the bargain, and who gave no consideration, can enforce the contract if he would have been benefited by the contract's performance.

   a. **Example:** A offers to paint B's building for $10,000, using paint sold by C. Can C enforce B's promise? (Under the conventional terminology used in such cases, *A* is the *promisee, B* is the *promisor*, and *C* is the *third-party beneficiary*.)

   b. **Original common law rule—promise unenforceable by third-party beneficiary:** [§569] The original common law rule was that in order to maintain an action on a contract, a person must have given consideration to, and be in privity of contract with, the party against whom he is seeking to enforce the contract. Hence, a third-party beneficiary could not enforce a contract.

   c. **Modern law:** [§570] Under modern law, a third-party beneficiary may sue and recover in appropriate cases. [Lawrence v. Fox, 20 N.Y. 268 (1859); 81 A.L.R. 1289] The problem is, what kinds of cases are appropriate?

2. **Traditional Modern Law Test—Third Party Must Be Donee Beneficiary or Creditor Beneficiary:** [§571]   Even under modern law, not every person who would benefit by performance of a contract can bring suit upon it as a third-party beneficiary. Under the traditional test, popularized by Restatement First, third-party beneficiaries are divided into three classes: (i) creditor beneficiaries, (ii) donee beneficiaries, and (iii) incidental beneficiaries. Creditor and donee beneficiaries can bring suit under the contract; incidental beneficiaries cannot.

a. **Creditor beneficiary:** [§572]   A third party is a "creditor beneficiary," and can enforce the contract, if the promisee's primary intent was to discharge a duty he owed to the third party. [Rest. 2d §302]

(1) **Example:** A owes $1,000 to C. A (the promisee) then makes a contract with B (the promisor) under which A agrees to render a performance to B, and in exchange B promises to pay C (the third-party beneficiary) the $1,000 owed by A to C. C is a creditor beneficiary and can bring suit against B if B fails to pay her the $1,000.

(2) **Rationale:** Permitting a creditor beneficiary to enforce a contract is justified for two reasons.

(a) **Prevents unjust enrichment:** [§573]   First, permitting a creditor beneficiary to enforce the contract prevents unjust enrichment of the promisor. The promisor has received consideration for his promise to perform for the benefit of the third party, and he should not be permitted to retain the consideration and not perform.

(b) **Prevents excessive litigation:** [§574]   Permitting a creditor beneficiary to sue also saves unnecessary litigation. The creditor beneficiary is allowed to sue the promisor directly, instead of being forced to sue the promisee, who would in turn sue the promisor for breach of contract.

(3) **Must there be an actual duty owing?** [§575]   Is it necessary, to establish creditor-beneficiary status, that the promisee owed an actual duty to the third party, or is it sufficient that the promisee believed he owed such a duty?

(a) **General rule—promisee's intent determinative:** [§576]   The general rule is that a third-party beneficiary is a creditor-beneficiary if the promisee *intended* to satisfy an obligation he *believed* he owed the third party, whether or not he actually owed such an obligation. Under this rule, it is sufficient if there is a *supposed* or *asserted* duty owing to the third party. [Hamill v. Maryland Casualty Co., 209 F.2d 338 (10th Cir. (1954)]

(b) **Example:** C has asserted a claim of $1,000 against A. A contests the claim, but decides he will pay C anyway. Shortly thereafter, B buys goods from A. As consideration for the goods, B agrees to pay $1,000 to C. It subsequently develops that C's claim against A was in fact invalid. Under the general rule, C is a creditor beneficiary and can enforce B's promise.

b. **Donee beneficiary:** [§577] Restatement First defined two types of donee beneficiaries. Either type can enforce the contract.

(1) **Intent to confer a gift:** [§578] Under Restatement First, a third-party beneficiary is a "donee beneficiary" if the promisee's primary intent in contracting is to *confer a gift* upon the beneficiary (*i.e.*, to confer upon the beneficiary a right against the promisor to some performance neither due nor asserted or supposed to be due from the promisee to the third party). [Rest. 1st §133]

(a) **Example:** A, who is dying, wishes to give her cottage to C, A's favorite niece. To achieve this objective, A makes a contract with her husband, B. By the terms of the contract, A agrees not to change her will, under which her husband is the principal legatee and will inherit the cottage. In exchange, B agrees that on his death he will leave the cottage to C. C is a donee beneficiary, and can enforce the contract.

(2) **Intent to confer a right to performance:** [§579] A third-party beneficiary is also a donee beneficiary under Restatement First if the promisee intended to confer upon the beneficiary a *right against the promisor to some performance, other than as a gift*. A test of whether a third-party beneficiary is a donee beneficiary of this type is whether recognition of the right to performance in the beneficiary is necessary or appropriate to effectuate the intent of the parties to the contract, and the circumstances indicate that the promisee intends to give the beneficiary the benefit of the promised performance.

(a) **Example:** Auto dealer A contracts with X Insurance Company that X will indemnify anyone who purchases an auto from A for loss due to fire or theft within one year after the purchase. C purchases a car from A, with A's statement that C is insured by X. C is a donee beneficiary, because giving C a right against A is necessary to effectuate the contract between A and X.

(b) **Example:** Testator employs Attorney to draft a will leaving all of Testator's estate to B. B is a donee beneficiary of Attorney's promise to draft such a will, because allowing such a suit is necessary to effectuate Testator's intent that his estate (or its value) end up in B's hand. [Lucas v. Hamm, 56 Cal. 2d 583 (1961)]

c. **Incidental beneficiaries:** [§580] Under the Restatement First terminology, third parties who would be benefited by performance of a contract, but who are neither creditor beneficiaries nor donee beneficiaries, are "incidental" beneficiaries and cannot bring suit under the contract.

(1) **Example:** A contracts with B to build a house on B's land. Construction will greatly enhance the value of neighboring property owned by N. If B

breaches the contract, and N brings suit against B, N will lose, because she is only an incidental beneficiary. It was clearly not A's intent to confer a gift on N or a right against B, and recognition of such a right would not be necessary to effectuate the contract between A and B.

(2) **Example:** A contracts with B to build a house on A's land. The contract requires A to use roofing materials manufactured and sold by Y. If A breaches the contract, Y cannot bring suit against her. It was clearly not B's intent to confer a gift on Y or a right against A, and recognition of such a right would not be necessary to effectuate the contract between A and B. Therefore, Y is only an incidental beneficiary.

3. **Restatement Second Terminology:** [§581]   Restatement Second substitutes the term *"intended beneficiary"* for the terms "creditor" and "donee" beneficiaries. Restatement Second retains the term "incidental beneficiary." Thus under the terminology of Restatement First, a donee or creditor beneficiary can bring suit to enforce a contract but an incidental beneficiary cannot, while under the terminology of Restatement Second, an intended beneficiary can bring suit while an incidental beneficiary cannot. However, although the *terminology* has changed, the *tests* remain largely the same. Under Restatement Second section 302(1), "a beneficiary of a promise is an intended beneficiary if recognition of a right to performance in the beneficiary is appropriate to effectuate the intention of the parties and either (a) the performance of the promise will satisfy an obligation of the promisee to pay money to the beneficiary; or (b) the circumstances indicate that the promisee intends to give the beneficiary the benefit of the promised performance." Essentially, the test in section 302(1)(a) is equivalent to the Restatement First test for creditor beneficiaries, and the test in section 302(1)(b) is equivalent to the Restatement First test for donee beneficiaries.

4. **Defenses that Can Be Asserted by Promisor Against Beneficiary:** [§582]   Assuming that a third-party beneficiary is one who can bring suit under a contract, the question arises, what kinds of defenses can the promisor assert against the beneficiary in such a suit?

   a. **Defenses that promisor could have asserted against promisee:** [§583]   The promisor can assert against a third-party beneficiary any defense that the promisor could have asserted against the promisee concerning formation or performance of the contract. [Williams v. Paxson Coal Co., 31 A.2d 69 (Pa. 1943)]

      (1) **Example:** A agrees to paint B's house in exchange for B's promise to pay $5,000 to C to satisfy a claim that C has against A. C is a creditor beneficiary and can bring suit against B. However, if, for example, A was guilty of fraud, or failed to paint B's house, B could assert these matters as a defense in an action by C against B for nonpayment.

   b. **Defenses that promisee could have asserted against beneficiary:** [§584] Suppose the *promisee* would have had a defense against the beneficiary? For example, suppose that in the last example, A could have asserted a defense against C if C had sued A on C's preexisting claim against A?

(1) **Creditor beneficiary cases:** [§585] As a practical matter, the issue whether the promisor, B, can assert a defense that the *promisee* has against the beneficiary is likely to arise only in a creditor-beneficiary context, like the last example. Unless there was a preexisting relationship between the promisee and the beneficiary, such that the promisee owed or appeared to owe an obligation to the beneficiary, there would not be much likelihood that the promisee would have a defense against the beneficiary. To put it differently, the concept of a defense implies that there is a claim against which the defense can be asserted. Only in the creditor-beneficiary context will the beneficiary have a claim against the promisee prior to the contract at issue.

(2) **Problem of interpretation:** [§586] The issue whether the promisor, A, can raise a defense of the promisee, B, against the beneficiary, C, is to some extent a problem of interpretation. If A's promise is interpreted as a promise to *pay whatever liability that B was under to C*, then A could raise any defense B could raise. If, however, A's promise is interpreted as a promise to *pay a given amount of money to C*, then A cannot raise such a defense. The courts normally tend to give the latter interpretation, and therefore generally do not allow a promisor to raise against a beneficary a defense that the promisee could have asserted against the beneficiary. [*See* Rouse v. United States, 215 F.2d 872 (D.C. Cir. 1953)]

c. **Rights of beneficiary against promisee; rights of promisee against promisor**

(1) **Donee beneficiary contracts:** [§587] If a third-party beneficiary is a *donee beneficiary*, then by definition the promisee did not owe the beneficiary a preexisting obligation. Accordingly, if the promisor fails to perform, the beneficiary cannot sue the *promisee*, because the promisee owed the beneficiary no obligation. Correspondingly, the *promisee* cannot recover *damages* against the promisor for failure to perform, because the promisee has suffered no loss, since the performance of the contract would have benefited the beneficiary, but not the promisor. However, under the modern trend of authority, the promisee *can seek specific performance* of the promisor's promise, for the very reason that the legal remedy is inadequate. [Crocker v. New York Trust Co., 245 N.Y. 17 (1927)]

  (a) **Example:** A and B contract with each other to share the costs of supporting their aged uncle, C. If A refuses to pay her share, B cannot sue A for damages but may seek specific performance of A's promise.

(2) **Creditor beneficiary contracts:** [§588] If a third-party beneficiary is a *creditor* beneficiary, then by definition, the promisee owed the third party a preexisting obligation. Therefore, if the promisor fails to pay the beneficiary, the beneficiary can sue the promisee on the original (preexisting) obligation. Correspondingly, the promisee can sue the promisor for a failure to perform, because as a result of such a failure the promisee's obligation to the beneficiary, which the promisor agreed to discharge, instead remains outstanding.

5. **Termination or Variation of Third-Party Beneficiary's Rights:** [§589] Even though a third-party beneficiary is a donee or creditor—or intended—beneficiary, until

the beneficiary's rights *vest* they can be cut off or varied by a modification of the contract entered into by the promisor and the promisee. On the other hand, once a third-party beneficiary's rights vest, an agreement between the contracting parties cannot impair or vary the beneficiary's rights under the contract. There are several different approaches to the issue of when vesting occurs.

a. **Restatement First view:** [§590]   Under one approach, adopted in Restatement First, a distinction is drawn between creditor and donee beneficiaries. Under this approach, a *donee beneficiary's* rights vest upon the making of the contract. [Rest. 1st §§142, 135, comment a]   In contrast, a *creditor beneficiary's* rights vest only when he detrimentally relies or brings suit on the contract. [Rest. 1st §143]

b. **Restatement Second view:** [§591]   Under a second approach, adopted in Restatement Second, the rights of *any* intended beneficiary, whether creditor or donee, vest when, but only when, the beneficiary: (i) *manifests assent* to the promise in a manner invited or requested by the parties; (ii) *brings suit* to enforce the promise; or (iii) *materially changes position* in justifiable reliance thereon. [Rest. 2d §311]   Most modern courts would probably go along with this approach.

(1) **Comment:** It is important not to overemphasize the concept of vesting in the law of third-party beneficiaries. Unlike property law, where vesting is very important, in the law of third-party beneficiaries vesting is relatively unimportant. The issue of vesting is significant to only one, very limited question: can the promisor and the promisee modify a contract that the third party could have enforced in the absence of the modification? If the third-party beneficiary's rights have vested, the answer to that question is no. If the third-party beneficiary's rights have not vested, the answer to that question is yes. But in any event, you normally do not need to consider whether vesting has occurred *unless* the promisor and the promisee have attempted to modify the contract, and the third-party beneficiary could have enforced the contract in the absence of the modification. So, for example, vesting is normally irrelevant in determining whether a third-party beneficiary *can* enforce a contract, and whether, if he can enforce the contract, there are *defenses* against him other than modification.

6. **Assumption of a Mortgage:** [§592]   An assumption agreement is an agreement under which one person (the promisor) assumes (*i.e.*, undertakes) to perform the obligations already owed by another (the promisee) to a third person. The third person in an assumption agreement is a creditor-beneficiary, because by definition the promisor has assumed an obligation the promisee owed to the third person. A common type of assumption agreement involves mortgages. A mortgage is an interest in property that secures a debt. A person who sells property that is subject to a mortgage often requires the purchaser to assume the mortgage debt.

a. **Purchaser "assumes" mortgage debt:** [§593]   Suppose a purchaser of real estate assumes (agrees to pay) an existing mortgage on the real estate as part of the purchase transaction. In that case, the mortgagee is a third-party creditor beneficiary of the buyer's promise. Therefore, if there is a deficiency owing after the mortgage lien is foreclosed, the mortgagee can sue not only the original mortgagor, but also the assuming purchaser. [Corning v. Burton, 102 Mich. 86 (1894)]

b. **Purchaser takes "subject to" mortgage:** [§594]   In some cases, a purchaser of mortgaged property merely takes the property *"subject to"* the mortgage, rather than assuming the mortgage. In such cases, there is no assumption agreement, and the mortgagee therefore has no action against the purchaser for payment of the mortgage debt. In the event of default, the mortgagee's remedy is to foreclose the lien and sue the original mortgagor—the seller—for any deficiency judgment.

  (1) **Compare—effect:** Note the difference in the effect on the mortgagee between assuming a mortgage and taking subject to a mortgage:

  (a) *If the transferee assumes the mortgage,* the mortgagee can either foreclose her lien or sue the transferor *or* transferee on the mortgage debt and get a personal judgment against one or both.

  (b) *If the transferee merely takes subject to* and does not assume *the mortgage,* the mortgagee retains her security interest in the property and can foreclose her lien on the property or can sue the mortgagor on the mortgage debt and get a personal judgment against the mortgagor, but cannot sue the transferee on the mortgage debt and obtain a personal judgment against the transferor.

c. **Purchaser assumes a mortgage from seller who only took subject to the mortgage:** [§595]   Suppose A owns mortgaged real property and sells it to B. B buys *subject to* the mortgage rather than assuming the mortgage. B then sells the property to X, who *assumes* the mortgage. Is X liable to the mortgagee?

  (1) **Majority view:** The majority view is that X is *not* liable, on the ground that B did not intend to confer an unconditional right on the mortgagee, but either acted under the mistaken impression that he was liable, or intended to make X liable only if B was liable.

  (2) **Minority view:** There is, however, a minority view, that holds X liable in such a case. The theory is that B must at least have *supposed* he owed a duty to the mortgagee or he would not have gotten X to assume the mortgage. This supposed duty is sufficient to make the mortgagee a creditor-beneficiary, because a person is a creditor beneficiary if the promisor agrees to pay an actual *or* asserted or supposed obligation of the promisee (*supra,* §576).

B. ASSIGNMENT OF RIGHTS AND DELEGATION OF DUTIES

1. **In General:** [§596]   This section deals with problems that arise when a party to a contract seeks to either assign (transfer) a right arising under the contract or delegate a duty imposed under the contract to a third party.

  a. **Nature of an assignment:** [§597]   In general, an assignment is the transfer of an intangible right. In particular, in contract law an assignment is a transfer of a contract right.

(1) **Terminology:** [§598] In the law of assignments, the transferor is known as the *assignor;* the other (nonassigning) party to the original contract is known as the *obligor;* and the transferee is known as the *assignee.*

(2) **Effect of assignment:** [§599] An assignment of a contractual right operates to extinguish the right in the transferor and set the right up exclusively in the transferee. [Rest. 2d §317] Thus as a result of an assignment, the assignee has a direct right against the obligor. Under modern law, all jurisdictions recognize that an assignee is the real owner of the right transferred to her, and that she alone may enforce the assigned right against the obligor. The assignee is the real party in interest, insofar as that right is concerned, and may sue directly on the contract in her own name without joining the assignor.

(3) **Governing law:** [§600] Today, Article 9 of the U.C.C. is the most important source of law governing assignments. Article 9 covers almost all assignments, subject to specific exceptions. Article 9 applies (subject to the exceptions) to any transaction that is intended to create a security interest in personal property, including "goods, documents, instruments, general intangibles, chattel paper or accounts" and "to any sale of accounts or chattel paper." Sales of accounts and chattel paper (as opposed to the creation of security interests) are brought within Article 9 to avoid difficult problems of distinguishing between transactions intended for security and those not so intended. Accordingly, under Article 9 persons who purchase most types of claims are treated the same way as persons who take such claims as security for a debt.

   (a) **Definitions:** [§601] Among the key terms in section 9-102(1) are "account," "account debtor," "chattel paper," and "general intangibles."

      1) **Account debtor:** [§602] The term "account debtor" means the person who is obligated on an account, chattel paper, or general intangible.

      2) **Account:** [§603] An "account" is a right to payment for goods or services, whether or not the right has yet been earned by performance, that is not evidenced by an indispensable writing. The term covers most types of choses in action, that is, rights to receive payments that can be enforced at law.

      3) **Chattel paper:** [§604] The term "chattel paper" means a writing or writings that evidence both a monetary obligation and a security interest in specific goods.

      4) **General intangibles:** [§605] The term "general intangibles" covers miscellaneous types of contractual rights and other personal property. Examples are goodwill, literary rights, and rights to performance.

(b) **Exclusions**

1) **Types of claims:** [§606]   Article 9 of the U.C.C. does not apply to certain *types of claims*, such as wage claims, bank accounts, tort claims, and insurance benefits.

2) **Types of assignments:** [§607]   Article 9 also does not apply to certain *types of assignments*, such as:

a) Assignments of accounts or contract rights *as part of the sale of the business* out of which the accounts or contract rights arose;

b) Assignments of a *right to payment under a contract to a person who is also to render performance* under the contract (*i.e.*, to a delegee; *see infra*, §684);

c) Assignments for *collection purposes only*;

d) *Donative assignments*;

e) A transfer of a single account to an assignee in whole or partial satisfaction of an existing indebtedness.

b. **Common law:** [§608]   Many of the common law rules governing the assignment of contract rights have been drastically altered by Article 9 of the U.C.C. However, the common law rules are still important, partly as a background to understand the U.C.C. provisions, and partly because the common law rules still generally govern assignments that are expressly excluded from Article 9.

2. **Rules Governing the Assignability of Rights**

a. **General rule:** [§609]   The general rule is that all contract rights are assignable.

b. **Exceptions—nonassignable rights:** [§610]   A right may not be assigned if an assignment would "*materially change the duty* of the obligor, or *materially increase the burden or risk* imposed on him by his contract, or *materially impair his chance of obtaining return performance* or *materially reduce its value* to him." [Rest. 2d §317; *and see* similar provision in U.C.C. §2-210(2)—applicable to assignments of contracts for the sale of goods]

(1) **Rights whose assignment would materially alter the obligor's duty**

(a) **Personal service contracts:** [§611]   Rights may not be assigned where the effect would be to require the obligor to perform *personal services* to the assignee. [Davis v. Basalt Rock Co., 107 Cal. App. 2d 436 (1951)]

1) **Example:** A employs B to paint her portrait. Later, A attempts to assign her rights under the contract to her uncle C. C may not compel B to paint his portrait.

2) **Rationale:** The performance of personal services for anyone other than the original obligee could materially change the nature of the obligor's duties. Wherever such services are involved, the law implies that the personal relationship between the obligor and the obligee is important. Therefore, the obligee cannot transfer her rights to another.

3) **What constitutes personal services?** [§612] The test of what constitutes personal services, for these purposes, is whether the performance so involves the personality or personal characteristics of the obligor that it would be unfair to require the obligor to render the performance to a third person.

   a) **Examples:** Examples of contracts for personal services, rights under which cannot be assigned, include contracts for the services of a painter, a lawyer, a physician, an architect, or the like. On the other hand, repair or construction contracts are usually *not* interpreted as involving personal services. Therefore, a contractor normally can be required to render his performance to an assignee of the person for whom the contractor originally agreed to perform the work.

(b) **"Requirements" and "output" contracts:** [§613] A contract in which one party, A, has the right to compel the other party, B, to buy all the goods A can produce (*i.e.*, an "output" contract), or to provide all the goods A needs in his business (*i.e.*, a "requirements" contract), is generally not assignable by A. Because the assignee might have far different output or far different requirements than A, the assignment could materially vary the duty of B. [34 A.L.R. 1184]

(2) **Rights whose assignment would materially vary the risk assumed by the obligor:** [§614] Rights under a contract cannot be assigned if the assignment would require the obligor to assume a materially different risk than the risk originally contemplated.

(a) **Insurance:** [§615] The most obvious application of this principle is to insurance policies. Such policies are contracts predicated upon a designated risk assumed by the insurer in connection with a named insured. Because the risk assumed in insuring one person necessarily differs from the risk assumed in insuring any other person, the right to be insured under a specific policy is generally not assignable. This is true not only as to life insurance, but also as to liability and casualty insurance. The risks created by one person's conduct, or ownership or operation of property or a business, are different from another's.

   1) **Right to insurance proceeds:** [§616] While the right to be *insured* may not be assignable, the right to *benefits* under an insurance contract—*i.e.*, the right to payment of money on the happening of the contingency that is insured against (such as the death of the insured or the destruction of insured property)—generally *can*

be assigned. Requiring the payment of money to an assignee, rather than to the named insured, does not materially vary the insurer's obligations or risk.

(b) **Credit:** [§617]   Where personal credit is involved, a substitution of debtors will vary the obligee's risk. Therefore, a right to the extension of credit generally cannot be assigned.

1) **Example:** A agrees to loan money to B in one month, the loan to be secured by B's promissory note. B decides she does not want the loan, and she attempts to assign A's promise to make the loan to her needy friend, C. C cannot compel A to take his promissory note in place of B's, because C's credit may not be as good as B's.

2) **Purchase money mortgages:** [§618]   The same principle applies where a seller of real estate has agreed to accept a mortgage on the property as part of the purchase price and the buyer attempts to assign his rights under the contract of sale.

a) **Example:** A agrees to sell Blackacre to B for $50,000, payable $20,000 in cash and the balance in installments that will be secured by a mortgage on Blackacre executed by B. Prior to the closing, B attempts to assign all of her rights under the contract to C. Most authorities would hold that the assignment is ineffective, on the ground that C's credit is not the same as B's. Although the property that is to serve as security for the debt remains unchanged, the personal obligation of C on a mortgage note is different from the personal obligation of B. [American Lithographic Co. v. Ziegler, 103 N.E. 909 (Mass. 1914)] (Of course, B could go through with the purchase, execute the mortgage herself, and then transfer title to C. However, B would then be subject to the personal liability for which A had bargained.)

3) **Assignment that would materially change contract terms:** [§619]   Even if an assignment will not materially change the duties of the obligor, materially increase the burden of risk imposed on him by the contract, materially impair his chances of obtaining return performance, or materially reduce the value of that performance to him, so that rights under the contract are assignable, an assignment will not be allowed to alter the material terms of the contract.

a) **Example:** A contracts to deliver goods to B at B's place of business. B assigns her rights under the contract to C, whose place of business is across town. The assignment is not effective to change the place of delivery. If C wants the goods, he must accept delivery at B's place of business.

3. **Partial Assignments:** [§620]   Rights under a contract may be transferred to one assignee or divided up among several assignees. Alternatively, the assignor may assign only some rights and retain the balance.

    a. **Early rule:** [§621]   At early common law, a partial assignment was held to be ineffective on the theory that it increased the burden on the obligor, because she would have several persons to pay instead of one and the possibility of increased litigation. However, a partial assignment was enforceable *in equity* if the partial assignee joined in her suit not only the obligor, but also all the partial assignees and also the assignor if he retained any rights under the contract.

    b. **Present rule:** [§622]   Today, partial assignments are generally enforced even at law. However, it is still usually necessary to join all of the other partial assignees as parties (and also to join the assignor if he retained any rights under the contract), unless joinder is not feasible and it is otherwise equitable to proceed without joinder. [Rest. 2d §326; *see* Civil Procedure Summary]

4. **Requirements for an Effective Assignment:** [§623]   Any manifested intention by a party to a contract to make a present transfer of rights under the contract to another person will constitute an assignment. However, the assignor must intend to transfer the right to the other person without further action; *i.e.*, make a *present* transfer. [Rest. 2d §324] If the assignor intends only to make a *future* transfer, there may be a valid contract *to* assign, but there is not a present assignment. (Note, however, that an assignor may make a present transfer of a right that is to arise in the future; *see infra*, §639.)The right that is assigned must be adequately described, and *present words of assignment be used.*

    a. **Test:** [§624]   The test for "present words of assignment" is whether the language used manifests an intent by the assignor to divest himself completely and immediately of the right in question and transfer the right to the assignee. The word "assign" need not be used. Words such as "sell," "transfer," "convey," "give," etc. will usually suffice.

        (1) **Consideration:** [§625]   Consideration is not required for an assignment; a gratuitous donative assignment is effective. However, an assignment that lacks consideration may be revocable. [Harriman v. Bunker, 106 A. 499 (N.H. 1919); *and see* below]

    b. **Formalities**

        (1) **Common law:** [§626]   Under the common law, no formality is required for an assignment. Therefore, absent a statute to the contrary, an oral assignment is just as effective as a written one. However, the lack of a writing may make a *donative* assignment revocable (*see infra*, §§629, 634). [Jemison v. Tindall, 99 A. 408 (N.J. 1916)]

        (2) **U.C.C.:** [§627]   U.C.C. section 9-203 provides that, with certain exceptions, a security interest is not enforceable against the debtor or third parties unless the debtor has signed a written security agreement describing the assigned collateral, or the assigned collateral is already in the assignee's pos-

session, for example, where the collateral consists of a claim embodied in a negotiable instrument that has been transferred to the assignee. The term "security interest" is broader than it seems—it includes *any* interest of a purchaser of accounts or chattel paper that is subject to U.C.C. Article 9. [U.C.C. §1-201(37)]

(a) **General Statute of Frauds:** [§628] Assignments not covered by U.C.C. section 9-203 are governed by the general Statute of Frauds provision contained in U.C.C. section 1-206. That section provides that except in the cases described in section 9-203 (and in contracts for the sale of goods or securities, which are covered by other, more specific U.C.C. Statute of Frauds sections—2-201 and 8-319), a contract for the sale of personal property is not enforceable by way of action or defense beyond $5,000 in amount or value of remedy, unless there is some writing which indicates that a contract for sale has been made between the parties at a defined or stated price, reasonably identifies the subject matter, and is signed by the party against whom enforcement is sought or by his authorized agent.

5. **Revocability of Assignments:** [§629] An assignment for consideration is irrevocable. However, a *gratuitous* assignment is ordinarily revocable at any time by the assignor, subject to certain exceptions described below. [Rest. 2d §332]

a. **How revoked:** [§630] A gratuitous assignment is effectively revoked by any of the following:

(1) The assignor's *later assignment of the same right* to another (whether or not consideration was paid for later);

(2) The *death of the assignor*;

(3) The *bankruptcy of the assignor*;

(4) A *notice of revocation* given by the assignor to either the assignee or the obligor; or

(5) An *acceptance by the assignor of payment or performance directly from the obligor.*

b. **How made irrevocable:** [§631] A gratuitous assignment is irrevocable under the following circumstances [Rest. 2d §332]:

(1) **Delivery of tangible token:** [§632] If a "chose" (*i.e.*, a claim) is represented by a "tangible token," delivery of the tangible token makes a gratuitous assignment irrevocable. A claim or chose is represented by a tangible token if the claim or chose normally can be enforced only by surrender, or proof of possession, of a document that represents the claim or chose, *e.g.*, a savings-account passbook, a negotiable instrument, or a stock certificate.

(a) **Restatement test:** [§633] Under the Restatement, a tangible token is defined more broadly, to include any document or thing of a type customarily accepted as a symbol or evidence of the right assigned. [Rest. 2d §332]

c. **Writing:** [§634]   The general rule is that a gratuitous assignment is also irrevocable if the assignment is made in a writing that is delivered to the assignee.

d. **Estoppel:** [§635]   If the assignee of a gratuitous assignment detrimentally relies on the assignment, the assignor may be estopped to revoke the assignment.

e. **Performance:** [§636]   A gratuitous assignment becomes irrevocable if, prior to revocation, the assignee receives payment or performance from the obligor, or obtains a judgment against the obligor by enforcing the assigned right.

f. **Novation:** [§637]   A gratuitous assignment is irrevocable if the assignee, the assignor, and the obligor all mutually agree that the assignor should be substituted for the assignee, so that the assignor's rights and duties under the contract are discharged. Such a three-way agreement is known as a "novation."

6. **Effectiveness of Assignments of Future Rights:** [§638]   As used in the law of assignment, "future rights" refers to rights *expected* to arise under (i) an existing or (ii) a future contract. At common law, there is a marked difference in the assignability of these two types of future rights.

a. **Future rights under an *existing* contract:** [§639]   At common law, rights expected to arise in the future under an existing contract are generally freely assignable, even though the right is conditional on such matters as the assignor's performance under the contract. [Rest. 2d §321]

b. **Future rights under an *existing* business relationship:** [§640]   Furthermore, some authorities at common law allow the assignment of a right to payments that are expected to arise out of a "continuing business relationship," even though there is no existing contract. (For example, Farmer assigns to T payments he expects to receive for his crop from a granary with which he has been doing business.) [Rest. 2d §321]

c. **Future rights under a *future* contract or business relationship:** [§641]   At common law, rights under a future contract or future business relationship are not assignable. The theory is that an assignment is a transfer, and a person cannot transfer something that he does not have. [Herbert v. Bronson, 125 Mass. 475 (1878)]

(1) **Equitable relief possible:** [§642]   Even at common law, however, although an attempted assignment of rights under a future contract or a future business relationship is ineffective as an assignment, if it is given for consideration, the attempted assignment is treated as a ***contract*** to assign the right if and when it does arise. Therefore, if the right does arise, equity may grant specific performance of the contract by compelling the assignment to be made at that point. [Holt v. American Woolen Co., 150 A. 382 (Me. 1930)]   However, because such an assignment is enforceable only in equity, equitable considerations govern. Thus the assignment will not be en-

forced if a subsequent bona fide purchaser acquired the right after it came into existence, provided the purchaser took without notice of the prior assignment. Nor will such an assignment be enforced against attaching creditors of the assignor who had no notice of the attempted prior assignment. [Stokely Bros. v. Conklin, 26 A.2d 147 (N.J. 1942)]

d. **U.C.C.:** [§643] For the most part, the common law rules concerning the assignment of future rights have been changed by the U.C.C. Article 9 explicitly recognizes the validity of an assignment of future rights and gives the assignee of such rights priority over most competing claimants, provided a financing statement describing the assignment is properly filed. [U.C.C. §9-204; *see infra,* §681] Recall, however, that Article 9 does not apply to all assignments. (*See supra,* §606-607.)

7. **Effect of Contractual Provisions Prohibiting Assignment**

a. **Traditional view:** [§644] At common law, a contractual provision prohibiting the assignment of rights under a contract is valid, both as to the parties and as to any assignee with notice thereof. [Rest. 2d §319; *and see* Rest. 2d §317] However, such provisions are not favored, because they interfere with free alienability. Accordingly, although the general common law principle is that such provisions are valid, the courts have adopted a number of rules that effectively reduce the force of the common law principle.

(1) **Prohibition on assignments are construed as promissory in nature:** [§645] If a contract contains only a *promise* not to assign the contract (*e.g.,* a provision that "No assignment hereof shall be made," or that "A agrees not to assign this contract without the prior consent of B"), the promise is said to destroy the *right,* but not the *power,* to make an assignment. Accordingly, although the obligor (the nonassigning party) will have an action against the assignor for breach of the contractual provision prohibiting assignment, the assignment will be valid as between the assignee and the obligor. Unless the assignment causes special injury to the obligor, only nominal damages could normally be recovered in the obligor's suit against the assignor.

(2) **Contractual prohibitions in the form of a condition:** [§646] If a prohibition against assignment is phrased as a condition, rather than as a promise (*e.g.,* "any assignment hereof shall be void," or "in the event of an assignment, this contract shall terminate"), at common law the provision is generally given full force and effect. Such a provision is said to destroy not only the obligee's right, but also his power, to assign, so that an assignment in violation of the provision is unenforceable.

b. **Restatement approach:** [§647] The Restatement nominally retains the principle that contractual prohibitions on assignment are enforceable, but adopts strong rules of construction against such provisions, as follows [Rest. 2d §322]:

(1) **Contract term that prohibits assignment of "the contract":** [§648] A contractual provision that prohibits an assignment of "the contract" is to be

construed to bar only the *delegation* by the assignor of his duties or conditions, not an assignment of rights under the contract.

(2) **Contract term that prohibits assignment of rights under the contract:** [§649]   A contractual provision that prohibits an assignment of rights under the contract (as opposed to prohibiting an assignment of "the contract") is to be interpreted:

(a) To give the obligor a *right to damages* in the event of a prohibited assignment, but *not* to render the assignment ineffective;

(b) *Not to forbid assignment of a right to damages for breach* of the whole contract or the assignment of a right arising out of the assignor's due performance of his entire obligation; and

(c) To be *for the benefit of the obligor,* and not to prevent the assignee from acquiring rights against the assignor, nor to prevent the obligor from rendering performance to the assignee as if there were no such prohibition.

c. **U.C.C. approach**

(1) **Contractual prohibition ineffective:** [§650]   U.C.C. section 9-318(4), which is applicable to most commercial assignments, provides that a term in any contract between an account debtor and an assignor is ineffective if it prohibits assignment of an *account.* (Recall that U.C.C. section 9-106 defines an "account" as any right to payment for goods or services, whether or not the right has yet been earned by performance, and an "account debtor" as the person who is obligated on an account.) Broadly speaking, therefore, U.C.C. section 9-318(4) denies the enforceability of contractual prohibitions of assignments of payments due or to become due under assignments to which Article 9 is applicable.

(2) **Right to damages assignable:** [§651]   Similarly, U.C.C. section 2-210(2) provides that the right to *damages* for breach of a *sales* contract is assignable, even in the face of an express contractual prohibition on assignment thereof.

8. **Wage Assignments:** [§652]   An assignment of wages to be earned in the future under an existing contract of employment is effective, under the principle that future rights expected to arise under an existing contract are assignable. (*See supra,* §629.) [McDonald v. Hudspeth, 129 F.2d 196 (10th Cir. 1942)]

a. **Employment terminable at will:** [§653]   This is true even where the existing employment contract is terminable at will by the employer or employee, so that there is no assurance that assigned wages will be earned under the contract. [Duluth S.S. & A. Railway v. Wilson, 167 N.W. 55 (Mich. 1918)]

b. **Statutory restrictions:** [§654]   However, many states have statutory restrictions on the assignability of future wages. For example, California Labor Code section

300 permits such an assignment only if a separate written instrument containing the consent of the employee's spouse (or the employee's parent, if the employee is a minor) has been filed with the employer. Even then, under the statute such an assignment is valid only to cover "necessaries of life" furnished to the employee by the assignee.

c. **Constitutional issue:** [§655]   Wages are usually assigned as security for a loan. If the debtor-employee fails to repay the loan, the creditor can go directly to the employer and force the employer to pay the assigned wages to the creditor rather than to the employee. In effect, therefore, the wage assignment is a substitute for suing the employee and garnishing her wages if she fails to pay a judgment, but without the protection of a judicial hearing. A constitutional question has arisen whether such a practice constitutes a "taking" of the employee's property (her wages) without due process of law in violation of the Fourteenth Amendment— *i.e.*, whether the employee must be afforded some sort of notice and judicial hearing before the creditor is permitted to enforce the wage assignment. [*See* Sniadach v. Family Finance Corp., 395 U.S. 335 (1969)—notice and hearing required before *garnishment* of an employee's wages] To date, the courts have upheld private enforcement of wage assignments, on the ground that no "state action" is involved, and the procedural safeguards of the Fourteenth Amendment therefore do not apply. [Bond v. Dentzer, 494 F.2d 302 (2d Cir. 1974)]

9. **Rights, Liabilities, and Defenses After Effective Assignment:** [§656]   An effective assignment extinguishes the assigned right in the assignor and sets it up in the assignee. Thereafter, only the assignee is entitled to performance from the obligor (*supra*, §§522-623).

a. **Rights of the assignee against the obligor**

(1) **Right of direct action:** [§657]   An assignee can enforce his rights by a direct action against the obligor. Suit may be maintained by the assignee in his own name.

(2) **Effect of notice to obligor:** [§658]   Once the obligor has knowledge of the assignment, he must render performance to or pay the assignee. If the obligor renders performance to or pays the assignor, he does so at his own risk. [Nelson v. Fernando Nelson & Sons, 5 Cal. 2d 511 (1936)]

b. **Defenses available to the obligor against the assignee**

(1) **General rule:** [§659]   The general rule concerning defenses that the obligor may assert against an assignee is set out in U.C.C. section 9-318, which for the most part reflects the common law. Under section 9-318, a defense that is contract-related can be asserted by the obligor against the assignee, whether the defense arises before or after notice of the assignment is given. A defense is "contract-related" if (i) the defense asserts that the contract under which rights were assigned was not validly formed (*e.g.*, a defense that the original contract lacked consideration), or (ii) the defense arises *under* the contract (*e.g.*, a claim that the assignor or the assignee has performed defectively).

(2) **Holder in due course and waiver of defenses:** [§660]   The general rule that an obligor can assert contract-related defenses against the assignee is modified if (i) the assigned claim is represented by a negotiable instrument and the assignee is a holder in due course, or (ii) the assigned claim arose under a contract in which the obligor waived his right to assert, against an assignee, defenses he might have against the assignor.

(a) **Holder in due course:** [§661]   If a claim is embodied in a negotiable instrument, the claim is assigned by assigning or transferring the instrument. A negotiable instrument is one that, among other things, contains an unconditional promise or order to pay a sum certain in money, and no other promise, order, obligation or power. The most common examples of negotiable instruments are promissory notes and checks. An assignment or transfer of a negotiable instrument to a holder in due course is called a "negotiation." A holder in due course is an assignee who takes the claim for value, in good faith, and without notice of any defense. If a negotiable instrument is negotiated (*i.e.*, transferred) to an assignee who is a holder in due course, the obligor cannot assert even contract-related defenses against the holder, except for certain limited defenses relating to contract formation, such as incapacity and duress.

(b) **Waiver-of-defense clauses:** [§662]   A similar result can be achieved, even in an assignment of a claim that is not embodied in a negotiable instrument, by a waiver-of-defense clause. This is a clause in the contract under which rights are assigned, which provides that the obligor agrees that he will not assert against an assignee any defenses he may have against the assignor.

(c) **FTC rule:** [§663]   A Federal Trade Commission rule now effectively limits both the holder-in-due-course doctrine and waiver-of-defense clauses in consumer credit sales. Under this rule, a person who sells consumer goods or services on credit must include a *notice* in any consumer credit contract or note that any assignee (including any holder) of the contract takes subject to all claims and defenses that the consumer-debtor could assert against the seller. The language of this notice deprives the instrument of its negotiability by rendering it conditional. The rule also makes it unlawful for such a seller to accept as payment the proceeds of a loan made by a creditor to whom the buyer was referred by the seller, or who is affiliated with the seller through a contract, business arrangement, or common control, unless an equivalent notice is contained in the contract or note given by the buyer to the creditor. The language becomes part of the contract between the creditor and buyer-debtor, and will bind them and thereby grant the defenses to the buyer-debtor. [16 C.F.R. §§433.1, 433.2]

1) **Rationale:** The purpose of the FTC rule is to reallocate the burden of any loss resulting from seller misconduct in the consumer market from the innocent consumer-purchaser to a creditor/lender who finances the transaction by purchasing the consumer's note or

lending on the security of such a note. Such a creditor/lender is likely to be in a better position than the consumer to police the seller.

(d) **Consumer protection statutes:** [§664]   Some statutes governing retail installment contracts provide that an assignee of such a contract takes subject to all "equities or defenses" of the buyer against the seller-assignor—even defenses that did not exist at the time of the assignment. [Cal. Civ. Code §1804.2]

(e) **Modification after notice of assignment:** [§665]   Suppose an assignor assigns certain rights under the contract, such as a right to one or more payments, but otherwise continues to perform the contract. After the assignment has been made, and after the obligor has been given notice of the assignment, the assignor and the obligor modify the contract in good faith. Does the modification affect the rights of the assignee?

1) **Traditional view:** [§666]   The traditional view is that the modification does not affect the assignee's rights, because an obligor who has received notice of an assignment deals with the assignor at his peril (*see* §658, *supra*).

2) **Modern trend:** [§667]   However, U.C.C. section 9-318, recognizing commercial realities, provides that in the case of commercial assignments, a "modification of or substitution for [a right to payment that has not yet been fully earned by performance] made in good faith and in accordance with reasonable commercial standards is effective against an assignee." [*See also* Rest. 2d §338] U.C.C. section 9-318 applies only to rights not yet fully earned by performance. Even under U.C.C. section 9-318, a modification between the obligor and the assignor cannot affect rights that have been fully earned.

(2) **Unrelated defenses:** [§668]   Unlike contract related defenses, defenses that are unrelated to the contract under which the rights were assigned (*e.g.*, a claim by the obligor against the assignor under *another* contract) can be asserted against the assignee if, but only if, the defense accrued *before* the assignee gave the obligor notice of the assignment.

c. **Rights of assignee against assignor—warranties of assignor:** [§669]   In every assignment for consideration the assignor impliedly makes the following warranties:

(i) That the *assigned right actually exists*, and is subject to no limitations or defenses other than those stated or apparent at the time of assignment;

(ii) That any *document or paper with regard to the assignment is genuine* and what it purports to be;

(iii) That she has *the right to assign* the assigned right—*i.e.*, that she has made no prior assignment of the same right; and

(iv) That she will do nothing in the future to defeat the assigned right; *i.e.*, she will *not attempt a subsequent assignment* of the same right.

[Rest. 2d §333]

(1) **Warranties not impliedly made:** [§670]   There is no implied warranty that the obligor is solvent or able to perform or that he will perform. [Galbreath v. Wallrich, 102 P. 1085 (Colo. 1909)]

10. **Priority of Competing Assignees:** [§671]   Suppose an assignor assigns the same right to two or more assignees. In a contest between the prior and the subsequent assignee, which assignee prevails?

   a. **Common law:** [§672]   The common law is relatively well-settled in two kinds of cases—those in which the prior assignment is revocable and those in which the assigned claim is embodied in a tangible token.

   (1) **If prior assignment revocable:** [§673]   Under common law, if the prior assignment is revocable—because, for example, it is gratuitous and oral—a subsequent assignment revokes the prior assignment, and the subsequent assignee therefore prevails over the prior assignee. [Rest. 2d §342]

   (2) **Tangible token:** [§674]   Under common law, the subsequent assignment also prevails if the assigned claim is represented by a tangible token and the prior assignee left the token in the assignor's possession—at least if the subsequent assignee gave value and took possession of the token. The rationale of this rule is that an assignee who leaves a tangible token in the assignor's possession should be estopped from claiming priority over a subsequent assignee, because by leaving the token in the assignor's hands the prior assignee allowed the impression to be created that the assignor still owned the claim.

   (3) **Other cases:** [§675]   If the first assignment is not revocable and the claim is not represented by a tangible token left in the assignor's hands, there are three competing rules at common law: the "New York rule," the "English rule," and the "Massachusetts rule."

   (a) **"New York rule":** [§676]   Under the New York rule, as between successive assignees of the same right, the first in time (*i.e.*, the prior assignee) prevails. The rationale of the New York rule is that once an irrevocable assignment is made, the assignor has no further interest left to assign. The subsequent assignee therefore gets nothing, because there is nothing to get. [Salem Trust Co. v. Manufacturers' Finance Co., 264 U.S. 182 (1923)]

   (b) **"English rule":** [§677]   Under the English rule, as between successive assignees of the same right the first assignee to give notice to the obligor prevails—provided that the assignee who first gave notice to the obligor paid value and did not have notice of the prior assignment. [Haupt v. Charlie's Kosher Market, 17 Cal. 2d 843 (1941); 110 A.L.R. 774]

1) **Rationale:** The rationale of the English rule is that it is easy for an assignee to give notice to the obligor, and if the prior assignee does give such notice, a person who is offered an assignment of the same claim has an opportunity to find out that the claim has already been assigned by checking with the obligor, who in effect functions as a sort of private recording office. In the absence of an official recording system, unless an assignee gives such notice to the obligor, a subsequent assignee will have no way of finding out that the claim was already assigned. (A dishonest assignor who wants to assign the same claim twice is not likely to advise the subsequent assignee that the claim has already been assigned.) The English rule provides an incentive to give such a notice.

(c) **"Massachusetts rule":** [§678]   Under the Massachusetts rule, if the prior assignment is revocable, it is revoked by the subsequent assignment. If the prior assignment is not revocable, the prior assignee prevails unless the subsequent assignee acquires the assignment in good faith and for value, and either:

1) Takes from the assignor a tangible token representing the claim;

2) Collects the claim from the obligor;

3) Obtains a judgment against the obligor; or

4) Secures a novation from the obligor.

b. **U.C.C.:** [§679]   Article 9 of the U.C.C. has radically changed the rules on priority between competing assignees of contract rights subject to the Code. Under the Code, most assignments are protected in order of their filing. [U.C.C. §9-312]   To achieve that result, Article 9 employs two basic concepts: attachment and perfection.

(1) **Attachment:** [§680]   A security interest under Article 9 normally ***attaches*** when the creditor enters into a security agreement with the debtor for value, and either puts designated elements of the agreement in writing or obtains possession of the collateral. [U.C.C. §§9-203, 9-204] When the security interest attaches, it becomes enforceable against the debtor. [U.C.C. §§9-201, 9-203(1)] In theory, it is also enforceable against third parties, such as competing assignees, but in practice it is normally enforceable against third parties only if it is "perfected."

(2) **Perfection:** [§681]   In most cases, a security interest under Article 9 is perfected only by filing, in a designated state office, a financing statement that describes the collateral and sets forth the parties' names and addresses.

A very few security interests are perfected "automatically" upon attachment (*i.e.*, upon creation of the security agreement in the manner specified by Article 9). For example, purchase-money security interests in most consumer goods are perfected in this way. In addition, a secured party can perfect his security interest without filing by taking *possession* of the collateral. [U.C.C. §9-105] In the case of accounts or other intangible personal property, however, there is usually nothing to possess, unless the intangible is embodied in or evidenced by a tangible token.

(a) **First to file:** [§682] Where a security interest is perfectible by filing, then as among competing assignees the first assignee to file prevails, even if that assignee's security interest was created *after* the security interest of another assignee, and even if she *knew* of the other assignee's security interest when she filed. [U.C.C. §9-312(5)]

(3) **Transactions covered:** [§683] The U.C.C. provisions apply both to outright sales of accounts of contract rights and to assignments for security purposes. However, recall that Article 9 does not apply to certain types of claims and certain types of transactions. (*See supra,* §§606-609.) In addition, under Article 9 a financing statement does not have to be filed to perfect certain security interests, such as an assignment of accounts that do not, alone or in conjunction with other assignments to the same assignee, transfer a significant part of the assignor's outstanding accounts. [U.C.C. §9-302(1)(e)] (Note, however, that a number of states, including California, have rejected this last exclusion.) Where there are successive assignments of a claim that is not covered by Article 9, priority between the successive assignees continues to be governed by the common law.

11. **Delegation of Duties**

a. **Nature of a delegation:** [§684] A delegation of a contractual duty is an appointment by a party to a contract of another person to perform the party's contractual duties.

(1) **Terminology:** [§685] The party who delegates a duty is called the *"obligor"* or the *"delegant."* The other original party to the original contract, to whom the delegated duty is owed, is called the *"obligee."* The party to whom the duty is delegated is called the *"delegee."* [Rest. 2d §318]

(2) **Novation:** [§686] A *delegation* should be distinguished from a *novation.* A novation is a three-party agreement under which the obligee agrees to completely discharge the original obligor and accept another in the obligor's place. Thus, a novation is a substitution of parties to the contract. A delegation does not have this substitutional effect. The original obligor remains liable for the performance of all obligations, although the delegee is also liable—both to the obligor, with whom the delegee has directly contracted, and to the obligee, who is a creditor beneficiary of the delegee's promise to perform the obligor's duty under the original contract.

b. **What duties are delegable:** [§687]   Any contractual duty can be delegated unless the obligee has a substantial interest in having the original obligor perform the duty personally. Thus, except where performance by a delegee would vary materially from the performance promised by the obligor, a contractual duty may be performed by a delegee without constituting a breach of contract. [Rest. 2d §318; U.C.C. §2-210(1)]

   (1) **Application**

        (a) **Personal services:** [§688]   The principal example of a nondelegable duty is a duty to perform *personal* services. If the contract requires performance by, for example, a painter, an author, a teacher, or a lawyer, the duty to render this performance cannot be delegated to another—no matter how competent—without the obligee's consent.

        (b) **Other contracts:** Most other contractual duties are delegable—for example—duties to manufacture or deliver goods, or to construct or repair buildings.

   (2) **Effect of contractual restriction on delegation:** [§689]   Provisions in a contract that limit either party's right to delegate duties are normally enforced. Such provisions evidence the parties' intent that the services involved are personal, so that performance by another would not constitute the bargained-for consideration. Unlike restrictions on assignment, restrictions on delegation do not clash with the policy in favor of free alienability.

c. **Effect of valid delegation of duties:** [§690]   A valid delegation of duties does not excuse the delegant from his duty to perform. However, as between the delegant and the delegee, the delegation places the primary responsibility to perform on the delegee. The delegant becomes secondarily liable—as surety—for performance of the duty. [Crane Ice Cream Co. v. Terminal Freezing & Heating Co., 128 A. 280 (Md. 1925)]

   (1) **Compare—assignment of rights:** [§691]   Contrast this rule with the effect of a valid assignment of rights, which operates to extinguish the rights of the assignor and set those rights up entirely in the assignee.

   (2) **U.C.C.—right of obligee to demand assurance:** [§692]   In contracts for the sale of goods, a delegation of performance entitles the obligee to demand assurances of performance from the delegee. [U.C.C. §2-210(5); *see* Sales Summary]

d. **Effect of attempt to delegate nondelegable duty:** [§693]   An *attempt* to delegate a nondelegable duty is not a breach of contract, because the original obligor (the delegant) remains liable for performance in any event. However, if the original obligor indicates to the obligee that he will not perform personally, that may be a sufficient repudiation of the obligor's duties under the contract to constitute an anticipatory breach of contract (*see* further discussion, *infra*, §§792 *et seq.*).

e. **Rights of the obligee against the delegee**

(1) **Promise to assume duties:** [§694]   Usually, as part of a delegation of duties the delegee expressly or impliedly promises the delegant that he will perform the duties owed by the obligor/delegant to the obligee. Such a promise constitutes a typical assumption agreement (*see* §593, *supra*), in which the obligee is a creditor beneficiary of the delegee's promise, and therefore may sue the delegee for nonperformance.

(2) **Implied assumption of duties:** [§695]   In some cases, one party to a contract simply "assigns" the contract to another, who does not expressly agree to perform the assignor's duties under the contract. The question then arises whether the courts should imply a promise by the assignee of the contract to perform the assignor's duties from the fact that the assignee has accepted benefits under the contract.

(a) **Traditional view:** [§696]   The traditional view, associated with *Langel v. Betz*, 250 N.Y. 159 (1928), which involved the assignment of a contract for the sale of land, was that the mere acceptance by an assignee of benefits under the assigned contract was not sufficient to imply a promise by the assignee that he would perform the assignor's duties under the contract.

(b) **Modern view:** [§697]   The trend of modern authority today is the other way. A growing number of courts, and the Restatement, hold that where a contract that is wholly or partially executory on both sides is assigned, the assignment is normally to be construed as a delegation, and acceptance of the assignment is normally to be construed as acceptance of the delegation, *i.e.*, as an assumption of duties under the contract. The result is the same, therefore, as if the assignee had expressly assumed the duties; *i.e.*, she is liable to both the assignor and the obligee in the event of nonperformance.

1) **Rationale:** Absent evidence to the contrary, it is the probable intent of the assignor and assignee in such cases that the assignee bear the burdens, as well as receive the benefits, of the contract. [Rest. 2d §328; Imperial Refining Co. v. Kanotex Refining Co., 29 F.2d 193 (8th Cir. 1928)]

a) **Note:** In deference to *Langel v. Betz*, *supra*, Restatement Second provides that "the ALI expresses no opinion as to whether the general rule Restatement Second adopts (that an assignee of a contract impliedly promises to perform the duties thereunder) applies to land-sale contracts. [Rest. 2d §328]

2) **U.C.C.:** [§698]   The modern view is adopted in the U.C.C. Section 2-210(4) provides that an assignment of "the contract," or of "all my rights under the contract," or an assignment in similar general terms, is an assignment of rights and, unless the language or the circumstances indicate the contrary—as where the assignment

is for security—is also a delegation of performance of the duties of the assignor, and that the acceptance of the assignment by the assignee constitutes a promise by the assignee to perform those duties. This promise is enforceable either by the obligee under the original contract, or by the assignor.

(3) **Effect of tender by delegee:** [§699]   If duties are delegable, and a delegee makes a satisfactory tender of performance to the obligee, the latter must accept it or the duty is discharged.

V. PERFORMANCE AND BREACH

chapter approach

If a contract has been formed and has consideration, and there are no defenses to formation, you should ask:

1. Did a party fail to perform in *good faith*, even though she did not violate the literal terms of the contract?

2. If one party failed to perform, were there any *express* conditions to that party's performance? If so, were the conditions fulfilled? If not, was fulfillment of the conditions excused?

3. Was there any *implied* condition to performance by the nonperforming party? In particular, was the other party required to have rendered performance, or to have made a tender of performance before the nonperforming party came under a duty to perform?

4. If a party who was required to perform first did not perform *perfectly*, did he nevertheless perform substantially? If so, he may be able to sue on the contract.

5. If a party to the contract who was required to perform first did not perform substantially, was the *contract divisible*? If so, performance of part of the contract may allow recovery as to that part.

6. If *both* parties failed to perform, was one party's failure to perform justified because the other party had committed a material breach?

7. Did a party *repudiate* the contract, even though the time for that party's performance had not yet arrived? If so, the other party might be able to bring suit under the doctrine of anticipatory breach.

8. Did it appear that a party would be *unable* to perform, even though the time for performance had not arrived and that party had not repudiated? If so, the other party might be entitled to assurances that performance would occur.

9. Was a failure to perform excused by *impossibility* or *frustration*?

10. Was the contract *discharged* by a mutual rescission, a release, an accord and satisfaction, or acceptance of a full-payment check?

A. OBLIGATION TO PERFORM IN GOOD FAITH

1. **In General:** [§700]   Under modern contract law, each party has an obligation to perform in good faith. For example, U.C.C. section 1-203 provides that "Every contract or duty within this Act imposes an obligation of good faith in its performance or enforcement." This concept permeates the entire U.C.C. Similarly, Restatement Second

section 205 provides that "Every contract imposes upon each party a duty of good faith and fair dealing in its performance and its enforcement." Under the obligation to perform in good faith, a party who does not breach any *explicit* provision of an agreement may nevertheless have breached its duty of good faith.

2. **What Constitutes Good Faith?** [§701]   Exactly what constitutes good faith is not always so clear. U.C.C. Article 1 ("General Provisions"), section 1-201(19), defines good faith to mean "honesty in fact in the conduct or transaction concerned." However, U.C.C. Article 2 ("Sales"), section 2-103(1)(b), provides that "unless the context otherwise requires . . . 'good faith' *in the case of a merchant* means honesty in fact *and* the observance of reasonable commercial standards of fair dealing in the trade." (Emphasis added.) The Comment to Restatement Second section 205 states: "Good faith performance or enforcement of a contract emphasizes faithfulness to an agreed common purpose and consistency with the justified expectations of the other party. It excludes a variety of types of conduct characterized as involving 'bad faith' because they violate community standards of decency, fairness or reasonableness. . . . A complete catalogue of types of bad faith is impossible, but the following types are among those which have been recognized in judicial decisions: evasion of the spirit of the bargain, lack of diligence and slacking off, willful rendering of imperfect performance, abuse of power to specify terms, and interference with or failure to cooperate in the other party's performance."

   a. **Example:** S agreed to sell four houses to B for $800,000. As B knew, S did not own the houses, but instead intended to purchase them at a foreclosure sale. B then attended the foreclosure sale herself and outbid S for the houses, acquiring them for $780,000. By entering into the contract with S to purchase property that B knew S would have to purchase at the foreclosure sale, B impliedly agreed that she would do nothing to prevent S from acquiring the property at the sale. Presumably, if B had not interfered, S could have purchased the houses for the same price that B paid. S would then have been able to sell the houses to B under the contract. B has not acted in good faith, and S is entitled to damages of $20,000, representing the difference between the contract price and the amount B paid at the foreclosure sale, which is the amount S would presumptively have paid if B had not outbid him.

   b. **Compare:** S promises to sell 1,000 bales of hemp to B, delivery to be made in six months. S contemplates obtaining the hemp on the open market. During the interim, B buys large amounts of hemp from other sources. B's large purchases drive up the market price and make it difficult for S to obtain the 1,000 bales ordered. B has not acted in bad faith, because it is reasonably to be anticipated that a purchaser will buy from other sources of supply. [Iron Trade Products Co. v. Wilkoff Co., 116 A. 150 (Pa. 1922)]

B. EXPRESS CONDITIONS

1. **In General:** [§702]   A contract may expressly provide that a party does not come under a duty of performance unless some condition is fulfilled. In such a case, the party's failure to render performance will normally be justified if the condition was not fulfilled.

2. **Definitions**

a. **Condition:** [§703]   For contract law purposes, the term "condition" normally means either (i) a state of events that must occur or fail to occur before a party's performance under a contract comes due, or (ii) a state of events whose occurrence or nonoccurrence releases a party from its duty to render performance under a contract.

b. **Express condition:** [§704]   The term "express condition" normally refers to an *explicit contractual provision* providing that a described state of events must occur or fail to occur, before a party's performance under a contract comes due, or an explicit contractual provision providing that if a described state of events occurs or fails to occur a party will be released from its duty to render performance under a contract. To put this differently, an express condition is an express statement in the contract providing either (i) that a party to the contract does not come under a duty to perform unless some state of events occurs or fails to occur; or (ii) that if some state of events occurs or fails to occur, the obligation of a party to perform one or more of his duties under the contract is suspended or terminated.

c. **Usage:** [§705]   In strict usage, the term "condition" refers only to states of the world, and the term "express condition" refers to contractual provisions. In general legal usage, however, the term "condition" is often used to refer to contractual provisions as well as states of the world, and this latter usage will sometimes be followed in this book.

3. **Express Conditions and Promises Distinguished**

a. **In general:** [§706]   A *promise* is an undertaking to perform or refrain from performing some designated act. An *express condition* is a provision whose fulfillment creates or extinguishes a duty to perform on the part of a promisor under a contract.

b. **Differences in legal effect of promises and conditions**

(1) **Breach and liability:** [§707]   An unexcused failure to perform a promise is always a breach of contract and always gives rise to liability, however minimal. Nonfulfillment of a condition is *not* a breach of contract, and does not give rise to liability.

(2) **Excuse of performance:** [§708]   Breach of a promise by one party may or may not excuse the other party's duty to perform under the contract. Nonfulfillment of a condition normally will excuse a duty to perform that was subject to the condition.

(3) **Interrelation of conditions and promises:** [§709]   If a party's promise to perform is subject to an express condition, there can be no breach of contract by that party until the condition has been fulfilled.

(4) **Example:** A contracts to loan B $50,000 on June 1 if the market value of B's gold-mine stock equals $100,000 on that date. The attainment by the

stock of a market value of $100,000 on June 1 is an express condition to A's duty to loan the money. If the state of affairs specified in the express condition occurs (*i.e.*, if the stock has a market value of $100,000 on June 1), A's duty to perform comes due, so that if A fails to loan the money, she will be liable for breach. If the state of affairs specified in the express condition does not occur, A's duty to perform does not come due and will never arise; *i.e.*, unless the gold-mine stock has a market value of $100,000 on June 1, A is under no duty to loan B any money. But because the provision concerning the value of B's stock was a condition and not a promise, the failure of B's stock to have a market value of $100,000 on June 1 is not a breach of contract and does not give rise to liability.

4. **Reasons for Using Express Conditions:** [§710]   Why would parties use an express condition rather than a promise? In some cases, it is because the relevant party is not willing to promise that the state of events in question will occur. For example, in the last example, neither A nor B may be willing to promise that the stock will have a value of $100,000 on June 1. Another possible reason for using express conditions rather than promises is to avoid the doctrine of substantial performance. (*See infra*, §§759-771.) Under that doctrine, if A promises some performance to B, A can sue B even if he, A, has performed his promise only **substantially** (rather than perfectly). A slight deviation from the promise renders A liable to B for damages, but might not prevent A from insisting on B's performance. On the other hand, if the contract states expressly that B shall incur no obligation to A unless A's performance is perfect or meets some other stated criterion, then B will not be liable under the contract if A performs only substantially, unless the condition is excused. (*See infra*, §§728-736.)

5. **Interpretation of a Provision as Express Condition or Promise:** [§711]   The determination whether a particular contractual provision is an express condition or a promise—or both—is of far-reaching importance. Such a determination may control whether one of the parties is in breach of contract, and will fix the rights and duties of the parties under the contract.

   a. **Parties' intent controls:** [§712]   Ordinarily, it is not difficult to determine whether a particular provision is a promise or an express condition. The issue depends on the parties' intent, and the words used by the parties will indicate that intent. However, cases may arise where the contract language is ambiguous and the court must interpret a provision to determine whether the parties intended a specified state of affairs in the contract to be (i) an undertaking by a party, so that it constitutes a promise, or (ii) to make a promise conditional, so that it constitutes an express condition.

      (1) **Example:** B enters into a contract to buy S's car. The contract provides, "it being understood that the car must be capable of a speed of 125 miles per hour." S's car cannot attain that speed. If the speed term is a condition, the failure of the car to reach 125 miles per hour discharges B's duty to buy the car, but does not give rise to any cause of action against S. If the speed term was a promise by S, the failure of the car to reach 125 miles per hour affords B an action against S for breach of contract.

b. **Where parties' intent unclear:** [§713] There is no stock formula to resolve ambiguities concerning whether a given provision is a promise or a condition. The ultimate test is the intention of the contracting parties, and each case therefore must be decided on its own facts. However, the following factors should be considered:

(1) **Words used:** [§714] Words such as "provided," "if," and "when" usually indicate that an express condition rather than a promise was intended. Words such as "promise" and "agree" usually indicate a promise.

(a) **Note:** Words by themselves might not be determinative.

1) **Example:** Suppose C Insurance Company issues a policy to O, insuring O's house against fire, and one of the policy provisions reads: "Insured *agrees* not to keep gasoline on the premises." Although phrased in terms of a promise, the provision is really a *condition* of the insurance. C would have no cause of action against O for breach of contract because O kept gasoline on the premises, but O's doing so would constitute a failure of the condition upon which C had agreed to insure, and would therefore excuse C's duty to pay in the event of a loss by fire attributable to the gasoline.

2) **Compare:** A contract provision that "all obligations hereunder are conditional upon submitting the matter to arbitration in the event of a dispute" might be interpreted as an enforceable promise by each party to arbitrate. [*See* Hamilton v. Home Insurance Co., 137 U.S. 370 (1890)]

(2) **In case of doubt, construe provisions as promises:** [§715] In case of doubt, contractual provisions will ordinarily be construed to be promises rather than express conditions.

(a) **Rationale:** Such a construction generally operates to give effect to the parties' expectations. First, failure to perform a promise will entitle the other party to damages, while failure to fulfill a condition imposes no liability. Second, failure to fulfill a condition normally excuses performance by the party whose performance is subject to the condition, and therefore effectively terminates the contract, which is a relatively drastic outcome. In contrast, a breach of promise may give rise only to an action for damages, without terminating the obligation to perform. [Green County v. Quinlan, 211 U.S. 582 (1909)] Thus if a contractual provision is an express condition, one party may lose his right to an agreed exchange after he has relied substantially on the expectation of that exchange by preparation or performance. When it is doubtful whether an agreement makes an event a condition of an obligor's duty, an interpretation is preferred that will reduce the risk of forfeiture. Interpreting a contractual provision as a promise decreases the risk of forfeiture; interpreting a contractual provision as a condition increases the risk of forfeiture.

(b) **Example:** In the car-sale example *supra,* §712 ("it being understood that the car must be capable of a speed of 125 miles per hour"), the provision would probably be interpreted as a promise rather than as an express condition. Therefore, if S fails to deliver a car that is capable of 125 miles per hour, B would be entitled to sue for breach of promise.

(c) **Example:** On May 29, A contracts with Trucker T to transport certain merchandise. A agrees to pay T $1,000 "provided T leaves Los Angeles with the goods immediately and delivers the goods to A's agent in New Orleans on June 1." T delays leaving Los Angeles, but is still able to deliver the goods to A's agent in New Orleans on June 1. Is A's obligation to pay the freight to T conditional on T's having left immediately on May 29? Unless it was shown that T's leaving "immediately" had some special importance to A, the provision would probably be construed as a promise, the nonperformance of which would entitle A to damages (if any) but would not excuse A's duty to pay the freight. A contrary interpretation might be appropriate if it appeared that T's leaving immediately had some special significance to A.

6. **Implication of a Promise from a Condition:** [§716]   In some cases, a contractual term that operates as an express condition also gives rise, *by implication,* to a promise relating to the condition.

   a. **Example:** On June 1, R agrees to assign a lease on Native American land to V for $13,000, payable that day. The assignment is "subject to approval by the Secretary of Interior." R promises to return the $13,000 if the Secretary does not give V approval by December 31. The Secretary does not approve the assignment by that date, but V did not press the Secretary for such approval. V sues for return of the $13,000. V is not entitled to the $13,000. Although the Secretary's approval is an express condition, it also gives rise, by implication, to a promise by V that he will seek the Secretary's approval in good faith.

7. **Provision Both Promise and Express Condition:** [§717]   In some cases, a provision may be both a promise and a condition—*i.e.*, a party may commit (promise) to bring about a given state of events, and the contract containing that commitment may also expressly state that the other party's duty to perform under the contract is conditioned on the occurrence of the state of events.

   a. **Example:** Trucker T promises to get A's goods to New Orleans by June 1, and the contract expressly provides that A will have no duty to pay T any of the freight unless the goods arrive by that time. Getting the goods to New Orleans by June 1 is both a promise by T and an express condition to A's liability.

8. **Conditions Precedent and Conditions Subsequent**

   a. **Conditions precedent:** [§718]   A "condition precedent" is a condition that must occur *before* a party has a duty to render performance under a contract.

   b. **Conditions subsequent:** [§719]   A "condition subsequent" is a condition in which occurrence or nonoccurrence of the relevant state of events *extinguishes* or *terminates* a duty to perform that had previously arisen. For example, assume E agrees to work for R for a specified period unless E is admitted to law school during that period. E's duty to remain in R's employ is subject to the condition subsequent that she not be admitted to law school. [*See* Hartman v. San Pedro Commercial Co., 66 Cal. App. 2d 935 (1944)]

c. **True conditions subsequent vs. conditions subsequent in form only:** [§720] True conditions subsequent are rare. Many provisions are *worded* as conditions subsequent *in form*, but are conditions precedent in *substance.*

   (1) **Example:** C Insurance Company insures P against loss by fire. The policy provides, "any liability of the insurer under this policy is discharged if either (i) proof of loss is not submitted within 30 days after the accident, or (ii) suit is not brought against the insurer for the claimed loss within 12 months from the date of accident." The proof-of-loss provision is a condition subsequent in form, but in substance it is a condition precedent to the insurer's duty to pay, because that duty does not arise unless and until a proof of loss is filed within 30 days after the accident. In contrast, the provision requiring suit within 12 months is a true condition subsequent. This condition has the effect of a private statute of limitations. The insurer's duty to pay arises when the proof of loss is submitted, but if the suit is not brought within 12 months, the duty is effectively discharged. [Brandyce v. Glob & Rutgers Fire Insurance Co., 252 N.Y. 69 (1929)]

d. **Procedural effect of condition subsequent:** [§721] A plaintiff is normally required to allege in his complaint, and to prove, that all conditions precedent to the defendant's duties have occurred or that there is some excuse for the nonoccurrence of such conditions. That is, the burden of pleading and burden of proof of the occurrence of conditions *precedent* is generally on the plaintiff. In contrast, the burden of pleading and the burden of proof of the occurrence of conditions *subsequent* is generally on the defendant.

   (1) **Note:** Statutes in many jurisdictions provide that in pleading the occurrence of conditions precedent, it is sufficient to allege generally that all such conditions have occurred. The defendant then has the burden of denying, specifically and with particularity, any condition precedent that he alleges has not occurred. [*See, e.g.,* Fed. R. Civ. P. 9(c)]

9. **Conditions of Satisfaction**

a. **Performance to satisfaction of promisor as condition precedent to promisor's duty to perform:** [§722] Assume A promises to paint B's house, and B promises to pay A $1,000 provided B is "satisfied with the work done." Because B's satisfaction is a condition precedent, B is not under a duty to pay unless she is satisfied. The problem is how B's satisfaction is to be measured. In particular, the problem is whether B's *personal* satisfaction is required. The modern trend is to construe a provision requiring the promisor's satisfaction according to the subject matter of the contract.

(1) **Subject matter involves mechanical fitness, utility, or marketability:** [§723] In contracts involving mechanical fitness, utility, or marketability (*e.g.*, construction or manufacturing contracts), a condition of satisfaction is interpreted to be fulfilled by a performance that would satisfy a *reasonable person.* It is therefore immaterial that the promisor was not personally satisfied if a reasonable person would have accepted and approved the performance tendered. [Duplex Safety Boiler Co. v. Garden, 101 N.Y. 387 (1886)]

(2) **Subject matter involves personal taste or judgment:** [§724] On the other hand, where the contract involves personal taste or personal judgment, a condition of satisfaction is interpreted to be fulfilled only if the promisor is personally satisfied. For example, contracts for portraits, for dental work, or for tailoring all require the promisor's personal satisfaction. [Mattei v. Hopper, 51 Cal. 2d 119 (1958)]

    (a) **Lack of satisfaction must be honest and in good faith:** [§725] However, even where a condition requires personal satisfaction, the condition will fail to be fulfilled only if the promisor's lack of satisfaction is honest and in good faith. Therefore, if the promisor refused to examine the promisee's performance or otherwise rejected the performance in bad faith, the condition of satisfaction will be excused. [Williams v. Hirshorn, 103 A. 989 (N.J. 1918)]

        1) **Comment:** Although technically the reasonableness, as opposed to the honesty, of the promisor's dissatisfaction is irrelevant if the subject matter of the contract involves personal taste or judgment, a lack of reasonability is *evidence* that the promisor's dissatisfaction was not in good faith. [Mattei v. Hopper, *supra*]

  b. **Performance to the satisfaction of a third person:** [§726] In many contracts, an express condition requires the satisfaction of a third person rather than a party to the contract. In particular, construction contracts often include a condition requiring the satisfaction of the owner's architect or engineer. When the satisfaction of a third person is a condition, most courts take the position that the condition requires the personal satisfaction of the third person. As in the case where a party's personal satisfaction is required, however, a condition that requires a third person's personal satisfaction will fail to be fulfilled only if the person's dissatisfaction is honest and in good faith. [Thompson-Starrett Co. v. La Belle Iron Works, 17 F.2d 536 (2d Cir. 1927)] Moreover, under a minority view, such a condition is excused if the third person acted under a gross mistake. [Rest. 2d §227]

10. **Conditions Relating to Time of Payment:** [§727] Frequently a contract provides that payment is to be made upon the occurrence of a certain event. For example, Contractor agrees to pay Subcontractor for Subcontractor's work "five days after Owner shall have paid Contractor therefor." This kind of provision appears on its face to make the occurrence of the designated event (in the example, payment by the Owner) a condition to payment by the promisor. However, the courts distinguish, in such cases, between (i) provisions that should be interpreted as a promise to pay that is enforceable only if the condition has occurred and (ii) provisions that should be inter-

preted as an unconditional promise to pay, with payment **postponed** until occurrence of the event designating the time of payment. If the second interpretation is given, the courts hold that if the event designating the time of payment does not occur, payment must nevertheless be made within a reasonable time.

a. **Example:** Contractor agrees to pay Subcontractor "as funds are received by Contractor from Owner." Most courts hold that such a provision falls into the second category, so that Contractor must pay Subcontractor even if Owner becomes insolvent. [*See, e.g.,* J. Dyer Co. v. Bishop International Engineering Co., 303 F.2d 655 (6th Cir. 1962); *but see* Mascioni v. Miller, Inc., 261 N.Y. 1 (1933)—contra]

   (1) **Rationale:** In the absence of a special contractual provision, the insolvency of an owner would not be a defense to a claim by a subcontractor against a contractor. The parties can change that result by contract, but the court will not construe a contractual provision to change the result unless the provision does so very explicitly.

11. **Excuse of Express Conditions:** [§728]   Normally, there is no obligation to perform a contractual duty unless all applicable express conditions have been fulfilled. In some cases, however, a condition may be **excused**, so that a duty must be performed despite the fact that the condition has not been fulfilled.

   a. **Excuse of condition by prevention or hindrance:** [§729]   A condition will be excused if the party favored by the condition wrongfully prevents or hinders the fulfillment of the condition. A party to a contract cannot take advantage of his own wrongful conduct to escape liability under the contract.

      (1) **Example:** C contracts to build a house for O, and O promises to pay C $40,000 for the house "on presentation of a certificate of completion from my architect, A." Presentation of the certificate is a condition to O's duty to pay. C finishes the house, but O improperly bribes A not to give the certificate of completion. The condition is excused.

      (2) **Example:** A has given B an option. It is a condition to the exercise of the option that B "tender the purchase price to A at A's office during business hours on January 15." If A goes into hiding or otherwise refuses to see B on the date set, the condition is excused. [Unatin 7-Up Co. v. Solomon, 39 A.2d 835 (Pa. 1944)]

      (3) **Element of "wrongfulness":** [§730]   To excuse a condition, the prevention or hindrance must be wrongful. This does not require a showing of bad faith or malice. Rather, it essentially means that in light of the terms of the contract, the objective of the contract, and the circumstances, the other party would not have reasonably anticipated the type of prevention or hindrance that occurred.

      (4) **Termination of a business:** [§731]   Many contracts are conditioned on the continued operation of a business. In such a case, whether closing down the business constitutes wrongful prevention, and therefore excuses the condition, depends on the type of contract involved and the reason for the closing.

(a) **Requirements and output contracts:** [§732]   Assume A contracts to sell her factory's output to B for the next five years. It is a condition to A's duty to perform that her factory *has* output. Suppose that one year after the contract is made, A closes down the factory. Is the condition that A's factory have output excused? Most courts hold that the answer depends on whether A had valid economic reasons for the closing *other than* losses resulting from her contract with B. [Neofotistos v. Harvard Brewing Co., 171 N.E.2d 865 (Mass. 1961)]   The Comment to U.C.C. section 2-306 states, "A shut-down by a requirements buyer for lack of orders might be permissible when a shut-down merely to curtail losses would not."

(b) **Agreements conditioned on "profits":** [§733]   Similarly, if a contract between A and B requires A to pay B a designated share of the profits from A's business, the existence of profits from the business is a condition to A's obligation. What if A sells the business?

　　1) **Example:** S sells his factory to B for $100,000 plus an additional $25,000 if B makes any profit from the business in the first year of operation. Prior to the expiration of one year, B sells the business. The condition of having made a profit during the year is excused. B is liable for the additional $25,000 if S can show that the value of the business was $25,000 greater than the amount B paid for it. [Du Pont De Nemours Powder Co. v. Schlottman, 218 F. 353 (2d Cir. 1914)]

b. **Waiver:** [§734]   A party by words or conduct may waive his right to insist on the fulfillment of a condition upon which his duty of performance depends. This subject is discussed *supra,* at §§127-129.

c. **Impossibility:** [§735]   Impossibility or impracticability excuses the fulfillment of a condition if fulfillment of the condition is not a material part of the agreed exchange and forfeiture would otherwise result. (For further discussion of the doctrine of impossibility/impracticability, *see infra,* §§810-826.)

(1) **Example:** A, an insurance company, issues to B a policy of accidental injury insurance, which provides that notice within 14 days of an accident is a condition of A's duty. B is injured as a result of an accident covered by the policy but is so mentally deranged that he is unable to give notice for 20 days. B gives notice as soon as he is able. Since the giving of notice within 14 days is not a material part of the agreed exchange, and forfeiture would otherwise result, the nonoccurrence of the condition is excused and B has a claim against A under the policy. [Rest. 2d §271, Ill. 2]

d. **Forfeiture:** [§736]   If the nonfulfillment of a condition would cause a disproportionate forfeiture, fulfillment of the condition may be excused unless the fulfillment of the condition was a material part of the agreed exchange.

(1) **Example:** A, an ocean carrier, carries B's goods under a contract providing that it is a condition of A's liability for damages to cargo that "written notice

of claim for loss or damage must be given within 10 days after removal of goods." B's cargo is damaged during carriage, and A knows of this. On removal of the goods, B notes in writing on the delivery record that the cargo is damaged, and five days later informs A over the telephone of a claim for that damage, and invites A to participate in an inspection within the 10-day period. A inspects the goods within the period, but B does not give written notice of its claim until 25 days after removal of the goods. Since the purpose of requiring the condition of written notice is to alert the carrier and enable it to make a prompt investigation, and since this purpose had been served by the written notice of damage and the oral notice of claim, the court may excuse the nonoccurrence of the condition to the extent required to allow recovery by B. [Rest. 2d §229, Ill. 2]

C. IMPLIED CONDITIONS

1. **In General:** [§737]   Recall that for contract law purposes, a "condition" means either (i) a state of events that must occur or fail to occur before a party's performance under a contract comes due or (ii) a state of events whose occurrence or nonoccurrence releases a party from its duty to render performance under a contract. The term "express condition" normally refers to an *explicit provision* providing that a described state of events must occur or fail to occur before a party's performance under a contract comes due, or an explicit contractual provision providing that if a described state of events occurs or fails to occur, a party will be released from its duty to render performance under a contract. Often, it can be *implied* that the duty to render performance under a contract is conditional upon the occurrence of some state of events, even though the contract does not explicitly so state. In that case, there is said to be an "implied" or "constructive" condition that the relevant state of events must occur before the performance of one or both parties comes due.

2. **Implied Conditions of Performance:** [§738]   By far the most important and common type of implied condition to the duty of each party to a contract to render performance is that the *other party* has either rendered *its* performance or made a tender of its performance. For example, suppose A and B make a contract under which B will paint A's house by May 30, and A will pay B $3,000 on June 1. It is then an implied condition to A's duty to pay $3,000 that B shall have painted the house.

    a. **Dual effect:** Note the dual legal effect of B's failure to paint A's house by June 1: (i) The failure is a breach of contract, for which *B* will be liable in damages. (ii) The failure is nonfulfillment of an implied condition to *A's* duty to pay on June 1, so that A does not come under that duty.

3. **Implied Conditions of Cooperation and Notice:** [§739]   Conditions other than performance or tender by the other party may also be implied conditions. For example, implied conditions of cooperation and notice are common.

    a. **Implied condition of cooperation:** [§740]   Under an implied condition of cooperation, the obligation of one party to render performance is impliedly conditioned on the other party's cooperation in that performance.

(1) **Example:** A promises to deliver certain goods to the "No. 2 loading dock" of B's factory. It is an implied condition to A's duty to deliver the goods that such a loading dock exists, that the dock is reasonably accessible for making a delivery, and that B permits A to make the delivery at the dock.

b. **Implied condition of notice:** [§741] Often, it is a condition to one party's performance of a duty under a contract that the other party give him *notice* that the performance is due. A condition of notice is most commonly applied where a party could not reasonably be expected to know a fact that triggered the duty to perform unless such notice was given.

(1) **Example:** L leases a building to T and promises to maintain and repair the interior of the building as necessary. It is an implied condition to L's promise to repair that T will give L reasonable notification of the need for repairs and will permit L to enter to make the repairs. T therefore cannot sue L for failure to make a needed repair unless he has first notified L that the repair is required, and given T an opportunity to make the repair.

D. ORDER OF PERFORMANCE [§742]

As pointed out above, in many cases one party to a contract is not obliged to perform unless and until the party has completed or tendered her performance. Sometimes, a contract explicitly provides for the relative order, or sequence, of the parties' performances, so that it is clear which party's performance is an implied condition to the other's performance. Often, however, a contract does not explicitly provide for the order or sequence in which the performances are to occur. Contract law has developed a number of rules governing the issue of order of performance when a contract is not explicit on the subject. These rules are phrased in the language of conditions because they address the issue: Under what circumstance is the duty of performance of one party, A, conditional on the actual performance or tender of performance by the other party, B?

1. **Performance That Takes Time Is a Condition to Performance That Will Not Take Time:** [§743] If one party's performance will take some period of time, while the other's performance can be accomplished in a moment of time, the performance that takes time must occur first. Accordingly, completion of the performance that will take time is an implied condition to the duty to render the performance that will not take time.

   a. **Example:** A promises to paint B's house in consideration of B's promise to pay $3,000. The completion of A's performance (which will take time) is an implied condition to B's duty to pay (which will not take time).

   b. **Example:** A promises to serve as B's private secretary. B promises to pay $800 a month for A's services. The completion of A's performance each month is an implied condition to B's duty to pay A each month.

2. **Earlier Performance Is Condition to Later Performance:** [§744] If one party promises to perform at a date *prior* to that on which the other party promises to perform, the first party's performance is an implied condition to the other's duty to perform.

a. **Example:** A promises to deliver a horse to B on March 1, in return for B's promise to pay A $500 on April 1. A's delivery of the horse is an implied condition to B's duty to pay.

3. **Performances to Occur Simultaneously at Fixed Time—Conditions Concurrent:** [§745] If both performances can be rendered simultaneously or nearly simultaneously, and the contract fixes the *same time* for both performances, tender of performance by each party is an implied condition to the other party's duty to perform; *i.e.,* neither party is obliged to perform unless and until the other party tenders performance. In such cases, each party's performance is said to be an *implied condition concurrent* to performance by the other.

    a. **Example:** S contracts to sell her car to B for $10,000. The contract states that both the purchase price and the car are to be exchanged on July 1. Tender of each performance by each party is an implied condition concurrent to the other party's obligation to perform. If B fails to tender the purchase price on July 1, S's duty to deliver the car never arises. If S fails to tender the car on July 1, B's duty to pay never arises.

    b. **Effect:** The legal effect of conditions concurrent is much the same as that of other implied conditions. If the condition concurrent is fulfilled (*i.e.,* if tender is made by one party) the other party's duty to perform arises. If the condition concurrent is not fulfilled (*i.e.,* if tender is not made) the other party's duty never arises. Accordingly, in a sales contract that does not involve a credit term, there is ordinarily no breach of contract by the seller until the buyer tenders payment, and no breach of contract by the buyer until the seller tenders delivery. Tender by either party is sufficient to make the other party's duty to perform absolute; lack of tender means that the other party's duty does not arise.

4. **No Time Set For Either Performance and Performances Can Occur Simultaneously:** [§746] The same rule applies if no time is set for performance of either promise and the promises are capable of being performed simultaneously or nearly simultaneously. In such a case, tender of each performance by each party is an implied condition concurrent to the other party's duty to perform.

    a. **Example:** S contracts to sell her car to B for $10,000. No time is specified. Payment and delivery are conditions concurrent to each other.

5. **Time Set For One Performance But Not Other:** [§747] The same rule also applies if both promises can be rendered simultaneously or nearly simultaneously and a time is set for one party's performance but not for the other's.

    a. **Example:** On June 1, S promises to sell her car to B in consideration of B's promise to pay $2,000 for the car. No time is set for B's performance. Payment and delivery on June 1 are implied conditions concurrent to each other.

6. **Anticipatory Repudiation:** [§748] A performance or tender that would normally be an implied condition to the other party's performance or tender will be excused if the other party repudiates the contract prior to the time when performance was to occur.

a. **Rationale:** One purpose of this rule is to avoid forcing the innocent party to remain in readiness to perform, and to tender performance, on the date set in the contract.

b. **Ability to perform:** [§749] Although a party who is the victim of a repudiation does not have to make a tender, or hold himself ready to make a tender, he may be required to show that but for the repudiation he had the *ability* to perform.

(1) **Example:** A agrees to sell stock to B, delivery on July 1. On June 1, A repudiates. B can sue A without making a tender of payment, but B may be required to show that he had the financial ability to tender payment.

c. **Anticipatory repudiation as a breach:** [§750] In addition to excusing the nonrepudiating party from holding himself ready to perform and from tendering performance, the nonrepudiating party can normally sue the repudiating party for breach even if the time for performance has not yet arrived. This aspect of the doctrine of anticipatory repudiation (or "anticipatory breach"), as well as further details of the doctrine, are discussed in *infra*, at §§792-809.

7. **Prospective Inability to Perform:** [§751] Sometimes it becomes apparent, prior to the scheduled time of performance, that one party to a contract will be unable to perform when the time comes for her performance. This is known as "prospective inability to perform" or "prospective failure of performance." The prospective inability to perform of one party, A, excuses the other party, B, from holding himself ready to perform, rendering performance, or tendering performance, as an implied condition to A's duty to perform. (If A's prospective inability to perform is caused by A's *voluntary conduct*, it may also constitute an anticipatory breach, with an attendant immediate right of action for B. *See infra*, §792.)

a. **Example:** S enters into a contract to sell Blackacre to B on June 1 for $40,000. On May 25, S conveys the property to X. By her conduct in conveying Blackacre to X, S has made it appear that she will be unable to perform her promise to convey Blackacre to B on June 1. S's prospective inability to perform excuses the condition that B hold himself ready to perform, or make an actual tender, on June 1, in order to put S in breach of contract.

b. **Facts constituting prospective inability to perform:** [§752] The following recurring fact patterns are illustrative of a prospective inability to perform.

(1) **Vendor's conveyance or encumbrance of contracted-for property:** [§753] After contracting to sell land or goods to A, B conveys or mortgages the property to a third person, retaining no apparent right to reacquire the property before the date set for conveyance. B's conduct constitutes a prospective inability to perform. [Rest. 2d §264; James v. Burchell, 82 N.Y. 108 (1880)]

(2) **Promisor's making of an inconsistent contract with another:** [§754] The same result follows if the promisor makes a contract with another that is inconsistent with his contractual obligation to the promisee. [Rest. 1st §318(c)]

(a) **Example:** On June 1, M hires S as a sales representative, and S agrees to report to work on July 1. However, on June 2, S goes to work for another company under a one-year contract. By accepting such employment, S has made it appear that he will be unable to work for M. S's prospective inability to perform excuses M from holding herself ready to employ S.

(b) **Contracts not inconsistent:** [§755]   Where it is possible to render service to both the promisee and another, the fact that the promisor has entered into a contract with another is not a prospective inability to perform his contract with the promisee.

(3) **Insolvency:** [§756]   Insolvency or bankruptcy of a party to whom credit is to be extended under a contract does not constitute prospective inability to perform so as to excuse the solvent party's duty of performance. However, insolvency or bankruptcy may justify the solvent party in suspending performance until he has received either the remaining performance or an adequate assurance that the remaining performance will occur.

(a) **Example:** A promises to paint B's house on August 1, and B promises to pay A $1,000 on September 1. On July 15, A discovers that B is insolvent. A's duty to paint B's house on August 1 is not discharged, but A has the right to insist on either payment in cash on the date of performance or an adequate bond securing payment on September 1. [Hanna v. Florence Iron Co., 222 N.Y. 290 (1918)]

(b) **Goods:** [§757]   The U.C.C. specifically provides that in contracts for the sale of goods, insolvency of either party gives the other the right to demand assurances of performance before proceeding further with his own performance under the contract. [U.C.C. §2-609; *see* below]

(4) **U.C.C.:** [§758]   Under the U.C.C., either party to a contract for the sale of goods has the right to demand "adequate assurance of performance" from the other party if reasonable grounds exist for believing the other party's performance may not be tendered. Until such assurance is given, the first party has the right to suspend any peformance due *by* him. An unjustified failure to comply with a reasonable demand for assurance for a period exceeding 30 days constitutes a repudiation of the contract as a matter of law. [U.C.C. §2-609]

(a) **Restatement:** The Restatement takes the position that a comparable principle should apply to all contracts, not just contracts for the sale of goods. [Rest. 2d §251]

E.   DOCTRINE OF SUBSTANTIAL PERFORMANCE [§759]

As shown above, normally the occurrence of performance or tender by one of the parties to a contract, or by each party in the case of conditions concurrent, is an implied condition to the other party's duty to render performance. In other words, if A's performance is to come first, B does not come under a duty to perform until A has performed; if A and B are to perform simultaneously, neither A nor B comes under a duty to perform until the other tenders. However, an implied condition of prior or simultaneous performance will usually be satisfied by *substantial* performance, as opposed to perfect performance. In other words, if A's performance is a condition to B's performance, the condition will usually be satisfied by A's *substantial* performance. If that has occurred, B will come under a duty to perform even though A's performance is not perfect, unless perfect performance either is an *express* condition (*see supra*, §§702-705), or is required by some exception to the substantial performance doctrine. (Note also that if A has substantially performed, B can sue A for the damages resulting from the fact that A's performance was not perfect. *See infra*, §768.)

1. **Significance:** The significance of the substantial performance doctrine is that in cases where the doctrine is applicable, a party can bring suit on the contract as a plaintiff, for expectation damages (*see infra*, §841), even though he has breached the contract by not rendering a perfect performance.

   a. **Offset:** However, the defendant is entitled to offset any remedy against him by the amount of damages he incurred as a result of the plaintiff's breach.

2. **Rationale:** If A promises to build a house for B, and B promises to pay $40,000 for the house, the law implies that A's performance is a condition to B's duty to pay the contract price. But if A has done everything except to install three doorknobs or one light switch, it seems unfair—and not a necessary implication—to deny A contractual recovery, subject to an offset for damages.

3. **What Constitutes "Substantial" Performance?** [§760]   Whether a less than perfect performance is nevertheless "substantial," within the meaning of the substantial performance doctrine, is a question of fact, to be governed by the circumstances of each case. The test is whether the performance meets the essential purpose of the contract. [Plante v. Jacobs, 103 N.W.2d 296 (Wis. 1960)]   Among the factors to be considered are the extent of the contracted-for benefits that the innocent party has received, the extent to which damages will be an adequate compensation for the breach, the extent to which a forfeiture will occur if the doctrine is not applied, and the extent to which the breach was wrongful or in bad faith.

   a. **Willfulness:** [§761]   At one time, it was often stated that the doctrine of substantial performance was inapplicable if the plaintiff was guilty of a willful or intentional breach of contract. The modern view, however, is that even a conscious and intentional departure from the contract will not necessarily defeat recovery. Rather, willfullness is to be considered as one of several factors involved in deciding whether there has been substantial performance.

4. **Application**

   a. **Construction contracts:** [§762]   The doctrine of substantial performance has been applied primarily in cases involving construction contracts, where it would be unjust to allow an owner to retain the value of a building free of charge just because the contractor made some small deviation from the agreed specifications.

   b. **Contracts for the sale of goods—U.C.C.:** [§763]   In theory, the U.C.C. adopts a "perfect tender" rule, rather than the substantial performance doctrine, in cases involving contracts for the sale of goods. Under the perfect tender rule, substantial performance is insufficient for a seller of goods. Instead, under this rule the seller must make a tender of goods that conform "perfectly," rather than merely substantially, to the contract specifications in order to put the buyer under an obligation to take and pay for the goods. [U.C.C. §2-601]

(1) **Exceptions:** [§764] However, the U.C.C. makes a number of exceptions to the perfect-tender rule—so many, in fact, that when all is said and done there is little left to the rule.

    (a) **Time for performance not yet expired:** [§765] Under U.C.C. section 2-508(1), where a tender of goods is rejected because the goods do not conform to the contract, and the time for performance has not yet expired, the seller has the right to notify the buyer of an intention to cure, and then has the right to make a conforming delivery within the contract time.

    (b) **Installment contracts:** [§766] Under U.C.C. section 2-612, if a contract for the sale of goods is an installment contract (*i.e.*, a contract calling for periodic deliveries and payments), the buyer cannot reject an installment, even though the installment does not conform to the contract, if: (i) the nonconformity of the installment does not substantially impair the value of the whole contract; (ii) the nonconformity can be cured; and (iii) the seller gives adequate assurance of cure.

    (c) **Reasonable grounds for believing tender conforms:** [§767] Under U.C.C. section 2-508(2), even if the defect in goods cannot be cured within the contract time, and the contract is not an installment contract, the perfect tender rule is not applicable if the seller had reasonable grounds to believe the tender would be acceptable, despite the defect, with or without a money allowance. In such a case, the buyer can reject a nonconforming tender, but the seller can then notify the buyer of his intention to cure the defect, and if the seller retenders a conforming delivery within a reasonable time, the buyer must accept it.

5. **Damages:** [§768] As noted above, under the substantial performance doctrine, a party who has substantially performed is entitled to enforce the contract—that is, to sue for expectation damages (*see infra*, §841). However, the other party is entitled to an offset for damages resulting from the fact that the performance was not perfect. [Plante v. Jacobs, *supra*]

    a. **Cost of completion:** [§769] Normally, the measure of damages for the failure to perform perfectly is the amount it would cost to repair the deficiency in the performance, or to make the work conform to the contract. This measure is known as "cost of completion" damages. [23 A.L.R. 1436]

    b. **Diminution in value:** [§770] However, if repair or reconstruction would involve "substantial economic waste," or if cost-of-completion damages would be disproportionate to the end to be served, the measure of damages will be the amount by which the deficiency in the performance diminishes the value of the performance.

(1) **Example:** Builder and Owner make a contract under which Builder will construct a house for Owner for $350,000. One of the specifications of the contract is that Builder will use Acme plumbing pipes. Instead, Builder uses Baker plumbing pipes, which are functionally identical to Acme pipes. The problem does not come to light until construction is completed. The cost of completion (*i.e.*, the cost to remedy the defect) would be $200,000: $50,000 to tear apart the house to get at the pipes, and $150,000 to replace the pipes and repair the house. That measure of damage will not be awarded. Instead, damages will be the amount by which the use of Baker pipe diminishes the value of the building as compared to its value if Acme pipe had been used. [Jacob & Youngs, Inc. v. Kent, 230 N.Y. 239 (1921)]

6. **Remedy in Restitution:** [§771] Even if the breaching party has ***not*** rendered substantial performance, he may have a right to recover in restitution for the value of performance rendered to and retained by the innocent party. In theory, the recovery in restitution is measured by the benefit conferred, minus an offset for damages. In practice, however, the measure of restitutionary recovery where the performance is incomplete but readily remedial is usually the unpaid contract price less the cost of completion, up to the value of the benefit actually received by the defendant. This formula may often result in the same recovery as would be granted if there ***had*** been substantial performance.

F. DIVISIBLE CONTRACTS

1. **In General:** [§772] A contract is said to be divisible if it is possible to apportion the parties' performances into matching or corresponding pairs that the parties treat as equivalents.

   a. **Example:** A promises to build a garage for B for $10,000, a pool for $18,000, and a tennis court for $7,000, for a total price of $35,000. Unless circumstances indicate otherwise, the contract is divisible into three pairs of matched parts: building the garage and paying $10,000; building the pool and paying $18,000; and building the tennis court and paying $7,000.

   b. **Significance:** [§773] If a contract is divisible, a party who has performed one or more parts is entitled to collect the contract price for those parts, even though he breaches other parts.

      (1) **Note:** Because there is still one contract (even though it is divisible), the right to collect the contract price for the parts performed is subject to an offset for damages resulting from breach on the other parts.

   c. **"Entire" contract:** [§774] A contract that is not divisible is said to be "entire." To say that a contract is "entire" means only that the need to show substantial performance of the whole contract as a condition to bringing suit on the contract cannot be avoided by bringing suit on individual parts of the contract.

   d. **Employment contracts:** [§775] If an employment contract or a statute requires periodic salary payments (for example, $1,000 per month), courts usually hold the contract to be divisible. Therefore, if an employee breaches the contract he may nevertheless recover wages for each period he has completed, minus an offset for damages resulting from his breach. [Clark-Rice Corp. v. Waltham Bleachery & Dye Works, 166 N.E. 867 (Mass. 1929)]

G. MATERIAL VS. MINOR BREACH [§776]

An actual breach of contract, at the time performance is due, always gives rise to an immediate cause of action for *damages*. However, not every breach also *excuses the other party's duty of performance.* For example, if C has contracted to build a $100 million commercial building for A, and C puts the wrong doorknobs on some doors, C will be liable for damages, but A will not be excused from performing. Whether a breach by one party excuses the other party's duty of performance depends on whether the breach is *"material" or "minor."*

1. **Distinguishing Material from Minor Breach:** [§777]   There is no hard-and-fast line between what constitutes a material breach and what constitutes only a minor breach. Every case must be decided on its own facts.

   a. **Relevant factors:** [§778]   The following six factors are normally relevant to determining whether a breach is material or minor:

      (1) *The extent to which the breaching party has already performed.* A breach at the outset ("in limine") is more likely to be considered a material breach.

      (2) *Whether the breach was willful, negligent, or the result of purely innocent behavior.* A willful breach is much more likely to be held material.

      (3) *The extent of uncertainty* that the breaching party will perform the remainder of the contract.

      (4) *The extent to which, despite the breach, the nonbreaching party will obtain (or has obtained) the substantial benefit bargained for.*

      (5) *The extent to which the nonbreaching party can be adequately compensated* for the defective or incomplete performance through his right to damages.

      (6) *The degree of hardship* that would be imposed on the breaching party if it was held that the breach was material and that he therefore had no further rights under the contract.

   b. **Repudiation:** [§779]   A repudiation consists of words or conduct that a reasonable person would interpret as an expression of refusal to render any further performance. An act that would otherwise constitute only a minor breach will be treated as a material breach if accompanied by a repudiation. For example, if A is under a contractual duty to paint B's factory for eight hours a day for 10 days, and A paints only 7½ hours on the third day, that would probably in itself be only a minor breach. However, if A's action was coupled with an express repudiation of the balance of the contract, it would be treated as a material breach.

c. **Effect of parties' agreement:** [§780]   The contract itself may expressly or impliedly make the time, manner, or other detail of performance a matter of bargained-for importance as to one party or the other. If so, deviations from the agreed performance that otherwise would be regarded as only minor breaches will instead be considered material.

(1) **Example:** A promises to pay B $1,000 to paint A's house by June 1, it being understood that A has planned a wedding in the house for June 8. Under these circumstances, any delay past June 1 could be considered a material breach.

(2) **"Time is of the essence" provision:** [§781]   Most courts hold that where the contract contains a provision that "time is of the essence," even a slight delay in performance will constitute a material breach.

(a) **Liberal view:** [§782]   To avoid forfeitures, some courts hold that if the overall circumstances indicate that the date set for performance was not of great importance to the parties, a minor delay will not constitute a material breach even though the contract contains a provision that time is of the essence. [Katemis v. Westerlind, 120 Cal. App. 2d 537 (1953)]

2. **Effect of Material Breach:** [§783]   A material breach has two effects. First, it gives rise to an immediate cause of action for breach of the entire contract. Second, it excuses further performance by the innocent party.

3. **Effect of a Minor Breach:** [§784]   A minor breach of contract also gives rise to an immediate cause of action for whatever damages were caused by the breach. However, a minor breach does *not* give rise to a cause of action on the entire contract. A minor breach may *suspend, but it does not excuse,* the other party's duty of further performance. Therefore, if a breach is minor, the breaching party is still entitled to enforce the contract, subject to an offset for whatever damages resulted from the minor breach.

a. **Example:** A agrees to paint B's factory for eight hours a day for 10 days. On the third day, A paints only 7½ hours, but does not repudiate the contract. A would be liable for whatever damages B sustained as a result of the breach, but the breach would not give B the right to sue for breach of the entire contract or to terminate the contract, nor would it excuse B's duty to pay A subject to an offset for damages resulting from the breach.

4. **Response to Breach:** [§785]   Suppose that A and B have an ongoing contract. In the midst of the contract B commits a breach, but does not repudiate; on the contrary, B wants to continue performing. How may A respond?

a. **Material breach:** [§786]   If B's breach is material, A may (i) *sue B for damages* resulting from the breach but let the contract continue or (ii) *terminate* the contract and sue B for breach of the whole contract ("total breach").

b. **Minor breach:** [§787]   If B's breach is not material, A can sue B for damages resulting from the breach. However, A *cannot terminate* the contract. In fact, if A terminates the contract, A himself will be in total breach, and **B can sue A**. Therefore, a decision by A as to whether a breach by B is material or minor is fraught with danger, because if A guesses wrongly that the breach is material and terminates the contract, A will end up owing substantial damages to B.

5. **Material Breach vs. Substantial Performance:** [§788]   The concept of material breach bears an obvious relationship to the doctrine of substantial performance. Both ordinarily distinguish between what could colloquially be called "major" or "very important" breaches, on the one hand, and "minor" or "less important" breaches on the other. It is sometimes said that the two are the opposite sides of the same coin: If a party has substantially performed, then any breach he may have committed is not material; if a party has committed a material breach, his performance cannot be substantial. Although this view of material breach and substantial performance as mirror-image doctrines may hold true in many cases, it is not true in all cases, and it masks an important difference between the two concepts. This difference can be seen in the following example:

a. **Example:** A and B are parties to a contract that A has breached in some way. If A has generally, but not perfectly, completed his performance and B refuses to pay the contract price on the ground that A has committed some breach, A would try to invoke the doctrine of substantial performance. A's purpose in invoking the doctrine would be to enable him to sue B on the contract, for the contract price (minus damages resulting from his breach), rather than being remitted to a suit based on benefit conferred. In contrast, if, while A is still attempting to perform after committing some breach, B orders A to stop performing and terminates the contract on the ground of A's breach, A may argue that although he breached, the breach was not sufficiently serious to justify B's response (*i.e.*, the breach was not material). As a corollary, A would argue that because his breach was minor, B himself has committed material breach in terminating the contract. B, of course, would argue just the opposite: that A's breach was material and allowed B not only to terminate the contract but to sue A for total breach.

b. **Summary:** In short, the doctrine of substantial performance is usually invoked by a party who has breached the contract in some way but nevertheless has and wants to sue for the entire contract price—subject to an offset for damages—despite his own breach. In contrast, the concept of material breach is usually invoked when one party, A, has breached; the other party, B, has terminated on the ground of A's breach; and A argues that B had no right to terminate (and that B is himself in breach for terminating), while B argues that he did have a right to terminate, and furthermore that he can sue A for total breach.

   (1) **Substantial performance:** [§789]   To put this more generally, the doctrine of substantial performance concerns the question: When can a party who has breached a contract nevertheless bring suit under the contract to recover damages for nonpayment for the work that he has performed, and when is he instead limited to an action based on the other party's unjust enrichment?

   (2) **Material breach:** [§790]   Similarly, the concept of material breach concerns the questions: Can the victim of a given breach (i) invoke the sanction

of terminating the contract and (ii) bring suit for damages for breach of the whole contract ("total breach")? Or is the victim of breach (i) not permitted to invoke the sanction of termination, (ii) limited to an action for damages for "partial breach," and (iii) himself in breach if he tries to terminate the contract?

(3) **Significance:** [§791]   As a consequence of the difference between substantial performance and material breach, the concept of material breach may arise in cases where the doctrine of substantial performance would not. For example, suppose A commits a breach very early in his performance. If B terminates the contract, A could not invoke the doctrine of substantial performance because he has hardly performed at all. However, A may be able to invoke the concept of material breach and claim that his breach was insufficiently material to justify B's response of terminating the contract. Accordingly, a breach may be immaterial even if there is no substantial performance.

H. ANTICIPATORY BREACH [§792]

As described above, if either party to a contract, in advance of the time set for performance, *repudiates* the contract, the repudiation excuses the other party from holding himself ready to perform, rendering performance, or tendering performance. In addition, the innocent party may generally treat anticipatory repudiation as a *present material breach* of contract, and bring an immediate action for the entire value of the promised performance. [U.C.C. §2-610]

1. **Acts Sufficient:** [§793]   The repudiation need not be by *words*. A voluntary act that disables the promisor from performing will also constitute a repudiation (for example, the promisor's making inconsistent contracts with another; see *supra*, §754).

2. **Insistence on Terms Not Part of the Contract:** [§794]   Insistence upon terms that are not contained in a contract constitutes an anticipatory breach. Similarly, there is an anticipatory breach if a party to a contract demands a performance to which he has no right under the contract, and states that unless his demand is complied with he will not render his promised performance.

3. **Requirement of Unequivocal Repudiation:** [§795]   Only a positive, unconditional refusal to perform as promised in the contract will constitute an anticipatory repudiation. A mere expression by the promisor of "doubt" that he will be able to perform is not sufficient to constitute a repudiation. Such expressions may, however, constitute a prospective inability to perform, permitting the other party to suspend counterperformance. (*See supra*, §§751-758.)

   a. **Example:** A is under a contractual duty to buy 100 tons of coal per week from B for one year, beginning June 1. In August, A says to B, "Unless the demand for steel increases, I may stop buying coal under our contract after October." This is not a sufficient repudiation to constitute an anticipatory breach.

4. **Exception Where Nonrepudiating Party Has Completed Performance:** [§796] The doctrine of anticipatory breach does not apply where, at the time of repudiation,

the *only remaining duty of performance* is the duty of the repudiating party. These are referred to as cases where only a unilateral obligation remains. In such cases, an anticipatory repudiation does not give rise to an immediate cause of action for breach, and the innocent party must wait to sue until there is an actual breach at the time set for the other party's performance.

a. **Example:** O offers to pay A $1,000 in three installments, beginning on December 1, if A can increase O's sales 50% by June 1. A does so. On September 1, O says, "I'm not going to pay you under that contract." A has no immediate cause of action against O; he must wait until the installments become due.

b. **Example:** A promises to pay B $1,000 on July 1 in consideration of B's promise to paint A's house by June 15. B promises and completes the painting on time, but A repudiates on June 17. B has no cause of action until the payment is due.

c. **Compare:** S agrees to convey title to Blackacre to B on November 1, and B agrees to pay $5,000 upon receipt of the deed. On October 1, B repudiates. Here, S has an immediate cause of action for damages, because at the time of the repudiation duties were owed by S as well as by B.

d. **Narrower view of the exception:** [§797] Some authorities adopt a narrower view of this exception to the doctrine of anticipatory breach. Under this view, the doctrine is inapplicable only if the sole remaining duty of the repudiating party is to pay a sum of money. Under a still narrower view, the exception is applicable only if the sole remaining duty is to pay money in installments.

e. **Comment:** As a practical matter, the exception to the anticipatory breach rule for cases where only a unilateral obligation remains almost always arises in cases where the only unperformed duty is to pay money in installments. In many (though by no means all) of these cases, even though the promisee has no *duties* left to perform, the promisor's continuing duty remains subject to some *condition* or *contingency*. For example, the promise may be to make fixed payments to the plaintiff during his life or while he is totally disabled. In such cases, the exception can be explained on the ground that it may not be possible to know, at the time of the repudiation, how many installments must eventually be paid, because it may not be known how long the relevant condition will persist. An obvious problem caused by the exception is that the plaintiff may end up having to bring a series of lawsuits. In most cases, however, the defendant will probably conform its conduct to the court's decision, and thereafter make payments voluntarily. If the defendant does continue to withhold installments, even after an adverse judgment on the earlier installments, the courts are unlikely to require the plaintiff to keep bringing suits. For example, in such a case the court could issue a decree for specific performance ordering future installments to be paid as they fall due.

5. **Retraction:** [§798] The general rule is that a repudiating party may retract his repudiation at any time prior to the date set for his performance, unless the innocent party has either accepted the repudiation or has changed her position in detrimental reliance thereon. [U.C.C. §2-611(2); Clavan v. Herman, 131 A. 705 (Pa. 1926)]

a. **Example:** B repudiates her executory land sale contract with S. In reliance thereon, S sells the property to T. B cannot subsequently retract his repudiation and sue S for damages for nonperformance because S's reliance bars the retraction. [Rayburn v. Comstock, 45 N.W. 378 (Mich. 1890)]

6. **Date for Determining Damages**

a. **General rule:** [§799]   The general rule in cases of anticipatory repudiation is that where damages are measured by the difference between contract price and market price, market price is measured at the time required for performance under the contract and not the time of the anticipatory repudiation.

b. **U.C.C.:** [§800]   In the case of contracts for the sale of goods, which are governed by the U.C.C., there is some ambiguity as to how damages are measured for anticipatory breach, at least in the case of breach by the seller.

(1) **Breach by buyer:** [§801]   Under U.C.C. section 2-708, the measure of damages for repudiation by the *buyer* is the difference between contract price and "the market price *at the time and place for tender*." (Emphasis added.)

(2) **Breach by seller:** [§802]   In the case of breach by the seller, U.C.C. section 2-712(1) provides that "After a breach [including a repudiation]   the buyer may 'cover' by making in good faith and without unreasonable delay any reasonable purchase of or contract to purchase goods in substitution for those due from the seller." U.C.C. section 2-713(1) provides that "the measure of damages for . . . repudiation by the seller is the difference between the market price at the time when the buyer learned of the breach and the contract price."

(a) **Majority view:** [§803]   The majority view is that the phrase "learned of the breach" in section 2-713(1) means "learned of the *repudiation*." Under this view, in the case of a breach by the seller in a contract for the sale of goods the buyer's damages are measured by the difference between the contract price and the market price *at the time the buyer learned of the repudiation.*

(b) **Minority view:** [§804]   Under a minority view, the phrase "learned of the breach" in section 2-713(1) means "learned at the time the seller's performance *was due* that the seller would not perform." Under this view, the buyer's damages are measured by the difference between the contract price and the market price *at the time tender* by the seller was required under the contract.

(c) **Alternative view:** [§805]   Under still a third view, the phrase "learned of the breach" in U.C.C. section 2-713(1) must be read in light of the phrase "without unreasonable delay" in U.C.C. section 2-712 (the "cover" provision), *supra*. Under this view, the buyer's damages are measured by the difference between the contract price and the market price a *reasonable time after the buyer learned of the breach*. (A "reasonable time," in this context, would be the time required for the buyer to find an alternative source of supply in the market. In a rapidly changing market, this might be almost the same as the time at which the buyer learns of the breach.)

7. **Duty of Innocent Party to Mitigate Damages:** [§806] The innocent party in the case of an anticipatory repudiation owes a duty to mitigate the damages arising from the repudiation. If she fails to do so, she is not entitled to recover the damages she could have otherwise avoided. If the innocent party is in the midst of rendering performance when the other party repudiates, she must *stop* unless doing so would involve greater damages than completing the performance (as where leaving goods half-manufactured would result in total waste). If the innocent party is supposed to *receive* performance, she must look elsewhere for the performance that was due under the contract, if failing to do so would increase her damages.

8. **Prospective Inability to Perform:** [§807] If one party's prospective inability to perform (*see supra,* §§751-758) is caused by her *voluntary conduct*, it may constitute an anticipatory breach, with an attendant immediate right of action for the other party.

    a. **U.C.C.:** [§808] Under the U.C.C., either party to a contract for the sale of goods has the right to demand "adequate assurance of performance" from the other party if reasonable grounds exist for believing the other party's performance might not be tendered. This rule applies even where the prospective inability to perform is not the result of the promisor's voluntary act (for example, if a buyer learns that the seller's source of supply is on strike). Until such assurance is given, the first party has the right to suspend any performance due by him. Accordingly, in the coal example (*supra,* §795) where A says, "Unless the demand for steel increases, I may stop buying coal under our contract after October," even though A's statement is not an anticipatory breach, it may give B grounds for suspending performance and demanding assurance. An unjustified failure to comply with a demand for assurances for a period exceeding 30 days constitutes a repudiation of the contract as a matter of law. [U.C.C. §2-609]

    b. **Restatement:** [§809] The Restatement takes the position that comparable rules should apply to all contracts, not just contracts for the sale of goods. [Rest. 2d §251]

I. CHANGED CIRCUMSTANCES—IMPOSSIBILITY AND FRUSTRATION

1. **General Rule:** [§810] Performance of a contract will normally be excused if the performance has been made "impossible"—more accurately, impracticable—by the occurrence of an event whose nonoccurrence was a basic assumption on which the contract was made, unless the adversely affected party has explicitly or implicitly assumed the risk that the contingency might occur.

    a. **What constitutes impossibility?** [§811] At one time, it was commonly said that for a performance to be excused by changed circumstances the change had to be such as to render the performance "impossible." In practice, however, the courts have normally only required that the performance be rendered *impracticable*, and that the other elements of the general rule were fulfilled. The U.C.C.

has explicitly adopted the impracticability test for contracts for the sale of goods [U.C.C. §2-215], and modern cases now tend to adopt that approach. Therefore, the term *"impossibility,"* for purposes of contract law, *includes impracticability,* and should be so understood. Remember, however, that not every type of impossibility/impracticability is an excuse for nonperformance. The impracticability must involve the occurrence of an event whose nonoccurrence was *a basic assumption on which the contract was made, and the adversely affected party must not have assumed the risk of that event occurring.*

2. **Recurring Types of Impracticability Cases**

a. **Supervening illegality or act of government:** [§812]   A promisor's performance is excused if performance has become illegal due to a supervening change in the law after the time of contracting or due to some other act of government. [Rest. 1st §458]

(1) **Examples:** Examples of such supervening changes include new zoning ordinances or building laws [Cordes v. Miller, 39 Mich. 581 (1878)], and governmental embargoes on certain exports [Millar & Co. Ltd. v. Taylor & Co. Ltd., [1916] 1 K.B. 402].

b. **Supervening destruction or nonexistence of subject matter:** [§813]   A promisor's duty to perform is excused if the subject matter of the contract or the specified means for performance is destroyed or becomes nonexistent after the contract is entered into, without fault of the promisor. [Rest. 1st §460; *and see* U.C.C. §§2-613, 2-614]

(1) **Examples:** A contract to use an auditorium for entertainment purposes is discharged by the destruction of the auditorium. [Taylor v. Caldwell, [1863] 3 Best & S. 826] A contract to drive logs downstream is discharged if the river is too low to drive logs on. [Clarksville Land Co. v. Harriman, 44 A. 527 (N.H. 1895)]

c. **Specific source of supply contemplated:** [§814]   A seller's duty to furnish goods under a contract of sale may be excused by the failure of a particular source of supply that was contemplated or specified by both parties to the contract. For example, a contract to sell potatoes to be grown on specified land is discharged by failure of the crop. But if no particular land was either specified or contemplated by the parties, the promisor's duty to supply potatoes is not excused, even though the promisor intended subjectively to fulfill the contract from the crop which failed. [Anderson v. May, 52 N.W. 530 (Minn. 1892)]

(1) **Where seller is a middleman:** [§815]   Ordinarily, failure of a middleman's source of supply will not be a defense because ordinarily in a contract with a middleman no particular source of supply is contemplated by *both* parties. However, failure of a middleman's source of supply may excuse the seller *if*: (i) the source of supply is shown to have been contemplated or assumed by the parties at the time of contracting as the exclusive source of supply; and (ii) the seller has taken all due measures to assure himself that the supply will not fail. Therefore, a refusal by a middleman's exclusive

source to supply goods is not an excuse for a middleman who could have assured himself of supply by entering into a contract with the exclusive source, but failed to do so. [U.C.C. §2-619, comment 5; Canadian Industrial Alcohol Ltd. v. Dunbar Molasses Co., 258 N.Y. 194 (1932)]

d. **Construction contracts—destruction of work in process:** [§816] Suppose O engages C to build a house on her property at a designated location, and after C has performed most of the work, the building is accidentally destroyed by fire due to the fault of neither party. The general rule is that a contractor's duty to construct a building is *not* excused by destruction of the work in progress. Construction is not rendered impracticable because the contractor can still rebuild. If the contractor fails to rebuild, she will therefore be in breach of contract. Furthermore, she will not be permitted any recovery in restitution for the work that was destroyed, because no benefit has been conferred on the owner. [School District v. Dauchy, 25 Conn. 530 (1857)]

    (1) **Note:** However, the duty of the contractor to perform *on time* may be excused by destruction of the building. Thus, for example, a provision requiring the contractor to pay liquidated damages for delay (*see infra*, §§904-913) may be inoperative for whatever period is reasonably required to rebuild. [U.S. Fidelity & Guaranty Co. v. Parson, 112 So. 469 (Miss. 1927)]

e. **Contracts to repair—destruction of the premises to be repaired:** [§817] The result is different where a contractor is hired to renovate or repair an existing building, rather than build a new one. In such cases, where the building is destroyed by fire or other calamity, the contractor's duty to continue performance is excused, and to the extent that the contractor has already performed, it is allowed to recover in restitution for the reasonable value of the work done prior to the destruction of the building. [28 A.L.R.3d 788]

f. **Land sale contracts—destruction of improvements:** [§818] Under the traditional rule, a purchaser of real property is deemed to be the equitable owner of the real property from the time the contract is executed. As the equitable owner, the purchaser bears the risk of loss or destruction to improvements on the real property, so that destruction of improvements does not excuse the purchaser's duty to pay. However, a number of modern jurisdictions have changed the rule, so that the risk of such loss is on the seller until the closing or until change in possession. In these jurisdictions, destruction of the improvements prior to closing or change of possession excuses performance.

g. **Sale of goods—destruction of the goods:** [§819] Under the U.C.C., if a contract involves goods that were *identified when the contract was made*, then if the goods are destroyed without fault of either party and before the risk of loss passed, the contract is avoided. [U.C.C. §2-613] If goods are to be shipped to the buyer, the risk of loss passes to the buyer when the seller duly delivers the goods to the carrier, *unless* the contract requires the seller to deliver the goods at a particular destination, in which case the risk of loss passes when the goods are tendered to the buyer at that destination. If no shipment is involved, the risk of loss passes upon the buyer's receipt of the goods if the seller is a merchant; otherwise, the risk of loss passes to the buyer upon tender of delivery. [U.C.C. §2-509]

h. **Death or illness in personal service contracts:** [§820]   In the case of a contract to render or receive personal services, death or incapacitating illness of the person who was to render or receive the personal services excuses both parties from the duty to perform. For example, if A promises to paint B's picture, either A's or B's incapacitating illness would excuse both parties.

(1) **What constitutes "personal services"?** [§821]   The best test for whether services are "personal," within the meaning of this rule, is whether the right to receive the services could be validly assigned or the duty to perform the services could be validly delegated. (*See supra*, §§687-688.)

3. **Temporary Impracticability:** [§822]   Impracticability that is temporary rather than permanent merely *suspends* (rather than excuses) the promisor's duty while the impracticability continues. After the impracticability ceases, the duty reattaches if, *but only if*, it appears that performance thereafter would not substantially increase the burden on either party or make the performance different from that which was promised.

a. **Example:** The leading case on this point is *Autry v. Republic Productions,* 30 Cal. 2d 144 (1947). Here the court first held that the drafting of an actor into the Army to serve during 1942-1945 rendered the actor's performance of a motion-picture contract, which was to expire in 1943, temporarily impossible of performance. The court then concluded that the actor's duty to perform did not reattach upon his discharge from the Army, because in the interim there had been substantial changes in the value of the dollar and in tax laws, which would have imposed a material detriment on the actor, not contemplated by either party when the contract was signed in 1938.

4. **Partial Impracticability:** [§823]   If (i) the promisor's performance is rendered only partially impracticable, (ii) the remainder of performance is not made materially more difficult or disadvantageous thereby, and (iii) the promisor is still able to render substantial performance, the promisor remains bound to render the performance as so modified, and the promisee remains bound to accept it with an appropriate offset.

a. **Example:** Contractor agrees to build a house for Owner, using Acme pipe. After the contract is made, Acme Pipe Company goes out of business, and Acme pipe therefore cannot be obtained. The contractor's duty to use Acme pipe is excused, but the contractor remains under a duty to construct the house and use substituted pipe, and the owner is under a duty to pay for the house, subject to an offset for the change in pipe.

b. **U.C.C.:** [§824]   The U.C.C. adopts a counterpart of this principle in section 2-614(1): "(1) Where without fault of either party the agreed berthing, loading, or unloading facilities fail or an agreed type of carrier becomes unavailable or the agreed manner of delivery otherwise becomes commercially impracticable but a commercially reasonable substitute is available, such substitute performance must be tendered and accepted."

5. **Recovery in Restitution For Part Performance:** [§825]   If either party has rendered part performance prior to the circumstances that excuse completion of perfor-

mance, that party may recover in restitution for the reasonable value of the part performance. [McGillicuddy v. Los Verjels Land & Water Co., 213 Cal. 145 (1913)]

    a. **Reliance:** [§826] Under an emerging, minority rule, if A and B have a contract, and A's performance is excused by impracticability, B can recover the value of her *reliance*, even though the reliance did not result in a benefit to A, if justice so requires.

6. **Frustration:** [§827] Even if performance of a contract is not made impracticable by changed circumstances, performance may be excused under the doctrine of *frustration* where the *purpose* or *value* of the contract has been destroyed by a supervening event that was not reasonably foreseeable at the time the contract was entered into. This doctrine arose from the famous *Coronation Case, Krell v. Henry,* [1903] 2 K.B. 720, in which the English court held that performance of a contract for licensing rooms from which to view a coronation procession was excused by the unexpected cancellation of the procession. There clearly was no impracticability—the rooms could still be licensed and paid for—but the whole value of the contract had been destroyed by cancellation of the coronation.

    a. **Example:** A promises to pay B a certain sum for advertising A's hotel in a souvenir program, and B promises to print and sell the program as a souvenir of a yachting race. The outbreak of war forces indefinite postponement of the race, but B nevertheless publishes the program. A's duty to pay is excused by the doctrine of frustration, because cancellation of the race totally destroyed the value of advertising in the program.

    b. **Example:** Hotel Co. promises to pay a monthly sum to a Golf Club for permitting hotel guests to play on Golf Club's course. The hotel then burns down. Hotel Co.'s duty to pay is excused under the doctrine of frustration. [LaCumbre Golf & Country Club v. Santa Barbara Hotel Co., 205 Cal. 422 (1928)]

    c. **Compare:** Tenant leases a building in which to sell cars. Due to a war, new cars are no longer available. Tenant's duty to pay is not excused by the doctrine of frustration. The value of the lease is not totally destroyed, because the tenant can either sell used cars or sublet the building to someone else to use for a different purpose. [Lloyd v. Murphy, 25 Cal. 2d 48 (1944)]

J. DISCHARGE

1. **In General:** [§828] This section considers problems that may arise under certain methods by which contracts can be discharged—in particular, mutual rescission; release; accord and satisfaction; and full-payment checks.

2. **Discharge by Mutual Rescission:** [§829] If a contract is still executory on both sides, it can be discharged by an express agreement between the parties to rescind or "call off" the contract. Such an agreement is itself a binding contract, adequately supported by consideration, because each party surrenders its right to require performance by the other.

a. **Executory duties on both sides:** [§830]   A contract can be discharged by mutual rescission only if the duties are executory on *both* sides. If one of the parties has completed performance, a mutual rescission is no longer possible, because a mutual rescission involves both parties giving up a right to the remainder of a performance owing under a contract. (However, in such cases, the contract might still be discharged by other means.)

b. **Modification:** [§831]   A mutual rescission should be distinguished from a *modification*. In a mutual rescission, each party gives up the right to require further performance by the other. In a modification, either the contract continues, with modified duties on one or both sides, or only one party gives up a right. The latter case often raises a problem of consideration under the legal duty rule. (*See supra*, §§76-114.)

c. **Formalities:** [§832]   A mutual rescission need not be in writing unless the agreement to rescind would effect a retransfer or reconveyance of an interest in land or a sale of goods within the Statute of Frauds. For example, an agreement to rescind a contract for the sale of land, where title has already passed, would operate as a sale of the land, and therefore would have to be in writing under the "interest-in-land" provision of the Statute of Frauds. (*See supra*, §501.)

d. **Third-party beneficiary contracts:** [§833]   Recall that if a third-party beneficiary's rights have "vested," a mutual rescission is not effective to vary the obligation to the third party. (*See supra*, §589.)

3. **Release:** [§834]   A contract may be discharged by the execution and delivery of a release in which the maker expresses his intention to extinguish contractual rights existing in his favor, provided the release is supported by adequate consideration.

   a. **Minority abolishes consideration requirement if release in writing:** [§835]   By statute in a number of states, a written release is effective to discharge a contract even without new consideration. The writing is accepted as a substitute for consideration. [*See* Cal. Civ. Code §1541]

      (1) **U.C.C.:** [§836]   U.C.C. section 1-107 provides that any claim arising out of an alleged breach of contract for the sale of goods (or any other contract falling within the U.C.C.) is effectively discharged by a written release, signed and delivered by the aggrieved party, although no consideration is given.

4. **Accord and Satisfaction:** [§837]   A contract can be discharged by an accord and satisfaction, in which one contract or performance is substituted for another. Recall, however, that an executory (unexecuted) accord gives rise to special problems. (*See supra*, §§119-126.)

5. **Payment-in-Full Check:** [§838]   A contract may be discharged by a check that is marked "payment in full" or the like, even though the check is for less than the amount claimed to be due, if the check is cashed by the party to whom the check is sent, provided certain conditions are met. (For example, the difference between the amount of the check and the amount of the claim must reflect a good faith dispute.) The law of full-payment checks is discussed *supra*, at §§109-114.

VI. REMEDIES

chapter approach

If you have determined that there is a valid and enforceable contract and a breach, you need to consider the appropriate remedies for that breach. There are two basic types of remedies: damages (an award of money) and specific performance (an order from a court to a party to perform as promised).

Damages: There are three basic measures for damages:

— *Expectation damages:* This measure is the usual means of compensating the victim of a breached *bargain.* Expectation damages give the victim enough money to put him in the position he would have been in if the promise had been performed. Remember that expectation damages are limited to reasonably foreseeable damages, so that not all consequential damages will necessarily be recoverable. Also remember that there is a duty to mitigate damages.

— *Reliance damages:* This measure is generally used where a promise is enforceable only because of reliance, as in the case of a relied-upon donative promise. Reliance damages give the breach victim her costs, so that she is put back into the position she would have been in had the promise not been made.

— *Restitutionary (or quasi-contract) damages:* This measure is usually awarded when: (i) a party has conferred a benefit on another under an unenforceable contract, (ii) a losing contract (*i.e.*, one where the victim of the breach would have lost money had the contract been performed) was breached, or (iii) a benefit was conferred at a precontractual stage and no contract was ever formed. Restitutionary damages give the promisee the reasonable value of the benefit he has conferred on the promisor.

Specific performance: Specific performance is available only where the remedy at law is inadequate. This includes cases where the subject matter is unique, including all contracts for interests in land and contracts for the sale of unique goods. Specific performance will never be awarded to force someone to work under a service contract, even if the services are unique, but some courts might issue an injunction against the breaching party to prevent him from working for others.

A. INTRODUCTION [§839]

There are two basic types of remedy in contracts: damages (*i.e.*, an award of money) and specific performance (*i.e.*, an order from a court to a contracting party to perform as promised).

B. BASIC MEASURES OF DAMAGES

1. **Damage Measures:** [§840]   There are three basic types of damage measures:

a. **Expectation damages:** [§841]   Expectation damages are based on the ***contract price*** and have the purpose of placing the victim of a breach in the position he would have been in if the promise had been performed. Expectation damages give the injured party the ***benefit of the bargain*** and are usually used where the promise broken is enforceable because it was part of a bargain (*see supra*, §24).

(1) **Incidental damages:** [§842]   Incidental damages are comprised of elements such as the cost of shipping goods to and from a buyer who has wrongfully rejected the goods, the costs of storing and insuring goods pending resale after a buyer wrongfully rejects them, and the cost of going to the market to purchase substitute goods or of advertising a resale. If the injured party incurs such incidental damages, they are normally added to the expectation damages to which he is entitled.

b. **Reliance damages:** [§843]   Reliance damages are based on the nonbreaching party's ***costs*** (including opportunity costs) and have the purpose of putting the nonbreaching party in the position he would have been in had the promise not been made. This measure usually is used where the promise is enforceable because it is relied upon, as in the case of a ***relied-upon donative promise*** (*see supra*, §§16-23).

c. **Restitutionary (or quasi-contract) damages:** [§844]   Restitutionary damages (sometimes referred to as "quasi-contract damages") are based on the reasonable value of a ***benefit conferred*** by the promisee on the promisor, and have the purpose of stripping from the promisor the gain derived from the promisee. Restitutionary damages are often associated with the law of restitution, rather than the law of contract, and are therefore sometimes not thought of as "contract damages." In a contract setting, the restitution measure of damages is most commonly used in three situations:

(1) Where a party has ***conferred a benefit under a contract that turns out to be unenforceable*** because of some defense (*e.g.*, because the contract is within the Statute of Frauds and is not in writing);

(2) Where there was an enforceable contract and a breach, but the ***contract was a losing one*** for the innocent party, and she is better off with restitution damages than with expectation damages; and

(3) Where ***no contract was formed, but a benefit was conferred in a precontractual stage***, while the parties looked toward or believed they had concluded a contract (as where a benefit was conferred during, and as part of, preliminary negotiations that eventually broke down).

2. **Other Classifications of Damages:** [§845]   Damages are also divided into other categories other than expectation, reliance, and restitution, such as: general vs. special damages, liquidated damages, punitive damages, and damages for emotional distress.

3. **Approach:** [§846]   Because most contracts (and most contracts questions) involve bargains, and expectation damages are the normal remedy for breach of a bargain, a discussion of the limitations placed on expectation damages (*i.e.*, foreseeability, cer-

tainty, and mitigation) and on specific performance will follow immediately. Then, specific expectation damage measures and the availability of specific performance in certain recurring types of cases (such as contracts for the sale of goods or provision of services) will be discussed. Finally, damages for emotional distress, punitive damages, liquidated damages, and restitutionary damages will be addressed.

C. LIMITATIONS ON EXPECTATION DAMAGES

1. **The Principle of *Hadley v. Baxendale*:** [§847]   Under the principle of *Hadley v. Baxendale*, 156 Eng. Rep. 145 (Ex. Ch. 1854) a party injured by a breach of contract can recover only those damages that (i) should "reasonably be considered [as] arising naturally, *i.e.*, according to the usual course of things," from the breach or (ii) might "reasonably be supposed to have been in the contemplation of both parties, at the time the contract was made, as the probable result of the breach of it." The two branches of the court's holding are known as the first and second rules of *Hadley v. Baxendale*.

   a. **General and consequential damages:** [§848]   On the basis of the two rules of *Hadley v. Baxendale*, contract law has conventionally distinguished between general and direct damages, on the one hand, and special or consequential damages, on the other hand.

      (1) **General damages:** [§849]   General or direct damages are the damages that flow from a given type of breach without regard to the particular circumstances of the victim of the breach. General damages are never barred by the principle of *Hadley v. Baxendale*, because by their very definition such damages should "reasonably be considered . . . [as] arising naturally, *i.e.*, according to the usual course of things" from the breach. For example, if a seller breaches a contract for the sale of goods, it follows naturally that the buyer suffers damages equal to the difference between the contract price and the market price or cost of cover (*i.e.*, cost of buying substitute goods). This difference can normally be recovered as general damages.

      (2) **Consequential damages:** [§850]   Special or consequential damages are the damages above and beyond general damages that flow from a breach as a result of the buyer's particular circumstances. Typically, consequential damages consist of lost profits (although other kinds of consequential damages may occur). For example, suppose a seller breaches a contract for the sale of a die press that the buyer plans to use rather than resell. The buyer's consequential damages are the difference between (i) the profits he actually earned after the breach and (ii) the profits he would have earned if the die press had been furnished as promised.

         (a) **Reasonable foreseeability:** [§851]   Today the principle of *Hadley v. Baxendale* is normally restated to mean that consequential damages can be recovered only if, at the time the contract was made, the ***seller had reason to foresee that the consequential damages were the probable result of the breach.***

1) **Example:** Seller contracts with Buyer to sell Buyer a steam boiler, delivery to be made in 10 days. Buyer is a commercial laundry and needs the boiler to meet rapidly expanding demand. No comparable boiler is then available on the market. Seller breaches. If Seller knew or should have known of the special circumstances concerning Buyer's needs and inability to buy a substitute boiler promptly, so that the buyer's loss of profit if the boiler is not delivered is reasonably foreseeable, Buyer can recover the lost profits as consequential damages. If Seller neither knew nor should have known of the special circumstances, Seller is liable only for Buyer's general damages.

2. **Certainty:** [§852]   Damages can be recovered only if their amount is *reasonably certain* of computation. Damages that are not reasonably certain of computation are referred to as "speculative." Where the amount is not reasonably certain, the plaintiff can recover only nominal damages (*see infra,* §903).

   a. **Application to profits:** [§853]   The certainty limitation is encountered frequently where the damages in question are lost profits. Courts often differentiate between lost profits for a new business and lost profits for an existing business.

      (1) **Existing business:** [§854]   Profits for an existing business generally are not treated as speculative and are recoverable since future profits can generally be estimated from past profits.

      (2) **New business rule:** [§855]   If the result of a breach is to prevent the nonbreaching party from setting up a new business (*e.g.,* a breach by a landlord of a lease of commercial space to a new retail business), the courts in the past were reluctant to award lost profits, because profits of a new business are inherently speculative. Today, however, the tendency is to examine each case on its own merits and to allow recovery of lost profits even in the case of a new business if the profits can be determined with reasonable certainty, *e.g.,* by comparison with similar businesses in the vicinity.

   b. **Modern trend:** [§856]   In general, the modern trend is not to cut off damages on the ground of uncertainty unless the uncertainty is fairly severe. For example, the U.C.C. provides that, "the remedies provided by this Act shall be liberally administered. . . ." [U.C.C. §1-106]

3. **Duty to Mitigate:** [§857]   An injured party is not permitted to recover damages that could have been avoided by reasonable efforts. This principle is often referred to as the duty to mitigate damages. The application of this principle varies according to the type of contract involved.

   a. **Contracts for the sale of goods:** [§858]   Under the U.C.C., if the seller fails to deliver, the buyer has a right to cover (*i.e.,* buy substitute goods and recover damages; *see infra,* §868. If the buyer fails to cover, she will be barred from recovering any consequential damages that she could have prevented by covering. [U.C.C. §2-715(2)] Similarly, if the buyer repudiates the contract prior to delivery, the seller cannot run up the damages by incurring freight charges for packing, delivery, and so forth. If the goods are still in the process of manufacture at the time of repudiation, the seller must stop production, unless completion would facilitate resale and thereby reduce the damages for which the buyer is liable. [U.C.C. §2-704(2)]

b. **Employment contracts:** [§859]   If the employer wrongfully terminates the employment, the employee is under a duty to mitigate by looking for a comparable job. (*See infra,* §891.)

c. **Construction contracts**

(1) **In general:** [§860]   A contractor is under a duty to not add to the owner's damages by continuing to work after the owner breaches the contract. In particular, a contractor cannot recover for his expenses in continuing construction after the owner repudiates the contract. [Rockingham v. Luten Bridge Co., 35 F.2d 301 (4th Cir. 1929)]

(2) **Replacement job:** [§861]   A contractor is usually not under a duty to secure an alternative construction job during the period in which he would have been working on a canceled contract, because he is not required to take additional business risks as a result of the owner's breach. Even if the contractor does take on another job during that period, his profits on that job would normally not reduce his damages, because he probably could have taken on the other job, even if the owner had not breached, by hiring extra workers. However, if the owner can show that the contractor would not have been able to take on the new job but for the owner's breach, the profits on a new job should reduce the contractor's damages.

d. **Expenses incurred in mitigating damages are recoverable:** [§862]   Expenses incurred by the nonbreaching party in a reasonable effort to mitigate damages are recoverable as incidental damages, whether or not the effort was successful.

(1) **Example:** The fees paid to an employment agency by a wrongfully discharged employee are added to the employee's damages, whether or not the job search was successful.

D. SPECIFIC PERFORMANCE [§863]

Specific performance is an equitable remedy wherein the court orders a breaching party to perform. Historically, courts of equity will act only where there is no adequate remedy at law. Thus, specific performance is available only where damages (the "legal" remedy for breach of contract) are not an adequate remedy. There are a number of cases where damages are not an adequate remedy; in particular, where the contract concerns a unique subject matter or where damages cannot be measured with reasonable certainty. Special rules concerning when specific performance (or an equivalent remedy) will or will not be granted are discussed below, in connection with recurring types of cases.

E. EXPECTATION DAMAGES AND SPECIFIC PERFORMANCE IN SPECIFIC CASES

1. **Contracts for the Sale of Goods:** [§864]   A number of remedies are available when

a party breaches a contract for the sale of goods. The nature of these remedies depends on whether it is the seller or the buyer who has breached.

a. **Breach by seller:** [§865]   In the case of a breach of contract for the sale of goods by the seller, the buyer's remedies fall into two major categories. One category consists of the buyer's remedies when the buyer has accepted goods that are defective and the seller cannot or does not want to rightfully revoke his acceptance. Typically, an action in this category is for breach of warranty. The second category consists of the buyer's remedies when the seller fails to deliver or the buyer properly rejects or revokes acceptance.

   (1) **General damages for breach as to accepted goods:** [§866]   If the buyer has accepted goods that do not conform to the contract, there will be a breach of warranty. For breach of warranty, the buyer may recover the loss resulting in the ordinary course of events from the seller's breach as determined in any reasonable manner. Unless special circumstances show proximate damages of a different amount, the usual measure of damages for breach of warranty is the difference between (i) the value of the goods accepted and (ii) value that the goods *would have had if they had been as warranted*.

   (2) **General damages where seller fails to deliver or buyer rightfully rejects or revokes acceptance**

      (a) **Difference between contract price and market price:** [§867]   In a contract for the sale of goods, one formula to measure damages for breach by the seller where the seller has failed to deliver or where the buyer has rightfully rejected or revoked his acceptance is the difference between (i) the *contract price* of the goods and (ii) the *market price* of the goods at the time the buyer learned of the breach.

      (b) **Cover:** [§868]   Alternatively, the buyer can "cover"—*i.e.*, purchase substitute goods from other sources. If the buyer covers in a commercially reasonable manner, she can recover the difference between (i) the *contract price* and (ii) the *cost of cover* (*i.e.*, the cost of the substitute goods). [U.C.C. §2-712]

   (3) **Specific performance and replevin:** [§869]   The traditional test for determining a buyer's right to specific performance in a contract for the sale of goods is whether the goods are "unique." Today, contracts for the sale of goods are governed by the U.C.C., which has expanded the traditional rule.

      (a) **U.C.C. provisions:** [§870]   U.C.C. section 2-716(1) gives the buyer a right to specific performance "where the goods are unique *or in other proper circumstances*." In addition, section 2-716(3) gives a buyer a right comparable to the remedy of replevin (*i.e.*, an action to be awarded possession of the goods in question) "if after reasonable effort he is unable to effect cover for the goods or the circumstances reasonably indicate that such an effort will be unavailing," and the goods either were in existence when the contract was made or were later identified to the contract.

1) **Comment:** The official comment to U.C.C. section 2-716 states that Article 2 "seeks to further a more liberal attitude than some courts have shown in connection with specific performance of contracts of sale."

(4) **Buyer's incidental and consequential damages:** [§871]   In a proper case, the buyer may also be able to recover incidental and consequential damages.

   (a) **Incidental damages:** [§872]   Incidental damages resulting from the seller's breach include: (i) expenses reasonably incurred in inspection, receipt, transportation, and care and custody of goods rightfully rejected; (ii) any commercially reasonable charges, expenses, or commissions in connection with effecting cover; and (iii) any other reasonable expense incident to the delay or other breach.

   (b) **Consequential damages:** [§873]   Consequential damages resulting from the seller's breach may include any loss resulting from general or particular requirements and needs of which the seller at the time of contracting had reason to know and which could not reasonably be prevented by cover or otherwise, and injury to the person or property proximately resulting from any breach of warranty.

(5) **Damages for late performance:** [§874]   If the seller breaches by *late* performance, the goods were to be resold by the buyer, and the seller knew or had reason to know that the goods would be resold, the buyer can recover damages for reduction in the market value of the goods between the time performance was due and the time performance was rendered.

b. **Breach by buyer**

(1) **General damages measures**

   (a) **Market damages:** [§875]   If a buyer refuses to purchase the goods she has contracted for, the seller can recover from the buyer the difference between (i) the *contract price* of the goods and (ii) the *market price* at the time and place for tender under the contract.

   (b) **Lost profits:** [§876]   If the market price/contract price formula is inadequate to put the seller in as good a position as performance would have, then the measure of damages is the profit (including reasonable overhead) that the seller would have made from full performance by the buyer. This is called the "lost profits" or "lost volume" measure.

      1) **"Profits":** [§877]   As used in this formula, "profits" means:

         a) Contract price minus the seller's cost of purchasing the goods, where the seller is a dealer; and

         b) Contract price minus manufacturing costs, where the seller is a manufacturer.

2) **Application:** [§878]   The lost profits or lost volume measure normally is available for a seller where the goods are relatively homogeneous and in relatively deep supply.

3) **Example:** Seller is a boat retailer, who purchases standard model boats from Manufacturer M for resale. Seller pays M $9,000 for each boat. Buyer agrees to purchase a boat from Seller for $13,000. The boat is on Seller's showroom floor. Later, Buyer refuses to take delivery. Seller then sells the same boat to T for $13,000. Seller can recover $4,000 from Buyer—the $13,000 contract price minus Seller's $9,000 cost. *Rationale:* If Buyer had gone through with the contract, Seller would still have sold a boat to T, because Seller's boats are identical. Seller would then have had two $4,000 profits—one from Buyer and one from T. Thus, to put Seller in as good a position as she would have been in if Buyer had not defaulted, Seller needs to recover $4,000.

(c) **Resale:** [§879]   Alternatively, the seller can resell the goods in good faith and in a commercially reasonable manner and then recover from the buyer the difference between (i) the *contract price* and (ii) the *resale price*. [U.C.C. §2-706]

(2) **Action for the price:** [§880]   The seller's counterpart to a suit for specific performance is an action for the price of the goods (as opposed to damages). A seller can maintain an action for the *full contract price* if: (i) the buyer has breached by refusing to purchase goods that have already been "identified to the contract" and (ii) the seller is *unable to resell* after reasonable efforts, or such efforts would be unavailing.

(a) **"Identified to the contract":** [§881]   If the relevant goods are in existence when the contract is made, they are "identified to the contract" when they are set aside as the goods to which the contract refers. If the relevant goods are not in existence when the contract is made, then identification to the contract occurs when the seller ships, marks, or otherwise designates the goods as the goods covered by the contract. [U.C.C. §2-501]

(b) **Example:** Buyer orders calendars imprinted with Buyer's name. Seller manufactures the calendars, but before they can be shipped, Buyer repudiates the contract. Because there is probably no market for calendars with Buyer's name on them, Seller can bring an action for the full contract price.

(3) **Incidental damages:** [§882]   In a proper case, the seller can recover incidental damages resulting from the buyer's breach. These include any commercially reasonable charges, expenses, or commissions incurred by the seller in the transportation, care, and custody of the goods after the buyer's breach that are incurred in connection with the return or resale of the goods or otherwise result from the breach.

2. **Contracts for the Sale of Realty**

a. **Breach by seller**

(1) **Damages:** [§883]   Many states hold that where the seller breaches a contract for the sale of realty by refusing to convey, the purchaser's damages remedy is limited to out-of-pocket costs, such as payments made on the purchase price and expenses incurred in connection with the purchase (*e.g.*, title charges and escrow fees), and the purchaser is not entitled to recover the difference between contract price and market value unless the seller's refusal to convey was in bad faith.

(a) **"Bad faith"** [§884]   As used in this context, "bad faith" means either that: (i) the seller knew at the time she made the contract that she did not have good title, or (ii) the breach involved a *deliberate* refusal to perform, as opposed to an inability to convey good title due to some unknown easement or the like. [*See* Cal. Civ. Code §3306]

(b) **Effect:** [§885]   If the seller's breach was in bad faith, the buyer can measure damages by the difference between: (i) *market price* and (ii) *contract price*, even in states that ordinarily restrict the buyer to recovery of out-of-pocket costs.

(2) **Specific performance:** [§886]   Rather than seeking damages, a buyer of real estate is entitled to the remedy of specific performance, in the form of a decree ordering the seller to execute a deed in the buyer's favor. Damages are considered an inadequate remedy because every piece of land is unique to some extent and because (for that reason) the value of land is always to some extent conjectural.

b. **Breach by buyer**

(1) **Damages:** [§887]   If a contract for the sale of realty is breached by the buyer, the seller is entitled to recover the difference between the contract price and the fair market value of the land in question. [68 A.L.R. 137]

(2) **Specific performance:** [§888]   Alternatively, the seller can get specific performance in the form of a decree ordering the buyer to take title to the land and pay the agreed price. The seller's right to specific performance is based on mutuality of remedy and the need for a formal termination of the buyer's interest in the land.

(a) **Effect:** [§889]   The seller's remedy of specific performance is normally not intended to actually make the buyer specifically perform (*i.e.*, by paying the purchase price). Rather, it is a mechanism to clear the seller's title by cutting off the buyer's rights, and also to establish the seller's damages through a resale of the property. To achieve these objectives, a decree of specific performance against a buyer of property will normally provide that if the purchase price is not paid by a given date, the right of the buyer to "redeem" the property by paying the price is cut off or "foreclosed." Usually, once the foreclosure date passes, the seller can resell the property and claim damages against the buyer for the deficiency, that is, the difference between the original contract price and the price at which the property was sold at the foreclosure sale.

3. Employment Contracts

a. **Breach by employer:** [§890]   If an employer discharges an employee in breach of an employment contract or otherwise commits a material breach, the employee is entitled to recover (i) the *remainder of her wages* minus (ii) the *wages the employee actually received* in a substitute employment, or the wages she *would have received* had she properly attempted to mitigate damages.

   (1) **Mitigation:** [§891]   If the employer wrongfully terminates an employment contract, the employee is under an affirmative duty to exercise reasonable efforts to locate a position *of the same rank and type of work in the same locale*. The burden usually is on the *employer* to show that such other positions were available. [Copper v. Stronge & Warner Co., 126 N.W. 541 (Minn. 1910)]

   (2) **Example:** An actress hired for the female lead in a musical to be filmed in Los Angeles is *not* required to accept substitute employment as the lead in a dramatic western to be produced in Australia; the latter role is not comparable to the former role. [Parker v. 20th Century Fox, 3 Cal. 3d 176 (1970)]

b. **Breach by employee:** [§892]   If an employee quits in breach of contract or otherwise commits a material breach, the employer is entitled to recover the difference between (i) the *employee's wages* and (ii) the *wages the employer must pay to a replacement*.

   (1) **Example:** S contracts to work for M for one year at $2,000 per month, but quits after one month to take a better job. M has to pay $2,500 per month to get a qualified replacement. M's damages are $500 per month times 11 months, or $5,500.

c. **Specific performance:** [§893]   Employment contracts are not specifically enforceable by either the employee or the employer. The objection to specific performance is that it is unwise to attempt to extract from an unwilling party a performance involving personal relations.

   (1) **Injunction:** [§894]   Although the courts will not order an employee to work for the employer, in some cases the courts will enjoin an employee from working for a competitor of the employer. Often such an injunction is tantamount to ordering specific performance, because the employee may be unable to get a job except with a competitor. Accordingly, Restatement Second adopts the rule that a "promise to render personal service exclusively for one employer will not be enforced by an injunction against serving another if its probable result will be to compel a performance involving personal relations the enforced continuance of which is undesirable or will be to leave the employee without other reasonable means of making a living." [Rest. 2d §367(2)]

4. Construction Contracts and Other Contracts for Services

a. **Terminology:** [§895]   The most common type of service contract is a construction contract, in which a contractor provides services to an owner. The same terminology will be applied herein to other service contracts; *i.e.*, the service provider will be referred to as the contractor, and the person receiving the services will be referred to as the owner.

b. **Breach by owner:** [§896]   If the owner commits a material beach of a construction contract, the contractor is entitled to recover (i) the *contract price,* minus (ii) the *out-of-pocket costs* remaining to be incurred by the contractor at the time of breach, with (iii) an *offset for amounts already paid* by the owner.

   (1) **Alternative formula:** [§897]   Under an alternative formula, the contractor is entitled to recover (i) its *lost profits* on the contract, plus (ii) its *out-of-pocket costs* prior to breach, again with (iii) an *offset for amounts already paid* by the owner. Normally, the two formulas, although they look very different, produce the same result, unless the contractor has made a losing contract.

c. **Breach by contractor**

   (1) **Cost of completion:** [§898]   If the contractor commits a material breach, the owner can usually recover damages based on the difference between the contract price and the *cost of completing the contract* by retaining a substitute contractor. [125 A.L.R. 1242]

   (2) **Diminished value damages:** [§899]   However, if the cost-of-completion measure would lead to substantial economic waste or would be unreasonably disproportionate to the value to be gained by the owner, the courts will measure the owner's damages by the *diminution in value* measure—the difference between (i) the *value of what the owner received* and (ii) the *value of what the owner would have received* if the contractor had performed the contract in full. (*See supra,* §770.)

   (3) **Damages for minor breach:** [§900]   If a contract is breached by rendering a performance that is defective, but not materially so (*e.g.*, a house built with the wrong doorknobs), damages normally are measured essentially in the same way as for material breach—by either: (i) the *cost of correcting the defect* (cost of completion) or (ii) the *difference between the value of the performance promised and the value of the performance rendered* (diminished value).

d. **Specific performance:** [§901]   The general rule is that a contract for construction will not be specifically enforced. This is partly because damages are usually an adequate remedy and partly because of the incapacity of the courts to superintend the performance. However, the courts can and often do grant specific performance of such contracts where they believe damages are not an adequate remedy and the problems of administration do not seem insurmountable.

5. **Late Performance in Contract for Carriage:** [§902]   Where a contract for carriage (*i.e.*, of transportation) is breached by *late performance* by the carrier, the subject matter of the contract involves goods that were to be sold by the shipper, and it was reasonably foreseeable to the carrier that the goods were to be sold, the shipper can recover damages for reduction in the market value of the subject matter between the time performance was due and the time it was rendered. Otherwise, the damages for late performance by a carrier are often measured by the reasonable daily rental value of the subject matter of the contract, multiplied by the days of delay, or, if that is not easily determined, the prevailing rate of interest on the capital investment involved. [Wood v. Joliet Gaslight Co., 111 F. 463 (7th Cir. 1901)]

F. NOMINAL DAMAGES [§903]

Any breach of contract, no matter how slight, normally entitles the aggrieved party to damages. If the party cannot prove any loss, the court will award "nominal" or "token" damages, *e.g.*, $1.

G. LIQUIDATED DAMAGES [§904]

A liquidated damages provision is a provision in a contract that fixes the amount of damages that will be recoverable in the event of a breach. The enforceability of such a provision depends on whether the court finds it to be a valid liquidated damages provision or a penalty. If the court determines that the provision is a penalty, it is not enforceable, and the innocent party is limited to whatever actual damages she can prove.

1. **Contract Terminology Not Controlling:** [§905]   The name the parties give such a provision is not controlling. A provision calling for "$10,000 as liquidated damages in the event of breach" may be shown to be a penalty and therefore not be enforceable.

2. **Requirements for Valid Liquidated Damages Provision:** [§906]   To be enforceable, a contractual provision fixing damages must meet two requirements:

   a. **Damages difficult to estimate:** [§907]   First, at the time the contract was made the actual damages that would result in the event of breach must be impracticable or extremely difficult to ascertain or estimate.

   b. **Reasonable estimate:** [§908]   Second, the amount of the damages fixed in the provision must be a reasonable forecast, at the time the contract is made, of the damages that would result from a breach.

   c. **Example:** Contractor A promises to pay Owner $300 *per day* for any delay in completing a building contract. When completed, the rental value of the building will be only $300 *per week*. The contractual provision is unenforceable as a penalty.

3. **Subsequent Events:** [§909]   If a liquidated damages provision was valid when made, the general rule is that the provision will be enforceable even though subsequent conditions have rendered actual damages ascertainable, or even though it is clear from the way things turned out that actual damages differ materially from the liquidated damages.

a. **Minority view:** [§910]   Some courts treat a liquidated damages provision as unconscionable if the liquidated damages are clearly disproportionate to the actual damages.

b. **U.C.C. position:** [§911]   Under the U.C.C., in contracts involving the sale of goods a liquidated damages provision is enforceable if the amount fixed is reasonable in light of the "anticipated or actual harm caused by the breach."

4. **Deposits:** [§912]   A deposit may serve the same function as a liquidated damage provision if the innocent party was allowed to retain the deposit even if the deposit exceeds the actual damages. On the recovery of deposits in such cases, *see infra*, §§929-930.

a. **U.C.C. section 2-718:** [§913]   In the case of contracts for the sale of goods, deposits are governed by U.C.C. section 2-718. U.C.C. section 2-718(2) provides that where the seller justifiably refuses to deliver goods because of the buyer's breach, the buyer is entitled to restitution of any amount by which the sum of his prior payments (including a deposit) exceeds (i) the amount set in a valid liquidated-damages provision, or (ii) if there is no such provision, 20% of the value of the performance, or $500, whichever is smaller. U.C.C. section 2-718(3) provides that the buyer's right to restitution under section 2-718(2) is subject to an offset to the extent that the seller establishes damages other than liquidated damages.

H. PUNITIVE DAMAGES [§914]

As a general principle, punitive damages are not available for breach of contract, partly on the theory that "the mere availability of such a remedy would seriously jeopardize the stability and predictability of commercial transactions, so vital to the smooth and efficient operation of the modern economy." [General Motors Corp. v. Piskor, 281 Md. 627 (1977)] However, there are some important exceptions to the general principle.

1. **Tort:** [§915]   Punitive damages are available if the conduct constituting the breach is independently a tort.

2. **Good Faith:** [§916]   Punitive damages may be available for a breach of the duty of good faith, on the theory that a breach of good faith is tortious.

a. **Insured vs. insurer:** [§917]   The application of this exception has been relatively limited. Its most significant application has been in suits by insureds against their insurance companies for failure to settle or defend in good faith.

b. **Employment contracts:** [§918]   Some cases have also applied the exception in cases involving a breach of an employment contract by an employer and in certain other limited contexts.

(1) **Contrary view:** [§919]   At least one court has held that punitive damages are not available for breach by an employer of the duty of good faith under an employment contract, at least where the breach consists merely of discharging the employee. [Foley v. Interactive Data Corp., 47 Cal. 3d 654 (1988)]

c. **Denial of contract:** [§920]   The California Supreme Court has held that a party to a contract may incur tort liability when, in addition to breaching the contract, it seeks to shield itself from liability by denying, in bad faith, that a contract exists. [Seaman's Direct Buying Service, Inc. v. Standard Oil Co., 36 Cal. 3d 752 (1984)] However, this rule does not appear to have been adopted outside California.

I.   DAMAGES FOR EMOTIONAL DISTRESS [§921]

Damages for emotional distress are ordinarily not allowed, with two exceptions.

1. **Bodily Injury:** [§922]   Damages for breach of contract for emotional distress may be awarded where the emotional distress accompanies bodily injury.

2. **Personal Interests Involved:** [§923]   Damages may also be awarded for emotional distress where the contract was of a type that involved *personal*, as opposed to strictly commercial financial, interests, so that emotional distress was a particularly likely result. Common examples of such cases are contracts of innkeepers and guests, contracts for the carriage and proper disposition of dead bodies, and contracts for the delivery of messages concerning death.

   a. **Example:** A contracts to construct a house for B. A knows when the contract is made that B is in delicate health and that proper completion of the house is of great importance to B. Because of delays and departures from specifications, B suffers nervousness and emotional distress. In an action by B against A for breach of contract, the element of emotional distress will **not** be included as a loss for which damages may be awarded. [Rest. 2d §353, Ill. 1.]

   b. **Compare:** A, a travel company, sells B a holiday travel package at a hotel in Switzerland. The hotel is not at all as A described, and B's vacation is ruined. B can recover for his emotional distress.

J.   RESTITUTIONARY DAMAGES

1. **Unenforceable Contract Situation:** [§924]   Restitutionary damages are available to recover the value of a benefit conferred on another where the benefit was conferred under a contract that is unenforceable because of the Statute of Frauds, the doctrine of impossibility, or other comparable excuses, such as mutual mistake.

   a. **Example:** A pays B $500 for B's promise to sing at A's wedding. B develops laryngitis and cannot sing at the wedding. Although B will be discharged from the contract under the doctrine of impossibility (*see supra,* §§820-821), A can recover the $500 as restitution.

2. **Breach of Contract Situation:** [§925]   Restitutionary damages may also be awarded, as an alternative to expectation damages, against a party who has *materially* breached a contract. Thus, if A and B have a contract and B commits a material breach, A can usually elect to either: (i) bring an action on the contract to recover expectation damages, or (ii) bring an action in *quasi-contract* for restitutionary damages to recover the reasonable value of the benefit conferred on B prior to B's breach. The

restitutionary damages normally will be measured by the market value of the plaintiff's (A's) performance, rather than the actual enrichment of the defendant (B), which could be less than the market value of the performance.

a. **Losing contracts:** [§926]   Normally, if the defendant has committed a material breach, the plaintiff will prefer expectation damages to restitutionary damages, because expectation damages usually are larger and easier to prove. The major exception is where the plaintiff has made a losing contract. In such a case, the benefit conferred on the defendant, measured by market value, will be greater than the contract price upon which expectation damages would be based. The general rule is that a suit can be brought for restitutionary damages where the defendant is in material breach, even if the contract is a losing one. To put this differently, the general rule is that if one party is in material breach, the other party can choose between expectation damages and restitutionary damages, and if she chooses restitutionary damages the contract price does not set a limit on the value of the benefit conferred. (However, the contract price is *evidence* of the value of the benefit conferred.)

b. **Exception for full performance:** [§927]   The general rule is not applied where the innocent party has fully performed. In such cases, the innocent party is limited to the contract price for her performance.

c. **Return of what has been received:** [§928]   Because restitutionary damages are based on the benefit the defendant received from the plaintiff, it is a condition to a suit for restitutionary damages for breach that the plaintiff has returned to the defendant what the plaintiff has received, so that the plaintiff recovers only the value of the net benefit to the defendant. Alternatively, the value of what was received will be deducted from the plaintiff's recovery.

3. **Plaintiff in Default:** [§929]   Under modern law, even a party who is in material breach, and therefore could not sue on the contract, may be able to bring an action to recover the value of the benefits she has conferred on the other party, subject to an off-set for the innocent party's damages. Such cases are known as "plaintiff in default" cases, because the plaintiff is allowed to bring a suit even though she is in material breach of contract.

a. **Application:** [§930]   This kind of recovery can apply to a deposit that was made by the breaching party, to the extent that the deposit exceeds the innocent party's damages and to the extent that the deposit was not also agreed upon as a liquidated damages provision (*see supra*, §912).

b. **Measure of damages:** [§931]   In an action brought by a plaintiff in default, the plaintiff's recovery will usually be measured by the amount by which the defendant has actually been enriched, *limited by the contract price*, rather than the market value of the plaintiff's performance.

c. **Significance:** [§932]   Recall that a party who has substantially performed a contract can bring suit *on the contract* even though he has not performed perfectly, subject to an offset for his breach. Therefore, a party who has substantially performed does not need to bring an action for restitutionary damages as a plaintiff in default. However, if plaintiff's default is not minor, but is so significant that he has not even rendered substantial performance, a suit for restitutionary damages as a plaintiff in default would be appropriate.

d. **Willful breach:** [§933]   At one time, the majority view was that if a breach was willful, the breaching party could not recover restitutionary damages for the benefit conferred. Modern courts are increasingly inclined to allow even a willfully breaching plaintiff to recover on this theory, in order to prevent unjust enrichment of the defendant. [Britton v. Turner, 6 N.H. 481 (1834)]

REVIEW QUESTIONS

FILL IN
ANSWER

CONSIDERATION

1. A executes a written guaranty to B of a debt then due from C. The guaranty is stated to be in "consideration of $1 paid to me by B, receipt of which is hereby acknowledged." Is A's guaranty binding if the dollar is never paid? _____

2. A and B were involved in a traffic accident in which B sustained serious personal injuries. A has agreed to pay B $5,000 for B's promise not to sue him.

    a. Assume that B had been advised by his attorney that he had no valid claim against A, but B nevertheless still honestly believed that he could win in front of a sympathetic jury. Could B enforce A's promise to pay $5,000? _____

    b. Assume that B realized he had no valid claim against A, but that A was still willing to pay him $5,000 for a written release. If B executes the release, can he enforce A's promise to pay $5,000? _____

3. Manufacturer A orally agrees to sell retailer B for $1 each as many Frisbees as B may choose to order within the next 30 days.

    a. A cancels before B places an order. Is A liable? _____

    b. Assume that the contract provided that A was to sell B "as many Frisbees as B needed for her retail store" (instead of as many as she "chose" to order). Would A be liable for canceling? _____

4. A places an order with B for all of A's computer service requirements. B's order form specifies "all orders subject to cancellation by B without notice at any time."

    a. The next day A wishes to get out of the deal. Is there a contract binding A? _____

    b. Suppose the order form said "All orders are subject to cancellation on 30 days' written notice by B." Is there a contract binding A? _____

    c. Assume that the contract was otherwise enforceable, but that it contained the following provision: "A shall have the right to terminate all obligations hereunder if the services are not performed efficiently, as determined by A in his sole and absolute discretion." In light of this provision, is there a binding contract? _____

5. Dealer contracts to sell a car to Bob, a minor, for $1,000. Later, Dealer realizes that Bob is a minor, and refuses to go through with the sale on the ground that a minor's promise is not sufficient consideration. Can Bob enforce the contract? _____

6. A promises to assign to B a patent owned by A, in exchange for B's promise to pay A $10,000. B's obligation is conditioned on the favorable termination of pending litigation concerning the patent's validity. Is B's promise valid consideration for A's promise?

7. Homeowner signs an agreement with Broker under which Broker is given the exclusive right to sell Homeowner's house during the next three months, for a specified commission. The next day Homeowner seeks to cancel, asserting that Broker did not give any consideration, and therefore there is no contract. Can Homeowner cancel?

8. The XYZ Bank is robbed. It posts a reward offer of $10,000 for information leading to the arrest of the robber. Officer Smith captures the robber. May she recover the reward?

9. A promises to design and build a racing car for B for $10,000. A has almost completed performance when he realizes that the contract is a losing proposition and tells B that he cannot complete the car unless B pays him an additional $3,000. B promises. Is B's promise enforceable?

10. Builder contracts to build a house for Owner, to be completed by June 1. Builder subcontracts the electrical work to Sparks, to be completed by May 15. Owner fears delay by Sparks and promises him a $500 bonus to make sure the job is finished on May 15. If Sparks finishes on time, can he enforce Owner's promise?

11. A borrowed $1,000 from B and executed a 6% interest-bearing promissory note due on June 1.

    a. Assume that on May 15, A tells B that she will not be able to pay the $1,000 and offers to satisfy the debt by delivering shares worth $700. B accepts and takes delivery of the shares. B then sues A for $300. Can B recover?

    b. Assume that on June 1, A delivers a check to B for $700, marked "payment in full," and B cashes the check. Can B later sue for the balance?

12. Able, a carpenter, told his friend and neighbor, Clutz, that he would be happy to give Clutz some help in building his new garage. When the garage was completed, Clutz said to Able, "I really appreciate your help. I'll help you paint your house in return." However, Clutz later changed his mind.

    a. Can Able enforce Clutz's promise?

    b. Assume that Clutz made his promise just after Able began helping. Would it then be enforceable?

13. Minister was employed by XYZ Church for 40 years. On Minister's retirement, there was no adequate pension plan. Therefore, two months after Minister's retirement, wealthy Parishioner promised to pay Minister $500 per month for life.

a. Is Parishioner's promise enforceable as a contract?

b. Would it make any difference whether Parishioner's promise was oral or in writing?

c. Assume that in reliance on Parishioner's promise, Minister contracted to purchase a home in a retirement village which Minister would otherwise have been unable to afford. Is Parishioner's promise enforceable?

d. Assume that Parishioner's promise to pay Minister $500 per month for life was conditioned on Minister's continuing to write sermons for the XYZ Church "if requested by the Church." The Church never made any such request. Is Parishioner's promise enforceable as a contract?

14. Debtor owes Friend $1,000 which is barred by the statute of limitations.

a. Assume Debtor telephoned Friend and promised to pay the $1,000. Can Friend enforce this promise?

b. Assume Debtor wrote to Friend, "I know I owe you $1,000, but I won't pay it." Does Debtor's written acknowledgment of the debt make it now enforceable?

c. Assume Debtor wrote to Friend, "I will pay you $700 of what I owe you, when I sell my car." Can Friend now enforce the $1,000 debt?

d. Would the answer to any of the above be different if Debtor's promise was to pay a debt which had been discharged in bankruptcy (rather than barred by the statute of limitations)?

15. A purchases B's car and promises to pay $3,000 for it. Shortly thereafter, A discovers that B fraudulently misrepresented the mileage and condition of the car. Even so, A likes the car and tells B that he will pay him for the car. Is A's new promise enforceable?

16. A becomes ill while driving across country. She stops at a farmhouse and seeks aid. Farmer takes A in and nurses her back to health. On leaving, A promises to send Farmer $5,000 for his efforts. Is A's promise enforceable as a contract?

17. A loaned money to B on a promissory note. B died penniless and without repaying the loan. B's father, however, agreed to repay B's debt "in order to clear my son's good name." Is the father's promise enforceable?

MUTUAL ASSENT—OFFER AND ACCEPTANCE

18. In the course of a television interview, actress Amy stated, "I'm always having problems with my weight . . . I'd give a thousand dollars for the secret of staying thin!" Buford wrote Amy a letter stating, "The secret of staying thin is to eat less and exercise more. You owe me $1,000." Is Buford entitled to the $1,000?

19. Is there an enforceable contract in any of the following cases?

    a. Alice telephoned the Elite Grocery Co., with whom she maintained an account, and ordered 100 pounds of prime beef for a dinner party. No mention was made of price. Elite billed Alice $5 per pound ($500), which was the regular posted price of such beef at the store. Alice refuses to pay claiming that she could have purchased the same quality meat elsewhere for $300. Is she contractually bound to pay the full $500? _____

    b. Arturo contracted to furnish janitorial services to Ben's offices for one year at a set price. At the end of the one-year period, he continued his services for three more years. Ben paid the contract price for the first two years but now refuses to pay for the last year. Is Ben bound to pay the contract price? _____

    c. Betty was seriously injured in a traffic accident. While she was unconscious, bystanders summoned Dr. Dudley, who performed a delicate operation on Betty, and later sent her a bill for $1,500. Is Betty contractually bound to pay this amount? _____

20. Has a contract been formed if—

    a. A writes B, "I am eager to sell my house. I would consider $20,000 cash." B promptly replies, "You've got a deal!" _____

    b. Clothing Store advertises a well-known brand of suits "regularly priced at $220, today only $150." Customer comes to the store in response to the ad, selects a suit, and tenders $150. _____

    c. A sends B a "letter agreement" for certain construction work which states "formal contract to follow." B writes "accepted" across the "letter agreement," signs it and returns it to A. _____

    d. Merchant A writes to Merchant B, "Dear B, I can quote you flour at $20 a barrel in carload lots for immediate acceptance." B writes, "Send three carloads." _____

21. A advertises in the newspaper that he will be auctioning off all of his household goods at a specified time and place.

    a. Is A bound to proceed with auction? _____

    b. If, during the course of the auction, A feels that the bids are too low, can he withdraw the goods? _____

    c. Assume that the auction is announced to be "without reserve." B makes a bid, but immediately changes his mind and yells "I revoke," before the fall of the hammer. Is B bound by his bid? _____

22. On March 1, A wrote to B offering to sell her house for $40,000. The letter stated that the offer would remain in effect for only five days.

    a.   Assume B received the letter on March 3, and sent an acceptance letter on March 7. Has a contract been formed? _____

    b.   Assume that the house was destroyed by fire on March 6, and B sent her acceptance letter the next day unaware of this. Is there a contract? _____

    c.   Assume A telephoned B on March 5, saying "I revoke my offer." B replied, "You can't revoke because you promised that the offer would remain in effect for five days." If B immediately delivered a written acceptance, is there a contract? _____

    d.   Assume that on March 5, A and B signed a memo in which A agreed to keep the offer open until March 10, for which B was to pay $100. On March 8, A telegraphed B revoking the offer. Can B accept the offer on March 9? _____

    e.   Assume that on March 4, with A's knowledge and approval, B had an expensive engineer's report made on A's house. Can A still revoke her offer? _____

23. A offers to sell to B a parcel of land for $5,000.

    a.   Assume B replies "I will pay you $4,800 for the parcel." Later that day, B says, "OK, I'll pay the $5,000," but A now refuses to sell. Is there a contract? _____

    b.   Assume B's first reply was, "Will you accept $4,800?" Would B's subsequent "acceptance" of the $5,000 offer form a contract? _____

    c.   Assume that B mailed a rejection to A, but later the same day B changed her mind and telegraphed an acceptance to A. The acceptance was in fact received by A prior to the rejection. Is there a contract? _____

    d.   Suppose B had mailed an acceptance to A, but later that day changed her mind and telegraphed a rejection, and the rejection was received by A *prior* to the acceptance. Is there a contract? _____

24. A mails an order to B for certain computer services. B replies: "Order acknowledged; will receive our attention and advise shortly."

    a.   Is there a contract? _____

    b.   Two days later, B writes A "accepting" the order, but stating that services cannot be provided for six weeks. Is there a contract? _____

25. Father writes to Daughter, who is living away from home, as follows: "I am old and lonely and miss you terribly. If you'll come back home and take care of me for the rest of my life, I'll make you sole beneficiary of my will. You

don't need to promise—in fact, you can terminate the arrangement at any time if it doesn't suit you. Just come."

   a.   If Daughter gives up her career and moves back home and starts to take care of Father, can Father later revoke his offer? _____

   b.   Assume Father does not revoke, but after a few years Daughter tires of the arrangement and moves out and leaves Father alone. Can Father sue Daughter for breach of contract? _____

26. A makes a written application for life insurance through an agent for B Insurance Company, pays the first premium, and is given a receipt stating that the insurance "shall take effect on approval of the application" at B's home office. B's home office approves the next day, but the day after, before notice of approval has been sent, A dies. Was A covered by the insurance policy? _____

27. A posts a $100 reward for return of his dog. B reads the reward offer, searches for and finds A's dog, and returns it. Can B collect the $100 even though he never notified A that he was going to accept the reward offer? _____

28. Rich writes to Lender stating, "If you will lend my brother, B, $1,000, I will guarantee repayment." On receipt of this letter, Lender loans the money to B. If Lender fails to notify Rich that she has done so within a reasonable time, can Lender enforce Rich's guarantee? _____

29. A posts a $100 reward for return of his lost dog. In the meantime, B has found the dog and returns it to A, unaware of A's reward offer. If he later finds out about the reward, can B collect the $100? _____

30. Which, if any, of the following offers can be accepted *only* by performance? _____

   (A) A orders goods from B on specified terms and further states, "Ship at once."

   (B) A offers a reward of $100 for a lost diamond bracelet.

   (C) A says to B, "I'll pay you $15 to mow my lawn this afternoon."

   (D) A says to B, "If you finish that table you are making and deliver it to my house today, I'll give you $100 for it."

31. A sends an order for 1,000 12-inch Frisbees to B Manufacturing Co., with instructions to ship immediately.

   a.   Suppose that B immediately ships the goods by common carrier. The next day, and before receipt of the Frisbees, A wires a revocation of his order. Is there a contract? _____

   b.   Suppose B was out of 12-inch Frisbees, and therefore shipped 11.5-inch Frisbees instead. Is there a contract at the time of shipment? _____

32. B has been renting A's house for many years, and has offered to buy it on several occasions but A has refused. Finally, A sends B a letter stating, "I'm now ready to sell the house at the price we have been discussing over the past several years. Knowing that you want the house, I'll consider that we have a deal, unless I hear from you otherwise." B makes no reply to this letter but does **not** wish to purchase the house at this time. Is there a contract?

_____

33. A mails B an offer to lease B's house for $1,000 per month; the offer states "reply immediately."

   a. B immediately telegraphs acceptance, but the telegram is lost and never received by A. Is there a contract?

   _____

   b. Assume that B mailed the acceptance but had accidentally misaddressed the envelope to A, and as a result it ended up in another city. However, the postmaster in the other city happened to know A personally, and forwarded the letter to A, who received the letter several days later. Is there a contract?

   _____

34. Art mails Bob an offer to sell him a restored Model T Ford for $2,000. Ignorant of Art's offer, Bob mails Art an offer to buy the same car for the same amount. On receiving Bob's letter, Art decides the car is worth more, and notifies Bob he will not sell. Is there a contract?

   _____

35. Ajax Oil Co. leases one of its service stations to Don. The lease provides it is "terminable at will of Ajax." Prior to signing the lease, Don questioned Ajax about this clause, and was assured that it would not be exercised so long as Don's sales exceeded 50,000 gallons per month. Ajax later attempts to terminate the lease, even though Don's sales are in excess of the figure stated.

   a. Is evidence of Ajax's oral promise admissible under the parol evidence rule?

   _____

   b. Assume that the lease provided Ajax could terminate only "for good cause." Would Ajax's oral promise to Don be admissible?

   _____

DEFENSES TO FORMATION AND ENFORCEMENT

36. Builder offers to build a house for Owner at a specified price. Owner accepts.

   a. If Builder does not state a completion date for the house, is there a contract?

   _____

   b. Suppose Builder hires Foreman at a monthly salary of $1200, payable weekly, but two days later Builder fires Foreman without cause. Was Builder legally obligated to employ Foreman for a reasonable length of time?

   _____

   c. If Builder's offer included no plans or specifications, is there a contract?

   _____

   d. Assume that Builder's offer does contain plans and specifications except as to paint and wallpaper, which are to be "selected at a later date." Has a contract been formed? _____

37. A agrees to sell to B "whatever amount of coal you will need to run your factory this winter," at $100 per ton. Is this agreement sufficiently definite to constitute a contract? _____

38. A agrees to employ B for one year as a sales manager. Is there an enforceable contract in the following cases, assuming that A breaches before B begins to work?

   a. A promises to pay B "a salary to be settled between us at the end of each month." _____

   b. A promises to pay B "a fair share of the profits derived from your services." _____

   c. A promises to pay B "half the profits on any increased sales after you come to work." _____

   d. A promises to pay B a salary of $1,500 per month "provided my sales volume is sufficient to enable me to pay this amount." _____

   e. No provision is made for salary. _____

39. Benny is a large retailer of toys. He anticipates a seasonal rush on Frisbees, and therefore contracts with Ajax, a Frisbee manufacturer, to purchase "as many Frisbees as you can produce within the next 30 days, at a price to be determined by you."

   a. Is the contract sufficiently certain as to quantity? _____

   b. Is the contract sufficiently certain as to price? _____

40. Manufacturer Ajax agrees to sell to retailer Benny 5,000 Frisbees, in sizes and colors "to be selected" by Benny from Ajax's stock, the price per Frisbee depending on the size and color chosen. Benny refuses to select any. Is there a contract? _____

41. A offers to sell to B a packet of diamonds for $50,000. B agrees to buy.

   a. Assume that A had misjudged the quality of the stones, and that their fair market value was really $100,000, and that B was aware of A's error. Is there a contract? _____

   b. Assume that A had miscounted the number and weight of the stones in the packet, and that B was aware of A's error. Is there a contract? _____

42. Bess owns two cars of equal value—a Ford and a Chevrolet. Bess offers to sell "my car" to Abe for $2,500. Abe accepts with the intent of purchasing the Chevrolet and later demands delivery of that car. Bess refuses on the ground that she honestly was intending to sell only the Ford. Is there a contract? _____

43. A is injured when the bus on which he is riding crashes due to the negligence of the driver. The ticket purchased by A contains a provision in large size print stating that the carrier shall not be liable for injuries caused by its agents and employees. Is A bound by this provision?

44. Retailer S sells a vacuum cleaner to customer B, at more than three times the price at which B could have purchased the same vacuum cleaner from other stores in the same community. Does B have any defense?

45. L orally agrees to lease a large factory building to T for one year. The building is worth several million dollars, and the rent is $10,000 per month. Is the oral lease enforceable?

46. A and B orally agree to work together in the development of a tract of real estate which A owns, and to split whatever profits are obtained. After the property is fully developed, it is sold at a big profit, but A refuses to give B any share. Is the oral agreement enforceable?

47. S orally agrees to sell 1,000 Frisbees to B, for the price of $1,000.

    a. Assume that the Frisbees are to be shipped in two shipments; and that after sending the first shipment, S changes his mind and refuses to send the balance of the Frisbees. Can B enforce the oral agreement against S for the balance of the goods?

    b. Assume that B had made a down payment of $200, but S has not shipped anything. Can he enforce S's promise to sell him the 1,000 Frisbees?

    c. Assume that the Frisbees were to be specially manufactured by S with B's name and advertising slogan permanently imprinted thereon; and that after S had completed production, but before shipment, B canceled his order. Can S enforce the oral agreement against B?

48. Which, if any, of the following types of oral agreements fall within the Statute of Frauds provisions applicable to contracts not to be performed within one year?

    (A) Lifetime employment contract.

    (B) A lease of personal property terminable at will.

    (C) A five-year option to purchase personal property.

49. Charley is an employee of Aerospace Co., and has recently been transferred to a new city. Charley wishes to lease a house in the new city from Lessor. Lessor telephones Aerospace for a reference on Charley.

    a. Assume that Aerospace told Lessor, "Don't worry about Charley's credit. If she doesn't pay the rent, we will." Lessor then rents to Charley. If Charley defaults, can Lessor recover from Aerospace?

b. Assume that Aerospace told Charley to negotiate her own lease with Lessor, and orally assured Charley that Aerospace would pay whatever rent was charged by Lessor. Can Aerospace refuse to pay on the ground that its promise was oral? _____

50. Do the following writings satisfy the Statute of Frauds?

a. S and B orally agree on sale of S's 100-acre farm for $1,500 per acre. They date and sign the following memorandum: "Agreement this date re sale of S's farm to B. $1,000 paid on purchase price; balance due when deed delivered.(signed)" _____

b. An oral agreement for the sale of goods is followed by the following signed memorandum:

"Jan. 15. Received $100 down on purchase price of 500 Frisbees. Balance due on delivery within 10 days. (signed)" _____

c. An otherwise sufficient memorandum of an oral agreement for sale of Blackacre is signed by X "as agent of Seller." X has authorization from S, the owner of Blackacre, to sell it on S's behalf, but X's authority is only oral. _____

51. If a contract fails to comply with the Statute of Frauds, may the seller recover in restitution for any benefits conferred thereunder? May the buyer? _____

52. Ajax orally promised to pay Bob a salary of $20,000 per year for five years and his moving expenses, if Bob would quit his present job and come to work for Ajax in another city. Bob agreed to do so, but requested a written contract. Ajax assured him that the company attorney would prepare such a contract as soon as possible, but Ajax needed Bob to start at once. Accordingly, Bob sold his house, moved his family, and commenced to work for Ajax. He was fired without cause two months later. Can Bob enforce Ajax's oral promise (no written contract ever having been executed)? _____

53. A, a 15-year-old, has run out of money while on a trip away from home. B gives him food, a place to sleep, and his bus fare home, in exchange for A's promise in writing to pay B $200 to cover these costs. Is A's promise enforceable? _____

54. Distraught with loneliness, wealthy A engages B as a traveling companion, and promises to pay B $2,500 per month for such companionship. A has a long history of emotional instability. Can B enforce A's promise? _____

55. S sells a chemical apparatus to B, knowing that B intends to use the apparatus to make moonshine in violation of the law. Can S recover the contract price for the apparatus from B? _____

56. A local statute requires all chiropractors to be licensed. C, who is not licensed, contracts with and performs chiropractic services for B, for a specified fee. B refuses to pay.

a. Can C recover the contract fee?   _____

b. Can C recover the reasonable value of his services in restitution?   _____

THIRD PARTY RIGHTS AND OBLIGATIONS

57. Larry claims that his co-worker, Bob, owes him $200. Bob has always disputed Larry's claim. Even so, in order to avoid further embarrassment on the job, Bob asks his Employer to pay Larry $200 from Bob's paycheck then due. Employer agrees. If Employer fails to do so, can Larry enforce Employer's promise?   _____

58. Consumer group enters into an agreement in which company promises to refund the price of a defective widget to any purchaser who bought a widget within a specified time. Can A, who bought a widget during that time, enforce the promise?   _____

59. A contracts to purchase B's grocery store, and as part of the purchase price, agrees to pay off the bills owing to B's suppliers, one of whom is C.

a. Assume that C learns of the sale of B's business, and informs A and B of his assent, but takes no action because A has a good reputation and he expects that A will pay off C's bill as agreed. However, A and B revise their contract, so that A is not obligated thereunder to pay off C. Does C have a valid claim against A?   _____

b. Assume that A failed to pay off supplier C, and that there is no defense to enforcement of the A-B contract. C now demands payment from B, the original debtor. Can B sue A *without first paying off C*?   _____

60. A contracts to purchase B's grocery store, and as part of the purchase price, A agrees to give B's parents a 10% discount on any groceries purchased by them from the store during the forthcoming year.

a. Assume that later, in order to resolve a dispute between themselves, A and B change their agreement so as to cut out any discount to B's parents. Still later, B's parents find out about the discount deal in the original contract. Do B's parents have any valid claim against A?   _____

b. Assume that B's parents' rights had vested in time. Assume further that when A took over the grocery store, he found considerably less inventory than B had represented. If B's parents now sue A for their discount, can A assert the inventory shortage as a defense to their suit?   _____

61. Are the following enforceable as third party beneficiary contracts?

a. Father promises Son that he will not sell the family home, in exchange for Son's promise to pay Daughter's college tuition. Daughter sues to enforce Son's promise.   _____

b. Bank agrees to loan money to A, so that A can pay off a debt A owes to B. B sues to enforce Bank's promise. _____

62. A owns a house on which there is a $70,000 mortgage owing to Bank. A sells the house to B.

   a. If B is aware of the mortgage and expressly takes "subject to" it, does B become *personally* liable to Bank in the event of default? _____

   b. Assume that B later resold the house to C, and that C expressly "assumed" the mortgage debt. In the event of default on the mortgage, is C personally liable to Bank? _____

   c. Assume that Bank fails to recover from either B or C and therefore sues A (original owner). Can it recover? _____

63. Are the following assignments effective?

   a. Arthur is about to undergo a serious operation. He mails the following letter to his friend, Bruce:

   > "Dear Bruce: I want you to have the debt owed me by Cooper and will write him a letter telling him so.(signed)"

   Arthur dies before Bruce receives this letter, and before writing to Cooper. Can Bruce enforce the assignment? _____

   b. To settle a bona fide dispute with Bruce, Arthur orally assigns to him a half interest in a $1,000 negotiable promissory note payable to Arthur which Arthur retains in his possession. Later, Arthur refuses to share the payments with Bruce. Can Bruce enforce the assignment? _____

64. Which, if any, of the following contract rights are assignable?

   a. Amy is employed as a sales representative for Homecare Products. She receives a salary, but her employment is terminable at will. Can Amy make an effective assignment of her *future wages*? _____

   b. Amy is employed as a real estate salesperson by Ajax Realtors. She receives no salary, but a share of each commission obtained by Ajax on sales she procures. Can Amy make an effective assignment of her share of *future commissions*? _____

   c. Amy is writing a book of her memoirs, which several publishers are anxious to publish. Can Amy make an effective assignment of the royalties she will receive on this book before signing with a publisher? _____

   d. Amy is planning to marry, and engages Claude to design an original wedding gown for her, for which she pays $1,000 in advance. Shortly thereafter, she breaks her engagement. Can Amy make an effective assignment of her right to have Claude design a gown to her friend Beatrice, who is also planning to marry? _____

e.   Amy has contracted with Coconut Grower to supply her with as much coconut oil as she needs for her cosmetic manufacturing business, at $100 per quart. Can Amy make an effective assignment to Barbara, who is also a cosmetics manufacturer, of her contract with Coconut Grower?

f.   Amy owns a cosmetics manufacturing plant on which she carries a fire insurance policy. If Amy sells the plant to Barbara, can she make an effective assignment of the fire insurance policy to Barbara without the insurance company's consent?

g.   Bank has agreed to loan Amy $100,000 for use in her cosmetics business. If Amy sells the business to Barbara before the loan is consummated, can Amy make an effective assignment to Barbara of her right to the bank loan?

65.   Aaron is a plumbing contractor. He contracts to furnish labor and material for the plumbing in a large office building being constructed by Baker, for the sum of $100,000.

a.   Assume that the contract contains a provision stating "neither party shall assign this contract without the other's consent." If Baker sells the building to Cooper during the course of construction, can Baker make an effective assignment of her rights to Aaron's services without Aaron's consent?

b.   Assume that the contract provision stated that "any assignment of any right hereunder without the other party's consent shall be null and void." Can Aaron, after finishing the job, make an effective assignment of his right to the $100,000?

c.   Assume that the contract provision stated "no assignment of this contract shall be made." Can Aaron *delegate* to another plumber, Potter, the duties to perform his contract with Baker?

66.   Ann signed a contract under which she is obligated to pay $5,000 to Belle for dancing lessons. Belle immediately assigned the monies due under this contract to Chester, who immediately notified Ann of the assignment. Chester is now suing Ann to enforce payment. Would the following be valid defenses for Ann to assert against Chester?

a.   Ann was unaware that she was signing a contract: she thought it was a contest entry form.

b.   Belle gave her only half the dancing lessons she promised.

67.   Alice buys a vacuum cleaner from retailer Ben. She promises to pay for it in six monthly installments of $50 each. Ben assigns the contract to First Finance Co., who paid value and took without notice of any defense. First Finance Co. sues Alice for nonpayment.

a. Is it a valid defense for Alice that, before she was aware of the assignment, Ben promised to refund her the price of a defective refrigerator purchased in another transaction?

b. Would the answer to the previous question be the same if the contract Alice signed contained a provision in which she agreed to *waive* defenses in favor of any assignee?

68. By way of a gift, Amos tells Bob, "I hereby assign to you the $10,000 debt owed to me by X." Later, however, Amos makes a written assignment of the same debt to Chris. As between Bob and Chris, who is entitled to collect the debt?

69. By way of a gift, Amos signs a letter to Bob reading "I hereby assign to you the $10,000 debt owed to me by X." Later, however, Amos changes his mind and sells his claim against X to Chris, who is a bona fide purchaser. As between Bob and Chris, who is entitled to collect the debt?

70. Employee borrows money from Bank, and assigns as security his wages then due from Employer. The next day, Employee makes a similar loan from and assignment to Finance Co. (which has no knowledge of Bank's interest). Finance Co. notifies Employer of its assignment before Bank does. Assume no restrictions on wage assignments.

a. As between Bank and Finance Co., which is entitled to priority?

b. Is the question of priority here affected by the U.C.C.?

c. Suppose that Employer actually *paid* Employee's wages to Finance Co., in response to their notice of assignment. Would Bank have a valid claim against Finance Co. for a share of the wages?

71. After Actor had contracted to star in Producer's new play, he received a better offer to appear in a film. Therefore, he assigned all of his rights and duties under his contract with Producer to Standby.

a. Standby is ready and willing to perform. Is Producer obligated to accept Standby's performance?

b. Assume that Producer is willing to allow Standby to perform instead of Actor. If Standby walks off the job halfway through the contract, can Producer sue *Actor* for damages?

72. Archer contracts to purchase Baker's farm for $50,000. With Baker's consent, Archer "sells, transfers and assigns" to Childs his contract with Baker. Can Baker sue Childs for performance?

PERFORMANCE OF CONTRACT

73. Able signs a contract to buy Baker's house for $67,500 "if I am able to obtain a mortgage loan for $60,000, at 7% interest, payable over 20 years." Assume

that Able tries but is unable to obtain the described loan, and therefore refuses to proceed with the purchase. Is Able in breach of contract? _____

74. Broker procures a buyer for Owner's house. Owner promises to pay Broker a commission of $1,500 "on close of escrow." If thereafter, the buyer refuses to proceed with the sale (and hence escrow never closes), is Owner under any duty to pay the $1,500 to Broker? _____

75. Borrower borrows money from Friend, promising to repay "as soon as I am able." If Borrower thereafter refuses to seek employment, and therefore has no money, is he under any duty to repay the loan? _____

76. Club charters an airplane from Airline for "flight from San Francisco to depart 10:00 A.M., June 1, to arrive in Papeete, Tahiti, 6:00 P.M., June 2." Due to mechanical delays the flight is 10 hours late in departure. Assume no statutes are applicable.

   a. Is Club obligated to pay the charter fee? _____

   b. Is Airline liable to Club for breach of contract? _____

77. Buyer orders 1,000 Frisbees from Seller at a price of $1 each. No credit term is agreed upon but Buyer reserves the right to return any or all of the Frisbees within 30 days after delivery.

   a. Is Buyer obligated to pay for the Frisbees during the 30-day period? _____

   b. If Seller sues Buyer for the price, does Seller have to *prove* that he made complete delivery of the goods? _____

   c. If Seller sues Buyer for the price, does Seller have to *prove* that Buyer made no return of any of the goods during the 30-day period? _____

   d. Assume that Buyer intended to sell the Frisbees at the County Fair, and that his order therefore stated: "Buyer reserves right to cancel this order if County Fair is not held this year." If Seller sues Buyer for the price, does Seller have to *prove* that the County Fair was held? _____

78. Farmer engages Digger to dig a new water well on Farmer's property. Farmer agrees to pay Digger $2,000 "provided the well water is fit for human consumption as determined by the State Water Board." Digger brings in a new well, but the State Water Board finds the water unfit for human consumption.

   a. If Digger can prove that the State Water Board has applied *unreasonably* strict standards in testing the water, can he collect from Farmer? _____

   b. Assume that Farmer's promise to pay was "provided that the well water is of a quality *satisfactory* to me" (Farmer); and Farmer now says that the quality is unsatisfactory. If Digger can prove that Farmer is acting *unreasonably*, can he enforce Farmer's promise to pay the $2,000? _____

79. Owner gives Broker a written listing to find a buyer for Owner's house. Nothing is said about Broker having the right to show the inside of the house to prospective purchasers. If Owner refuses to allow Broker to show the inside of the house (and Broker is therefore unable to obtain a purchaser), can Broker collect the commission provided in the listing agreement? _____

80. Owner contracts to sell his house to Purchaser for $50,000, and to repair a broken toilet therein prior to the date set for closing. On the date set for closing, Owner tenders a deed, but has still not fixed the toilet. If Purchaser refuses to proceed with the purchase, can Seller enforce the contract? _____

81. Owner agrees to sell her house to Buyer for $25,000. The contract provides that the purchase price is to be paid by Buyer, and the deed is to be delivered by Owner, on June 1. On that date, nothing happens.

   a.   On June 2, can Owner sue Buyer for breach? _____

   b.   On June 2, can Buyer sue Owner for breach? _____

82. Bertha advertises a car for sale. Andy offers to purchase the car for $2,000, payable $200 per month for the next 10 months. Bertha says, "I accept." In the absence of any other understanding, is Bertha entitled to hold onto the car until she receives the full purchase price? _____

83. Artist agrees to paint a portrait for Lawyer, in exchange for which Lawyer agrees to draft a will for Artist. Artist gets very busy and puts off Lawyer's portrait, and Lawyer therefore never draws a will for Artist, although she clearly had time to do so. Can Artist recover damages from Lawyer for breach of contract? _____

84. Arthur promises to move in and care for his wealthy Uncle for the rest of his life, in exchange for which Uncle promises to pay Arthur $500 per month and also to name him sole beneficiary of his estate.

   a.   If Uncle later, *without cause*, refuses Arthur's care and orders him to leave, can Arthur enforce Uncle's promise to name him as sole beneficiary? _____

   b.   Assume that Uncle never ordered Arthur to leave, but became increasingly disagreeable as he grew older, making if far more difficult for Arthur to care for him. Would Arthur be excused from his duty to care for Uncle for the rest of his life? _____

85. Owner signs a written listing authorizing Broker to sell Owner's house, and requiring Owner to pay Broker a commission "on closing of the sale." Thereafter, Broker interests Purchaser in the property, and Purchaser signs a written agreement to buy Owner's house on the terms of the listing. Prior to closing, however, Purchaser wrongfully refuses to perform. Owner could, but does not, file legal action against Purchaser, and hence the sale never "closes." Can Broker recover any commission from Owner? _____

86. Owner hires Manager to collect rents and manage Owner's apartment house for a period of five years, for which Manager is to be paid 5% of the gross rentals received by Owner. At the end of the first year, Owner sells the apartment house, and the purchaser does his own managing. Can Manager now sue for damages? _____

87. Owner contracts to sell his house to Purchaser, purchase price to be paid and deed to be delivered on June 1.

   a. Assume that on May 1, Owner tells Purchaser that he is involved in divorce litigation and that his wife will not release her interest in the property. Purchaser therefore does not tender payment on June 1. If Owner tenders clear title on June 1 (Owner's wife releasing her interest), is Purchaser in breach? _____

   b. Assume same facts as in previous paragraph, but assume further that Purchaser told Owner on May 1 that in view of Owner's pending divorce litigation, Purchaser would look elsewhere for a house. If Owner thereafter clears his title, and gives Purchaser notice thereof *before* June 1, can Owner enforce the contract? _____

88. Sam agrees to sell his car to his friend, Bob, for $1,000, the price to be paid and car transferred within 10 days.

   a. The next day, Sam receives a better offer from Fred, and accepts Fred's offer (still not delivering the car, however). Bob learns of this and buys himself another car. If the deal with Fred falls through, can Sam enforce Bob's promise to buy the car? _____

   b. Would the answer be the same if Sam was a new car dealer and the car sold to Bob was part of his stock? _____

   c. Suppose that the day after the agreement was made, Bob declared bankruptcy. Relying on this, Sam sold the car to another. On the tenth day, Bob tenders the $1,000. Is Sam in breach? _____

89. Owner leases a vacant lot to Promoter for 10 years. Promoter agrees to erect a car wash thereon, and to pay Owner as rent "one-third of the profits received from operation of the car wash."

   a. If Promoter never gets the car wash built because she is unable to obtain financing, can Owner enforce the lease? _____

   b. If Promoter in fact erects the car wash, but hires her family and friends at such exorbitant salaries that there are *no* profits, can Owner recover any rent from Promoter? _____

   c. If after operating the car wash for awhile, Promoter determines that it cannot be operated profitably and hence closes it down, can Owner recover future rent from Promoter? _____

90. To settle divorce litigation, Wife releases her marital rights in certain property, and Husband agrees to pay Wife $10,000 a year for five years. After the first installment is paid, Husband informs Wife that he will make no further payments to her. Can Wife bring suit immediately for the remaining four installments?

_____

91. Ace contracts to manufacture and deliver 10,000 spark plugs to Beta on April 1, which Beta needs on that date to keep its assembly line running. On February 1, Ace advises Beta, "I'm having trouble locating the raw materials I need to fill your order, and may not be able to deliver on time." Beta immediately notifies that it will purchase its spark plugs elsewhere. If Ace is in fact able to manufacture spark plugs, and tenders delivery on April 1, is Beta in breach if it refuses to accept delivery?

_____

92. In January, Amos contracted to sell his house to Beulah for $70,000, the purchase price to be paid and deed to be delivered on June 1.

a. On March 1, Beulah writes Amos, "I've had second thoughts about buying your home. I won't pay you that amount of money, unless you repaint the house and fix up the yard." Could Amos sue Beulah for breach of contract upon *receipt* of this letter?

_____

b. On April 1, Beulah writes Amos, "I'm no longer concerned about the paint and yard work. However, my attorney has just advised me that your title is defective, and not to proceed with the purchase. Of course, I have to follow his advice. Sorry." If in fact Amos has a clear and perfect title, can he sue Beulah for breach of contract *on receipt* of this letter?

_____

c. Assume that, notwithstanding her letters to Amos, Beulah tenders the full purchase price on June 1. Can Beulah still enforce the contract?

_____

d. Assume that after receipt of Beulah's letters, Amos had replied, "You have no valid excuse for breaking our contract. I expect you to pay the full purchase price on June 1, as agreed." However, not hearing anything further from Beulah, Amos decided not to wait until June 1, and resold the property to another. If Beulah shows up with the full purchase price on June 1, is Amos in breach?

_____

93. Developer contracts with Builder to install sewers in a large housing tract, for a price of $100,000, construction to start in six months. Before Builder has done anything, Developer writes him a letter stating, "I have decided to have another company install the sewers instead of you. Send me a bill for whatever expenses you have incurred."

a. If, instead, Builder goes ahead and procures the supplies, equipment and labor which he will need to perform the contract, and shows up on the job site ready to perform, can he enforce the contract for the full $100,000?

_____

b. Assume that it was Builder who repudiated the contract before any performance. Developer waits until the end of the six-month period to see if

Builder will change his mind, and then hires another contractor. Consequently, Developer then has to pay $10,000 more because costs of construction have increased in the interim. Can Developer recover the $10,000 from Builder?

94. Owner contracts to sell his house to Purchaser for $50,000, and June 1 is the date set for closing. The contract requires Purchaser to pay the purchase price in five equal installments of $10,000 each, due January 1, February 1, March 1, April 1, and May 1. Purchaser makes the first four payments but is unable to raise the final $10,000.

    a. Can Purchaser enforce the contract against Owner on June 1?

    b. Can Owner enforce the contract against purchaser on June 1 *without first tendering a deed* to the property?

95. Don orders 1,000 cases of spaghetti from Giovanni, to be delivered in five equal monthly shipments (200 cases each). A total purchase price of $5,000 is specified, but the time for payment is not mentioned.

    a. Assume that Giovanni delivers the first shipment, and demands payment of $1,000 (200 cases at $5 each), but Don refuses to pay until the balance of the order is received. Can Giovanni sue and recover for the 200 cases delivered?

    b. Assume that Giovanni had delivered the first two shipments (totaling 400 cases), but then received a better offer from one of Don's competitors, and therefore cut off any further shipments to Don. Under such circumstances, could Giovanni sue and recover for the 400 cases delivered?

    c. Assume that the contract stated: "This contract is indivisible, and Don shall pay nothing whatsoever unless and until full and complete delivery is made." If Giovanni had delivered 800 cases, and then his plant was shut down by a strike, so that he was unable to make the final delivery, could he recover anything for the 800 cases delivered?

96. On March 15, Archie contracts to buy Bunker's house, closing to occur on April 30. However, on April 15, Bunker requests a 60-day extension because he has not yet found a place to move, and Archie good-naturedly agrees.

    a. Assume that on April 30, Archie changes his mind and tenders payment and requests a conveyance, and Bunker refuses. Is Bunker in breach of contract on that date?

    b. Assume that on April 29, Archie notified Bunker that he was unwilling to stick by his promise to extend closing for 60 days, and demanded a conveyance not later than May 15. Could Archie enforce the contract by proper tender on May 15?

    c. Assume that the sale closed on May 15 as demanded by Archie. Is Archie entitled to recover anything from Bunker for Bunker's use of the property during the two-week period?

97. Alana contracts to purchase a sofa from Furniture Store. When it is delivered she notices that it is badly stained, but accepts it anyway. Later she refuses to pay for the sofa because of the stain. Was her acceptance a waiver of the defect?

98. Owner engages Contractor to build a house. The contract calls for Owner to make progress payments upon completion of various portions of the construction, as evidenced by certificate signed by Architect. Owner makes the first three progress payments to Contractor without the certificate. Has Owner waived the right to insist upon the Architect's certificate before making future progress payments?

99. Alpha engages Builder to remodel her kitchen and to install therein new Frigi-Queen built-in appliances. Because Frigi-Queens are in short supply, Builder installs another brand of appliances which has a reputation as good as Frigi-Queen.

   a. Alpha refuses to pay Builder for the remodeling because of the unauthorized substitute of brands. Can Builder collect the contract price from Alpha?

   b. Assume that the reason for the substitution of brands was simply that Builder was unable to get as good a discount on Frigi-Queen appliances as he could on the brand he installed. Can Builder collect the contract price from Alpha?

   c. Assume that Alpha's contract with Builder provided "any deviation or substitution without Alpha's consent shall render this contract void, and she shall be under no obligation to pay Builder anything." Can Builder collect the contract price from Alpha?

   d. Assume that in addition to substituting appliances without Alpha's consent, Builder also failed to install the proper electrical wiring, so that the appliances installed are constantly shorting out. Could Builder recover anything from Alpha—on the contract or in restitution?

100. Alpha contracts with Builder to build her a new house on a lot she owns. Builder had almost completed the house when it was struck by lightning and destroyed. Builder sues Alpha for the contract price less cost of completion. Will he recover?

101. Alpha goes to XYZ Department Store and orders new Frigi-Queen built-in appliances, to be delivered to her home. She and her husband plan to install the appliances themselves. XYZ is short of Frigi-Queens, and therefore delivers another brand which has as good a reputation, and costs the same. Alpha refuses to accept delivery of the appliances. Can XYZ collect from Alpha for its loss of profit on the sale?

102. Don orders 1,000 cases of spaghetti from Giovanni, 200 cases to be shipped "immediately," and 200 cases on the first of each month thereafter. The agreement requires Don to pay $5 per case, *i.e.*, $1,000, on receipt of each shipment.

a. If Giovanni delays the first shipment to Don for more than two weeks, is Don justified in canceling the contract and rejecting any later shipments from Giovanni? _____

b. If Don was more than two weeks late in paying Giovanni for the first shipment, is Giovanni justified in canceling the contract and refusing further shipments to Don? _____

c. Assume that the order form signed by Don contained a "time is of the essence" clause. If Don was only one day late in making the first payment, would Giovanni be justified in canceling the contract and refusing any further shipments? _____

d. Assume that the final shipment by Giovanni was timely, but contains only 150 cases. Must Don accept and pay for this short shipment? _____

103. Alpha contracts with Builder to build her a new house on a lot she owns.

a. During the course of construction, Builder encounters rapidly rising prices of labor and materials. It turns out that it will cost Builder **double** the amount he estimated when contracting with Alpha. Is he in breach if he refuses to complete the job? _____

b. Builder is injured while on the job site, and suffers a broken leg. Because of this, he is unable to return to the job within the period specified in the contract. Is he in breach if he fails to complete the house on time? _____

c. Assume the contract required Builder to construct Alpha's house "in accordance with City Building Code" standards. If the City thereafter changes its Building Code, so as to make performance of the contract by Builder more expensive, is he excused from performing for the same price? _____

104. Lew leases to Ted for 99 years a large tract of undeveloped land at a rental of $5,000 per month, upon which Ted is to erect a large shopping center (as per agreed plans). Shortly thereafter, a zoning ordinance is enacted which restricts development of the property to single family residences.

a. Is Ted's obligation to erect the shopping center discharged? _____

b. Is Ted entitled to cancel the lease (*i.e.,* is his obligation to pay the rent discharged)? _____

105. Wanda agrees to sell her prize-winning poodle to Brenda for $1,500, and to ship the poodle cross-country to Brenda by air carrier the next day.

a. If, unknown to either party, the poodle had died the night before they contracted, could Brenda sue Wanda for damages for nondelivery? _____

b. Assume that Wanda delivered the poodle to the air carrier, but the poodle was killed in a crash of the plane. Could Wanda sue Brenda for the $1,500 purchase price? _____

c. Assume that all air carriers were grounded by bad weather, and Wanda shipped the poodle to Brenda by truck instead. If Brenda refused to accept the poodle because of the delay, could Wanda enforce the contract? _____

106. Lew executes a written lease to Ted for 99 years covering a large tract of undeveloped land, which Ted planned to develop as a shopping center. Later, the land is zoned to prevent this use, and the parties agree in writing to cancel the lease.

a. If Lew later changes his mind and sues to enforce the lease, is he bound by the agreement to cancel? _____

b. Would the answer be the same if the agreement to cancel was oral? _____

107. Ted signs a contract to purchase a tractor from Larry for $10,000, payable within 30 days following delivery. Upon delivery, Ted complains of various defects in the tractor. Although he does not regard Ted's complaints as reasonable or justified, Larry agrees in writing to reduce the purchase price by $500.

a. If Larry later changes his mind, and sues to collect the full purchase price, is he bound by his agreement to reduce the price? _____

b. Would the answer be the same if the agreement was oral? _____

108. Sandy owes Pete $1,500 on a personal loan, which she finds difficult to repay. Sandy offers to pay off the loan by painting Pete's house, and Pete gladly agrees to this because he was planning to have his house painted anyway, and the cheapest bid he got was $1,800.

a. If Sandy later changes her mind and refuses to paint Pete's house, can Pete sue Sandy (1) for the original $1,500 debt *and* (2) for the extra $300 it cost him to get his house painted? _____

b. If Sandy actually painted Pete's house, but did a poor job, could Pete later sue Sandy for the $1,500 original debt? _____

c. Suppose that it cost Pete $500 to correct and complete the paint work which Sandy was supposed to do. If Sandy gave Pete a check for $100 marked "in settlement of all claims re my paint job" and Pete cashed this check, can Pete thereafter recover from Sandy for the balance of the damages? _____

DAMAGES

109. If a seller willfully and in "bad faith" refuses to perform a contract for the sale of goods, is an award of exemplary damages proper? _____

110. Duke orders 10,000 Frisbees to be manufactured by Easy according to Duke's specifications and carrying Duke's brand name and advertising. If Easy tenders delivery and Duke wrongfully refuses to accept, can Easy thereafter recover the full purchase price? _____

111. Alpha contracts with Builder to remodel her kitchen.

 a. Before Builder starts to work, Alpha's house is accidentally destroyed by fire. Builder tenders performance. Can he recover from Alpha his loss of profits on the remodeling job? _____

 b. Assume that the fire had taken place *after* Builder had started the job. Can he recover anything from Alpha? _____

112. Martha agrees to sell her house to John for $70,000. The fair market value of the house is $72,000. Martha's title proves defective so that she cannot convey marketable title. Can John recover $2,000 damages? _____

113. Producer hires Designer to design and create the costumes for a new Broadway show, for the sum of $25,000. The contract requires that all costumes be completed one week prior to opening date.

 a. If Designer is one day late in completing the gowns, but this delay causes no postponement of the show or other loss to Producer, can Producer recover anything from Designer? _____

 b. If Designer is two weeks late in completing the gowns, and the delay results in a loss of over $100,000 to Producer—extra salaries to cast, theater rental, etc.—can Producer recover this entire amount from Designer (less, of course, $25,000 contract price)? _____

 c. If Designer fails to complete the costumes at all, and as a direct result Producer has to cancel the show entirely, can Producer recover the *profits* which he claims he would have made had the show opened on time? _____

114. Tom Johns, a leading singer, contracts to appear for one week in the floor show at the Starburst Hotel, for the sum of $25,000.

 a. Assume Starburst management notifies Johns well in advance of his starting date that they have changed their mind and have hired someone else for the week in question. Can Johns recover the full $25,000 from Starburst? _____

 b. In a suit brought by Johns against Starburst, is the burden on Johns to prove that he could not find other suitable employment during the week in question? _____

 c. Assume that Johns had started to perform as agreed, but the third night he showed up drunk, got in a fight with the management, walked off the job, and refused to return. Starburst rushed in Danny Davis, Jr. as a replacement. Can Johns recover anything from Starburst for the two nights he worked? _____

 d. Would the answer to the preceding question be the same if (instead of walking off the job) Johns had become seriously ill and was unable to perform for the balance of the week? _____

115. Alpha hires Builder to remodel her kitchen, as per agreed plans, for a total price of $4,000, due on completion, and which (after deducting cost of labor and materials) will result in a net profit of $1,000 to Builder.

a. If Alpha notifies Builder before he starts the job, or has incurred any costs, that she has changed her mind and does not wish to proceed, can Builder still recover his lost profits ($1,000)?

        _____

b. Would the answer to the preceding question be the same if Alpha proved that Builder had free time as a result of not having to remodel her kitchen, and made no effort to seek other jobs during this period?

        _____

c. Assume that Builder walks off the job when it is half finished and that the value of the work done is $2,000. Assume further that it costs Alpha $3,000 to have another contractor come in and finish the job. Can Alpha recover the full $3,000 from Builder?

        _____

d. Assume that Alpha had insisted upon the following provision in the contract: "In event Builder fails to complete the work by (agreed date), he must pay Alpha $50 for each day's delay thereafter." If there is a delay in completion which is Builder's fault, can Alpha recover $50 per day in addition to her other damages?

        _____

116. Acme orders 1,000 Frisbees from Baker, and pays a premium price of $1.50 each (regular price is $1 each) in consideration of Baker's promise to deliver no later than July 1. The contract also provides that if Baker is late in delivery, he must pay Acme $500 as a "penalty." If Baker is two weeks late in delivery, but Acme suffers *no* actual damage because of the delay, can it recover the $500?

        _____

ANSWERS TO REVIEW QUESTIONS

1. **YES** A guaranty of an *existing* debt must be supported by consideration to be enforceable. However, most courts will enforce a written guaranty which *recites consideration* (even though the consideration has *not* in fact been paid). [§§30, 35]

2.a. **YES (modern view)** Modern courts hold that forbearance to sue is a valid consideration if the claimant *honestly* believes he has a valid claim *regardless of the reasonableness* of his belief. [§§39-40]

b. **PROBABLY** Some authorities (including the Restatement) take the view that release constitutes consideration even if there is neither a reasonable basis for the claim released nor a good faith belief in its validity. [§42]

3.a. **NO** B gave no consideration because her promise to purchase as many as she "chooses" was an illusory promise. *Note:* Nor can A's agreement be enforced as a "firm offer" because it was oral. "Firm offers" between merchants must be signed and in *writing*. [U.C.C. §2-205] [§§46, 225, 233]

b. **YES** This would be a "requirements" contract, and B's promise is not illusory. [§§68-72]

4.a. **NO** A provision giving a promisor the right to cancel at will and without notice renders his promise illusory; hence no contract. [§47]

b. **YES** B has made a real promise, since he must supply A's service requirements for a minimum of 30 days. [§§48, 50]

c. **YES (modern view)** Even though the term "absolute discretion" is used, the modern (and U.C.C.) interpretation requires the exercise of *good faith*; hence no power to terminate at will, and promise therefore not illusory. [§§53, 73]

5. **YES** Even though a minor's promise is voidable, it is sufficient consideration to support a counterpromise. Thus, a minor can always enforce a contract even though it cannot be enforced against him. [§51]

6. **YES** A *conditional* promise is sufficient consideration provided the condition does not give the promisor the alternative of canceling the obligation. Here, B had no such right, and hence his promise is good consideration. [§53]

7. **NO** Even if Broker did not expressly promise to do anything, there was at least an *implied promise* to use *reasonable or best efforts* to find a buyer, since this was a contract for exclusive dealing. This implied promise is sufficient consideration to support Homeowner's promise to pay a commission. [§§65-67]

8. **NO** It would be against public policy to allow a public officer to claim a reward for performing an act which is within the scope of her duties per the legal duty rule. In this case, the officer had a *public* duty to capture the robber. Thus, she is not entitled to recover the reward. (*Compare:* If the acts required to obtain the reward were *not within the scope* of the officer's preexisting duty, the result would be contra.) [§§76-80]

9. **PROBABLY NOT** Many courts would **refuse** to enforce the promise on the ground that A was already under a contractual duty to perform, and his continued performance therefore imposes no "legal detriment" under the legal duty rule. A liberal trend is to enforce the promise **without consideration** if the unforeseeable difficulties render the demand for additional compensation **fair** and equitable in light of the circumstances. (The U.C.C. permits modification of a contract for the sale of goods without consideration, but the contract here will probably be found to be a contract for services rather than for the sale of goods.) [§§84-85, 87, 91-92]

10. **SPLIT OF AUTHORITY** Yes under the majority rule, although not under the minority view. *Note:* This is a case where the preexisting duty is owed to a third person (Builder), rather than the promisor (Owner). [§88]

11.a. **NO** Payment of a lesser sum in exchange for discharge of the preexisting debt is not sufficient consideration for the discharge **unless** each party suffers **some** detriment. However, payment before maturity or in a **different medium** constitutes two of the many acceptable changes to the original transaction to constitute sufficient "detriment." [§§99-100]

b. **YES** In the absence of some **bona fide dispute** as to the amount due, payment of a lesser sum does not discharge the debt and B can sue for the balance, even if she agreed to accept the smaller amount in full discharge of B's obligation; there is **no** "accord and satisfaction" because no consideration. [§§99, 797-798, 115, 838]

12.a. **NO** A promise based on "moral consideration," because of gratitude or a prior favor, is not enforceable in most jurisdictions. Although some courts hold that a promise based on a moral obligation is enforceable to the extent the promisor was enriched by the promisee's action, in this case it is not clear that Clutz ever came under a moral obligation. [§§6, 131, 144]

b. **YES** Under these circumstances, the promise would have tended to **induce** Able to help in the completion of the garage. Hence, there would be bargained-for consideration for Clutz's promise, and it would be enforceable. [§24]

13.a. **NO** Parishioner was intending a gift; no bargaining intent. (Even if the promise were deemed bargained for, it would relate to Minister's prior services and hence would be "past consideration.") [§§130, 131]

b. **NO** The fact that a promise is in writing does not make it enforceable. By statute in some states a writing may raise a **presumption** that there is an adequate consideration, but that presumption is rebuttable by proof of the real consideration (or lack thereof) for the promise. [§§11, 12]

c. **DEPENDS** On whether such reliance could have been reasonably expected. Under the doctrine of "promissory estoppel," courts will enforce a relied-upon **gratuitous** promise, if the reliance was reasonably expected by the XYZ Church. (However, the promise may be enforced only to the extent of the reliance.) [§§17, 19]

d. **YES** This appears to be a bargain; Minister has bound himself to perform services on a condition beyond his control. The fact that Minister's promise may have little tangible value is immaterial *if* the promise is really bargained-for; as is the fact that the Church, rather than Parishioner, receives the "benefit" of Minister's promise. (But note that if the promise is put in merely for show, as a mere recital of consideration, it may be deemed merely nominal consideration, and Parishioner's promise might therefore be unenforceable.) [§§25, 31, 53]

14.a. NO (majority)   Most states require that the promise or acknowledgment of a debt barred by the statute of limitations be in *writing* or that the debtor make part payment of the barred debt. Thus, Debtor's oral promise would not be enforceable. [§137]

b. NO   The courts may imply a promise to pay from an *acknowledgment* of the debt, but a promise cannot be implied from a *refusal* to pay the barred debt. [§136]

c. NO   But Friend can enforce the promise on the terms contained therein—*i.e.,* $700 when Debtor sells the car since it is the new promise and not the old debt that is enforceable. [§134]

d. MAYBE   In "a.," Friend might be able to enforce the *oral* promise. *Reason:* In most states there is *no* requirement that a promise to pay a debt discharged by bankruptcy be in writing. However, under the Bankruptcy Reform Act, a promise to pay a debt discharged in bankruptcy is enforceable only if several stringent requirements are met, and not enough information is given here to determine whether, under the Act, the agreement here is enforceable. [§142]

15. YES   A's preexisting duty (to pay $3,000) was *voidable* because of the fraud. A had the option of rescinding or ratifying the sale. His new promise is enforceable *without new consideration* and is not subject to the fraud defense. [§139]

16. SPLIT   Farmer's services were apparently rendered *without* expectation of payment and are therefore regarded as mere "moral" consideration for A's promise; hence, unenforceable in most states. However, the trend of authority is to enforce such a promise to the extent of the benefit conferred. [§§144-147, 128]

17. NO   The promise to discharge the son's debt is apparently based only on moral consideration, and is not binding on the promisor. Even under the modern view, a promise based on a moral obligation will normally not be enforced where the promisor did not receive a direct economic benefit. [§150]

18. NO   Whether a person intends to be contractually bound is measured by an *objective* standard. Thus, if a *reasonable* person would have realized that Amy's offer was made in jest (no true bargaining intent), there is no contract—even if Buford took her seriously. [§154]

19.a. YES   A contract may be "implied in fact" from the *conduct of the parties*. Here, the fact that Alice maintained an account with Elite indicates that she had done business there before. Hence, she should have known that they would bill her the regular store prices, and by telephoning an order without mentioning price she *impliedly agreed* to pay that price, unless it is manifestly unreasonable. [§156]

b. YES   Again, a contract may be implied from the conduct of the parties. Arturo's continuing performance was an implied offer to extend their contract each year, and

Ben's acceptance is implied from his conduct in permitting Arturo to continue and by paying the contract rate for the first two years. [§156]

c. **NO**   Since Betty was unconscious, she did not expressly or impliedly agree to anything. However, Dudley can still recover from Betty through an implied-in-law contract in order to prevent unjust enrichment (and in cases such as this, to encourage rendering services in an emergency). As a matter of policy, the law will fictionally imply a request by Betty for Dudley's services. But, in implied-in-law contracts only the *reasonable value* of the services is recoverable . . . which might be less than the $1,500 billed by Dudley. [§157]

20.a. **NO**   An offer must evidence a *present* contractual intent. A's words suggest an *invitation* to B to make an offer. B's purported "acceptance" is actually the offer, which A is free to accept or reject. [§§161-162]

b. **NO**   Advertisements to the public are generally held mere invitations for an offer, on the ground that the advertiser has not committed itself to an unlimited quantity of the goods. [§163]

c. **DEPENDS**   On *parties' intent* as to effect of letter agreement. If both parties intend to be bound only by the written contract, the "letter agreement" would be deemed preliminary only. Otherwise, it will be enforceable. (This assumes that the letter of intent would be sufficiently definite to enforce but for the addition of the words "formal contract to follow.") [§§443-446]

d. **PROBABLY**   "Quoting" of prices is commonly understood only as *inviting* an offer. But here, since it was directed to a specific person (B), and A added the words "for immediate acceptance," most authorities would hold this manifests an intent to make a binding offer. [§170]

21.a. **NO**   The advertisement of an auction is an *invitation* for offers, and is not in itself an offer. [§172]

b. **YES**   Unless the property is *explicitly* put up for sale "without reserve," the auction is deemed to be "with reserve" which permits the seller to withdraw the goods at any time before the fall of the hammer (acceptance). [§175]

c. **NO**   Even though the *seller* is bound to sell the goods at an auction without reserve, this does not prevent a bidder from revoking his "acceptance" prior to the fall of the hammer. [§174]

22.a. **YES**   An offer terminates by operation of law after expiration of the period of time specified in the offer. The period commences to run on the date of actual *receipt* of the offer or on the date it would normally be received. Since the offer was received on March 3 and there does not appear to be an unreasonable delay in the transmission, the five-day acceptance period would commence to run on March 3. As the acceptance was dispatched within five days, a contract was formed. [§§183, 307]

b. **NO**   Destruction of the subject matter prior to acceptance terminates the offer. [§251]

c. **NO**   The general rule is that offers are revocable even though there may be an express promise not to revoke. And, a written offer can be revoked orally. The revocation must be communicated to the offeree and becomes effective upon **receipt**. Since A learned of the revocation prior to dispatch of the acceptance, no contract was formed. [§§219-222, 225, 230-233]

d. **YES**

If the offeror receives **consideration** to keep the offer open, she cannot revoke during the stated period because an **option** will be created. *Compare:* Under the U.C.C., a written offer by a merchant, containing words of firmness, cannot be revoked for the time stated or a reasonable time (but in no event more than three months) even absent consideration. [§§233, 263]

e. **NO**

The trend of authority is that an offeror may be estopped to revoke where the offeree has **foreseeably and reasonably** relied to her detriment on a promise to keep the offer open. [§228]

23.a. **NO**

B's $4,800 counteroffer terminated her power of acceptance. B's "acceptance" thereafter did not form a contract. [§192]

b. **YES**

B's question is neither a rejection nor a counteroffer, but an inquiry. A's offer would therefore still be open, and B's acceptance would create a contract. [§193]

c. **YES**

Generally, an acceptance is effective on dispatch unless there has been a **previous** rejection. In such event, acceptance is effective only on **receipt**. However, since A in fact received the acceptance prior to the rejection, a contract was formed. (But if A regards the later-arriving rejection as a repudiation of the acceptance, and relies on it, B will be estopped from enforcing the contract.) [§§342, 333]

d. **YES**

Under the *Adams v. Lindsell* rule, the contract was formed on dispatch of the acceptance, even though A **learned** of the rejection first. (If, however, A relied on the rejection and contracted to sell the property to C, B should be **estopped** to assert the contract.) [§§347-348]

24.a. **NO**

To be effective, an acceptance must be unequivocal (here, B has apparently put off a decision). [§§196, 192]

b. **DEPENDS**

Ordinarily, an acceptance must be a mirror image of an offer (except where the U.C.C. applies). Since A's order did not specify time for provision of services, the law will imply a term of "reasonableness" based on the nature of the contract, custom and usage in the community, and prior dealings between the parties. If six weeks is reasonable, the variance in the "acceptance" would not prevent formation of a contract. [§§203, 408-409]

25.a. **NO**

Father's offer is for a unilateral contract. (He is bargaining for Daughter's lifetime care, not for a mere promise.) Since the performance will take time to complete and the offeree has **started performance**, the offer **cannot** be revoked under the principle of the Restatement (Second) §45. [§§241-242]

b. **NO**

Father specifically did **not** bind Daughter to anything. Her caring for Father was merely the start of her acceptance of his offer for a unilateral contract. [§288]

26. **YES**

In a bilateral contract situation, the offeree must use "reasonable efforts" to communicate the return promise *unless* the offer expressly *dispenses* with notice (which seems to be the case here). [§265]

27. **YES** — Ordinarily the offeree of a *unilateral* contract need not notify the offeror that he intends to perform or is performing the act. [§269]

28. **NO (majority rule)** — While the offeree ordinarily does not need to give notice that performance has begun, she usually does have to give notice within a reasonable time after performance is completed, unless the offeror has waived notice, or the performance itself would come to the offeror's attention in reasonable course. If she doesn't give such notice, the offeror's obligation is discharged. (However, a minority does not require notice in *guaranty* situations.) [§§270-272]

29. **NO (majority rule)** — Even though B performed the act bargained for, he did not do so with the *intent* of accepting A's offer. Hence, no contract. [§275]

30. **(B)** — Where it is clear from the circumstances that the offeror is not interested in a return promise, the offer is for a *unilateral* contract and can be accepted only by performance. In (A), (C), and (D) it is not clear whether the offer can be accepted only by performance, or whether a promise to perform would be sufficient. In such case, Restatement Second construes the offer as inviting acceptance *either* by performance or by *promise* to perform (*i.e.,* bilateral contract). [§§286-288]

31.a. **YES** — Under U.C.C. section 2-206(1)(b), an offer to buy goods for prompt or current shipment can be accepted *either* by notice (promising to ship) *or by actual shipment*. Note that where an offeree chooses to accept by shipment, he must also *notify* the offeror that shipment has been made "within a reasonable time"; otherwise, the offeror could treat his offer as having lapsed before acceptance. [U.C.C. §2-207] Here, however, B had no opportunity to notify A of his shipment; A's revocation therefore was too late. [§290]

b. **YES** — Shipment is an acceptance under section 2-206(1)(b), above, even if the goods shipped are nonconforming. *But*, the shipment of such goods is also a *breach* of the contract formed by the shipment, so that the buyer can either reject the goods, or take delivery and sue the seller for any damages. (The seller can avoid this by notifying the buyer that the shipment is offered only as an accommodation.) [§290]

32. **NO** — A's letter cannot be regarded as an "acceptance" of any outstanding offer by B. Rather, it is itself an offer. The mere fact that an offeror states that silence will constitute an acceptance does not deprive the offeree of the right to remain silent *without* acceptance. (*Compare:* If B had remained silent *with the intent* of accepting, silence would constitute an acceptance.) [§§292-295]

33.a. **YES** — Under the rule of *Adams v. Lindsell,* an acceptance of an offer is effective upon dispatch (mail), *if* dispatched by an *authorized* means of communication. The issue here is whether a telegraphed acceptance is an "authorized" means of accepting a mailed offer. The modern view is that where, as here, the offer fails to require any particular manner of communication, any *commercially reasonable* means is "authorized"—and telegraph would seem to fall in this category. [*See* U.C.C. §2-206(1)] [§§307, 309, 319-320]

b.	**NO**	Where an acceptance is misaddressed or sent by unauthorized means, it is effective as an acceptance only if it arrives on time. Here A's offer requested an ***"immediate"*** reply, whereas B's reply was in fact received several days beyond the normal time for mail delivery. Hence it would be concluded that A's offer had in fact lapsed before B's purported acceptance was received. [§327]
34.	**NO**	An offer must be ***communicated*** to the offeree in order to create a power of acceptance. Bob's offer to Art was therefore ***not*** an acceptance of Art's offer, but, rather, was a cross-offer. [§350]
35.a.	**NO (traditional view)**	If the lease appeared on its face to be the ***final and complete integration*** of the parties' agreement, the parol evidence rule would bar evidence of prior inconsistent agreements—unless there is a showing of ***fraud***—*i.e.,* making the promise with no intent to perform. [§§365, 386, 469]
b.	**YES**	To explain or interpret the term "good cause." Parol evidence is always admissible in the process of ***interpreting*** terms used in a written agreement. (While some courts might let in the evidence in "a." above on similar grounds, most courts would say either that the term "at will" needs no explanation, or that the evidence would contradict rather than explain the term.) [§388]
36.a.	**YES**	If the offer is silent as to the time for performance, the courts will generally imply that the contract is to be performed within a ***reasonable*** time. (*Compare* 38.e., below. Here the term is less essential, and more susceptible of objective determination.) [§408]
b.	**NO**	When the ***duration*** of the contract is omitted from the offer, the law normally implies that the contract will last for a reasonable time. ***But employment agreements*** are treated differently; they are normally deemed terminable at will by either party regardless of how the salary is to be paid, unless the employer has specifically limited his right to terminate the employee. [§§410-412]
c.	**NO**	Where there is a complete gap as to the ***subject matter*** of the offer, there can be no contract. (No basis for implication of "reasonable" terms here.) [§402]
d.	**YES**	If the term which the parties have left open is an ***essential*** term of contract, the offer is deemed too uncertain and there is no legal obligation until such future agreement. But selection of paint and wallpaper would seem to be only a ***minor*** term, and hence the agreement will be deemed enforceable. If subsequently the parties cannot agree on the term, the "reasonable" test will be applied. [§431]
37.	**YES**	This is a typical "requirements" contract. Even though the exact quantity is not stated, it can be supplied by an objective standard (Buyer's requirements). [§427]
38.a.	**NO**	"Agreements to agree" are too indefinite to enforce where, as here, the value of the subject matter (B's services) is not readily ascertainable. (And, there is no room for implication of a promise to pay the "reasonable" value of such services, because this is ***not*** what the parties agreed.) [§429]
b.	**NO**	Promise to pay a "fair" share too indefinite to enforce (same as "a.," above). [§407]

c. **YES**	Here, the amount due would be ascertainable by computation (sales increase and profits thereon); hence sufficiently definite. The key is the method of computation must make reference to an effective standard to be used. [§425]
d. **YES**	Most courts would agree that whether A *is* "able" to pay this amount *is* capable of objective determination (*e.g.,* by evidence as to normal accounting standards and business practices). [§442]
e. **NO**	The court could imply a "reasonable" salary, but would be unlikely to do so where performance had not begun, since there is no clear standard as to what a reasonable salary would be for such a position, and the omitted term is essential. [§402]
39.a. **YES**	For same reasons as in previous answer (except this is an "output" rather than a "requirements" contract). [§427]
b. **YES**	At common law, if one party had the unlimited right or choice to set the price, the promise was deemed too indefinite and illusory. However, under section 2-305 of the U.C.C., a contract for the sale of goods in which one party sets the price is enforceable, as long as it appears the parties intended to be bound; but A must set the price in good faith. [§§436-437]
40. **YES**	U.C.C. section 2-311 provides that a contract for the sale of goods is enforceable "even though the agreement leaves particulars of performance to be specified by one of the parties." Benny's refusal to select constitutes a breach. [§40]
41.a. **YES**	The rule concerning palpable unilateral mistake applies only to mechanical errors. However, a number of modern cases hold that if the mistaken party notifies the other party of a unilateral mistake before the nonmistaken party relies, the mistaken party can rescind the contract. Unless there is a fiduciary relationship between the parties, offeror's error in judgment as to *value* or quality—*even if known to offeree*—does *not* affect offeree's power of acceptance. [§457]
b. **NO**	The result is different where the mistake is a mere *mechanical* miscalculation, known to the offeree. Such an offer cannot be "snapped up" by the offeree. [§455]
42. **DEPENDS**	Bess is charged with knowledge that her offer was ambiguous because she owned two cars. If Abe was *also aware* that Bess owned two cars, there is a *misunderstanding*, both meanings are equally reasonable, and the contract will not be enforced if each party subjectively intended a different car. However, if Abe was not aware that Bess owned two cars, there is a binding contract on what Abe subjectively intended (the Chevrolet). [§461]
43. **NO**	Provisions excusing a party from liability for ordinary negligence (but not willful misconduct) may be enforceable where the parties are of equal bargaining power. But that is not the case here. Moreover, there is a public interest in a carrier's performance. Therefore, exculpatory clauses in contracts with common carriers which exculpate the carrier for bodily injuries caused by its negligence are generally held unenforceable as contrary to public policy. [§491]

44.	**DOUBTFUL**	No such defense was allowed at common law. But the U.C.C. now authorizes courts to refuse enforcement of "unconscionable" terms in contracts for sale of goods; and a *few* courts, at least, have held that gross overcharging by a retail seller may constitute "price unconscionability," at least in consumer transactions. [§486]
45.	**YES (most states)**	A lease of land (regardless of its value or the amount of rent) for *one year* or less does *not* fall within the Statute of Frauds in most states. [§488]
46.	**YES**	The Statute of Frauds applies to the transfer of any *interest* in real property, but an agreement to share profits or income from land *does not* constitute an "interest" in the land itself. Hence, it is not within the Statute and can be enforced although oral. [§502]
47.a.	**NO**	An oral contract for the sale of goods priced at over $500 is unenforceable under the Statute, except to the extent that it has already been performed. [§§508, 510]
b.	**NO**	Prior to enactment of the U.C.C., many courts held that a down payment made the entire contract enforceable. But under the U.C.C., the contract is enforceable only proportionately (to the extent of "goods for which payment has been made and accepted"). Here, B can recover his $200, or enforce S's promise as to 200 Frisbees only. [§510]
c.	**YES**	A contract to manufacture special goods for the buyer which are *not suitable for resale to others* (as here, with B's own advertisements thereon), is enforceable once the seller has made a "substantial beginning" in their manufacture. [U.C.C. §2-201][§513]
48.	**NONE**	The Statute of Frauds refers only to contracts which *cannot by any possibility* be performed within one year from the making of the contract.
	(A)	The lifetime employee may die within one year. (But note that some states have statutes which explicitly require lifetime contracts to be in writing.)
	(B)	The lease may be terminated within one year.
	(C)	The option may be exercised within one year. [§§522-524]
49.a.	**NO**	Under its suretyship provision, the Statute of Frauds requires a promise to answer for the debt of another to be in writing. [§525]
b.	**NO**	The Statute of Frauds does not apply where the promise is made directly *to the debtor*. Such a promise is enforceable though oral, assuming there is consideration. [§526]
50.a.	**NO**	Memorandum omitted one essential term—the price. [§530]
b.	**YES**	Under the U.C.C., less completeness is required; and even though the writing omits an essential term (here, price) it will be sufficient if it indicates that a contract for sale has been made. [§530]

c.	**YES**	At common law. But note that some states have "equal dignity" statutes which provide that where a contract is required to be in writing under the Statute, *the agent's authority* to execute such a contract *must also be in writing*. [§§535-536]
51.	**YES (AS TO BOTH PARTIES)**	Whether the contract is deemed *voidable* (unenforceable), or *void* (no contract at all), *either* party may still obtain restitution, in order to avoid an unjust result for *benefits* conferred even though there is no recovery under the contract. [§545]
52.	**PROBABLY YES**	Many courts hold that if a party represents that he will cause the agreement to be formalized in writing, he will be estopped to set up the Statute as a defense. Furthermore, there is a modern trend to enforce promises which are within the Statute but have been relied upon. [§547]
53.	**NOT AS A CONTRACT**	A minor's promise (even for necessaries) cannot be enforced as a contract. *However*, the other party (B) may recover the reasonable value of necessaries furnished to a minor in restitution, and the written promise is evidence of the value. [§§548-550]
54.	**YES**	Emotional instability does not mean a person lacks contractual capacity. A promise is enforceable unless the promisor was so deficient as to *lack understanding* of what he was doing. (*Compare:* Result would be different if promisor had *previously been adjudged* incompetent.) [§§551, 553]
55.	**YES (most courts)**	A valid contract is not made illegal by knowledge that the subject matter will be used for an illegal purpose that does not involve great moral turpitude. *Compare:* But if S somehow *facilitates* the illegality—*e.g.,* sets up the apparatus for B at a hidden location—S will not be permitted to recover. [§558]
56.a.	**NO**	Where a license or permit is required for the purpose of protecting the public from unqualified persons, a contract for services entered into by an unlicensed person is generally held illegal and unenforceable. [§566]
b.	**NO**	Where a license is required for protective purposes, the courts have refused to permit *any recovery* by the unlicensed person. [§566]
57.	**SPLIT**	Larry would not qualify as a creditor beneficiary under the older cases, which required a *legally enforceable* duty. Under the modern trend, however, a *supposed* or *asserted* duty is sufficient. [§§572-576]
58.	**YES**	A third party beneficiary need not be individually named in the agreement. It is sufficient if the class of persons of which he is a member and for whose benefit the contract was made is sufficiently identified. [§580]
59.a.	**SPLIT**	The issue here is whether C's rights have so "vested" as to prevent the contracting parties from changing their agreement. Under the traditional and Restatement views, a creditor beneficiary's rights vest when he assents to the contract, brings suit, or detrimentally relies thereon. Under these views, C would have a valid claim. The minority view is that a creditor beneficiary's rights vest only if he has detrimentally relied. (Such detrimental reliance might be found here, for example, if C failed to take some action to enforce his claim which he otherwise would have

taken but for A's promise; *e.g.,* filing suit to attach B's assets, or to garnish the funds payable on sale of B's business.) Under this view, C would not have a claim. [§§589-591]

b. **YES**   As between A and B, A is now the primary obligor on the debt to C (B having assumed the debt as part of the purchase); B is *surety* for A's performance. And, the surety can sue in equity for specific performance without first paying off the debt himself. [§588]

60.a. **SPLIT**   Most courts would say *"No"* applying the same rules as above; *i.e.,* a third party beneficiary's rights vest only when he or she learns of and assents to the deal, files suit, or otherwise detrimentally relies thereon. Here, the donee beneficiaries (B's parents) never found out until *after* the promise had been rescinded. A few authorities, however, take the view that a *donee* beneficiary's right vests automatically on the making of the contract (knowledge and assent not required). Under this view, B's parents would prevail even though A and B later agreed to eliminate the provision in question. [§590]

b. **YES**   The promisor can always assert against a third party beneficiary whatever defenses he could have asserted against the promisee (B) in connection with formation and performance of the contract. Here, the defense of fraud or material breach could have been asserted against the seller (B) and therefore also can be asserted against the third party beneficiaries. [§583]

61.a. **YES**   The primary purpose of the contract is determined by the *promisee's* (Father's) *intent*. It would appear from these facts that Father agreed to forbear the sale *in order to obtain a benefit* for Daughter. She would therefore have the right to enforce the contract against Son. [§588]

b. **NO**   Primary purpose of agreement is to benefit A, rather than A's creditor, B. [§581]

62.a. **NO**   One who only purchases "subject to" a mortgage has made no agreement to pay it. Hence, no third party beneficiary contract exists upon which any claim of personal liability could be based. [§594]

b. **SPLIT**   One view is that C is not liable because no actual duty to Bank was owed by B (*see* previous answer), and therefore there was no liability to "assume." The other view is that C is liable. B's apparent purpose was to guard against a *supposed* liability on her part, and that is enough to create a third party creditor beneficiary contract. [§595]

c. **YES**   The original obligor remains liable (as surety) notwithstanding another's assumption of the mortgage debt. [§593]

63.a. **YES**   A gratuitous assignment of a simple chose (debt) is irrevocable if made in a signed writing. The assignment should be deemed effective when the assignor has put the writing beyond his power of recall (here, by mailing) even though not yet received by assignee. That is, the writing must be delivered to the assignee. [§634]

b. **YES**   An assignment given for consideration is irrevocable, whether oral or in writing. [§629]

64.a. **YES**	Future rights under an existing contract are assignable even though the right is conditional. Hence, even though Amy's wages will only be paid if she remains employed by Homecare Products, the assignment is valid. (*But note:* There are often *statutory restrictions* on wage assignments.) [§§639-648]
b. **YES**	Even though Amy's commissions will be entirely dependent on her selling property, a *continuing business relationship* exists between her and Ajax, and her "business expectancies" are held assignable by most (not all) courts. [§640]
c. **NO**	Because there is as yet no existing royalty contract. Rights under a contract *not yet in existence* are not assignable. (However, if she does make a purported assignment thereof for a consideration, it will be treated as a contract *to* assign; and equity will grant specific performance if she ever finds a publisher.) [§§641-650]
d. **DEPENDS**	On whether Claude's designing for Amy so intimately involves her own personality or appearance that it would be unreasonable to require Claude to design for someone else (Beatrice). [§§611-612]
e. **NO**	This is a "requirements" contract. Barbara's "requirements" might vary significantly from Amy's and thus materially vary Coconut Grower's duties under the contract. [§613]
f. **NO**	Because it might materially alter the risk assumed by the insurance company (Barbara's operations might not be as safe as Amy's). If assignment of a right would change the risk in any material way, the right is nonassignable. [§§614-615]
g. **NO**	Where personal credit is involved, any substitution of debtors would materially vary the risk. Hence, the right to borrow money from another is a nonassignable right. [§610]
65.a. **YES**	Because of a policy favoring free assignability, the provision would probably be construed as affecting only delegation of the performance of duties. Such a provision destroys the *right*, not the *power* to make an assignment, despite the fact that the obligor will have an action for breach of the contractual provision. [§645]
b. **YES**	Even though this covenant is broad enough to affect Aaron's power as well as his right to assign, under modern law such restraints are normally unenforceable where the only right involved is to the receipt of money, for completed performance. [§650]
c. **NO**	A contract for plumbing installation is probably not a personal service contract. Even so, the provision against assignment of "the contract" is generally held *effective* to bar any delegation of duties. [§689]
66.a. **YES**	Lack of contractual intent is a "real" defense which can be asserted against any assignee. [§659]
b. **YES**	An assignee takes subject to all defenses against the assignor arising under the contract, even when the defense accrues after notification of the assignment (except where negotiable instruments are involved). [§§659, 660]

67.a. YES   An assignee takes subject to whatever defenses arise before the obligor receives *notice* of the assignment. [§659]

b. DEPENDS   At common law and under the U.C.C., such a waiver may be effective. But many states today have *statutes which void* such waivers in retail installment contracts for *consumer goods*. In such states, Alice could still assert her defense. [§662]

68. CHRIS   Since the assignment to Bob was gratuitous and oral, it was revocable, and was *revoked* by the subsequent assignment to Chris. [§673]

69. CHRIS   Even though the assignment to Bob was "irrevocable" (because in writing), Chris prevails because she paid consideration and took without knowledge of Bob's interest, and therefore has the stronger equity. [§675]

70.a. SPLIT   "New York" rule is first in time (Bank); "English" view is first to give notice (Finance Co.). [§§676-678]

b. NO   The U.C.C. provisions for filing of financing statements do not apply to wage claims. [§683]

c. NO   Under either the New York or English rule, an assignee who obtains payment is deemed to have a stronger equity and therefore prevails. [§§676-677]

71.a. NO   A duty to perform personal services is nondelegable. Indeed, Actor's attempt to delegate his duties may be regarded as an anticipatory breach of contract. [§§688-689]

b. PROBABLY NOT   A mere delegation of duties does not excuse the delegating party from his duty to perform. He remains secondarily liable in the event the delegatee fails to perform. However, the result is different if there is a *novation*; *i.e.,* if Producer was willing to discharge Actor from his contract and to make a *new contract* with Standby. Under the circumstances of this case, there was probably an implied novation, since once Producer accepts Standby, it is unrealistic to say that he continues to look to Actor as primarily responsible for full performance. [§§684, 686, 690]

72. PROBABLY NOT   The issue here is whether any *promise* by Childs to perform can be implied from his mere acceptance of the assignment. The traditional view was that it could *not*. While the modern trend is to imply a promise if consistent with the *parties' probable intent*—i.e., if Childs was to receive the benefits, he probably was also intended to bear the burdens—Restatement (Second) caveats whether this modern view applies (as here) to *sales of land*. [§§695-696]

73. NO   A cause of action for breach of contract lies only where the defendant has failed to perform an *unconditional* duty to perform. The issue here is whether the quoted phrase *conditioned* Able's promise to purchase Baker's house, or was a *covenant* binding Able to obtain the financing, so that he is in breach by failing to obtain it. In determining this, courts look to the *intent of the parties* as evidenced by the words used, custom and usage, and all the surrounding circumstances. Here, the word "if" suggests a condition, as does the fact that the event (obtaining financing) was not something subject to Able's absolute control; and as a matter of practical usage, most purchasers of real estate would regard the purchase as being conditional on obtaining satisfactory financing. Able may have implicitly promised to use reasonable efforts to insure that the condition was fulfilled, but he apparently did use such efforts. [§§102, 711-715]

74. **NO**   The quoted phrase would be construed as an express *condition* on Owner's duty to pay a commission because this is consistent with parties' probable intent (no sale, no commission due). Fact that third party is to perform supports construction as condition. [§709]

75. **YES**   Either on the theory that the quoted phrase was *not* a condition at all, but only a *covenant* as to the approximate time for repayment, or on the theory that Borrower implicitly promised to use reasonable efforts to become able to repay the loan. [§§711-716]

76.a. **PROBABLY**   Time is ordinarily *not* of the essence unless expressly made so. Moreover, the preferred construction of a doubtful provision is that it is a covenant rather than a condition of Club's obligation to pay. [§715]

  b. **YES**   Failure to perform a promise, regardless of the reason, constitutes a breach for which at least nominal damages (*infra*) would be available. [§§706-707]

77.a. **YES**   Unless otherwise agreed (by credit terms), payment is due on delivery of goods. [U.C.C.§2-310][§420]

  b. **YES**   The delivery of the goods was a constructive condition *precedent* to Buyer's duty to pay. And, the burden of proof as to the occurrence of a condition precedent is always on the plaintiff (here, Seller). [§718]

  c. **NO**   The right of return would probably be regarded as a *true condition subsequent* (*i.e.,* it would cut off Buyer's otherwise absolute duty to pay for the goods received). The burden of proof as to the occurrence of such a condition is a matter of *defense*—in this case, on Buyer. [§721]

  d. **NO**   Buyer's duty to pay is conditioned on the Fair's being held. Although *worded* as a condition subsequent (Buyer reserving right to "cancel"), it is really a condition precedent in effect—*i.e.,* no Fair, no duty to pay ever arises! But because it is *worded* as a condition subsequent, most courts would still impose the *burden of proof* on the defendant-promisor (Buyer). [§721]

78.a. **NO**   Most courts hold that where the approval or satisfaction of a third person (here, Water Board) is a condition, strict literal compliance is required; *i.e.,* it is *immaterial* whether the third person or agency was "reasonable" in withholding its approval. (Minority contra.) Dissatisfaction must be honest and in good faith, and although *reasonableness* is irrelevant here a lack of it is *evidence* that the promisor's dissatisfaction was not in good faith. [§726]

  b. **NO**   As long as Farmer was acting *honestly* in finding the water unsatisfactory. A condition of satisfaction is given literal effect where the object is a matter of personal taste (and water quality would seem to fit in this category). [§§724-725]

79. **YES**   On the theory that conditions "necessary" to the performance are *"implied in fact"*

conditions to the contract. The test is simply whether the parties, as reasonable persons, would have agreed upon these had they thought about it. (Here, the right to show the inside of the house would seem "necessary" to procure a purchaser for the house.) Failure of such a "necessary" condition excuses any duty of counterperformance; *i.e.,* Owner's refusal to allow Broker to show the house excuses the condition that Broker obtain a purchaser for the house, and renders Owner's duty to pay absolute. [§737]

80. **PROBABLY**   Owner's performance (to deliver deed and to repair toilet) was a constructive condition precedent to Buyer's duty to pay. But a *constructive condition can be excused by substantial performance* (*infra*) . . . and here the value of that which has been tendered (title to house) would probably be considered "substantial performance." Failure to repair the toilet would be an "immaterial breach" (*infra*), for which Buyer would be entitled to an *offset* of money damages. *Caution:* Result would be contra if parties made repair of the toilet an express condition (*e.g.,* "Buyer to pay *only when* title passes and toilet fixed"). In such a case, most courts would hold Buyer under *no* duty to perform. [§§742, 783]

81.a. **NO**   Payment by a Buyer is a covenant, as is delivery of deed by Owner. But each covenant is also a *constructive condition concurrent* to the other. The result is that until Owner delivers (or tenders) the deed, Buyer's *duty to pay does not arise*; and vice versa. [§§744-746]

   b. **NO**   For the same reasons. [§§744-746]

82. **YES**   Unless the parties otherwise agree, payment of the *full* purchase price is a *constructive condition precedent* to the seller's duty to deliver goods. [U.C.C. §2-511(1)] [§745]

83. **NO**   Where no time is fixed for the performance of either promise, each is a constructive condition concurrent to the other. Neither can place the other in breach without tendering her own performance. And, neither need proceed with performance unless the other is proceeding apace. [§745]

84.a. **YES**   Under doctrine of prevention. If Arthur has tendered the care for which Uncle was bargaining, and Uncle has refused it, the condition (Arthur's performance) is excused, and Uncle's duty to perform is absolute. (*Note:* The *remedy* here would probably be to impose a constructive trust against Uncle's estate at time of his death—"quasi-specific performance"; *see* Remedies Summary.) [§728]

   b. **PROBABLY NOT**   This is the kind of risk one assumes in a contract of this type. There is not sufficient "wrongfulness" to constitute prevention. Wrongfulness does not require a showing of bad faith or malice. Rather, it essentially means that in light of the terms of the contract, the objective of the contract, and the circumstances, the other party would not have reasonably anticipated such conduct. [§730]

85. **NO**   The doctrine of prevention does *not* apply here. Courts generally hold that prevention exists only where a party has done something affirmative to hinder occurrence of a condition (here, "closing of sale"). *Mere inaction is not enough.* Although every contract implies a promise of cooperation, passiveness is not deemed a breach of covenant. [§730]

86.	YES	Owner's sale of the property prevented Manager from rendering the services contracted for by Owner. Thus, Manager's further performance was excused. Majority view is that cause of action arises immediately (Manager need not wait five years). Manager is entitled to recover 5% of the rentals likely to be received during the next four years, less whatever he earns by reason of being excused from performing such services. (*See* discussion of mitigation, *infra.*) [§§729, 806]
87.a.	NO	Under doctrine of **prospective inability**, if it **reasonably** appeared that Owner would be unable to deliver clear title, Purchaser would be entitled to rely thereon in **suspending** his own performance until it appeared that Owner could perform . . . meaning that Purchaser would have a reasonable period after June 1 within which to pay. [§§751-754]
b.	SPLIT	Some courts hold Purchaser is justified in canceling in light of Owner's prospective inability. Other courts assert that there must be detrimental reliance on the prospective inability (*e.g.,* Purchaser buying another house, etc.) before Purchaser is excused. [§798]
88.a.	NO	Again, under doctrine of prospective inability (the seller having contracted to convey same property to another), the purchaser is justified in changing his position in reliance; and having done so, is discharged from contract. [§752]
b.	NO	If it reasonably appeared that Sam could obtain another car like the one in question within the 10-day period, there is no prospective inability to perform. [§754]
c.	YES	Insolvency or bankruptcy of the other may be relevant where credit was to be extended, but is immaterial where (as here) a **cash sale** is involved. (*Note:* Under U.C.C. section 2-609, Sam would have been entitled to demand assurances of performance from Bob upon learning of his bankruptcy.) [§755]
89.a.	YES	Inability to obtain financing does **not** constitute impossibility of performance; and hence Promoter's erecting and operating the car wash was not excused. However, the rent provision is too speculative to enforce. There is a basic problem of **uncertainty** as to the damages here because the profits from a business which has never been built cannot be ascertained. Owner would probably be limited to reasonable value of use of property. [§852]
b.	YES	The condition that there be "profits" is excused under the doctrine of prevention. Promoter's acts show breach of her **implied promise** to act reasonably in computation of "profits." Owner should recover a third of whatever profits **would have been** realized but for the excessive salaries charged (*i.e.,* using normal accounting and business practices). [§§729-733]
c.	DEPENDS	On whether Promoter acted reasonably in closing down the car wash. If in fact it reasonably appeared no "profits" can be earned, Promoter is **not** obligated to remain in business at a loss. (*Compare:* If the lease required rent payments based on a percentage of **sales or gross receipts**—rather than net profits—the result would be contra; *i.e.,* courts would find an implied promise to remain in business throughout the lease, whether run profitably or not.) [§§731-732]
90.	NO	A party to a contract cannot claim breach until the other performance is due. The

one exception is the doctrine of repudiation (anticipatory breach). But, this doctrine does not apply unless there are executory duties on **both** sides. Here, Wife has fully performed her side; only Husband's duties are executory. Hence, Wife cannot sue until the due date of each installment. [§796]

91. **YES**   Mere expression by the manufacturer of **doubt** as to ability to perform is not a repudiation (which requires words that are positive and unequivocal). Beta therefore was **not** justified in canceling the contract, and hence is in breach. *Note:* Under the U.C.C., Beta's remedy was to **demand adequate assurances of performance** by Ace. If Ace had failed to provide same within a "commercially reasonable" period of time, **then** it would be treated as a repudiation of the contract by Ace. [U.C.C. §2-609(4)] [§795]

92.a. **YES**   Beulah's letter demands performance of conditions which were not part of the sale, and to which she is not entitled. She is, therefore, refusing to perform as originally agreed; and this is sufficient repudiation. Under the doctrine of repudiation, the nonbreaching party is entitled to sue immediately for breach. [§798]

b. **YES**   A repudiation is a repudiation. The repudiator's good faith (here, reliance on advice of counsel) does not detract from the fact that she *is* repudiating. [§793]

c. **YES**   A repudiator **can retract** the repudiation—**unless** in the interim the other party notifies the repudiator that he accepts the repudiation (in which case contract discharged by rescission); or had changed his position in reliance thereon (*e.g.*, by selling to another; *see* below). Note, however, that the retraction must be made **in sufficient time** to enable the other party to perform. Here, if Beulah did not notify Amos that she was going ahead with the purchase until June 1, Amos would not be expected to stand by with a deed in his hand. Consequently, Amos would have a **reasonable time after** June 1 within which to tender delivery of the deed. [§798]

d. **NO**   The weight of authority is that the innocent party's demand that the contract be honored does not affect his right to rely on the repudiation; *i.e.*, the presence or absence of a breach is **dependent on the repudiating party's actions alone**. Here, Amos having relied on the repudiation, Beulah can no longer retract it and demand performance. [§798]

93.a. **NO**   The repudiatee owes a **duty not to enhance** damages. Ordering the supplies, equipment, and labor after the repudiation only enhanced the damages. Builder would be limited to whatever his **profits** would have been had he completed the job (*i.e.*, $100,000 minus his costs of performance). [§806]

b. **DEPENDS**   On whether Developer's delay in securing another contractor was "commercially reasonable." If it was **not**, then he owed a duty to mitigate damages, and cannot recover damages resulting from his failure to do so. [§806]

94.a. **NO**   Payment of the **full** purchase price is a **constructive condition precedent** to Owner's duty to convey. (Nothing less can be considered "substantial" performance.) Stated differently, a default in 20% of the purchase price is a "material" breach by Purchaser, which **excuses** any duty of performance by Owner. (*But note:* Purchaser probably would be entitled to recover his payments from Owner in **restitution** at least to the extent that such payments exceeded any damage suffered by

Owner as the result of Purchaser's breach.) [§§759-770]

b. **YES** Normally, tender and payment are constructive conditions concurrent, meaning that neither party can place the other in breach until he first tenders full performance himself. [§719] However, here there is a "material" breach by Purchaser on May 1, prior to the date Owner's performance is due. The "material" breach on May 1 *excuses* Owner's duty of counterperformance on June 1. Hence, he is entitled to sue Purchaser for breach without tendering deed. [§776]

95.a. **YES** This contract is divisible under U.C.C. section 2-307. The value of each case can be ascertained by dividing the total purchase price by number of cases; and each appears to have some proportionate value to Don. Under such circumstances the seller *can demand a proportionate part* of the purchase price. [§772]

b. **YES** As long as the contract *is* divisible, the breaching party can recover for the part performed, *even though his breach is willful* or in bad faith (here, to aid Don's competitor). [§773]

c. **YES** But only in restitution. In view of the express condition, no recovery on the contract would be allowed (full delivery was an express condition precedent to his duty to pay). But since the breach was nonwillful, relief in restitution would be proper for the reasonable value of the spaghetti delivered (might be *less* than the contract price, however). [§774]

96.a. **NO** Having agreed to the extension, Archie is estopped from asserting the original closing date to the extent that Bunker has relied thereon. Here, Bunker has apparently not prepared his title for closing on April 30 in reliance on the extension agreement, and hence is not in breach on that date. [§734]

b. **PROBABLY** A gratuitous waiver of condition *can* be retracted provided the other party has not relied to his detriment thereon. (Nothing here shows any reliance by Bunker on Archie's promise to extend for 60 days.) The only requirement is that the other party be given a *reasonable* period of time within which to perform; and here, the two-week period (April 30-May 15) would seem reasonable. [§129]

c. **NO** In the absence of some agreement to this effect, the condition (time for closing) is waived, and hence there is no breach of contract and no right to damages. The party waiving the condition assumes the risk of such loss or damages. [§734]

97. **DEPENDS** On whether she *notified* Furniture Store within a reasonable time after discovery of defect. Under the U.C.C. a buyer is barred from asserting any remedy against a seller if she does not notify the seller of breach within reasonable time of discovery. [U.C.C. §2-607(3)] [§§127-129]

98. **NO** Repeated waivers of a condition do *not* by themselves bar a party from asserting it in the *future*. (The result *might* be contra if elements of detrimental reliance or hardship were involved.) [§§127-129]

99.a. **YES** On the theory of substantial performance. Although Builder's performance (including installation of Frigi-Queen appliances) was a *constructive* condition precedent to Alpha's duty to pay, and there has been a partial breach in his performance (hence, the condition has **not** been performed), still the forfeiture would be too great, and thus, the courts will enforce the contract on the theory that the condition has been "substantially performed." Alpha will have a right to offset any damages she can prove by virtue of the unauthorized substitution. [§759]

b. **NO**

Because in such a case, his breach would be regarded as **willful**, and the doctrine of substantial performance is not applicable to willful breaches. [§793] *Note:* The tough issue is whether courts would allow restitutional recovery in such a case. Normally, restitutionary relief is not allowed to a willful wrongdoer. But where, as here, there would be tremendous unjust enrichment, courts may treat the breach as "trivial," and grant restitutional recovery (the reasonable value of Builder's performance) notwithstanding. [§§759, 761, 771]

c. **NO**

Because the doctrine of substantial performance does not apply where Builder's complete performance is (as here) made an **express** condition precedent to Alpha's duty to pay. But again, **restitutional relief might still be available** (*see* above). [§§771, 780]

d. **DEPENDS**

On whether Builder's performance falls short of being "substantial." This can only be determined by applying the standards set forth in Restatement section 251. The test is whether the performance meets the essential purpose of the contract. If it is **not** substantial (and facts here suggest this), Builder certainly cannot recover on the contract. Further, most courts will also **deny Builder any relief in restitution** even though there clearly could be an element of forfeiture in such cases. [§§760, 771]

100. **NO**

Here, the contract **is not** rendered impracticable of performance. The subject matter was a house **to be built** (not an existing house). Builder can rebuild, and hence the contract is **not** impossible of performance, although the time for completion would be extended accordingly. Builder suffers the cost of loss (no recovery in restitution either). [§777]

101. **NO**

The doctrine of substantial performance has no application to contracts for the sale of goods. Instead, the U.C.C. adopts the "perfect tender" rule. Alpha is free to reject any variation from what she ordered. The possibility of forfeiture, which is the basis for the doctrine of substantial performance, is not present here. [§763]

102.a. **DEPENDS**

On whether the delay in first shipment "substantially impaired the value of the contract." [U.C.C. §2-612(3)] *Compare:* If this were **not** an installment contract, the delay in delivery would probably be held a "material" breach. U.C.C. section 2-601 provides that if the delivery **fails in any respect to conform** to the contract the buyer may reject the whole. [§766]

b. **NO**

Delay in payment of money normally is **not** regarded as a "material" breach because the delay normally can be compensated for in damages. But the delay **would suspend** Giovanni's duty to make further shipments until payment is received. [§789]

c. **YES**

Where the parties have **expressly** made time of the essence, the courts generally give it literal effect. (*And see* U.C.C. section 2-703, which provides that if the buyer fails to make a payment due on delivery, the seller has the option to cancel the contract.) [§784]

d. **PROBABLY**	On the theory that the breach is minor and the contract is divisible—*i.e.,* the value of each case can be ascertained ($5 per case) and each apparently has the same value to Don. Under these circumstances, unless Don can prove that the 50-case shortage "substantially impairs" the value of that installment to him, he must accept and pay for the 150 cases (offsetting any damages caused to him by the shortage). [U.C.C. §6-612(2)] [§§772-775]
103.a.**YES**	Extra cost of performance does *not* discharge a contract on doctrine of impossibility. Some courts (minority) recognize *extreme* hardship cases, under a theory of "impracticability." But even here, the cost of performance would have to be more extreme. [§§810-811]
b. **YES**	The services to be rendered by Builder would appear to be delegable by him to another. Hence, his personal inability to perform does not discharge his duty under the contract. (*Compare:* If a *personal service* contract was involved, death or disability of the person to render such services *would* discharge the contract. But a construction contract is not generally so regarded.) [§§820-821]
c. **PROBABLY NOT**	This is *not* a case where his performance would be illegal by reason of supervening act of government. This is simply a case where his performance will be more expensive. Most courts would hold Builder *assumes the risk* of such changes. *Compare:* If the change was totally unforeseeable and the added costs were tremendous, rescission on the ground of mutual mistake might be possible. [§812]
104.a.**YES**	Where performance of a contract has become illegal due to change in law enacted after the contract was entered into, the duty to perform is discharged under the doctrine of impossibility of performance. [§812]
b. **DEPENDS**	On whether doctrine of frustration of purpose applies. Ted would have to show two things here: (1) that the enactment of this zoning restriction was *not reasonably foreseeable* at time of contracting; and (2) that the restriction *totally or nearly destroys* the value of the contract. The second element here is doubtful; *i.e.,* the holder of a 99-year lease might still be able to develop the property into residential tracts (although some buyers might decline to purchase because he could not convey the fee.) [§827]
105.a.**NO**	The death or destruction of the subject matter of the contract *at the time the contract* was entered into prevents the contract from arising. Hence, neither party could enforce. [§813]
b. **YES**	In contracts for sale of goods which involve shipment by carrier, the risk of loss is transferred to buyer at time goods are delivered to carrier (unless otherwise agreed). [U.C.C. §2-509] [§819]
c. **DEPENDS**	On whether her shipping by truck was a "commercially reasonable" decision under the circumstances. [U.C.C. §2-614] (If it was *not*, the inability to ship by air *would* constitute impossibility of performance to discharge contract.) [§813]
106.a.**YES**	The issue is whether the agreement to cancel (rescind) is itself enforceable. It is, if supported by consideration on both sides. Here, there clearly is consideration—each party having given up the executory obligations of the other. (Lew gave up

future rent, and Ted gave up the right to future use of the property.) [§829]

b. **NO**   Where the contract itself is required to be in writing under the Statute of Frauds (here, 99-year lease), most courts hold that any recession thereof must also be in writing to be effective. [§832]

107.a.**YES**   There probably is consideration here (resolving a bona fide dispute). However, even if there were not, an agreement to modify a *contract for the sale of goods* is enforceable *without* consideration. [U.C.C. §2-209] [§92]

b. **NO**   A written contract for the sale of goods can be modified orally *except* where the contract as modified falls within the Statute of Frauds, and contracts for goods priced at $9,500 fall within the Statute. [§508]

108.a.**YES**   The agreement to pay off the loan by having Sandy paint the house was an "accord"—supported by consideration, and effective itself as a contract. Hence, Sandy's repudiation is a breach for which she is liable in damages. [§837]

b. **DEPENDS**   On how "poor" a job Sandy did. If it was "substantial" performance, it would be sufficient to satisfy and discharge the original debt; Pete's remedy would be to sue Sandy for whatever it cost to repair or complete the job. If not "substantial," then the painting would not constitute a satisfaction of either the original debt or the accord agreement. [§§118, 759]

c. **NO**   *If* there is a *bona fide dispute* as to the amount due or the right to collect a debt, the creditor's cashing of a check marked "payment in full" is deemed an accord and satisfaction discharging any claim for a greater amount. [§838]

109. **NO**   Punitive (exemplary) damages are normally *not* recoverable in an action for breach of contract—no matter how "willful" the breach. (*Compare:* There may be exceptions where the breach also constitutes intentionally *tortious* conduct.) [§§914, 915]

110. **YES**   The normal measure of damages for breach of a contract for sale of goods is the difference between the contract price and market price at the time and place for delivery. *However*, where, as here, the goods are manufactured to buyer's specifications and are not resalable (bearing Duke's brand name and advertising) the seller can recover the full contract price. [§880]

111.a.**NO**   Destruction of the house *discharges* the contract under the doctrine of impossibility of performance. Here, the existence of a kitchen to "remodel" was the contemplated subject matter of the contract. Since it has been destroyed through the fault of neither party, *both* parties' duties of performance are discharged. [§817]

b. **YES**   He can recover the reasonable value of his performance (but *not* his loss of profits on the job). Where a contract is discharged by impossibility after performance has commenced, the performing party is entitled to *restitutional recovery* for the value of his performance. Even though his performance has not resulted in any real "benefit" to Alpha. Builder is entitled to recover the costs of his labor and materials. [§825]

112. **NO**	In contracts for the sale of realty, where the vendor breaches, the purchaser is limited to recovery of his "out of pocket" losses (down payment, title charges, etc.) unless "bad faith" is shown. [§883]	

113.a. **YES**   For each breach of contract *at least nominal damages* of $1 can be recovered. [§903]

b. **YES**   If such damages were *reasonably foreseeable* to both parties at the time of contracting. Under the doctrine of consequential damages, the breaching party is liable to the other for all damages the seller had reason to foresee were the probable result of the breach. Here, it would seem that a designer would be aware of the kind of damages Producer would suffer by reason of the delay, and hence should be liable therefor—even though they far exceeded the contract price. [§851]

c. **NO**   Because there is *not sufficient certainty* that there would be any profits, or how much. There is no satisfactory way of knowing whether a new Broadway show would operate at a profit or loss. [§§852-853, 906]

114.a. **DEPENDS**   On whether Johns made a bona fide effort to mitigate damages by finding other comparable jobs during the week in question. Even though the employer is clearly in breach, the employee is under a *duty to mitigate* damages. [§§857-859, 918]

b. **NO**   Failure to mitigate damages is a matter of defense, meaning the burden would be on Starburst to prove that such employment *was* available. [§§859, 891]

c. **YES (modern view)**   The modern trend, at least, is to allow recovery in *restitution* for the reasonable value of the services, even where the employee is clearly in breach and his breach is *willful*. Such recovery would be offset, however, by any loss or expense the employer suffers by reason of the breach (*e.g.,* losses in canceling show, costs incurred in hiring replacement above what would have been payable under the contract). Here, Johns should probably recover two-sevenths of $25,000 less any extra money paid to Davis for the remainder of the week. [§§929-933]

d. **NO**   Answer would be different, because illness on the part of a person who is to render personal services constitutes impossibility of performance, *discharging* the duty to perform the balance of the contract. *Result:* Johns could recover in restitution for the reasonable value of the nights he worked, *without any offset* for the cost of replacing him. [§§929-933]

115.a. **YES**   Where the owner breaches a construction contract before any work is done, the contractor's lost profits is the proper measure of damages. [§897]

b. **YES**   A contractor is *not* under any duty to mitigate damages resulting from the owner's breach. The theory is that every construction job involves its own peculiar business risks and the contractor should not be required to assume new or different risks because of the owner's breach. [§861]

c. **NO (most courts)**   Even if his breach was willful, many courts allow a contractor restitutional relief—*i.e.,* the *reasonable value* of that which he has performed. Hence, Builder is entitled to a $2,000 offset against the $3,000 damages claimed by Alpha. (Some courts contra because breach *willful*.) [§933]

d. DOUBTFUL To be enforceable as a valid liquidated damages clause, the actual damages must be difficult to ascertain; *and* the amount stipulated must be a *reasonable forecast* of whatever damages are likely to result. Here, the actual damages are certainly difficult to ascertain (value of loss of use of one's kitchen); but it is doubtful that the $50 per day figure is a reasonable forecast of actual damages—*i.e.,* it would not appear tied into the costs of eating out as opposed to cooking at home; or loss of use of that space in the house. Therefore, it is probably unenforceable as a penalty. [§§906-908]

116. PROBABLY The U.C.C. would allow recovery if the $500 was a reasonable forecast of *actual or anticipated* damages. [U.C.C. §2-718(1)] The fact that the provision was labeled a "penalty" does *not* by itself make it unenforceable. A strong argument here for enforceability is that Baker was paid a $500 premium for prompt delivery, and it would be unjust to allow him to breach and still retain the premium. Hence, the $500 "penalty" would appear to be a reasonable forecast of damages. [§§908, 912]

SAMPLE EXAM QUESTION I

Alfred Ohner and Ted Kwik had been friends for a number of years. They had served in the Army together during the Korean War, and Kwik had saved Ohner's life on one occasion by shooting a North Korean sniper who had drawn a bead on Ohner. Both lived in Denver, Colorado. In October 1989, Ohner finished construction of a new 100-unit apartment house in Denver called *The Crescent*. Ohner and Kwik then entered into a written contract under which Kwik rented *The Crescent* from Ohner for ten years, at a rental of $100,000 per year, beginning January 1, 1990. The parties contemplated that Kwik would take on management of *The Crescent* as his full-time business, and would pay all operating expenses, making a profit on the difference between rentals and expenses.

The Crescent was scheduled to be opened in January 1990. Based on projected expenses an annual rental of at least $2,000 per unit was necessary just to break even. The initial annual rental was set at $2,300 per unit, giving Kwik a projected profit of approximately $30,000 per year. All the units were quickly rented by January 1 under standard two-year leases for a term beginning January 1, 1990, and ending December 31, 1991.

By the time the 1990-91 leases were about to expire, annual operating costs for *The Crescent* had risen so high that in order to maintain a $30,000 profit, annual rentals for 1992-93 would have to be set at $2,600. However, by early 1991, several other luxury singles apartment houses had been built in Denver and were charging lower rents. It therefore proved extremely difficult to re-rent *The Crescent's* units for $2,600. In February 1992, Ohner told Kwik that it was obvious that Kwik was going to go broke unless he could lower his rentals to that of his competitors. To keep Kwik from going broke, Ohner told Kwik he was lowering the rental he charged Kwik from $100,000 to $70,000/year, effective retroactively to January 1, 1992, which would enable Kwik to make a $30,000 annual profit by renting *The Crescent's* units at $2,300/year. Kwik thanked Ohner profusely, and then began offering the vacant units at a $2,300/year rental on standard two-year leases ending in early 1993. Within a short time all the vacant units were leased.

In July 1992, Ohner and Kwik had a falling-out over a game of bridge. Kwik accused Ohner of cheating. Ohner was enraged and demanded that Kwik retract the statement. Kwik refused. Ohner then said, "That's it for us; our friendship is over. What I did for you on *The Crescent* is off, too. From now on, you pay me the regular rent."

What are Kwik's rights?

SAMPLE EXAM QUESTION II

On September 21, Prentice Farm Supplies Co. received from Dayview Seed & Grain Company an envelope containing clover seeds. On the face of the envelope was written, "No. 1 Red Clover seed, 5,000 lbs., like sample. We are asking 24 cents per pound." There was no covering letter.

On September 23, Prentice wrote to acknowledge receipt of the sample. In its letter Prentice advised Dayview that it had accumulated quite a stock of clover seed and preferred to wait a while "before operating further," but stated that it might nevertheless be interested if Dayview could come down somewhat on the price.

On October 4, Dayview wired Prentice: "We are now asking 23 cents per pound for the 5,000 lbs. of No. 1 Red Clover seed from which your sample was taken. We have been made an offer of 22 3/4 cents per pound."

On October 15, Prentice wired Dayview: "Your wire of October 4 is in our receipt. We accept your offer."

At the time of this telegram the market price of No. 1 Red Clover seed was 25 cents per pound. Dayview immediately wired back, "Re yours of October 15, we have no deal." Prentice then purchased 5,000 lbs. of No. 1 Red Clover seed on the market, at 25c/pound.

Prentice now brings an action against Dayview based on the above facts. Discuss.

SAMPLE EXAM QUESTION III

On August 15, Cheshire University requested bids from Bildgood, Inc., a large construction firm, and seven other contractors for the construction of a new dormitory for Cheshire's medical school. Under the terms of the bidding, the bids were to be submitted on October 5, and Cheshire had two days to award a contract. On October 4, Bildgood computed its total bid, which came to $1.55 million. The bid was submitted on October 5; it proved to be the low bid, and Bildgood was awarded the contract, which was signed on October 6. The other bids were $1.8, $1.9, $2.0, $2.1, $2.2, and $2.3 million, respectively.

In computing its bid, Bildgood had used an Addup Model 15 electronic desk calculator, which had been delivered to Bildgood by Addup on October 2. On October 7, Addup notified Bildgood that it had discovered a defect in the circuitry of some of its Model 15 calculators and asked Bildgood to check out its calculator in a certain manner. Upon running this check, Bildgood discovered that the calculator was defective. It promptly reran the raw data for the Cheshire bid on a mechanical adding machine and got a (correct) result of $1.95 million. On October 8, Bildgood notified Cheshire that its $1.55 million bid had been erroneous because of a defective electronic calculator; that the correct bid should have been $1.95 million; and that it would perform at this price but not for less. Cheshire insisted on performance at the contract price; Bildgood categorically refused. On October 9, Cheshire approached Alpha Construction, the contractor which had bid $1.8 million, but Alpha declined to take on the job, stating that in the interim it had taken on another major commitment. Three days later, Cheshire entered into a contract with Deutron Builders, which had entered the third-lowest bid, of $1.9 million. Cheshire then brought suit against Bildgood.

Discuss.

SAMPLE EXAM QUESTION IV

Assume the same facts as in Question III, above, except that Bildgood sues Addup. At the trial, Bildgood shows that before purchasing the Model 15 it acquainted Addup with its needs.

What result?

SAMPLE EXAM QUESTION V

John Ash was a lumber dealer in Bangor, Maine. Robert Beam was the owner of a large construction business, based in Philadelphia, Pennsylvania. Beam bought a substantial portion of his lumber from Ash.

On Wednesday evening, March 13, 1990, Ash gave Western Union the following message for transmission to Beam: "Will sell 5,000M laths,* delivered Philadelphia, nineteen dollars seventy net cash per M, late-May shipment. Answer quick." Ash wrote out this message personally in Western Union's Bangor office.

The message actually delivered by Western Union to Beam was as follows: "Will sell 5,000M laths, delivered Philadelphia, nineteen dollars net cash per M, late-May shipment. Answer quick." This message arrived on Thursday morning, March 14. On Monday morning, March 18, Beam sent the following telegraphic answer: "Accept your telegraphic offer on laths." Ash made no reply, but entered the order in his books. In late March the parties began corresponding concerning the exact date of shipment. Further correspondence between the parties in early April disclosed the error in the transmission of Ash's message. Beam then insisted he was entitled to the laths at $19.

What are Beam's rights?

_____

*Laths are long, thin strips of wood, which are used extensively in home construction. "M" stands for thousand.

SAMPLE EXAM QUESTION VI

Assume the same facts as in Question V, above, except that Ash sues Western Union and that Western Union defends in part on the basis of the following provision, which was printed at the top of the form upon which Ash wrote the message: "All messages are taken subject to the following terms: To guard against mistakes or delays, the sender of a message should order it *repeated*; that is, telegraphed back to the originating office for comparison. For this, one-half the regular rate is charged in addition. It is agreed between the sender of the following message and Western Union that Western Union shall not be liable for mistakes or delays in transmission or delivery, or for nondelivery, of any unrepeated message, whether happening by the negligence of its agents or otherwise, beyond the amount received for sending the same." Ash did not ask to have the message repeated. What are Ash's rights against Western Union if he did not ship the laths? (Assume this matter is governed solely by state law and not by federal statute or by the rules of any federal agency.)

SAMPLE EXAM QUESTION VII

Frances Fee owned a summer home in the mountains known as "Lakerest." Lakerest was a pleasant house surrounded by attractive scenery, but its chief attraction was that it fronted on the eastern side of Blue Heron Lake. This was a small artificial lake, ideal for swimming and boating during the summer months, which had been created by construction of a dam that retained the waters of Blue Heron Stream. The lake had been built as a reservoir and was owned by the state. Theoretically it was open to the public, but as a practical matter it was used almost exclusively by the owners of the houses fronting on the lake, since it was almost completely surrounded by private property and was relatively inaccessible.

On October 1, 1993, Fee agreed to sell Lakerest to Alice Aqua for $50,000. Section 5 of the contract of sale provided as follows:

> 5. Vendor acknowledges that purchaser has paid her a deposit of $10,000 on the property at the time of the execution of this agreement. The balance of the purchase price, $40,000, shall be payable at the closing, which shall take place on December 1, 1993. If the vendor is unable to convey good and marketable title at the closing, or if the improvements on said property shall be destroyed or materially damaged prior to the closing, said deposit shall be returned to purchaser, upon her demand, and neither vendor nor purchaser shall be liable for any damages. If the purchaser fails to pay the balance of the purchase price at the closing for any other reason, said deposit shall not be refunded.

On November 15, an earthquake tremor occurred near Lakerest. Although the tremor did no damage to any of the lakefront houses, it destroyed the dam which had retained Blue Heron Lake's waters. As a result, the lake's waters emptied out into the old bed of Blue Heron Stream, and the lake was destroyed. There was no prospect that a new dam would be built in the immediate future, and the stream that took its place was much too shallow for either boating or swimming.

When Aqua learned what had happened, she called Fee to tell her that she would not consider going through with the deal. Fee instituted an action against Aqua for breach of contract. Aqua counterclaimed for return of her $10,000.

On May 1, Fee sold Lakerest to David Dry for $35,000.

Discuss.

SAMPLE EXAM QUESTION VIII

Reflex Studios, Inc. entered into a contract with Alan Grume under which Reflex agreed to take photographs of Grume's wedding for $110, with a deposit of $25. Through the negligence of Reflex, no photographer showed up at the wedding, and no pictures were taken. You are Grume's lawyer. He asks you what are his rights. You quickly conclude Reflex is in breach. To what damages may Grume be entitled?

SAMPLE EXAM QUESTION IX

Albert Penn was a professional writer, specializing in American politics. Penn had a regular three-times-a-week newspaper column, and also wrote magazine articles and books.

Talia Tawker was a United States Senator. In late 1990, Tawker decided to seek the Democratic nomination for the Presidency of the United States in 1993. Tawker assembled a small campaign staff, and in August 1991, she approached Penn and asked him to do a "campaign" (*i.e.,* favorable) biography, running about 300 pages, for $5,000. Penn declined. Tawker then raised the price to $7,500, but Penn still declined, stating that he had a lot of irons in the fire, and did not want to commit himself to a single major project. Tawker then stated, "I really want to get you for this biography. I will tell you what. If you deliver a completed manuscript to me by April 1, 1992, I will pay you $10,000." Penn replied, "Right."

Soon after, Penn began work on the Tawker biography. On October 1, 1991, Penn had done most of a rough draft of the book, representing about half the total needed for a completed manuscript. On October 2, Tawker withdrew from the race, and telegraphed Penn, "Do not begin manuscript, as no longer needed."

What are Penn's rights?

SAMPLE EXAM QUESTION X

Wolf Chemical Company was a major chemical producer. Through its Raremetals Division, Wolf was engaged in the business of processing certain kinds of ores, including rutile, which contains the metal titanium. Wolf's Raremetals Division accounted for approximately 5% of its business.

Andrews Mines, Inc. was the owner of a rutile mine. The process of refining rutile to extract the maximum amount of titanium at the cheapest possible price is a highly skilled and very expensive one. Since Andrews had no processing facilities, it approached Wolf as a possible purchaser of its ore. On its part, Wolf was anxious to acquire a long-term assured source of rutile, which was then in short supply and promised to remain so for a considerable period of time.

On April 5, 1987, Andrews and Wolf entered into a contract under which Andrews agreed to sell to Wolf, and Wolf agreed to purchase, Andrews' entire rutile output through April 15, 1992. The price of rutile is figured per pound of unrefined titanium contained in the rutile. Prices are quoted and paid for unrefined titanium; not for rutile. Usually the purchase price of a batch of rutile is fixed by an assay (that is, by a scientific estimate) of the amount of unrefined titanium it contains. However, the agreement between Wolf and Andrews provided that promptly upon delivery of rutile by Andrews, Wolf would refine the rutile to extract the titanium, certify the amount of titanium it had extracted, and pay for that amount a price equal to 97% of the market price for unrefined titanium on the date of the certificate. Wolf's certificate would be conclusive as to the amount of titanium it had extracted, but any dispute concerning the market price of unrefined titanium on the date of the certificate would be submitted to arbitration.

On January 15, 1990, Wolf entered into a contract with Xavier, Inc., providing for the sale to Xavier of Wolf's Raremetals Division for $2 million. Xavier was a major tobacco company, which was attempting to diversify its operations.

Xavier promptly notified Andrews that the Andrews-Wolf contract had been assigned to it in connection with its acquisition of Wolf's Raremetals Division, and directed Andrews to address all further shipments to it (Xavier) at the former Wolf plant. Andrews promptly wrote to Wolf (with a copy to Xavier) that it did not recognize the validity of the assignment. Xavier replied that Wolf would continue to accept shipment of rutile from Andrews in its own name, and while such ore would be accepted on Xavier's behalf, Wolf would agree to be responsible for payment of the purchase price.

Andrews replied that it would not deliver any ore to Wolf or Xavier under such arrangements and began selling its ore on the market.

What are Xavier's rights against Andrews?

ANSWER TO SAMPLE EXAM QUESTION I

1. **Was There Consideration for Ohner's Modification of Kwik's Lease?** In February 1992, Ohner in effect agreed to modify the lease by promising to accept $70,000/year in full discharge of Kwik's obligation. The first issue is whether this modification is enforceable.

   a. ***Foakes v. Beer;* donative promise:** It has often been held that a promise to accept less than one is legally entitled to in satisfaction of the full obligation is not legally enforceable, on the ground that such a promise lacks consideration. (*See, e.g., Foakes v. Beer.*) Absent duress or unconscionability, it seems questionable whether this rule is sound, since in the usual case the promise is given as the price for a counterpromise, so that consideration is apparently present in the form of a bargain. In this case, however, it is arguable that Ohner's promise lacks consideration even if the rule of *Foakes v. Beer* is not applied, on the theory that it was ***donative*** in nature. The general rule is that a donative promise lacks consideration, *i.e.,* such a promise is unenforceable. (It may be that there was in fact a bargain here; that Ohner had an economic interest in keeping *The Crescent* fully rented, and that in exchange for Ohner's modification Kwik impliedly promised to lower rentals to $2,300/year, which he was not legally obliged to do. This construction, however, seems strained.)

   b. **Moral obligation:** Assuming the promise was donative, it may have been based on moral consideration. Although the usual rule is that moral consideration is insufficient to support a promise, there is some law that a promise based upon a moral obligation arising out of a material benefit conferred upon the promisor, or, perhaps, an output by the promisee, will be enforced, at least to the extent of the benefit conferred or the output. However, even under the modern view, a promise based on a moral obligation will normally not be enforced where the promisor did not receive a direct economic benefit. One may assume for purposes of this question that Ohner is continuing to profit despite the modification. Here Kwik had undoubtedly conferred a substantial benefit on Ohner—he had saved Ohner's life. On the other hand, it is not completely clear that Ohner was under a moral obligation to Kwik. Kwik's action was performed in the course of Kwik's own duties as a soldier, and at no apparent risk to himself. There is a difference between gratitude and moral obligation. Moreover, Ohner's rent concession does not seem to have been intended as a "repayment" to Kwik.

   c. **Reliance:** Reliance is viewed as either a substitute for consideration (bargain theory) or as consideration itself. The term promissory estoppel remains in wide use as a description of the principle that reliance may make a donative promise enforceable. Even if Ohner's promise was donative, under the principle of promissory estoppel, it would be ***legally enforceable*** if relied upon in a reasonable, foreseeable way, at least to the extent of the reliance. Certainly it was foreseeable that Kwik would lower the rentals on vacant apartments to $2,300/year. Ohner's promise should therefore be enforced at least as to those apartments rented at $2,300 in reliance on the promise.

   d. **Waiver:** It might be argued that rather than making a promise, in effect Ohner "waived" payment of $30,000. However, that should not make a difference in the result; any *Foakes v. Beer* type of transaction can be verbalized in the form of a waiver. Additionally, a waiver maybe retracted in this case as no separate consideration was given.

   e. **Modification without more:** Partly in recognition of the unsoundness of the rule of *Foakes v. Beer,* the tendency of the law may be to uphold any modification of an executory contract without the requirement of fresh consideration. Thus U.C.C. section 2-209(1) provides that "An agreement modifying a contract within this Article needs no consideration to be binding." Section 2-209 is inapplicable to Kwik and Ohner, since their transaction does not involve a sale of goods (although it might be utilized by analogy). However, Restatement (Second) section 89(a) provides that "A promise modifying a duty under a contract not fully performed on either side is binding . . . if the modification is fair and equitable in view of circumstances not anticipated when the contract was made." To the extent this section represents the law, it might be applicable to this case, on the premise that construction of the other singles apartments constituted "circumstances not anticipated when the contract was made." However, while Kwik and Ohner may not have specifically thought about the possibility of such construction, it was certainly a foreseeable circumstance.

    f.   **Completed gift:** Where the rule of *Foakes v. Beer* is applicable, there is a split of authority in contracts involving an ongoing performance by both sides as to whether an agreement to accept a lesser payment than due is enforceable to the extent that is executed. Insofar as the Ohner intention was donative, it is arguable that a completed gift has been made as to that portion of the rent actually forgiven prior to the retraction.

2.   **Is There a Violation of the Statute of Frauds?** In addition to the defense of no consideration, Ohner has a Statute of Frauds defense, since the transaction (i) involved a lease of more than two years; and (ii) could not be completed within one year from the making of the contract. Although there was part performance here, part performance does not take a contract out of the one-year provision unless performance is completed on one side. Some types of part performance may take a contract out of the interest-in-land provision, but mere payment is usually insufficient. Additionally, an action for damages may not lie, as the part-performance exception to the Statute of Frauds does not traditionally apply to actions at law insofar as interests in land are concerned. Kwik's reliance might take the transaction out of the Statute, but probably only to the extent of the reliance.

ANSWER TO SAMPLE EXAM QUESTION II

1.   The letter of 9/21 appears to have been an invitation to bid, rather than an offer, since no quantity was specified, and the letter was apparently unsolicited. The words, "we are asking" indicate preliminary negotiations as well.

2.   The letter of 9/23 was also an invitation to bid, insofar as it indicated Prentice might be interested if Dayview came down on the price.

3.   The wire of 10/4 might be deemed still another invitation (*i.e.,* an offering circular), but is better interpreted as an offer. As a wire, the communication seems individualized, and it is in response to an invitation (*i.e.,* the letter of 9/23). To be legally sufficient as an offer, a statement meet two criteria: (i) intent to make a bargain; and (ii) certainty and *definiteness* of terms. Generally speaking, a statement will not be considered an offer unless it makes clear: (i) the subject matter of the proposed bargain; (ii) the price; and (iii) the quantity involved. It is not absolutely clear that the entire 5,000 lbs. is being offered, but in light of the circumstances that seems to be a reasonable inference, despite the fact that the quote is per pound. The wire does not state terms of payment or delivery, but that does not seem fatal since reasonable terms could easily be implied. The reference to another offer might be construed to indicate that Dayview was only soliciting offers, but it seems at least equally reasonable to construe the reference to mean, "Since we already have an offer for 22 3/4c, our offer at 23c is a reasonable price, and in any event is not negotiable, so please do not bother to try to get us down in price again."

4.   If the offer does not state a period of time during which it will remain open, the offeree's power of acceptance lapses after the expiration of a reasonable time. Thus, under the circumstances, even assuming the 10/4 wire was an offer, the answering wire of 10/15 was not effective as an acceptance because it was not dispatched within a reasonable time, considering (i) the offer was by wire, indicating some

urgency (especially when set in the context of the original solicitation, which was by mail); (ii) Dayview apparently had an offer in hand, which it would not want to delay acting on for too long; and (iii) the market price of clover seed was apparently subject to serious fluctuations.

ANSWER TO SAMPLE EXAM QUESTION III

1. **Expectation Damages:** Cheshire will undoubtedly claim damages for breach of contract measured by its expectation—$.35 million, the difference between $1.55 million (its contract price with Bildgood), and $1.9 million (its contract price with Deutron). Should this claim succeed?

    a. **Palpable mistake:** Bildgood's mistake was of the kind normally called "unilateral"—that is, a mistake arising out of the calculations of one of the parties, rather than a mistake in the assumptions shared by both. Such a mistake is generally a defense when it is "palpable"—that is, when the nonmistaken party knew or should have realized that the mistake had been made—because in such a case the nonmistaken party's expectation is not worthy of much protection. On the other hand, if the mistake is "impalpable"—if the nonmistaken party neither knew nor should have known of its existence—the cases are split on whether the mistaken party has a defense in an action for expectation damages. The majority of the cases hold that he does not; but a minority, particularly the more recent cases, hold that he does.

    The first question therefore is whether the mistake was palpable. The fact that Bildgood, itself a contractor, did not realize the bid was unusually low speaks against this. But it is arguable that Cheshire was in a better position than Bildgood to realize that Bildgood had made a mistake because Cheshire could see the extent to which Bildgood's bid differed from all the others. How significant was this difference? The seven bids put in by the other contractors ranged from $1.8 million to $2.3 million, mostly at intervals of $.1 million. Bildgood's bid was $1.55 million, $.25 million less than the second lowest bid. On balance, this does not seem to be enough in itself to put Cheshire on notice. By hypothesis the winning bid will always be the lowest, so some interval between Bildgood's bid and the second lowest bid must be expected. The interval was admittedly substantial—but it was much less than the interval between the second lowest and the highest bids ($.5 million). Of course, a difference on the low side is frequently more striking than a difference on the high side, because costs set a lower limit, while nothing sets an upper limit. Nevertheless, in the absence of other evidence the range of the bids would not in itself seem enough to have put Cheshire on notice that a mistake had been made.

    b. **Impalpable mistake:** Assuming the mistake was impalpable, should it nevertheless serve as a defense to an action for expectation damages? Under the majority view, the answer is no, but certainly there is a modern trend that where the defendant has entered into a contract only by reason of his mistake it should be sufficient if he reimburses plaintiff for actual reliance. The rationale behind the cases rejecting this position is two-fold: (1) the courts should not defeat the legitimate expectation formed by the nonmistaken party as a result of the defendant's fault; and (2) unilateral mistakes are normally difficult or impossible to prove objectively—that is, since they normally occur in the defendant's own mental processes, they can normally be established only through proof of the defendant's subjective intent, and the courts have been noticeably reluctant in contract cases to let a party get out of a contract on the basis of such proof.

    Cheshire v. Bildgood, however, is distinguishable from the usual unilateral mistake case. First, the mistake did not occur in Bildgood's subjective mental processes. It occurred in the objective world of the calculator, and presumably is susceptible of completely objective proof. Second, Bildgood was not at fault in the making of the mistake: Rather, Addup had erred. In light of these factors, and since the trend of authority is in favor of limiting damages in such cases to reliance,

Bildgood's mistake should serve as a defense to a suit by Cheshire for expectation damages.

2. **Reliance Damages:** Assuming that Cheshire cannot recover expectation damages, what damages, if any, can Cheshire collect from Bildgood? The cases are agreed that even if unilateral mistake will serve as a defense to a suit for expectation damages, the nonmistaken party is entitled to reimbursement for reliance. (Of course, usually the mistaken party is at fault, while Bildgood was not; nevertheless, to the extent Cheshire relied on Bildgood's promise, it seems more appropriate to cast any resulting loss on Bildgood than on Cheshire.)

Cheshire appears to have relied on Bildgood's promise by accepting Bildgood's bid rather than another. If Bildgood had not made its incorrect bid, Cheshire would presumably have accepted the second-lowest bid, which was $1.8 million, and since bids are normally deemed offers, Alpha would have had to enter into the contract if its bid had been accepted within the two-day period. Therefore, Cheshire should be entitled to receive $.1 million, representing the difference between the contract price with Deutron ($1.9 million) and the price Cheshire would have had from Alpha ($1.8 million) but for Bildgood's mistake.

ANSWER TO SAMPLE EXAM QUESTION IV

1. **General Damages:** When Addup sold Bildgood the Model 15 there was an implied warranty of fitness. Therefore, Bildgood should be able to return the machine, or to collect damages equal to the difference between the value of the Model 15 as it is, and the value it would have if it met the implied warranty of fitness (which might be measured by the cost of repairs necessary to correct the defect).

2. **Special Damages:** In addition, Bildgood may be able to collect from Addup the amount of damages, if any, which Bildgood must pay to Cheshire. Unless Bildgood was guilty of contributory negligence (which seems rather unlikely), such amounts would be proximately caused by Addup's breach of implied warranty. The only question, therefore, would be whether such damages were foreseeable within *Hadley v. Baxendale* (which has not been changed by the U.C.C.). Today the principle of *Hadley v. Baxendale* is normally restated to mean that consequential damages can be recovered if, at the time the contract was made, the seller had reason to foresee that the consequential damages were the probable result of the breach. Since Bildgood had acquainted Addup with its needs, it was foreseeable when the contract was made that if the calculator was defective Bildgood might enter an incorrect bid. Further, *Hadley v. Baxendale* is primarily used by the courts to limit damages by cutting off claims for lost profits. A claim by Bildgood against Addup based on the damages (if any) Bildgood must pay to Cheshire would not be a claim for lost profits, but for out-of-pocket expenses, and would undoubtedly be treated sympathetically.

ANSWER TO SAMPLE EXAM QUESTION V

1. **Did Ash's Telegram Constitute an Offer?** Yes. The telegram was obviously individualized, appeared to contemplate the conclusion of a deal upon acceptance, and was specific as to the critical terms of price and quantity. It was somewhat vague as to delivery date, but not fatally so (the date seemed firm enough to satisfy Ash and Beam), and other terms (such as transportation) could be filled in by implication.

2. **Was Beam's Acceptance Timely?** Where an offer does not specify a time of acceptance, it must be accepted within a reasonable time or the power of acceptance will be terminated. What constitutes a reasonable time depends on the subject matter of the offer, its form, and its language. Here the subject matter of the offer was a standardized commodity which probably fluctuated in price, the form was a telegram, and the offer specifically stated, "Answer quick." All these factors imply that a reasonable

time was no more than a day (unless trade practice or prior dealing indicate otherwise). While it is true that only two business days passed before Beam sent his acceptance, nevertheless without more Beam's acceptance was probably too late.

Here, however, there was more: (1) The acceptance was *arguably* sent within a reasonable time. Therefore, if Ash did not regard the acceptance as timely, he was under an affirmative obligation to communicate that fact to Beam. (Under this theory, Beam's late-arriving acceptance operated as a counteroffer, and Ash's failure to object to the delay operated as an acceptance of the counteroffer by silence.) (2) Furthermore, in their correspondence, Ash and Beam acted as if a contract had been formed, and that in itself should suffice (*see* U.C.C. §2-207(3)).

3. **The Error in Transmission:** As between Ash and Beam, the mistake in transmission appears to be a *Peerless* type of mistake—that is, the kind of mistake usually known as a misunderstanding. Both parties seem to have acted reasonably: Ash reasonably thought he had a contract at $19.70; Beam reasonably thought he had a contract at $19. (It is possible that the market price for laths was so well established that Beam should have realized that the $19 price was mistaken, but there is no indication that was the case.) Conversely, Ash might have been careless in using the telegraph as a mode of communication, or in not having the telegram repeated. But that too seems unlikely. People use the telegraph every day. Assuming it is not customary to have telegrams repeated, it seems stretching things to characterize Ash as having been at fault. In fact, Beam himself used the telegraph, and there is no indication that *he* had the telegram repeated.

Nevertheless, the majority view is that in cases like this a contract is formed on the terms conveyed to the offeree by the intermediary. This view is sometimes rationalized on the theory that the intermediary's error may be laid to the offeror on the ground that he selected it as a method of communication, or that it was his agent. But selection of Western Union was not itself faulty for the reasons just discussed, and Western Union seems to be an independent contractor rather than an agent. Therefore, a minority view is that no contract is formed in such cases under a *Peerless* type analysis—*i.e.,* the parties have neither objectively nor subjectively intended to contract. Under either view, the intermediary may be liable for negligence for any loss suffered by either party.

ANSWER TO SAMPLE EXAM QUESTION VI

Assuming first that the disclaimer is invalid, if Ash did not ship the laths, he might sue Western Union for his lost profits. However, such a loss seems too speculative and uncertain to recover, since there is nothing to show that Beam would have accepted the correct ($19.70) offer. Furthermore, although disclaimers are always suspect on unconscionability grounds, the disclaimer in this case is probably valid. The clause was conspicuous (it was printed at the top of the form upon which Ash wrote his message), and was in relatively clear language. The facts that Western Union was in a monopoly position, that the clause extended to negligence, and that the loss was apparently caused by negligence, all argue for striking the clause down. However, Western Union's monopoly was limited to fast communication of written messages; other media were available for oral communication or slower communication of writings. Furthermore, Ash had a *choice*: This provision was not imposed upon him. He could have obtained the same service without being subject to this provision (albeit at a higher rate), by selecting the repeated-message alternative. Moreover, the type of loss involved here is economic rather than physical. Finally, to prohibit Western Union from employing its two-tier rate system would presumably increase the rates of all persons dealing with Western Union—including those who would rather take their chances on a mistake or delay and pay less. On balance, the clause should probably be given effect.

ANSWER TO SAMPLE EXAM QUESTION VII

1. **Fee's Claim**

   a. **Amount of damages:** A preliminary question in Fee's suit is the amount of her damages. If Fee is successful, she would be entitled to contract price ($50,000) minus market value at the time of breach. This is a general damages measure. While the question does not state what the market value was at the time of breach, the sale to Dry at $35,000 only two and a half months later is very strong, almost conclusive evidence of such value. In other words, if successful, Fee's damages would probably be $15,000 minus the $10,000 she already has.

   b. **Aqua's defenses**: This raises the question of whether Aqua has any defenses.

      (1) Aqua might claim that section 5 is a liquidated damages provision applicable to Aqua as well as to Fee. However, the provision is not a liquidated damages provision by its terms, and since such provisions are not favored, it should not be construed as such in the absence of clear language.

      (2) A second and much stronger defense is that of frustration of purpose. ("Impossibility" would not be applicable, because the performances of both parties are literally possible.) As in the case of *Krell v. Henry* where the plaintiff was buying not just a room, but a room with a view, so here Aqua was buying not simply a house, but a lakeside summer house. Even the name—Lakerest—indicates the integral significance of the lake. While frustration is a question of fact, and opinions can differ in a given case, Aqua should probably be excused under the defense of frustration.

      However, because this is a sale of land transaction, a special problem is raised. In many jurisdictions, the purchaser in a sale of land contract must perform even if there has been material destruction to improvements on the property ("rule 1"). Other jurisdictions hold that the risk of destruction is on the vendor until title passes ("rule 2"), or is on the party in or entitled to possession ("rule 3"). If the jurisdiction in which these suits are brought follows rule 2 or 3, there would be no special problem in this case above and beyond the ordinary problems raised by frustration. But what if the jurisdiction follows rule 1? Should the rule be extended to deny the defense of frustration, even if it would be available to Aqua in any case other than one involving sale of land? Probably not. First of all, literally the rule would not apply (since the lake is not an improvement on the property). Furthermore, since the rule is questionable in any event, it should not be extended—particularly in this case where the contract shows a clear intent to repudiate it.

2. **Aqua's Counterclaim:** Aqua should get her $10,000 back on grounds of frustration.

   Fee might argue that some courts have distinguished between money paid before the frustrating event and money remaining to be paid at that point. However, this distinction seems unsound. A stronger argument in Fee's favor is that the contract specifies that the deposit shall be returned under only two conditions (material destruction of improvements on the property or failure to make good title), neither of which has occurred, and that it goes on to provide that if the named "purchaser . . . fails to pay the balance of the purchase price at the Closing for any *other reason*, said deposit will not be refunded." However, the purpose of that clause seems pretty clearly to give the vendor a right to keep the deposit only if the purchaser *unjustifiably* fails to complete payment. For instance, suppose the improvements on the property had *not* been destroyed, but a fissure had opened up cutting the property in half; would the fact that such a condition was not specifically mentioned in the provision be a defense to a claim for return of the down payment? Frustration and impossibility problems arise precisely because the parties did not specifically foresee specific kinds of events; hence, without strong proof to the contrary, a general clause like this should not shift the risk of all unforeseen events on to the purchaser.

ANSWER TO SAMPLE EXAM QUESTION VIII

Since this was a contract for the sale of services, the normal measure of damages would be reasonable cost of completion, minus the unpaid portion of the price. However, completion now seems impossible—although perhaps damages might be measured by the cost of restaging the wedding and photographing the restaged version. (It is assumed that Grume could not have mitigated by hiring a substitute photographer in time or by getting a friend to take pictures.)

Where cost of completion is inappropriate, damages can usually be measured by the difference between the value of what the injured party ended up with and the value of what he would have ended up with had the contract been performed. In this case, however, the latter element is probably too uncertain to permit practicable measurement. A second problem with the alternative measure, as applied in this case, is that most of the value of the promised pictures would have been largely sentimental, and contract law normally protects only economic interests. Nevertheless, exceptions are sometimes made, particularly where the subject matter of the contract is a personal interest. Since that seems to have been the case here, sentimental value might be taken into account if damages can be assessed with certainty.

Grume might also seek damages for mental anguish. Again such damages are normally not permitted for breach of contract. But since this case specifically deals with a personal interest, and since the mental anguish was foreseeable and resulted from Reflex's negligence, such tort damages might be appropriate in this case.

In any event, Grume is of course entitled to restitution of his $25, as the contract is unenforceable in this situation.

ANSWER TO SAMPLE EXAM QUESTION IX

1. **Bilateral vs. Unilateral Contract:** The initial question is whether Tawker and Penn entered into a bilateral contract or whether Tawker merely made an offer to enter into a unilateral contract—that is, an offer that could be accepted only by performance of an act. If the parties had made a bilateral contract, Tawker's revocation is clearly ineffective. If Tawker's offer was for a unilateral contract, however, greater difficulties are presented.

   Tawker's words, at least, seem to call for an act—delivery of the completed manuscript by April 1, 1992. The words, however, are not necessarily decisive: some offers that seem to call for acts can be interpreted as calling for promises—*e.g.,* "I will give you $500 to paint my house."

   Restatement (Second) section 32 says that if an offer is ambiguous as to whether it calls for a promise or an act, either method of acceptance should suffice. This leaves open (i) whether the offer was ambiguous, and (ii) whether Penn made a promise. The answer to both questions seems to be "no." It will be recalled that in response to Tawker's second offer Penn had indicated that he did not want to be committed to a single major project—*i.e.,* did ***not*** want to make a promise. Tawker seems to have been responding to this reaction by setting up the transaction so that the money would serve as a lure, thus insuring performance through incentive rather than through commitment. It is true that Penn said, "Right," which response might evidence as exchange of promises, but the word is equally consistent with Penn saying, in effect, "Structuring the transaction in this way, so that I am not committed but will get $10,000 if I perform, is fine with me."

2. **Consequences If the Transaction Is Deemed to Be an Offer for a Unilateral Contract:** If the offer is for a unilateral contract, an initial problem is whether Penn was required to give notice that he had begun performance. Probably not. Tawker indicated that she would pay $10,000 if the manuscript was completed by April 1, and a reasonable person in Penn's position would probably not have felt obliged to give any notice, on the theory that he would either produce the manuscript by April 1 and get the $10,000, or not. Also, Penn's statement, "Right," might be taken to put Tawker on notice that Penn was at least seriously interested.

A second problem is whether the offer was revocable. In classical theory, an offer for a unilateral contract was revocable at any time prior to completion of the act required. Thus, if the Tawker-Penn transaction is deemed an offer for a unilateral contract, under classical theory, Tawker would have no obligation to Penn since the revocation occurred prior to completion of the act. However, it is now widely acknowledged that an offer for a unilateral contract generally ***cannot be withdrawn once performance has begun***, as was the case here, because of the offeree's ***reliance*** on the offeror's implied promise to hold the offer open. Thus, Tawker's countermand would be wrongful.

3. **Changed Circumstances:** Tawker might argue that she was excused by virtue of changed circumstances—specifically, her withdrawal from the race. This is not a case of impossibility—Penn could still finish the biography and Tawker could still pay for it. If Tawker has an excuse at all, therefore, it is under the doctrine of frustration—the book can no longer serve its intended purpose. However, it is unlikely that the frustration doctrine would be applied to this case. First, the book would still have some value to Tawker, even under the changed circumstances. Second, the changed circumstance was a result of Tawker's own decision and does not seem to be the kind of risk Penn should bear.

4. **Statute of Frauds:** The Statute of Frauds does not present a problem. The transaction involves services rather than goods, and performance could take place within one year.

ANSWER TO SAMPLE EXAM QUESTION X

Rights are normally assignable unless the assignment would materially vary the other party's corresponding rights, or, to use the U.C.C. terminology, the obligor has a substantial interest in the obligee's identity. Was that the case here?

If the Andrews-Wolf contract had merely called for the purchase and sale of rutile at a price keyed into the market, so that Wolf's only duty was to make payment, Wolf's rights certainly would have been assignable. However, here there was more: Wolf also had to ***refine*** the rutile to extract the titanium it contained, and to certify how much titanium it had extracted. This certificate was to be conclusive. That in itself indicates that Wolf's rights were not assignable, because clearly the identity of the person making such a certificate would be highly important to Andrews. Of course, despite the language of the contract, the certificate might not really be "conclusive" in the ordinary sense of the term, since it would probably be open to Andrews to show that more titanium had been extracted than was stated in the certificate. On the other hand, it would not be easy for Andrews to know how much titanium had actually been extracted, let alone prove it; in other words, Andrews had to place a fair amount of trust and confidence in Wolf, which it would not necessarily have in Wolf's assignee.

Furthermore, we are told that "the process of refining rutile to extract the maximum amount of titanium is a highly skilled and very expensive one." Since Andrews' payment depended on the amount of rutile extracted, it is clear that this also gave it a substantial interest in the identity of the refiner; refinement by a less skilled refiner would mean less payment for Andrews. Furthermore, one refiner might be willing to spend extra money to extract the maximum amount of titanium, whereas another might not. These considerations have particular force in this case, since Wolf was a major chemical company, experienced in the business, whereas Xavier was a newcomer.

Xavier might argue that since Wolf's *entire* Raremetals Division was being bought, as a practical matter the same organization would probably continue to run the refining operation. Nevertheless, on balance, Andrews appears to have a substantial interest in having the contract performed by Wolf, so that the contract would not be assignable without Andrews' consent.

Wolf's offer to accept shipment of the rutile is of no real significance; nor is its offer to be ultimately responsible for the purchase price, since it would be liable in any event under ordinary principles of contract law.

All this being so, Andrews is within its rights in declining to make further shipments under the contract.

TABLE OF CITATIONS TO
RESTATEMENT (FIRST) OF CONTRACTS

TABLE OF CITATIONS TO
RESTATEMENT (SECOND) OF CONTRACTS

TABLE OF CITATIONS TO
THE UNIFORM COMMERCIAL CODE

TABLE OF CASES

INDEX